# LAWRENCE D MOYO

# PURSUIT OF THE ELUSIVE DREAM

## Somewhere, Everywhere by all Means Possible

novum pro

© 2023 novum publishing

ISBN 978-3-99131-316-8
Editing: Hugo Chandler
Cover photos: HandmadePictures,
Agencyby | Dreamstime.com
Cover design, layout & typesetting:
novum publishing

www.novum-publishing.co.uk

**Climate neutral**
Print product
ClimatePartner.com/16547-2201-1002

＊

# Dedication

To my children: Gerald, Audrey, Lorraine and Valerie.

Know ye your roots, children, and
whence your power derives its force.
Be reminded that
it didn't
come easy.

# Introduction

Before writing this memoir, I often wondered how one takes the plunge and begins telling the story of a lifetime, especially one that includes grim childhood details of extreme poverty and a relentless search and waiting for a perceived life of comfort as I edged into adulthood. After mulling over the assignment before me and finally bringing together the bits and bobs of memories I have gathered about myself and the circumstances that have nurtured me, I am chuffed to bits to get started and commit these thoughts in the pages that follow. My wife, Margaret, son Gerald and daughters Audrey, Lorraine and Valerie have occasionally had the good fortune of listening to me telling them broken pieces of my life experiences during family mealtimes or while we relaxed in the lounge at home. With you, dear reader, my family can now sit back and watch me condense these reminiscences in a book they can read at leisure. The chapters in this book represent a selection from numerous recounts of events that I made to my family (including pieces that I may not have even told them) that, while nevertheless by no means exhaustive, constitute what will probably appear to some of you, my readers, as an unnecessarily obese volume. But I must remind you that this is the story of my life, so I feel there may be no apology that I can possibly offer for this hypertrophy of verbiage! For a long time, I kept promising my family I would start writing this memoir. Still, somehow for reasons to do with my inability to organise myself properly, I persisted in putting it off.

The title of this book, **"Pursuit of the Elusive Dream"**, is about Me. I talk extensively about myself in this book, and there are no holds barred. The memoir is published in my name 'Lawrence D Moyo' which name I have publicly been known as for the past sixty odd years. Otherwise, for all my years in middle primary school, part of my secondary school, the period of my training as a teacher and even a bit of my university education, I used a mixed bag of names which, from my unmerited position, I have the privilege to tell you that some of these names will have no bearing on your knowing anything about them, save to say most of them were completely at variance with my family names or the true names I have been known by. The multiplicity of these and often offending surnames, furtively stealing their way onto some of my school reports and other personal paraphernalia of the document type, arose principally from my quest in the 1960s to attend African government primary and secondary schools in Salisbury (now Harare).

For reasons associated with the political climate obtaining in Rhodesia (Zimbabwe) at that time, these places of learning enrolled in them only those black children of parents who had been authorised to live in rented municipal houses in African townships. Schools would without exception demand production of relevant documents to confirm that a child seeking enrolment was a bona fide child of parents who had permission to live in the African locations which by then had mushroomed in towns and cities all over Rhodesia (now Zimbabwe). Towns and cities were essentially European areas by designation in terms of the Land Apportionment Act brought into law in the parliament of Rhodesia (Zimbabwe) in 1930. In terms of that law, Europeans alone were entitled to live in urban areas while all those of colour were relegated to live far away in rural areas. In terms of that discriminatory law, therefore, it was illegal for black parents to send their children to attend schools outside their assigned tribal trust lands.

As most of my readers will probably be total strangers to me, I will get to share with them episodes or experiences I have never shared with them before. To be honest, except for perhaps my wife, my children, immediate family members, students I once taught in schools and colleges in Zimbabwe and in the UK, collegemates and workmates and a handful of close friends and associates, the great majority of my readers will not immediately recognise me.

8

It is true because we have never met anywhere for whatever reason. I am by no means a celebrity of any sort; it has never been my wish to be one. I am content and a freer man to be hidden in the inconspicuousness of my nonentity. Before we go too far, let me be categorical about one important matter: English is by no means my first language although, being colonial Rhodesia, it was the official medium of communication through which all teaching and learning in the school system were conducted. So, in my flat-footed, though not plodding prose style, I make a determined effort to express myself in writing intelligibly as I take you on a tour of a whole raft of my childhood and adult experiences in this book.

As you read through this book, it may seem that some of the anecdotes that I narrate will give you the sense of soliloquies or monologues. You may discover that at times, it appears as if I am having a conversation with myself. Now depending on your analytical ability and the level at which you reach your conclusions, you might be allowed through these seemly devices the rare opportunity to identify the invisible force, the inner workings of my psyche that sustained my spirit through the rigours and ravages of my childhood and adulthood when I was tossed about from pillar to post by circumstances beyond my control.

Some of the events I narrate were happy while others were probably sad. Within the sub-plots that surreptitiously emerge as the sequence of events in the book unfolds, I explore several themes, some of them probably controversial to my readers. In no order of priority or importance, therefore, some of the themes that I discuss are child and domestic abuse; racial discrimination and its effects on people's attitudes and behaviours; identity; equal rights; racism per se; 'hidden racism'; diversity; violence; deprivation and evils of individualism. By way of ventilating my thoughts on some of these themes, I have put myself in the centre as a by-product of the extent to which a stultifying environment, the negative outcomes of evil practices, attitudes and behaviours by other people can have the potential to frustrate or altogether kill off all hope and aspiration in budding youth. In my case and through hard work, sheer determination, and aspiration-flow, I adopt the 'fight' and not the 'flight' spirit. Indeed, like the proverbial phoenix, I rise from the ashes and face the challenges before me head-on to free myself from the evil clutches of deprivation and the malevolent attitudes of other forces. The forces I refer to symbolise human beings who do not believe that the things that are good for them must also correspond to the natural needs that are the same for everybody else. This book is an epic account of my heroic struggle to escape a life of grinding poverty and unhappiness.

My struggles as a school-going child to obtain a formal education in Enkeldoorn (Chivhu), Gwelo (Gweru), Selukwe (Shurugwi) and Salisbury (Harare) in pre-independence Zimbabwe are consistent with the Greek Philosopher Aristotle who says, 'the means we use to finally grasp those goods that we seek so that in the end we live well is by developing in ourselves and acquiring good habits in the form of intellectual and moral virtues.' Acquisition of those moral virtues will help us to choose our options correctly as we move through life. Possession of such virtues will also determine whether at the end of all our efforts, we will enjoy good living or not. Aristotle concludes his argument on possession of moral virtues by pointing out that if we do not choose our options correctly and therefore tend to make too many bad choices, we will be destined to live poorly. Then as the thread of my story unfolds and I become an adult, I am seized with the same mindset where, juxtaposed with the vexing issue of living the good life. Aristotle further emphasises that the goal of human life is to flourish, to live well and enjoy the comforts and conveniences that life has to offer.

Stretching his perspective further, Aristotle says some of the good things or the natural desires that we must accumulate, over the course of our lives, include health, pleasure, food, drink, shelter, clothing, knowledge, skills, love, self-esteem, aesthetic enjoyment, and honour. All our actions should aim at this goal.

With all these ideas at the back of my mind as I progress through my life of work and study in the Zimbabwean and UK corridors, I find myself ceaselessly on the move in search of better opportunities to obtain comfort and happiness, life chances, employment, and a better quality of life for myself and my family. In the full grasp of Aristotle's philosophy on living the good life, it will be noted in **'Pursuit of the Elusive Dream'** that my wife, Margaret, and I do not just concentrate on increasing our knowledge and skills about the nature of our occupations. I reserve a whole area of the book to talk about my work as a teacher and our children who I am proud to say were our biggest achievement and I single them out as 'our bundles of joy'. As parents who recognise that educational achievement is a key determinant of financial success, we spare no effort and cost in cultivating in them an appreciation of the value of acquiring a strong educational base. To this end, my wife and I invested heavily in ensuring they each attended top performing primary and secondary schools in Zimbabwe at the time so that they would be ready to face the challenges of life ahead of them and engage in making choices unconstrained by the circumstances in which they would live and work.

Earlier in the book, I present a caricature of my father as the basis of my origin and how his personality shaped me into the person I am today. My biological father, Timothy Dzenga Mudyara, was driven by an ambition to achieve fame as a small-scale farmer. He calculates that achieving fame as an African farmer would be his escape route from the negative effects of racial discrimination in colonial Rhodesia (now Zimbabwe) in which many blacks suffered. He uprooted himself from his rural home in Nharira Tribal Trust Lands (Mashonaland East Province) where I was born. Then against all odds, he embarked on a hazardous expedition as a small-scale farmer on soils of doubtful fertility in an area of unreliable weather patterns. It is in these provincial, rough, and dreary conditions where my childhood and early adolescence were nurtured. I project my father as a 'He-man' in the farm compound who has a mercurial temper. He rarely spoke to or smiled at me and my brothers, ever.

In the winter months of May, June and July when work in the fields is considerably reduced in the Rhodesian (Zimbabwean) countryside, his idea of relaxation in the evening is to sit quietly but seriously on a stool or chair by a fire at the 'dare' scratching or strumming lightly on a 'mbira' instrument, humming an old hunting song in accompaniment. Hardly anybody, including his wives, will make him smile. Yet when the summer rains begin falling in earnest in November following a long dry spell, seeing him feign a smile is an absolute revelation. I make this submission here and now because I spend the whole of my childhood years being brutally disciplined by that man. When things went wrong between you and him, it was you who got the worst end of the stick. He would pick up any hard object near him and hurl it at you. I cannot remember how many times he threw hoe or axe handles at me. Fortunately, I always quickly ducked away from his intended target, and he always missed his targets whenever he threw these missiles in a fit of temper. Otherwise, I would have had one of my lower limbs or both broken. In one incident, he threw an axe at me. The instrument of death missed me by a whisker; I ran round the corner of a brick building and the force of the axe was, luckily for me, wasted on the foundation stone. That man was hard.

In a large section of this book, I have no choice but to present a caricature, as best as I can, of him as a man who ultimately became my father. As a result of his over-indulgence in substance misuse, especially alcohol drinking, my father died of suspected liver cirrhosis in 1979. Presuming upon your goodwill, reader, I sincerely hope that the image of my father that I will portray in this narrative, without any intention on my part to exaggerate it, will not seem egregious to you. However, given that I sought to make it abundantly clear the nature of his character traits, I hope that by juxtaposition, it will also be easy for you to understand the difficult childhood I endured at his mercy.

As the story unwinds, I also write at considerable length about my mother, Leah, or 'Rheya' (nee Muguto). Expressing my thoughts about her in this book is like a blast from the past which I find therapeutic after some of the harsh realities of life I have encountered so far since she died over thirty years ago. Finding herself in a polygamous marriage with a husband none other than my father, she relentlessly worked so hard to set all her children up in the world, the seven of us, in grim circumstances of life as one of the farmer's three wives. She did so, at huge expense to her personal health, to equip us with capabilities which in later life would not find us wanting amidst a myriad challenges of life that lay ahead for each one of us, her seven children. In this book, I include a singular and colourful description of my maiden bus-ride from a bus terminus in Enkeldoorn (now Chivhu).

I highlight that flashback as an example of the immeasurableness of my mother's support for me by the painstaking efforts she takes to prepare me for that maiden journey and to personally accompany me to the bus station on foot. Up to that point in my childhood, I had never seen the inside of or travelled by bus or train before. So, in that description, I left my rural background behind to travel to Gwelo (now Gweru) aboard a bus and a train for the very first time. I will treasure forever the memory of my mother walking with me a distance of ten kilometres, with my clothes' case carefully balanced on her head because she wanted to see me off at the bus station, the very first time I had ever gone off on my own to travel on a bus. Having reached the bus station, it took a long time before the only bus to a place called Umvuma (now Mvuma) arrived. My mother and I waited for the bus to arrive in a crowd of other would-be passengers.

Then, orderly, and more civilised entrance routines into modes of public transport or the queues that have become commonplace today in banks, superstores and so on, were unheard of at that stage of my growing up in colonial Rhodesia (Zimbabwe). In other words, if it were not for my mother's mad dash when the bus arrived as she heaved and handed over my clothes' case to the bus conductor who stood on top of the bus carrier while I engaged in what amounted to a physical combat with other would be passengers in a brutal competition to enter the bus, there would have been a risk of my failing to catch that one and only bus on the day. I am eternally grateful to a countless of things my mother did out of her maternal instinct to support me, and my other six siblings, as a I grew up at the farm. In later life and a few years after the start of my teaching career, the gentle giant experienced complications arising from a broken marriage, high blood pressure and sugar diabetes, all these combined led to her passing on quietly on one dark night in March 1986, leaving me and my six other siblings to thrash our own paths through life and chart our own individual destinies.

In keeping with the policy of 'separate development' in colonial Rhodesia of my childhood, children of Africans who lived in 'reserves' or in 'lines' were supposed to attend schools and complete their education in their designated places of abode, appropriately called Tribal Trust Lands. The few government-funded primary and secondary schools found in urban areas for Africans at that time in Rhodesia (Zimbabwe) were meant to cater for just those few Africans who had left their homes in rural areas to come and find work as cooks, garden 'boys', waiters, labourers, cleaners etc. on properties that belonged to Europeans.

Those of us like me who unknowingly drifted to towns to look for school places but unfortunately did not have parents or close relatives with town passes that authorised them to live and work in European areas, were regarded as 'unregistered' for purposes of enrolment in the few available urban government schools. In the likely event that one did not find places to attend school in urban African townships, the only alternative one had was to return to seek enrolment in schools which did not exist in our rural areas. Thus, thousands of my counterparts suffered an abrupt end to their dreams of an education. However, mindful guardians, supported and assisted by kind and helpful political activist 'landlords' who rented houses in towns and cities, resorted to devious means whereby hapless children like me were enabled to continue with our education in urban government schools, untrammelled by prevailing restrictions.

For me finally to be able to attend schools in Harari Township (Mbare), I had no choice but to resort to the use of undercover names for my middle to upper primary school, as well as my secondary school education. The trick of using pseudonyms may have surprisingly worked for me in my quest to gain or complete my education. Yet the larger number of pseudonyms by which I was known, some of them double-barrelled and very offending, caused me serious grief and inconvenience in my first few years as a teacher. The utter confusion the litany of surnames on my personal profile presented fell on me. I made a solemn vow that before the time came for me to pass-on, my wife Margaret, and my children Gerald, Audrey, Lorraine, and Valerie would never be placed in the same predicament of finding themselves in possession of distorted identities as I had because I omitted to do the right thing when I was still alive.

Five years into my teaching career, and interestingly with my father assisting me, I used the services of a Notary Public to straighten things out officially. Consequently, I had the litany of undesirable and conflicting surnames that had been appended to me deleted, leaving me with just my clan name 'Moyo' as my official surname. In line with the practice at the time, I had already dropped my first name at birth, 'Kingston', when I was baptised and confirmed into the Roman Catholic Church in 1962. The only noteworthy survivor of the name-culling was my current middle name 'Dzenga' which I requested should be retained for spiritual and emotional reasons, remaining a permanent fixture in my name configuration until eternity. Most other people's names, especially those of members of my immediate and extended family, stated in this book are true and correct as this book goes to the publishers. But names that refer directly to owners of small patches of land in the neighbourhood as I grew up at Maronda Mashanu in Enkeldoorn (Chivhu), including other people I got myself mixed up with as a teacher trainee and while I offered my services as a teaching practitioner and educational administrator, were either omitted altogether or pseudonymised to protect the individual identities of the persons concerned. The full story of who exactly I am and who the 'VaRozvi' people in Zimbabwe are, is a long, tedious, and complicated one, which would need to be researched upon more deeply before a book could be produced separately on that subject.

Meanwhile, I will make a small input to assist my readers who will be wondering where I derived the inspiration to write a book of this magnitude with the emotive title: **'Pursuit of the Elusive Dream.'** In addressing this matter, I will consider the fact that although I am a British Citizen by naturalisation, not only am I not a native English language speaker but also that, for reasons I have already briefly outlined in paragraphs above, I did not have a proper grounding in studies of English Language and Literature as a fulltime secondary school pupil.

At the beginning of my teaching career in 1972, I embarked on studying by distance learning for my Advanced Level General Certificate of Education in 'Literature in English' through University of London. It was an ambitious programme of study involving me in extensive reading and analysis of selected masterpieces or books by renowned poets, playwrights, and fiction writers, namely, Geoffrey Chaucer (Canterbury Tales), William Shakespeare (Hamlet and Winter's Tale) and Charles Dickens (Hard Times and Great Expectations). I also read renditions by Charlotte Bronte (Jane Eyre and Sense and Sensibility). Except for wisps of 'Oliver Twist' and 'A Tale of Two Cities' by Charles Dickens that I had read for my studies for the Rhodesia Junior Certificate examinations in the English language, I was meeting the rest of these authors for the first time.

Without the assistance of qualified and experienced teachers to assist me, it would have been an uphill struggle for me to get to grips with the demands made on me to unpack the narratives pursued by these authors. After I had done justice to my struggles with the intricacies of studying 'A' Level Literature in English, my next focus as a fulltime undergraduate student studying for the Bachelor of Education Degree in English Language and Literature, was on the extent to which a mastery of language can be used as an effective tool to solve problems in society. That involved another ambitious and comprehensive programme of reading, writing of assignments and researching into publications by not only Sixteenth Century English metaphysical poets like John Donne, Andrew Marvell, etc but also Twentieth-Century fiction writings and poems by a whole line-up of African writers, e.g., Chinua Achebe, Wole Soyinka, Ngugi W Thiong'o, Charles

Mungoshi, Cyprian Ekwensi and several others. For the record, details of which I have included in the main body of this memoir, I narrowly missed finishing my primary school education, due to the socio-economic frustrations that prevailed in my country, Rhodesia (Zimbabwe) when I was growing up.

Without me voluntarily being able to make my choice at the end of my two years of secondary school whether I should wait for a chance for me to attend Form 3 in another school or to go for the inferior teacher training course, I had to take the route of starting training as a primary school teacher even if I only possessed an 'incomplete' secondary school qualification. Being one of literally thousands of hapless victims of a 'bottlenecking' system which severely restricted the upward mobility of those of us who came from poorer social backgrounds, I attended the first two years of my lower secondary school in 'donated' church buildings. The so-called secondary 'school' and the circumstances attached thereto had simply not been designed for teaching and learning by any stretch of the imagination. Halls and prayer rooms in these structures were subdivided into classrooms, mostly with mere cloth curtains, which we used as learning venues during the week. That secondary school was a community effort, forcibly brought into existence by political activists, in collaboration with pliant church authorities to provide a much-needed education to thousands of us who could not be accommodated in the one and only government-funded secondary school in the area. Community schools for African pupils did not exist, so they were not funded or catered for financially by the then Rhodesian government.

The government of the period I describe did not recognise the existence of such institutions for registration purposes, so I attended the first two years in a secondary school which had no learning materials. We had to bring our own textbooks and writing materials from home. All our teachers, most of whom did not possess any teaching qualifications, were paid their salaries from the school fees we paid. Surprisingly and by a miracle of mathematics, the one government-funded secondary school in the area was intended to absorb the thousands of us Standard 6 certificate holders from up to seven primary schools in the African township of Harari (Mbare)! Amidst these scenarios, I envied some of my colleagues I met later at university who spoke fluently of having sailed through their primary and secondary school education unperturbed by disturbances in their schooling, prior to starting university. On the contrary, I had the odious, if not altogether embarrassing, task of having to give broken accounts of how I had acquired my General Certificate of Education 'O' and 'A' Levels in dribs and drabs, and through private study most of the time. I can therefore safely admit that the reading culture that I have built up around myself, and the propensity for writing that has emerged thereof, did not occur by accident; they were direct outcomes of a burning ambition on my part, fine-tuned over the years to achieve and make progress in life; they were the result of my self-discipline, aspiration-flow, and tremendous willpower.

By now, my readers might have concluded in their assumptions that I am an omnivorous reader of fiction and non-fiction publications, most of them bordering on serious literature. You will be correct in making those assumptions. However, apart from the household names of English authors and African writers in English mentioned above, I am going to highlight one latter day Scottish novelist and physician, Archibald Joseph Cronin (born 1896 and died 1981), who has single-handedly influenced my writing style. His works combine realism and social criticism. I started by reading 'Hatter's Castle', his debut novel in 1931 when I was training as a school teacher; and I have read nearly all his thirty-seven publications including, among others, 'The Citadel', 'The Keys of the Kingdom', 'Beyond This Place,' 'The Green Years', 'The Stars Look Down', The Northern Light', 'Pocketful of Rye', 'The Judas Tree', and several others too many to include in this list. The recurring themes that run throughout Cronin's novels harp repeatedly on the struggle against poverty, the illusion of limitless ambition and the conflict between personal desire and conventional restraint. Aligning his themes with the title and contents of my memoir, as it were, A.J. Cronin seems adamant in maintaining that if one keeps on trying, even when all hope has evaporated, victory may still finally be wrested from the ashes of defeat. His prose style of writing, exerting a kind of lunar pull on my imagination, has literally infiltrated itself into every nook and cranny of my approach to writing.

In concluding these introductory remarks, this memoir owes its birth to my wife, Margaret, who not only coined the title based on her view that it neatly dove-tailed with the stories she had heard me recount. Also, she was convinced that the selected title provided me with an opportunity to ridicule and generally excoriate the contemporary colonial values that prevailed in Rhodesia (Zimbabwe) as I grew up. Margaret comprehensively re-edited the final copy, working from my original text rather than the one I would send to the publishers. My eldest daughter, Audrey, who is a senior lecturer and head of section in a local further education college, also deserves praise for her sterling contribution in the production of this final manuscript by formatting it using the latest version of 'Word'. She also reminded me respectfully to include details that I had omitted in the rough drafts. Working together with her mother, they also punctiliously checked my spelling and factual presentation. The duo spared no effort in labouring diligently to reduce my repetition, my stylistic inadequacies, and syntactical infelicities to the barest minimum. Let them also be accorded their fair share of credit or notoriety that will accrue from the publication of this memoir. I rest my case.

**Lawrence D Moyo**
**West Bromwich, Birmingham, United Kingdom**

# Chapter 1

# Tracing my Birth and Tribal Distinction
## plus a few related details

My father and mother were literate, both having acquired Standard 2 (Grade 4 or Year 4) levels of education, respectively. That was quite a magnanimous feat by virtue of the standards of educational achievements among most of the indigenous population in colonial Rhodesia (Zimbabwe) of eighty to ninety years ago. So, before they died, both within a time lapse of seven years, they would repeatedly state the obvious fact to me that I was born three years after the end of the Second World War; And that I was born in a round hovel in the grinding poverty and cramped conditions of an African village named Dzenga Kraal of the 'Mudyara Reserve' on 27 December 1948. Besides being a 'baby-boomer', those of my Christian readers might want to remember that I am one of the few people to have nearly been born on Christmas Day! Fifteen years later, my father transported me on his bicycle carrier and travelled with me to take out my first registration certificate (or 'Chitupa' in my native Shona language) in the District Commissioner's Offices at 'The Range', Charter (now Chikomba) District in the country then known as 'Rhodesia' (changed to 'Zimbabwe' on attaining independence from Great Britain in 1980). At the time of my birth, the authorities in 'colonial' Rhodesia did not attach much importance to the immediate registration of new-born babies who belonged to the indigenous population. In line with these arrangements (or lack of them) then, even accurate records of deaths were not properly maintained, so the majority of those in my age group throughout Zimbabwe (then Rhodesia) only became privileged enough to obtain birth certificates when, due to changes in legislation, it became standard practice for all black pupils to be in possession of birth certificates before we could be registered to sit either the 'Standard 6' (year 7 in the UK) or Rhodesia Junior Certificate (year 8 in the UK) Examinations with the Department for Native African Education. Also, my father played a big role in helping me obtain a birth certificate before I registered to sit for my Standard 6 (year 6 in the UK) examinations.

Please note this distinction: I am Rozvi or 'Murozvi' by tribe. This distinguishes me from other tribal groups in Zimbabwe; for example, the Karanga, the Zezuru, the Manyika, the Shangani, the AmaNdebele, the Tonga, the Ndau and the Korekore. My clan's name (mutupo) is 'Moyo', and my sub-clan's name (chidawo) is Dhewa/Bvumavaranda. The 'Moyondizvo, Dhewa, Bvumavaranda, vaRozvi vakapera nenda, sahai, vakadzi vanouya vomene etc, etc, etc' are the praise-poetry or incantations which emanate from our sub-clan 'chidawo'. The Kalanga tribe found in Matabeleland South must not mistakenly be characterised associates of the Karanga tribe. Researchers have established that the Kalanga are a distinct clan of the Rozvi-Moyo Empire who are believed to have played a big role in the building of Mapungubwe, Great Zimbabwe and Khami Ruins, centuries ago. The Kalanga tribe of Matabeleland therefore are not the same as the Karanga tribe of Masvingo Province, although some words in 'Kalanga' are mutually intelligible with the dialect of Karanga. The various descriptions about the vaRozvi people to whom I belong will also apply to the Kalanga. Before I leave this area, let me also briefly state that totems ('mitupo') play a huge role in the culture of Zimbabwean Africans. Totems differentiate them from other clans. The different sub-clan terms (zvidawo) Moyo, MaMoyo (in reference to our females), Dhewa, Bvumavaranda or Moyo-Chirandu or Moyo-Gono should not confuse readers because they refer to the same and only one tribal group, the 'vaRozvi.' If I were a young man looking for a wife and I met a young lady who was of the Moyo-Chirandu totem, I would be would probably be cautious enough not to persist with the relationship lest I ended up marrying one of my sisters! – as that is taboo and disallowed in my culture.

Before the advent of Christianity in the then Rozvi Empire, long before Europeans arrived in our part of Central Southern

Africa, polygamy appears to have been a widespread practice among the various Shona tribes, especially among those of royal descent royalty. My father was a product of a polygamous marriage. As recently as the 1970s, I heard there was a chief of the 'vaHera' people in the Nyashanu area near Buhera who had fifty wives, some of whom he could not recognise until they were introduced to him by court officials! Not far from me in the line-up, vaDzenga, my father's father and my grandpa is said to have had up to seven wives. My father, Timothy Tazvinga Mudyara, was the older of two sons in a family of seven siblings. His young brother, who passed on recently at the grand age of eighty=seven, was Rodrick Tinarwo Mudyara. Uncle Rodrick forms an integral part of this novelised autobiography, so I will be saying quite a bit about him in the course of writing this book. Timothy and Tinarwo had five sisters including Mandiyera, Mavis, Jasmine, Lucia and Enita. Their mother and Granny on my father's side of the family, Mbuya VaChemedza, was said to be wife number seven and the youngest wife of their father, vaDzenga. When it became possible for me to travel and retrace my origins, I went out of my way occasionally to visit my grandpa's grave which lies with his remains solidly cemented on a rock a few yards eastwards outside the Dzenga Kraal homestead in Nharira Tribal Trust Lands, Chikomba District. My grandpa sired a few other sons with the remainder of his senior wives.

These include Svahure (with his second wife Mbuya Dzivaidzo); Torongo (with his third wife Mbuya Mugwandavata); Mufari (with his fourth wife Mbuya Mhake); Tafireyi and Toendepi (with his fifth wife Mbuya Shingaidzo) and Gwature Moses (with his sixth wife Mbuya Tsongoni). With the existence of polygamy in his DNA, it was hardly surprising my own father, Timothy Tazvinga, ended up marrying three wives. Continuing to read this account, you will discover that he unsuccessfully attempted to marry a fourth wife, but he was prevented from doing so by economic restrictions that confronted him; the proposed marriage failed to materialise with all his plans ending up on the rocks. Following less than three years of the woman's stay at the farm homestead, my would be number 2 Stepmother 'Mainini', quietly packed up her few belongings and headed back to her parents' home in Manyene Tribal Trust Lands. We would never see or hear of her again. Her mysterious disappearance was attributed to her inability to conceive, so the rumour went.

Going further back beyond my father's father, 'Sekuru' or Grandfather vaDzenga, 'Sekuru' or Great-grandfather Mudyara was my great-grandfather. I know little about him except that he is among several of my ancestors in an exhaustive list which includes illustrious family houses and names such as Masakwa, Mukundwa, Munamati, Musarurwa, Madzorera, Kareya, Gwangava, Chirisamhuru, Tumbare and others I cannot name because the list stretches back into the blue mists of history. I have given that list of names and family houses following no order of priority, hence what would appear to be a mixed-up jumble to those of my peers within the dynasty who may presumably be more knowledgeable on these matters than I am. In Rozvi or indeed Shona culture, many names given to new-born babies almost always carry meanings arising from present, future, or recent events in the life history of the parents or even the extended family.

As you read through this chapter, you will come across names of people in my nuclear and extended family. I have taken a snapshot of some of these names in my family, and I now venture to explain how the people concerned ended with such labels attached to them. My father's marriage with his first wife, Jessica, was blessed with a son as their first child. They named the son 'Reuben'. However, he died in infancy due to a childhood illness. To remind him of his firstborn child ever, my father had that same name replicated in another 'Reuben' with his third wife, Marumbidza. Reuben II died as an adult several years later. Refusing to allow that name to be forgotten, his lastborn son with his second wife, my mother 'Leah or Rheya', was also named 'Reuben'. He is still alive and fit sixty years later. My brother Reuben was later christened Norman. However, if they had copied typical British Royal Family traditions, the lastborn in my mother's might have fittingly been named Reuben III! My young brother, who was born three years after me, was curiously named 'Irrigation' because my mother, who was at full term pregnancy, suddenly experienced birth pains and gave birth to him while she was making ridges in the marshes for a yam-like or 'tsenza' crop on a family patch of a (the then) communal irrigation scheme sited along the river valley below Mudyara Hill, 'Gomo rekwa Mudyara' in the Nharira Tribal Trust Lands. There being no other people of either gender in the vicinity to call upon for help when she felt the birth pangs, she took matters into her own hands and became her own mid-wife. My mother was so courageous because after giving birth, she is alleged to have wrapped up her new-born baby in whatever bits of blanket or shawl she had on her person and innocently walked back to her hut several miles away up the hill, carrying her baby in her arms. Years later in his early adolescence, Irrigation was baptised into the Roman Catholic Church and adopted the new name 'Wilfred'. One of my nephews, Bernard, was given the name 'Last' at birth. Last was his mother's first and only child. Unfortunately, Aunt Enita died on the day soon after giving birth to her son. A second brother from me after Irrigation (Wilfred) was named 'Wonder' because something wonderful happened. Jessica, my father's first wife and my mother 'Leah', father's second wife, curiously fell pregnant at the same time. One of the wives gave birth in the morning and the other delivered her baby in the evening of the same day. These were, and still are, rare occurrences that hardly ever happen in African communities.

My young brother was appropriately named 'Wonder,' arising from that event. My father's first wife gave birth to a girl child. Resulting from that unique event, the girl child was given an interesting name. She was named 'Fainah' suggesting that such an unusual event was the final one and that it might never happen again in the family. Wonder and Fainah might have been twins if their birth had been delivered by one woman. However, this was not so. It remains a puzzle in the extended family how it was biologically possible for my father's two wives to fall pregnant at about the same time, resulting in the mystery births. A related version pertaining to why my stepsister was named 'Fainah' was that after her birth, father is said to have resolved to have no more children with his first wife, Jessica, because Fainah was a girl child while he would have preferred a boy child. It is not explained why he would arrive at such a name-giving decision. Anyway, in making that decision and because he would have preferred all his children to be males only, my stepsister would understandably be the final girl child my father and his first wife would have. Hence the name 'Fainah' was given to my stepsister. In later life she was baptised into the Anglican Church and assumed a new name – 'Sylvia'.

At birth, my older brother Kufakunesu – the one I was born after – was given the name 'Kufakunesu', which literally means 'We live with death in our midst'. The question that would arise is why parents would decide to give their child a name like that. Here is why. It was said that for several years, my parents experienced difficulties in starting a family. An amazing story giving credence to the sequence of events describes how up to five of my older brother's siblings who came before him were either stillborn one after the other or were weaklings such that most of them died in their infancy. It must have been a stressful and heart-rending experience for my parents, especially my mother. When my older brother arrived and he seemed to cling dearly to life where his predecessors had all perished from infant illnesses, the name 'Kufakunesu' was chosen as the most appropriate label for him. It would remind my parents of the nail-biting hardships they went through before my brother arrived. In truth, my older brother was a belated blessing rather than a curse and they would always be reminded of that by his name. In later years, older brother Kufakunesu would take up the new Christian name 'Roland'. Sadly, typical of a disquieting feature, my predecessor – the male child who was born after older brother Kufakunesu (name unknown) – is said to have followed the same path as my older brother's predecessors. Reader, you might want to contrast this with the fact that after I was born, my mother would be blessed with five more births in the years that followed, none of whom died in infancy. I was christened 'Lawrence' in the

Roman Catholic Church at Gwelo (Gweru) in 1962, years after my birth. According to my deceased mother, my 'heathen' name 'Kingston' at birth had connections with two meanings that were interrelated. First, the 'VaRozvi' are spoken about in Zimbabwean folklore today as belonging to a dynasty of royalty.

For a long time before the arrival of the Portuguese traders and Matabele warriors between the sixteenth and nineteenth centuries, the geographical area that is called Zimbabwe today was once dominated and ruled by the Rozvi 'Mambos', 'Changamires' and/or Kings. That alleged paramountcy over other tribes during that period was toppled by forces beyond the control of the Rozvi rulers. Among them were the marauding Matabele warriors on the one hand and the eventual arrival of the colonial settlers from Great Britain in 1890 on the other. Then long after the enactment of the Rhodesian Land Apportionment Act of 1930 which took away all land rights from black Rhodesians, King George VI of the UK toured South Africa in 1947. That royal tour was extended to include His Royal Highness's tour to the colony of Southern 'Rhodesia' upon which his entourage travelled north across the Limpopo River and arrived at Salisbury (Harare) by train. My parents informed me that although I was born over a year after His Royal Highness's visit to 'Rhodesia', a fitting tribute to an event of such magnitude could only be made through local inhabitants in Rhodesia giving some of their male children names such as 'King', 'Kingsley' or 'Kingston,' as was the label finally decided should be attached to me.

The older of my two sisters, Shupikai (Lilian), who sadly died just over twenty years ago, was in her early forties when she passed on. She was named 'Shupikai' in reference possibly to the suffering the local Zimbabwean African community have continued to experience since especially the promulgation of the Rhodesian Land Apportionment Act of 1930 in the 'whites only' parliament of Rhodesia (now Zimbabwe). That evil law by the colonial authorities visited untold suffering on the black population, relegating nearly all of them to lives of absolute penury, persisting to this day despite 'uhuru' or independence. The rigours of that law triggered the nationalist politicians in the 1960s to confront colonial rulers with force of arms, leading to the liberation struggle that ended with the political independence of Zimbabwe in 1980. Unfortunately, the purposes for which the war of liberation from colonial rule was waged have recklessly been tweaked over the years, to suit the self-serving needs of a small clique of our 'liberators'.

So, for forty-two years since 'independence', the war against poverty in Zimbabwe has continued unabated with only a tiny fraction of those our people with links to the bureaucracy seeming to enjoy the true benefits of independence. There are no prospects pointing to the suffering of the people in Zimbabwe coming to an end in the immediate future. In a peculiar coincidence with the title of this memoir, searching for solutions that will bring an end to people's suffering in Zimbabwe is like searching for a needle in a haystack!

Out of the seven children my parents left behind when they died, I am the second born of five sons, all of whom are still alive. After me, 'Irrigation' Wilfred was born. Then there was 'Wonder' who was followed by the late Lilian Shupikai. My only surviving sister is Phyllis Winnie (now Mrs Bonga). The lastborn of my parents' family was Reuben Norman. He is still alive and well. Phyllis Winnie is the only one of all my siblings who later relocated and joined me here in the UK from Zimbabwe in the early 2000s together with her husband (my brother-in-law), Chipo Bonga. Four of my brothers and the bulk of my extended family still live in Zimbabwe. I frequently keep in touch with all of them by mobile phone calls, mobile phone messaging or other forms of media communications, e.g., Zoom, etc. Phyllis and I visit each other from time to time. She lives and works as a nurse in a small town in south-west England (Hampshire) called Liss, around a hundred and fifty miles from Birmingham where I live. Like my sister here with me in the UK, all my brothers are married and each of the marriages to their spouses has children in them.

To name the children in my siblings' marriages, if I can still remember all of them, older brother Kaston Kufakunesu (Roland)

and the firstborn in my mother's family, that is, his first child with his wife Faith, who unfortunately succumbed to the ravages of COVID-19 in mid-2021, was Carol Makawana followed by her brothers Knowledge, Lawson and Chamunorwa. My own first child with wife Margaret was Gerald who was followed by sisters Audrey Shingaidzo, Lorraine Vimbai and Valerie Hazvinei. Wilfred (Irrigation) and his late wife, Esther, had their first child Portia Ndakaitei with siblings who include Adelaide Shorai, Donaldson, King and Natalie. My young brother Gibson (Wonder) and his late first wife Theresa had a first daughter, Kudzai. Theresa bore five other children namely Fadzai, Tendai, Tanaka, Tapiwa and Tanyaradzwa. Following the passing on of his first wife, he re-married and the family have three children namely Mazvita, Tawanda and Blessing. With nine children altogether, seven girls and two boys, my young brother Gibson and his wives have the largest number of offspring. Our older sister (the late) Lilian Shupikai's first child was Martha. After her firstborn child Martha, subsequent to which she died from illness in 2002, she, however, had had three other children including Bruce, Marshall and Fortunate. Our second sister Winnie Phyllis (Mrs Bonga)'s first child was Takudzwa who was followed by Tatenda. The couple's third child and only daughter in that family is Mwaita. Then finally, the last of my brothers and the lastborn in the family is Reuben Mucheriwa Norman. With his wife Fungisai, they had a firstborn daughter, Chido. Two other children, a daughter, and a son, were born in Reuben Norman's family, namely Kudakwashe and Isheanesu respectively.

Were my parents still alive as I write on these pages in July 2022, they would have been grandparents to a total of thirty-one grandchildren and countless great-grandchildren! Combined with a long list of uncles, aunts, cousins, nieces, and nephews on both my father's and mother's sides of the family, I love my folks, dead or alive, who make up one great big family.

# Chapter 2

# The colony of 'Rhodesia' (Zimbabwe) where I was born: A brief historical preview to put you in the picture

In my days of youth or early adulthood, I never wished to be directly involved in activities that related to any forms of power-er relations between individuals such as the distribution of resources or status. Yet reflecting on this matter and whether I liked it or hated it, I gradually realised that the food I ate and the air I breathed as an infant, adolescent and adult were inextricably linked with the hateful subject to do with the politics of the land. I was born into a political environment whose toxicity was shaping the destinies of all the individuals targeted in the uneven distribution of land resources by the powers that ruled at the time. Against that background, allow me this opportunity to give you a brief description of the 'Rhodesia' (now Zimbabwe) into which I was born. After that I will try to characterise how the unfolding events negatively impacted my father who was in his mid-thirties at the time of my birth. I want you to imagine what the bruised and damaged personality that emerged from him because of the ill treatment meted out to indigenous inhabitants from the draconian land distribution laws of the 1930s did to his parenting capabilities in colonial Rhodesia.

The Berlin Conference held in Germany in 1884, paved the way for European nations to partition Africa amongst themselves, their objective being to obtain and divide amongst themselves the numerous mineral and agricultural resources from that continent at the expense of the indigenous African populations. By 1950, European settlers from Great Britain had arrived and had been in Zimbabwe (then Rhodesia) for nearly sixty years. The British South Africa Company (Pioneer Column) had marched into Salisbury (now Harare) in September 1890. The First Chimurenga War of 1896 by Rhodesian African Chiefs to resist white domination had been lost and violently put down because the new settlers had more superior weapons of war like guns, revolvers, and cannons. From then on, more settlers arrived in the country every day and continued to grab more land from the indigenous black people. Most of the European settlers continued acquiring more land from indigenous inhabitants not only because they wanted to use it for farming purposes but in many other cases for purely speculative reasons, they wanted to keep the land unused after acquiring it and resell it at a profit later. Not only that; the indigenous people also lost thousands of their cattle which were taken from them often by force. In 1930, a nasty law called the Land Apportionment Act was passed in the Rhodesian Parliament where there was not a single African member of parliament.

On the strength of that one felt legal swoop, the right of Africans to land ownership was rescinded; completely taken away from them, leaving all of them without any land they could call theirs. The Act partitioned land in Rhodesia – which later became independent Zimbabwe – into European areas and African 'Reserves' with the Africans being forcibly evicted from fertile land which they had worked on for generations and to which they were spiritually attached. Leaving their family shrines or indeed community grave sites behind, they were mostly moved in vast numbers to barren lands and resettled in areas far away from major roads and railway lines; thus depriving them of a means of survival and the enjoyment of the transport infrastructure.

Towns and cities were designated as white areas. The Act made no meaningful welfare provision for black people who chose to live in towns while they were employed at white-owned businesses and residential properties. The Land Apportionment Act resulted in negative social, economic and political ramifications on the indigenous people, most of them on their agricultural practices. So, immediately after the creation of Native Reserves, African agricultural production plummeted in value. The fact that they were forcibly moved from productive to unproductive dry and often rocky and small pieces of land hold caused large reduction in their crop and livestock production. These scenarios culminated in high levels of poverty, which, in turn, caused considerable hardship, suffering, stress and a feeling of hopelessness which affected the bulk of the African folk, off-loaded and abandoned, in 'reserves' dotted across the low-rain-fall areas of the 'Lowveld' in the colonial 'Rhodesia' of the time.

My Grandmother VaChemedza, father's elderly mother who was still alive and living with us on the small-scale farm in the late 1950s, had photographic memories of the events at the time the Land Apportionment Act was brought into law in the 1930s. She was a young mother at the time and possessed clear memories of the extent of suffering that was brought to bear upon indigenous Africans in Rhodesia at that time. In little shards of melancholy, she lamented.

"The biggest mistake made by the white people was that they took away from us all the land ownership rights upon which our whole culture was built." She recalled that her husband and my grandfather, VaDzenga, and many other men in the community who had undoubted connections to a recent history of tribal royalty and chieftainship had died miserably, having been stripped of their entitlement to these badges of honour and having lost the pride of ownership of those little things they prized so much and called theirs. She continued, "Increasingly, the human psyche of our people was indelibly scarred and many of our men not only lost their manliness; they also lost their beliefs in the concept of 'hunhu' or 'ubuntu', that is, that sense of black pride or that element of being who they were as Africans, which was deeply rooted in their cultural traditions."

It should also be noted that at the time of the Land Apportionment Act in 1930, estimates say that there were about fifty thousand European settlers in the then Rhodesia, compared with approximately 1,081,000 indigenous black people. Silly and meaningless taxes like, for example the 'Hut Tax', were imposed on Africans for the purpose of making life as uncomfortable and inconvenient for them as possible. The taxes were meant to compel them to go and look for employment as labourers on European farming estates and newly established mines.

The taking away (alienation) from indigenous Rhodesian Africans of their most productive land and reserving it for exclusive use by

Europeans, led to acute soil erosion that was consequent to overgrazing in the small and overcrowded portions on which they found themselves. The Land Apportionment Act caused widespread poverty among Africans, resulting in many of them seeking work as labourers, cooks, garden 'boys', cleaners etc on European farms, mines and properties in towns and cities. On return to the villages on brief weekend visits, many of the African workers were reported to have told sad tales of being subjected to frequent administration of corporal punishment and verbal abuse by their white bosses. They reported that they were constantly on the receiving end of generally humiliating treatment from their employers.

Nonetheless, even if towns were designated as 'white areas only', it is noted that by 1969, the urban black population outnumbered the urban white population by more than four to one. The rampaging poverty in the rural areas had caused people to 'drift' to towns and cities in search of jobs in mushrooming factories, European properties and a better quality of life. However, nearly all black town-dwellers lived in rented municipal homes in 'townships' located some miles away, almost always on the windward or western sides from town or city centres.

Meanwhile, the metropolitan cities of Salisbury (now Harare) and Bulawayo, Gwelo (now Gweru) and Umtali (now Mutare) then had, in sharp contrast, impressive office buildings and quiet, leafy 'white' suburban areas that ironically were partially ringed round by overcrowded black townships. In the end, the Land Apportionment Act of 1930 on whose livelihoods my black brother had depended, brought no benefit but rather outright suffering and misery. That is a characterisation of the backdrop against which my father survived as a young family man and in which I arrived just two years short of twenty years, following the promulgation of the notorious Land Apportionment Act.

Growing up on the farm, when I turned ten years of age it dawned on me that all the black-skinned people in my little community, my peers and I, appeared to be on the receiving end of a vicious cycle, a socio-political system which regarded people belonging to other racial groups, especially those like me who had accidentally been born with a darker complexion, to be inferior and lesser humans. However, I was still too young then to do anything about it. Add to this my blissful existence in the stultifying seclusion and deprived isolation of the farm environment. At my tender age and growing up in such rural and often restricted circumstances where opportunities did not exist for me to question the realities in my surroundings, I plodded on with life. It still worried me continuously why role models like my own father, Timothy, often displayed inconsistent behaviours or even split personalities whenever they came into the presence of Europeans. Somehow, I guessed that something had gone seriously wrong somewhere causing some, if not most, of my people to lose their confidence and relegate themselves to second or third grade status whenever a person of 'white' heritage appears on the scene. As I have already revealed, my father's elderly mother, VaChemedza, lived with us on the small-scale farm. She was probably in her late seventies.

She blamed it all on the sad sequence of events which took place when the Europeans arrived and settled in Rhodesia from Great Britain at the end of the eighteenth century. Then a young girl herself in the early 1900s, she had first-hand information about wave upon wave of British settlers arriving and settling in different parts of the Charter District and the rest of Rhodesia. My brothers and I would often get the chance to chat with Grandmother VaChemedza when she was sitting resting in her round hut. She would lower her voice and explain to us quietly lest some hidden 'white men' might be eavesdropping why most adult Africans in our community seemed to have no confidence in themselves; and that most of them appeared to have an inherited a permanent fear of all the people of a European heritage over the last seventy years since the 'white man' had made his first appearance in our part of the world:

"*First, there was the violent way in which the uprising against European occupation was put down by European forces in 1896. The force used by Europeans to squash down any future outbreak of another 'Chimurenga War' left many of our men (and women also) shaking with the fear of*

*God. Then the Land Apportionment Act of 1930 and the suffering it wrought upon most of us was the final straw. Taking ownership of land away from our men, land which linked directly with our Africanness, religion and spirituality, broke their fighting spirit, leaving them like maize husks. This inevitably led to the DNA of fear to flow relentlessly in the blood of all future black generations from then onward down the line. If you have noticed, that is probably why your father, as an example, often walks about with his back hunched, in a dazed fashion and he absolutely lacks confidence whenever he appears in the presence of 'Varungu' (Europeans). The latter have become our new masters before whom we must bow down on our knees as if they were our gods because we have lost our identities, our land and the animals we possessed to them."*

After completing his primary school education up to Standard 2 (year 4) at some remote rural church-run primary school in the Nharira Tribal Trust Lands, my father – like all young men in his village – had no choice but to look for work to support his growing family. Luckily, he was one of the lucky few men to find jobs as messengers at the nearby Native District Commissioner's Offices (Charter District) which were based at a place called 'The Range'. These government messengers underwent rigorous training following a scheme which approximated or resembled the training given to African police recruits who, on completing their training, would be employed as constables by the then British South Africa Police (now Zimbabwe Republic Police). At the end of their six months' training, it was believed 'messengers' were just as good law enforcers as ordinary police constables who however were only answerable to the orders or instructions given by the District Native Commissioner. They had a messenger number and a strict code of conduct whereby they carried out their duties. One of the nicknames of our current Zimbabwe Republic Police officers is 'Mabhurakwacha' which in fact is a bastardisation of the term 'Black Watchers'.

The original 'Black Watchers' were the 'messengers' who were employed at various District Native Commissioners' Offices throughout the country. My father was one of these hordes of 'messengers' who flanked the Native District Commissioner (who I am told they called 'Mambo' or Chief) riding on their shiny and well-polished government issue bicycles when the white man 'Mambo' on horseback toured areas in the district to ensure the black people living in the 'reserves' were abiding by the rules and not planning another uprising against white rule as had happened in 1896. Carrying on with the same theme of fear of Europeans and how Africans generally behaved whenever 'those without knees' (because European men often walked about in public wearing trousers, so their knees could not be seen), grandmother herself gave us a little account of her own behaviour one year when a group of men suddenly pitched up into the open space of the farm compound and she was alone with the children. It was a quiet and hot afternoon.

The farm homestead was almost deserted with all the adults away at their portions in the fields. I was one of the little children playing about in the farm compound. In our blissful ignorance, we were very surprised at the sudden appearance of these men 'on patrol', led by a white man who rode on a huge and well fed brown horse! The rest of the party supporting him were, of course, the district office messengers; half a dozen African men in ten-ounce khaki uniforms, wheeling their bicycles. It did not help to ease the tension when the huge, healthy-looking and well-polished horse ridden by the European Officer became impatient and began engaging in dressage. It lifted its front legs while dancing about recklessly, pound the ground below it with its rear ones with so much force we were inspired with the fear of God. Neighing with its mouth wide open, it displayed those absolutely huge canines while the white man tried to control its behaviour by pulling the reins. This sequence of events did not augur well with Grandmother VaChemedza, At the sight of the horse and the white man riding on it, she grew weak in the knees, flopped noisily to the ground and noisily started emptying her bladder, having lost control of the liquids that passed out of her system through that route.

Fortunately, she wore a very large skirt which, filled with wind, spread all around her on the ground as she threw herself to the ground, thus automatically protected her dignity from the white man and his African assistants. As my Granny continued sitting on the ground looking bemused, the white man asked in broken Shona vernacular, looking directly down at her from upon high, "Wena iwe Mbuya, hakuna mabhinya anozokunesa here kona?" (Old lady, are there any terrorists disturbing the peace here?).

This was her first experience of a white person talking to her directly. Although the white officer had used a few Shona words in a badly constructed sentence, she had not heard a single word, so she asked one of the African assistants to repeat the white officer's question. This was done. However, seeing that my grandmother was beside herself with fear and could hardly answer simple questions to do with the security situation in the area, the white man and his men quickly marched out of our farm homestead on their way to the next farm which was barely a mile away. The group of men lined up in single file as they went with the white man on his horse at the front and his black aides on shiny bicycles bringing up the rear. Look, this was in the early 1950s when I was still a toddler, yet the white man was still staying on guard and taking precautions nearly sixty years after the incident of the 'First Chimurenga War' of 1896 in which indigenous people took up arms to liberate themselves from colonial oppression.

As one of the senior messengers at the District Native Commissioner's Office at The Range in later years, I understand that my father would usually be entrusted with running errands on his bicycle delivering important and urgent messages between the Native Commissioner and local chiefdoms. As a trained and experienced Messenger at the District Native Commissioner's Office, he had power to effect arrests, so returning to the Mambo's offices from some of his two-week absences on 'patrol', he reportedly brought back to the said offices handcuffed miscreants he had arrested for breaking local laws or disturbing the peace. Oral evidence from those who were familiar with my father as a young 'messenger' confirmed that during his outreaches on 'patrols' he made dalliances with several women in and around the sprawling district, two of whom he had married at the time of my birth. His first wife, Jessica, came from the Muroore family, while Leah, his second wife, and my own mother, originated from the Muguto family. To this day, both families still reside in the Nharira Tribal Trust Lands, Chikomba District.

By the end of 1948, when yours truly was born, my father had risen through the ranks of the 'messenger' promotion structure at the District Native Commissioner's Offices. He occupied a high rank in terms of seniority, so he could be trusted to have certain responsibilities, which had previously been the preserve of the District Native Commissioner, delegated to him. You can be sure that as he went around the rural areas carrying out those 'Black Watcher' duties wearing the new 'Mambo' crown, there probably were many unrecorded exaggerations of authority committed. Despite the passing of the Land Apportionment Act in 1930, Africans persisted with their requests through authorities in Great Britain to be allowed to purchase some of the land available. In response to these requests, the white Rhodesian government acceded to the setting up of the Native Land Board in 1931.

The Native Purchase Areas Programme was only finally given the green light when purchase areas for Africans were seen as training grounds for the vanguard of mixing African peasantry, who it was hoped would help to educate traditional cultivations in the 'reserves,' through their farming examples. By the setting up of this land board, Africans would then only be allowed to purchase land in areas to be known as Native Purchase Areas. These were identified all over the country in terms of the quality of the land that was on offer for purchase by black Africans. This greatly varied from area to area. Worth noting was that where these purchase areas had had no prior European occupier, that was perhaps because of the poor quality of the soil and/or the paucity of adequate water supplies which had not attracted European buyers in the first place.

What that meant really was that areas identified as Native Purchase Areas were simply the remnants or scrag ends of the massive land grab by European settlers following the enactment of the Land Apportionment Act of 1930. These developments were unfolding under my father's watchful eye, employed as a senior Messenger at the District Native Commissioner's Offices at 'The Range', Charter (now 'Chikomba') District. While carrying out his duties at the Native Commissioner's Offices, he became aware that a large piece of land called 'Muckleneuk' to the south of Manyene Tribal Trust Lands near Enkeldoorn (now Chivhu), previously owned by an Anglican Missionary priest, Father Arthur Shearly Cripps, had been sold to the government. Typical of what was happening all over Rhodesia at the time, that arrangement was put in place so that Africans living in the Maronda Mashanu tribal trust lands could buy pieces of land from it as part of the Native Purchase Area Scheme. Maronda Mashanu Purchase Area would be too far away, about fifty miles from father's relatives in Nharira Tribal Trust Lands. He is reported to have wondered whether he should take the plunge and buy one of the pieces of land on offer in the new Maronda Mashanu African Purchase Area.

Information I obtained from Aunt Lucia, the only one of her seven siblings who is still alive, confirms that at about the same time, father's arrangements to marry his third wife, Marumbidza, had reached an advanced stage. That being so, it worried him that the small portion of land he had in the 'Reserves' could not cope with or accommodate a possible third wife and a growing brood of children. He was reported to have repeatedly said, "I want to own a larger piece of land which I will call mine. When that happens, I have ambitions to become a successful farmer." Owning a piece of land he would call his own was such a prize possession, so he threw his hat into the ring as one of the applicants for portions of land in the proposed Maronda Mashanu Native Purchase Area on ninety-nine-year leases. There was no cash up-front needed, so his application was successful. My father had massive pride in land ownership. To him, it was a badge of honour and a reminder of stories of the Rozvi people, our ancestors, who had lived in that part of Rhodesia long before European settlers arrived, and the Rozvi were renowned for their successful farming practices.

Then came the Second World War in the 1940s which diverted most of the resources, both human and financial, to the war effort in the British Empire and overseas. Pressure on resources and a general shortage of surveyors to mark out the farms for successful applicants delayed the whole programme until well after the war. Meanwhile, my father's family had grown by leaps and bounds. By 1950, he had sired two children with his first wife, Raphael Misheck and his sister, Faith. With Leah, his second wife and my mother, he had sired Roland Kaston Kufakunesu, yours truly (Lawrence) and my young brother, Wilfred Irrigation, who was probably then still a few months old.

The demarcation of the land purchased from Father Cripps into small farm allotments that would be called 'Maronda Mashanu Native Purchase Area' was finally undertaken and completed after the World War II. Most of the new farmers took up occupation of their allocations between 1950 and 1952. It was at this stage that my father is reported to have resigned his position as a government employee with the District Native Commissioner's Offices at The Range. It was at the same time narrators say, that he finally made the decision to marry his third wife, 'Marumbidza'. Her family came from the Chivese Village. Marumbidza already had a daughter, Chishamiso, from a previous relationship. My father did not mind. When all the logistics had been put in place and he had bidden family elders in the village farewell, Father moved home with whatever farm implements he owned from Dzenga Kraal to his new landholding at Farm No. 7, Maronda Mashanu Native Purchase Area on an unspecified date in either 1951 or 1952. He took along with him also his three wives and all their children; his mother (Mbuya Chemedza); his elderly and blind mother's mother (Mbuya aVhurai); and his three sisters Mavis, Jasmine and Lucia. His young brother Rodrick Tinarwo was presumably part of the great trek. I could not obtain information whether, as father moved bag and baggage, Uncle Rodrick was still training as a teacher at Kutama Mission or whether he had already given up his training as he finally did and started working as a Meteorological Assistant. My father, Timothy, also took with him all the few domestic animals he owned in Nharira Tribal Trust Lands, including a small herd of cattle, goats, sheep, chicken and donkeys – all of them, with the exception of chicken perhaps, driven to the farm on foot for the entire journey of sixty odd miles! thanks to the assistance given for this awesome burden by one of our older stepbrothers, the late Naison Dzenga, and Timothy's eldest son, Misheck (Raphael), who was already a hardy little boy of ten years of age or thereabouts.

Information from those who were older than I was confirms that I was a tiny little boy of around three to four years of age when the great trek from Nharira Tribal Trust Lands to Farm No. 7 at Maronda Mashanu Native Purchase Area took place. Who would remember anything of substance at that age?

# Chapter 3

# Fading memories of yours truly as a toddler

I am sure you do not expect me to tell you about my recollections of the journey my father and all his family travelled from Nharira Tribal Trust Lands to Farm No. 7, Maronda Mashanu Native Purchase Area (Chivhu). I have no memories whatsoever about that journey. I am told I was only just a little boy when that great trek took place in either 1951 or 1952. True, I was one of the children in the entourage, but I was still pretty much an infant who could not really respond meaningfully to the myriads of different perceptions around me. None of the adults still alive from that great trek has confirmed to me the mode of transport that was used to move a whole body of people from one part of the country to another. I understand that all the so-called 'feeder roads' from towns deep in rural areas in those years were gravel roads which were very badly maintained by whichever government department had the responsibility for roads and road traffic for African areas. Consequently, few bus owners would dare put their buses on such roads for fear of running–up huge maintenance costs. There is talk of just one rickety old bus from a small fleet owned by 'Chikati Bus Services' that used to ply the route between Buhera Township and Enkeldoorn (Chivhu). Folklore says that the bus stopped to drop off and pick up passengers at a remote township called 'Sadza'. Nobody will say whether my people were put on that bus to Enkeldoorn (Chivhu) or whether they made the whole journey on foot for the entire sixty or so kilometres. If indeed that was so what happened? Those of us who were mere infants would have to have been carried on adults' backs to complete that length of the journey!

The destination reached by my father and his family was a site just a couple of a hundred yards from the base of a mountain called 'Makumimai', a key geographical feature occupying the middle of my father's new farm. I will explain to you later the significance of the mountain's name. A few trees had been cut down by an advance party. Several round grass huts with thatched roofs had, it seemed, hurriedly been built so much so that, apart from looking clumsy and unsightly in appearance, some of these tumbledown shacks did not look strong enough to withstand storms that would usually be accompanied by strong gusts of wind.

At the western edge of the homestead was a large, tall, old 'Mutsubvu' tree which clearly was in season. Thousands of its black fig-like fruit made the boughs of the tree hang low, forming an umbrella-like canopy below it. Requests for better sanitary facilities, e.g., toilets, by my father's wives and the rest of the family members were summarily dismissed by my father. No provision had been made for these facilities by the advance party. He was far too busy with other chores at the farm to attend to what he considered to be small or unimportant matters.

Instead, he would tell everyone dismissively to relieve themselves behind bushes or thickets of trees, several of which surrounded the homestead. At the end of a busy day a year later, he would repeatedly be heard saying, "This is just a temporary home. I shall make sure we shall have proper and more hygienic places to relieve yourselves at the new site." I remember thinking, 'So there are plans to move to another site' because there being no plans to move to another site soon, the place we were calling home seemed to be 'the place' for the family to stay for a long time in the future.'

As time passed, I was also growing up physically, emotionally, and cognitively. My perceptual development enhanced my ability to begin making sense of the world around me. My first impressions appertained to human relations, and I obtained the bulk of these from interactions with my mother and my two brothers Kaston (later christened Roland) and Irrigation (later christened Wilfred). Outside of my mother's close-knit family would be other older children I began relating with. These were Misheck (later christened Raphael) and his sister, Faith, who I was made to understand were 'brother and sister' to me, whenever I met them in the sort of courtyard outside. They would talk to me, or I would start childish conversations with them. I also noticed that there were other older women in the homestead, including my father's other wives and his three sisters. I have a blurred memory of my older brother Caston (Roland), then six or seven years old, sitting beside me by a fire in the centre of a little round hut with its walls and roof made of grass. Thank God, I had this childish thought to myself, somebody had remembered to tie up two or three wooden rafters across the grass thatch using 'musasa' or 'mutondo' bark string. I feared the entire structure was in danger of collapsing into a rugged heap at any time with the threat that if that happened, we would be hidden under the unsteady structure. Anyway, let's return to the scenery in my mother's hut; Mother had just finished boiling some pumpkins, together with dry round nuts and was busy draining remnants of brownish water from the bottom of the clay pot before she began serving these foods as our evening meal. The lovely smell of the boiled pumpkins combined with that of the round nuts was simply amazing. The aroma was so attractive that it made you feel hungry; it made you want to start eating the food before it was served. Meanwhile, as mother waited for the pumpkins and the nuts to cool off a bit, prior to serving them lest we got scalded, buckets of sweat poured down her face.

At the same time, she drove off thick clouds of smoke that billowed from the ends of semi-dry logs of wood in the fire, with the open palms of both her hands moving back and forth in pendulum-like fashion. I was soon to learn that the multiple number of similar huts outside of my mother's hut belonged to other adults; all of whom I would address variously as 'Grandmother' (Ambuya), 'Big Stepmother' (Maiguru), Small Stepmother (Mainini). Aunt (Tete) and so on. Less than two hundred yards in a westerly direction from the homestead was a large structure which had many huge trees near its base and rocky boulders and outcrops as you looked up towards its summit. I found its sheer size frightening and mesmerising. Its structure projected from the bottom, rising to an astronomical height I had never seen before, and then levelling off on top at a receding angle, which gave you the image of a man's head losing its hair due to old age.

My older brother, Kaston Kufakunesu, informed me that the structure that arrested my attention so much was what was called a mountain. He promised me that when I became a little older, he would climb up the mountain with me to find out more about it. A short distance to the north of the homestead but just a stone's throw away from the edge of the huts was a large rectangular enclosure built of large wooden logs which crisscrossed each other. The wooden entrance door of this large structure had a padlock on it. I slowly got to know that this place was where hoofed four-legged animals with long tails, called cattle, were kept at night to prevent them from wandering off and getting lost while we slept. Then there was the ever present, pungent smell of cowdung. You could rest on it as it wafted past you each time you walked past the cattle pen. Beside the cattle pen were two smaller enclosures. From one of them pigs could be heard squealing and grunting recklessly. When one day I peeped inside this enclosure through the wide cracks in the wooden door, my nostrils were greeted by a powerful stench coming-up from the damp, moist floor that was littered with these porkies' smelly excrement. It was nauseating, to say the least. Chickens and ducks had their own small, in separate enclosures or spaces at specified locations at the edge of the homestead. From them, cocks crowed loudly early in the morning, waking everybody up. As the sun rose, chickens would be seen roaming round the homestead with their broods of chicks in tow, picking up bits of food, as their menu, including any rubbish they found on the dusty and windswept floor. Emerging from their own enclosures, ducks would be seen hobbling clumsily towards a rubbish dump where they would mingle with cackling chickens and squeaking chicks in a free for all for the feast of newly discovered worms or crickets. Imperceptibly, more of the adults in the environment fell into my radar range.

There were six shelters of similar appearance and size at the site we settled when we arrived from Nharira Tribal Trust Lands.

These places of human habitation were dotted all over the cleared ground, without following a particular pattern. My father occupied the hut in the centre. Each of his three wives had a hut to themselves which they shared as a kitchen and a bedroom with their children. My grandmother and her blind mother shared one of the huts. Additionally, Father's three spinsterish sisters Jasmine, Mavis and Lucia shared one of the huts also as a kitchen and a bedroom. Being a mere toddler myself, I would not know whether my stepbrother Misheck (who would be about eleven years old in 1951), stepsister Faith and my older brother Kaston, both of whom would be six and seven years old at that time, had started school or not. Reportedly born in 1940 or thereabouts, stepbrother Misheck (Raphael) was more than old enough to have started school and to be assigned more difficult tasks. For example, that he assisted by walking about sixty kilometres from Nharira to the farm at Maronda Mashanu, driving my father's herd of cattle and other livestock my father owned. At their ages of six and seven years, my older brother Kaston Roland and stepsister Faith would only be expected to assist with carrying out lighter duties, including helping their parents draw water, tidying up duties around the house and (in the case of Faith) fetching firewood from the forests nearby. Collecting firewood was not that much of a challenge as dead wood was in plentiful supply in the surrounding virgin bush.

At the impressionable age of five years or thereabouts, the only young children I could interact with in the homestead then were my young brother Irrigation (Wilfred) and my nephew Last (Bernard). They were still little children themselves with a two to three-year age gap between me and them. Thus in the first year or two of my life at the farm, I was very much a loner in the absence of other children of the same age as myself. Surprisingly and despite the massive age gap between them, Misheck (Raphael) and Kaston (Roland) appeared to have bonded well as a pair and I always observed them interacting freely with one another. As I did not have other agemates with to spend time with, the only choice left for me was to engage in 'baby-talk' with either

Irrigation (Wilfred) or nephew Last (Bernard) who were still babies. Being the older child, I credit myself for perhaps contributing a positive influence towards Irrigation (Wilfred's) and nephew Last's (Bernard's) speech development. I make this claim because by the time they were four years of age, the duo was quite loquacious and relatively more adept at language use than I was. Being of the same age, the two little boys spoke with each other more than with me.

Communication between my three aunts and I was minimal. They were already far too old as young 'girls' for me to interact with often. I did not often talk to the spinsters, and they did not volunteer to chat with me either except to exchange scant greetings with them when I met any of them outdoors near their hut. I have just described them as being spinsterish because all of them had passed their sell-by dates to continue using the term 'girls'. They were in their mid-twenties or older at the time of the big move from Nharira Tribal Trust Lands to the farm. They were a close-knit group, almost always together. If they were not in their hut, they would go as a group to fetch water from a spring well which was about a mile from the temporary site; or they would walk together into the nearby bushes to collect firewood. Otherwise in the winter months when there was little work to be done in the fields, they confined themselves to their hut. From this venue, they would occasionally dart across to my Granny's hut (their mother). Just to remind you Granny shared her hut with her blind old mother. The 'girls' would help with cleaning up or cooking of food for the elderly occupants both of whom were no longer spring chickens.

In the evenings after meals, all of us children, including the older ones like Misheck Raphael, Kaston Kufakunesu Roland and Faith, assembled in Granny's hut to listen and enjoy fantastic stories narrated by either Granny herself or her elderly blind mother. Even if the latter had lost her sight due to old age, her stories were spellbinding. Some of them were liable to be extravagant and camp, but despite all that, there was something enchanting about them. Nearly all the stories they told involved animals with the most enthralling clever rabbit almost always taking advantage of the baboon, making him look very foolish. Some of the hunting stories they told required us to participate by chanting certain parts of the story while the storyteller plodded on with the rest of the storyline. The narrators made us feel happy because bits of some of their stories made us laugh a lot. We would retire late on such nights following wild exchanges of banter. On moonlit nights when it was not very dark, we would gather in the courtyard and the older children would take turns in leading us to dramatise some of the stories the grannies had told us. We derived so much fun playing the roles of the different characters in the stories. Some of the dramatisations we laid on reflected what was happening in the community in which our farm was set.

After these nights of drama, I remember that even if I was still just a child, the storylines in the plays would continue to be subjects for intense conversation and discussion and even disputes among us. That was healthy for those of us who were growing up mentally and getting to grips with the realities of the world around us. From our numerous dramatisations of some of the stories in broad daylight later, how all of us role-played different characters and engaged in innocent exchanges of banter and uproarious laughter, the joy and camaraderie that flowed from these group efforts unwittingly assisted in enhancing my cognitive, social, and linguistic development.

The nights were invariably very quiet except on moonlit nights. Some nights in the first few months of my family's arrival at the farm were so dark that you could hardly see any objects within one's arms reach. There was something eerie and unpleasant about being up and about on a dark night. There was no way of knowing who you would meet or what strange animals of the night you would run into. Darkness itself held a vague queer terror among us children, even the bravest among us. My older brothers would always remind me it was taboo to whistle at night lest such reckless indulgences made the spirits angry or invited witches. Lions, leopards, hyenas, and other reptiles were the stuff with which we enjoyed the litany of stories narrated to us by our grannies. However, these animals and reptiles became sinister and uncanny under the blanket of solid darkness that was cast over our homestead promptly after sunset. None of us would dare call snakes by their names because, as adults whispered in our ears, those snakes would hear and might pay us visits while we slept. I could not imagine myself welcoming such creepy crawlies as visitors, and in the thickness of darkness for that matter. Instead, I was advised to call them 'string' or something to that effect. Consequently, I stayed close to my mother or my older brothers on dark nights. Better still, I always made sure comfort in numbers was my watchword as soon as night fell and that in the event of any danger or threat to my safety, others would intervene and prevent me from being injured or coming to any serious harm.

A cloudless night would present a completely different scenario. The full moon shone brightly from a cloudless sky. The happy voices of little children playing in the open spaces between the huts would clearly ring out. I, my little nephew Last (Bernard), young brother Irrigation (Wilfred) together with Wonder, Fainah (who were recent additions to the family and growing up very quickly) would engage in 'hide and seek' games at the end of which peals of laughter and shouts of joy broke out when the one hiding and their secret hiding place had been discovered.

I noticed that even older boys and older girls like my aunties Jasmine and Lucia would also remember their days as little girls on such nights and might even join us in the 'hide and seek games'. Elsewhere, my father's wives would often visit each other's huts, or they would walk over to the grannies' hut where they exchanged greeting pleasantries, chatted away or start singing familiar tunes until they returned refreshed to their huts late on those lovely nights. The only person who seemed unmoved or unaffected by these changes in the movements of the moon was my father. After he had partaken of his evening meals – each of his wives served him an evening meal separately – he quietly escaped to his own hut where he relaxed on his bed, keeping rigidly to himself. I have already pointed out that my aunties Mavis, Jasmine and Lucia were already old enough to attract attention from male suitors for marriage purposes, but they were still stuck with their older brother's family until a marriageable date in future, yet to be reached. It seemed standard practice for some of these old 'girls' to marry later in their lives. Anyway, on such pleasant nights, they would stand as a pair at the edge of the village whence they would be heard chattering inaudibly and clapping hands cheerfully, accompanied by little hops and jumps to punctuate messages of affection contained in missives they would have received from their male pursuers, who for the moment should remain strictly unknown to everybody else but themselves. Hence the whispers and inaudible chattering in the moonlit night.

Listening carefully in the brief intervals of the cacophony of those multitudinous noises in the moonlit night, it happened that I would sneak out to empty my bladder in the small bushes just behind the round, grass-thatched huts. I would hear rodents faintly squeak and rasp through the dry tufts of grass and fallen tree leaves on the ground below. Ah, I would think to myself, these are some of the nocturnal creatures whose night shift in search of food had started with the fall of dusk. Looking in the distance about a mile away, visibility became poorer, but all was peaceful and quiet, especially when there was no wind blowing. My father would soon have chopped down a few trees to clear the land and open new fields in preparation for the forthcoming planting season. However, the job was still to be completed, so several stumps the height of a man appeared to stand still in the semi-darkness like soldiers on parade. Uncertain of both my security and safety, I would short-circuit my passing of urine and dash back into the courtyard to regroup with the others lest those tree stumps were real people who could suddenly run towards me and abduct me! The thought of horrible things happening to me was terrifying. Then as I nipped along snapping dry wooden twigs beneath my feet, a surprised night owl would suddenly whoosh past me and flap its wings just over my head as it flew at the speed of an arrow to a hidden perch somewhere in the nearby trees.

Meanwhile, the moon would slowly glide across a clear, star-studded galaxy. Farther down the river valley, about a mile and a half away, I would occasionally hear a choir of frogs competing to sing in discordant tones and voices thanking God, as it were, for the abundant rainfall and the water that never stopped flowing in the river. Their music would mingle with the splashing sounds of water as it tumbled and tripped over rocks and snaked through rounded and rectangular crevices and stony outcrops on its long journey down the Chiputya River.

Such was the unique joy, feeling of liberation and of fear, that these moonlit nights ushered into my years of growing up. Already at that tender age of five or six years, I began to sense that there was a joy, a happiness in life that we seemed to be missing in our straitjacketed environment. My senses packed all these different impressions and others, too many to elaborate upon, into my subconscious.

# Chapter 4

# Never too early to know about 'consequences' and taking responsibility for my actions

Events moved on rapidly after my family settled at the farm. In the short space of two years, the large family had moved bag and baggage from the temporary site we had camped at on arriving from Nharira Tribal Trust Lands. The new site, a more permanent fixture and home for me until I turned just over ten years of age, was approximately two miles northwards from the old temporary site. Half-a-mile further north, and just beyond a small grove of 'misasa' trees, was the Chiwandire Farm homestead. The Chiwandire's were our nearest next door neighbours from the new farm compound. At between sixty and seventy hectares of land, their farm was comparatively smaller than our own ninety hectares. I was then a small boy of about seven years, leaving roughly three years' age difference between me and two other little boys, my young brother Irrigation (Wilfred) and my nephew Last (Bernard).

The two little boys were growing up very quickly and catching up fast with me due to my stunted physical development. Also repeating some details, there had been new additions to the family. Young brother to me, Wonder (later christened Gibson) and stepsister Fainah (later christened Sylvia) had reportedly been born on the same day in the year the family arrived at the farm from Nharira Tribal Trust Lands. The name 'Fainah' was allegedly linked with Father's disappointment when he discovered that Stepmother Jessica's new baby was a girl when he had wished her to be a boy. My father is said to have resigned himself to the unalterable fact of the infant baby girl's arrival. But he is believed to have vowed that 'Fainah' would be the last (the final!) baby girl my Stepmother Jessica would give birth to after the two girls Faith and Finah had been born before her.

Two or three years down the line, Stepmother Marumbidza gave birth to her first child, Tichaona (later Christened Newton) with Father. This man was keeping himself quite busy and active, allowing no time of respite for his hapless wives. Meanwhile, Marumbidza's first child (Chishamiso), who was her daughter from a previous relationship, had been allowed to join the rest of us at the farm. Chishamiso was perhaps a little bit older than Wonder and Sylvia when she joined us at the farm from Chivese Village in Nharira Tribal Trust Lands. The homestead was steadily filling up with children. Curiously, more offspring were in the pipeline. Then to everyone's surprise one day, following an absence of two days ostensibly to attend what was touted as a big farmers' conference in Manyene Tribal Trust Lands, Father arrived back at the farm homestead wheeling his bicycle upon which was a strange looking cargo.

Quietly sitting on the carrier of his bicycle was a young woman who my father, carelessly and without any show of compunction, introduced to his mother and sisters as his fourth wife. She was not introduced to either of his senior wives. I did not hear my mother and her other 'sisters' voice their consternation. However, from their body language, you could easily tell they were saying: "Oh no, not another woman in this harem! One would have thought the three of us were already a crowd!" As time passed, they would occasionally be heard asking, "Who has more than one wife in all the farms in the neighbourhood?"

Notwithstanding; whatever objections his senior wives might have entertained were never to be vented or expressed loudly. They dared not challenge my father on these matters without risking abuse or ill treatment. There were approximately twenty-eight small-scale farms in Maronda Mashanu Native Purchase Area. My father was the odd man out. He was the only one, as far as I knew, who was a polygamist. I had become aware that the land we were farming on had once been owned by an Anglican Priest named Father Arthur Shearly Cripps who, though late then, had founded the Maronda Mashanu community and that when he died in 1952, he had left the community with a strong Christian ethos. My father's polygamy, a practice that was regarded as heathen and unchristian in that community, became palpable.

Even those of us who were mere children began to question the truthfulness of the reason given for father's absence from the farm for two days, allegedly to attend a farmers' conference at an unspecified venue, somewhere in Manyene Tribal Trust Lands. As father appeared to have made no prior arrangements in advance of the arrival of his new wife, he made her share the hut and barn used by his mother. At the age of six or so years, I was old enough to read or analyse events as they unfolded, but I dared not ask any questions about these things I saw lest I got my wings clipped for going over the top. However, the reality was there before my eyes: the sudden arrival of a woman who my father said was his fourth wife ruffled quite a few feathers among his wives, resulting in what I term as matrimonial complications later.

To the west of our farm and stretching for endless miles both to the north and south was a farm that had vibrant grasslands as grazing areas for numerous herds of cattle and huge thick forests with trees closely packed together. Anyone unlucky enough to lose their way in the maze formed in the thick forests would need a well-trained team of 'lost and found' investigators to find them. The massive farmland, running parallel to our miniscule of a farm in the adjacent Native Purchase Area, belonged to none other than a European farmer who went by the name 'Kerry Schultz.' Pronouncing the tongue-twisting two names together was a bit of a mouthful for the local Shona-speaking people, so we simply called the farm Kerry's farm ('kwaKeri' in the local dialect) or Schultz's farm ('kwaChorosi'). To mark it off from the small and poorly maintained Native Purchase Area farms on its eastern side, a six-foot barbed wire boundary fence had been constructed probably years before the Native Purchase Area Scheme came into existence.

Along the fence were steel, circular prism poles of the same height holding up to six strands of the barbed wire and placed along the boundary fence at ten-yard intervals. Standing upright at ninety degrees all of them, the steel poles had been driven into the ground and secured in their holes with concrete. In between the poles were thinner, rectangular steel supports which had been attached to the strands of fence, using thinner but strong pieces of metal string. The six strands of barbed wire had been stretched so tautly that, notwithstanding the vagaries of weather changes, the wire did not dangle or become drab. Durable-looking and so professionally executed, the fence had been made to last until eternity. The message this piece of workmanship conveyed was that the white man's land was a no-go area and that the black native Africans who lived next door to it must keep out and dare not enter this prohibited area. In sharp contrast, many of the score or so of the small farms huddled together like a clutch of eggs, competing for space next to this huge farm, did not have any boundaries or perimeter fences between them.

In fact, the so-called boundary fences were something all the small-scale farmers could only dream about because they simply lacked the financial resources to undertake such expensive farm development projects. When opportunities were availed to some of the farmers later on, the fences which were erected were replaced by mere trigonometrical beacons as markers between farms which were of poor quality. The boundary fences subsequently erected between my father's and our neighbours Chiwandire, Tagarira and Chigwaza were characteristically the three-strand or four strand barbed wire fences. But the poor quality wooden poles and supports provided by the sparse bushlands on the farms held the fences up but only for very short periods. The strands of fence either became bedraggled dangled, or ultimately fell to the ground due to the untreated wood becoming ravaged by weather changes or eaten away by ants. Because there were no strong fences or perimeter boundaries between our neighbouring farms, farmers frequently quarrelled when cattle or other domesticated animals like goats or donkeys strayed into neighbouring farmers' fields and devoured the crops growing in them.

Our new homestead was sited at a place just as one went around the bend to reach the north of 'Makumimai Mountain' which rose majestically before it, approximately two hundred to two hundred and fifty yards from the base of this geographical feature. Often during the day and standing at the edge of the homestead, I would call loudly or whistle facing the slopes of the mountain. The sounds echoed several times in adjacent spurs and caves farther up the mountain side. Frighteningly, it was as if imaginary strangers living in places up against the mountain also called or whistled back in response. It was intriguing listening to the echoes returning to the homestead when nobody else was about. When I remembered I was alone in the farm compound and sensed my insecurity, I quickly abandoned the silly and senseless practice of whistling or calling at the mountain. Moments after I had stopped the habit, I would check again quietly, making sure that no sub-humans or total strangers had descended from the mountain cliffs and were walking towards our homestead to collect me or do horrible things to me.

Farmer Kerry Schultz's farm boundary fence cuts right across a third of the western side of Makumimai Mountain. After mounting the steeper northern slopes and briefly straddling the half-moon-shaped flat surface across the summit of the mountain, the huge fence and accompanying steel posts descended the mountain's gentler slopes behind it. On reaching the bottom of the mountain, the perimeter fence carried on across a small stream and by-passed my father's farm on the left and proceeded beyond Chigwaza's Farm to an unknown destination further on. As I looked at the positioning of the six-foot poles along the fence, they resembled a troop of soldiers lined up on parade, all of them standing upright with their hands straight down beside them in a ruler-straight line. The narrow strip of land along the Chiputya River, a mile east of our farm had been declared as 'crown land'. None of the local farmers owned it.

The farmers Chiwandire, my own father, Pfumojena, Tagarira, Pfende, Mashonganyika and Marisira further up the river, whose lands bordered along the river had prescribed limits beyond which they were not permitted to plough or grow crops. Across the river to the east from our farm was a small to medium size farm. That farm belonged to the Pfumojenas. Looking towards the east from Father's farm, the Pfumojenas Farm was on a bit to the left. In the south of the Pfumojenas was Father Arthur Shearly Cripps's approximately ten-hectare farm which had been retained as a spiritual centre in tribute to and in honour of the reverend gentleman. Since his death in 1952, his remains remained interred at his shrine aptly called Maronda Mashanu or 'Five Wounds'. The holy shrine was (and still is) less than a kilometre from the crown land along the Chiputya River and my father's farm in the west on the opposite side of the river. Father Cripps had named that river the 'River Jordan' because that was where the priest baptised newly converted Christians. The shrine was only about two kilometres from the farm homestead where I spent all my early and middle childhood.

On a quiet day in that rural neighbourhood, anybody could call with a raised voice and easily be heard from Pfumojena Farm homestead which was about two miles north of Father Cripps's shrine. The caller's voice could easily be picked up by anybody at Chiwandire Farm as well as by anybody working in the fields on my father's farm, both just across the river. One of Sekuru Pfumojena's daughters, Matimbe, was renowned for her loud voice which, when she called out, rang out like a church bell summoning parishioners to come to church, reaching far and wide. Before he died in 1952, Father Cripps – who reportedly lived a simple villager's life at the shrine – had maintained a small orchard with apple, banana, and orange plants. sixty-five years later or thereabouts, as I write this memoir after his death, some of the orange plants have survived the vagaries of weather to this day, yet nobody from among his parishioners in the local community voluntarily took responsibility upon themselves to take care of the orchard. The orange plants had grown tall. When the season was good, these orange trees produced yellow, juicy, sweet fruit.

At that stage of history that I write about and describe in this narrative, the late Reverend Father Cripps's shrine at Maronda Mashanu Mission did not have a perimeter fence around it. I do not know if it has one now, but the serenity and solitude that forever pervaded the shrine gave it a forbidding atmosphere. Yes, there was unwritten permission for us to graze our cattle in the area surrounding the shrine. But nobody could just walk into the grounds of that holy place without feeling a sense that you were trespassing on someone's property. However typical of childish impertinence, we little boys would often dare to sneak into Father Cripps' orchard to fetch some fruit.

I was seven years old or thereabouts when one day I was herding cattle not far from Father Cripps' orchard. It was a hot noon day, and I assumed my herd of cattle had had enough to eat. Leaving nearly all of them lying on the ground in the shade of huge trees just over the riverbank, I made a quick dash to Father Cripps' orchard to pick some ripe oranges, if I could find any. I did not have to go far, just three hundred yards or so away following a winded path through a small woodland. My wish was that if I found any of the juicy fruit in the orchard, I would quickly return and continue keeping an eye on my herd of cattle while munching my oranges. Barely ten minutes later when I was trying to reach the third yellow orange that dangled invitingly high up in the tree, I suddenly heard the shrilly voice of a woman calling loudly from a distance north of Father Cripps's shrine. Initially, I ignored it and desperately continued trying to bring the orange at the top of the tree down, using a long dry stick. The voice persisted:

"Kune ariko here mhiri uko-oo,
mombe mumunda kwaPfumojena-aa!
Ndati pane arikundinzwa here mombe
mumunda kwaPfumojena uko
Nhaiweeee-ee! KwaMudyara nhaiweeeeeee,
mombe mumunda kwa
Pfumojena dzapedza zviyo zvese nhaiweeeeeee eeeee!"

My father's farm was the nearest to that edge of the Pfumojena Farm, so the message conveyed by the woman was saying, the Pfumojena homestead was saying that two or so kilometres away – she could see a whole herd of cattle in rapoko's (zviyo), not far from Father Cripps' shrine. She was pleading; asking whether anyone who was nearer, anybody from my father's farm or the nearby Chiwandire's farm, ould run and take the cattle out of the field as they were snipping off the rapoko ears which had almost reached harvesting stage in the field. I hurriedly ran back to the site where I had left my herd of cattle, all resting under the shade of trees. I found the entire herd had gone! The woman's voice was still calling piercingly. Her thin but sharp voice was ringing in the air, and it lacerated through the hot afternoon atmosphere. Recognising the voice as that of a woman who was popularly known as Matimbe, I sensed danger. Throwing away the two oranges I held in my hands into the undergrowth, I ran through the bushes towards Pfumojena's fields.

My herd of cattle was all over the field. All of them were having a feast. I succeeded in driving those that had complied with my shouting out of the field. However, there was a small herd, lugubrious and ungainly to the point of caricature, which walked reluctantly as they chewed the rapoko ears that filled their mouths. You might have thought they wanted me to push them out of the field. I was subsequently successful in ejecting the whole herd out of the field. Looking around fearfully as I drove the cattle out of the field, I noticed that almost an acre of the field had been ruined.

Just as I reached the edge of the field with the remainder of the cattle intending to drive the whole herd across the river back to a grazing area in our farm, my father suddenly arrived on the scene. The shrilly voice of the woman at Pfumojena Farm two kilometres or so away from our farm had reached him while he was working in one of his fields. He and I drove the entire herd of cattle, some of them still chewing remnants of the rapoko (millet) ears in their mouths voraciously and swishing their tails in the process.

I was not too happy seeing him arrive to help me drive the cattle across the river. Looking around quickly as my father and I drove the cattle out of the field, I noted with dismay half that the field had been ruined. Before long, my father pretended to want to help me drive the cattle cross the river. "Er-r let's work together, Kingi, to get the whole herd cross the river. Over here, find a stick and get this cow near me to get across, eh!" he prompted. "I beg your pardon, Dad. What do you want me to do?" I asked nervously with my heart thumping against my ribs. It was clear the man had a hidden agenda. I quickly surmised that there was trouble on the way. Then before long, he thundered, "Where have you put your ears, you? I said get a move on, son. Please, don't waste my time. Drive this cow nearer me here and get it to cross the river like all the others are doing!"

I was tempted to thank him for his kindness in rushing over from our own farm just across the river to help me drive the cattle from the neighbour's rapoko field. However, what I could not understand was that he pretended to want to help me drive some of the cattle which were nearest to me rather than those at the extreme end nearer him. Of course, he had an ulterior motive. It quickly dawned on me that his trick was for me to be near to him. With me close at hand, he would find it easy to reach out, grab me and give me a beating for letting the cattle stray into other people's fields and eat their rapoko crop.

My only alternative was to make a run for it if I could. I suddenly broke into a sprint and tried to escape into the nearby bushes. That was a tactical error on my part. I had no chance with my father who had once been a policeman-like messenger at the District Commissioner's Offices. He wore a pair of shorts that day, so his mode of dress made it easy for him to run and catch up with a fleeing little boy. Holding both my thin wrists in the vice grip of his massive left palm, he obtained a fresh 'mutondo' stick off the main plant with one mighty tug of his right hand and he gave me the mother of all battering's. My loud wailing and grovelling for forgiveness and for him to let me go fell on deaf ears. My wriggling, jumping and wildly dancing about while he held me tightly with his left hand came to no avail.

It was such a pity that neither my mother nor any other adult was anywhere in the vicinity to intervene and stop him from continuing to unleash those vile strokes on me. He only stopped thrashing me and let me go when he became tired of landing the countless strokes all over my back and even on my clean-shaven head. That was the first time he had beaten me so brutally. It was my father's pattern of meting out punishment not just to me but to all his children, especially those of us boys.

After beating me so cruelly, he never bothered to find out how I felt or if his beatings had caused wounds on my skin or made my skin swell. Instead, he harshly ordered me to drive the cattle back into the grazing areas of our farm while he shuffled back to the field from whence, he had originally responded to the urgent call to remove stray cattle from the 'rapoko' field belonging to the Pfumojenas. Parts of my shaven head had bumps on it from the beatings. As my father walked back to his field of maize leaving me alone with the cattle, as if nothing had happened, I experienced a terrific headache. It felt as if I was carrying a thousand kilograms of metal objects on my head. That experience gave me a deep sense of injury not just to my body but also to my inner self; I hated my father with a passion for most of that afternoon.

Starting off as one of the many poor and unemployed village youths in Nharira Tribal Trust Lands, my father had no choice but to go looking for employment. While his agemates went looking for menial jobs at large European-owned farms nearby or as labourers in mines which were sprouting all over, he was lucky enough to be employed as a mere Messenger at the District Native Commissioner's Offices in the then Charter (now Chikomba) District. Securing that job at The Range while the great bulk of his agemates were getting employment as labourers on white men's farms and mines gave his ego an enormous boost. My father's ego was further inflated by the success and fame achieved within a short time as a senior messenger. He used his air of superiority to look down on other men, his own wives and children and everybody else.

His fame in the community as the most trusted messenger at the DC's Offices; often seen accompanying the white officers, the 'Mambos', when they toured 'native' villages sprawled across vast swathes of the district, grew like wildfire in the dry season. Even when he subsequently resigned from his job as a messenger to relocate to Maronda Mashanu to occupy his newly acquired small-scale farm, my father was not completely a stranger to his counterparts in the new African Purchase Area. He had been one of the messengers from the District Native Commissioner's Offices who local villagers frequently observed accompanying 'white' Land Development Officers or surveyors at the time when the land that would later be named 'Maronda Mashanu Native Purchase Area' was being demarcated into farms in the late 1930s! The man who had ridden on the crest of his wave just ten to fifteen years previously, then the villagers were looking at now, was a man who, though previously had been a farmer with a landholding in his name, and still enjoyed his old fame and popularity.

My father was tall but of medium build].

His bushy moustache and double chin that was always clean-shaven gave him a severe appearance. When he walked, his body was ramrod straight and his arms at the elbows were slightly parted from the thoracic area of his chest, giving people the impression that he was about to give somebody a good hiding, at any time, at the slightest provocation; and pounce on other men, my father often did, if they expressed a different opinion from his. He had a slight stammer in his speech, so whenever he lost his temper, and he could not get words out to vent his anger immediately, he resorted to the use of his fists. He was notorious for that behaviour at beer-drinking parties or group community efforts (nhimbes or majakwara) in the local African Purchase Area and the nearby congested 'Reserves' or 'Lines'.

There was one exception, though. One of the few men he dared not cross swords with was our neighbour, Mr Martin Chiwandire. Usually, the latter was a quiet man who was reticent about his past. He was renowned for his efficiency in putting up a good fight, having previously had stints working as a mine labourer in Johannesburg Gold Mines, back in the 'Wenela' days. The man had been exposed to the rough and tumble of life where he had dealt with rough riders of all sorts in that city known for its 'tsotsis', tricksters, and all kinds of social misfits, so he was no push-over. We used to call him affectionately 'Vamujubeki' meaning simply 'The Johannesburger'. My father would usually give this man a wide berth and treat him with great care lest it would be his turn to get thumped.

I have already hinted on my father's absence of feeling after the beating he gave me near Father Arthur Shearly Cripps's shrine the other day. I now attribute his character to the fact that he was sadly lacking in the soft touch. He rarely, if ever, engaged in small talk with any of us, his children. As it was, I rarely saw him playfully or affectionately talk to any of his wives. When the need for him to speak to any members of his family arose, it was with a voice that was loud, harsh, unpleasant, and punctuated with the rumbles of a thunderous storm. Being the father-figure in the homestead, all power and authority pivoted on him like a door hinge turns around a pin. He ruled his household with a strict code of ethics. His wives and all of us lived in perpetual fear of his fiery temper. There was no difference in the manner with which Father meted out justice on incidents of wrongdoing between adults and children in the home. The person he deferred to only was his mother, my Granny or his own mother's mother. The old English proverb 'When the cat is away, the mice will play' fitted in nicely with our circumstances. Whenever father was absent from the farm during the day, attending either a farmers' meetings somewhere or meeting with friends at beer-drinking parties out there in the 'reserves', all would be peaceful and quiet at the farm compound. We would all be very happy. If we were laughing and chatting away happily and he suddenly arrived in the homestead and entered the hut where we were gathered, the fear-free intercourse we were enjoying would end with the abruptness of a clap of thunder. The subdued lighting in the room rendered the atmosphere an air of foreboding. Like frightened rats, we would bolt out of the venue one by one to another where we felt safe from danger. Even from those safe venues where we had escaped to in the large farm homestead, we often picked up noises of disagreement between him and some his wives, especially my mother with whom he often picked quarrels of one sort or the other. Doors would be banged or slammed. Cries and squeals of pain would be heard as the victims of his brutal beatings escaped into the dark night. Often, the heavy punishments he meted out either to his children or his wives would be for comparatively minor offences ranging from failing to complete an assignment to letting a troop of baboons or monkeys raid a field of maize because you accidentally fell asleep at an appointed spot and thus failed to scare them away!

I have grown well beyond middle-age myself as I write this memoir, but I can never forget this day when, following a whole day's absence at beer-drinking parties in 'Mutasa Reserves' five miles away, he suddenly hobbled into the farm compound. It was around nine o'clock in the evening. Although stars twinkled in a cloudless sky, there was no moonlight, and the night was quite dark. My young brother Irrigation (Wilfred) and I were still awake. We sat chatting with our mother in her round hut before we would finally go to bed in our 'bedroom' in the main farmhouse. In the centre of the hut was a fire which had begun burning brightly due to the dry and old 'Musasa' logs mother had added to stoke it. In addition to the brightness the flames of the fire produced, a candlestick placed on a bare floor near the mantelpiece at the back of the hut produced its own light. On the fire was a huge three-legged metal pot in which mother was boiling pumpkins, some of which we were going to eat for our lunch meal on the following day. Father suddenly banged the door open and walked into mother's hut. Breathing heavily and without sitting down, he glared at us and mother in the candle-light. He was a big man and his whole frame filled the hut's entrance. Struggling to speak as he was clearly drunk, he ordered mother to leave the hut at once as he had a bone to chew with both Irrigation (Wilfred) and I. He rarely talked to us as, looking at each other in bewilderment, my young brother and I wondered what that was all about. The sequence of events that followed had obviously been carefully premeditated. As Mother was leaving the hut as ordered, Wilfred's attempt to leave together with our mother was fiercely resisted by Father.

Glowering at him angrily, he gave my young brother such a shove that he fell onto the floor by the kitchen mantelpiece while father slammed shut the home-made door with his gumboot shod right foot. Within a minute of mother stepping outside the hut, Father pulled from behind his back a thick freshly cut 'Mutondo' stick from somewhere under the bottom of his shirt. As soon as Irrigation (Wilfred) caught sight of the stick hidden under the shirt behind him, he became quite unsettled and started begging to be allowed to leave, rubbing his palms together and appealing for father to accept his plight: "Father, please let me go. I don't want you to beat me today. You can beat Kingston (Lawrence) today if you want, but please spare me the stick!"

Irrigation (Wilfred) was so terrified of being beaten, hence his employment of a charm offensive to persuade Father kindly to consider sparing him the rod; but our father flatly ignored what I think he may have interpreted to as my young brother's unintelligible mumbling. He prefaced his action, clearly premeditated, with a badly crafted little speech in which he accused us of an offence which he said had occurred a week or two before, none of which Wilfred or I could recollect: "I'm not going to have children who let the cattle you're grazing stray into my large maize field and allow them to eat most of the cobs of maize that were ready for picking. So, for your negligence, both of you Kingi and Irrigation, are going to get it thick today. I'm quite sure that after today's beating, there'll not be a repeat of the same carelessness from you."

My father started flogging us all over our bodies one by one. Although we squealed with pain and begged and shouted for forgiveness, jumping up and down with every stroke of the stick that landed on our bodies, the man continued beating us mercilessly. If any of us attempted to reach the exit where he firmly stood, he simply picked you up and hurled you like a lifeless object to the rear of the then dimly lit hut. It was darker in the hut then because as we danced and dashed about during the beating, one of us knocked over the candlestick leaving the atmosphere in semi-darkness except for the fragments of light that flickered from the dying embers of the fire that had been burning brightly in the centre of the hut. Wilfred and I were like trapped prisoners as father never bothered to take note of our plight. He seemed to enjoy thrashing us, his stick landing on either your head or bare skin of the body. We cried and shouted for help at the tops of our voices, but the man would not relent from applying the needless corporal punishment.

At the height of the hullabaloo, aided by the semi-darkness in the venue, Wilfred ventured to escape the beating once more through Father's parted legs, hoping he would get half a second's chance to open the door behind our tormentor and slip out. Unfortunately, that plan did not work. Father picked him up with the hooked fingers of his right hand and threw him right into the fire just in front of him, a process which knocked over the large three-legged pot in which pumpkins were cooking. The likelihood is that the man did not even notice what had happened. Some of the boiling water cooking the pumpkins on the fire may have spilled onto parts of Wilfred's body. He sustained very serious burns to his legs, buttocks, areas around his stomach and parts of his forearms. It was terrible.

Creeping out of the fire to the safety of the open space at the darkened back of the hut, his cries of, "I'm burnt! Help me please! I'm burnt and I'm in pain!" fell on deaf ears. During the goings-on inside her hut, mother had stood just outside the closed door struggling with her inner self as a mother as to how she could intervene and ameliorate our situation. Throwing all care to the wind and the danger she risked of the fire being turned on her, she decided she had to do something to help her children, especially on hearing Wilfred's cries of pain after he had been thrown into the fire. She forced open the home-made wooden door by pulling it with both her hands from the outside until it broke free from its hinges. She quickly threw it on the ground beside her, leaving the entrance wide open. On noticing this, father immediately switched his focus onto Mother who stood a few steps away ready to face the music from my father. It was frightening. With a furrowed brow, father would have gone for Mother and given her a thorough beating.

That would have happened if it were not for our Granny VaChemedza, father's own elderly mother, who suddenly appeared on the scene, awakened from her sleep in the hut next door, by the commotion in the dark night fifteen metres away from her hut. The only person Father had respect for was his own mother. When Granny implored him to stop in his tracks for whatever reasons he had to start assaulting Mother, Father reluctantly complied, and walked over to escape into his own bedroom nearby, huffing and puffing like a wounded bull. Meanwhile, Granny's sudden appearance on the scene offered us a much-needed respite and a window of opportunity to make good our escape to freedom. Taking our cue from Father's switch of focus, we discreetly slipped through his legs, through the open doorway and darted into the freedom of the pitch blackness of the night. Despite the limited light in our path to freedom, I held one of my brother's hands and he ran together with me through the darkness, both of us skipping over low bushes, rocky boulders, and tufts of drying grass until we reached an empty field with several stacks of freshly harvested maize stalks still carrying their cobs on them.

We had run to safety two or three kilometres away from the farm compound. I crept with my brother into the deep interior of one huge maize stack that I had selected. Creeping to the centre of the huge maize stack in pitch darkness, we also risked the danger of being bitten by snakes that usually also sought the same warmth and comfort that were found in these dark spaces. Wilfred had been badly burnt, so he was in severe pain which made him whimper quietly and shake noisily and uncontrollably throughout the night. It was dark where we hid, so I had no way of noticing the extent of my young brother's burns. But I really felt pity for him and the pain he was suffering.

At about midnight, I became anxious that if father came searching for our whereabouts, which was likely, it was going to be easy for him to locate where we were hidden. However, that did not happen, and I was assured we were in the relative safety of the maize stack and the warmth was good. Just before sunrise on the following morning, Wilfred and I quietly crept out of the maize stack. That was when I discovered to my horror the full extent and seriousness of my brother's burns. Unsightly blisters with liquid in them had formed in all those places he had received burns. Some of the dark and shiny skin dangled on his hands and legs. Meanwhile the intensity of his pain was increasing by leaps and bounds. I could not continue just looking at my sibling continue suffering, so without consulting anyone – I surmised that our mother might never have the opportunity to look for us and find out about how we had fared after the events of the night before – I made the bold decision to take my brother to the hospital in town for treatment even if it might entail my having to carry him on my back along the ten-kilometre route.

I was only about nine or ten years of age then. Chivhu (then Enkeldoorn) Hospital was, and still is, ten kilometres – approximately six miles – away from Father's farm which still exists to this day. I was surprised by the courage and tenacity Wilfred (Irrigation) displayed. He managed to walk slowly beside me the first two miles or so, with me holding one of his hands which did not have too many blisters on it. After passing a place called 'Benson' – named after an old white farmer who had either died or relocated elsewhere many years previously – it became hotter on a cloudless autumn day and my brother's pain increased rapidly. Part of his discomfort was also caused by the fact that he was becoming hungry, both of us having had no breakfast. He told me in a pitiful voice, "Brother King (Lawrence), I want to thank you for your decision to take me to Enkeldoorn (Chivhu) Hospital. But I am in great pain, and I can't walk no more." I had no choice but to carry Wilfred on my back for the remainder of the journey, about four miles; during which I stopped and rested several times in the cool shade of trees. I was afraid that father might ride on his bicycle and catch up with us as I carried my brother on my back along the main gravel road to Enkeldoorn. The destination was the hospital in Enkeldoorn (Chivhu), and I needed to get my brother there before sunset. We therefore changed tack, left the main feeder gravel road and snaked our way through secret pathways in Kerry's and another unknown white man's farms. Still quite some walking distance from the town, the blisters which had formed on Wilfred's body had begun to break open and some of the watery liquid gushed out of the openings thereby exposing the skin covered by the blisters to the air. This caused my young brother more pain and discomfort, making me also feel the pain he was going through. Along that dusty and secret network of paths passing by a place we popularly used to call 'Benson Corner', old buildings now crumbled to ruins, on our way to Enkeldoorn (Chivhu), my brother and I were like lost souls upon the vast expanse of a large body of water. Besides just the two of us walking through that lonely path, I had no one to ask for assistance to carry my brother! What intensified my predicament was also the fact that, having spent most of my childhood in the blissful obscurity of the farm environment, I knew absolutely nothing about ambulances, 'Casualty Department' or sections of hospitals that we today call 'Accident and Emergency.' Even if the ambulance service had started operating at Enkeldoorn (Chivhu) Hospital, I was too young and of had too much of a rural background to tell whether such facilities had ever existed at Enkeldoorn (Chivhu) Hospital. As for summoning an ambulance, I would have had no way of calling for one because of the secret paths I used to reach the town with my brother carried on my back. The ambulance driver would have found it difficult to reach us in the bush.

Exhausted, thirsty, and hungry, we finally arrived in the town well after five o'clock in the evening, only to be informed by a bystander outside the perimeter fence of the hospital that the 'Out-Patients Department' – I was hearing this term for the first time – was already closed for the day! I picked up my burden once more and carried my young brother to an address about a mile and a half downtown where an Uncle Chigonyati (on my mother's side) lived and worked as a General Hand. He lived at that address in a small two-roomed cottage or 'Boy's Kaya'.

Seeing the dastardly condition Wilfred was in, Uncle Chigonyati expressed anger at my father for perpetrating what he said was a scandal. In total disbelief, he scowled, "Oh, my God, this is hard to believe! What's all this, boys? What happened?" I explained without giving too many details and he retorted, "Typical of your father, Kingi. He is so rough he has no idea how to take care of his own wives and children. If the people at the hospital get to know about the things you've just told me, your father's going to be in serious trouble." Straight away, he begged both Wilfred and I not to reveal to the hospital authorities the true cause of Irrigation's (Wilfred's) injuries. Otherwise, Uncle Chigonyati feared, Father risked being arrested and sent to prison if the truth of what exactly happened was known.

At the crack of dawn the following morning, Uncle Chigonyati cooked maize meal porridge and prepared some hot mugs of tea for us. After tucking in our meal – of which Irrigation (Wilfred) only ate very little because he was in great pain – Uncle Chigonyati offered to transport him to Enkeldoorn (Chivhu) Hospital on his bicycle carrier. As Uncle wheeled his bicycle, I walked on the side holding my young brother so that he did not fall over. By eight thirty a.m. that morning, Irrigation (Wilfred) had quickly been admitted into hospital where he was confined for the next two months. To protect my father from possible arrest, thank God Uncle Chigonyati had suggested that we invent a story to the effect that (Wilfred) had accidentally fallen into a fire while playing with a group of other children at the farm. In line with Safeguarding and Child Protection rules that were in force at the time, the hospital authorities subsequently summoned our male parent to the hospital for a chat.

On reporting to the hospital as invited, he was severely reprimanded by the 'European' doctors who had invited him to establish what exactly had transpired leading to Irrigation (Wilfred) being so badly burnt. There were yet to be any African doctors in the whole of Rhodesia, (Zimbabwean) hospitals then, so the few European doctors available did the treatment rounds in both the European sections and the Native African hospital sections of both the In-Patient and Out-Patient wards.

The European doctors who chatted with my father warned him that should the hospital receive further reports of adult negligence from his farm again leading to children being hurt, they would not hesitate to press charges! That jolted him. Being interviewed by a team of European doctors, he apologised profusely in his unawareness that a story had been invented to protect him. In sharp contrast to his bossy conduct and behaviour in the woods at the farm where he seemed a demi-god and barked orders at everybody, his demeanour at the hospital was completely transformed in the interview with the white men. He had ridden his bicycle from the farm to attend the summons from the doctors. I had instead, unbeknown to him, walked to Enkeldoorn (Chivhu) separately to visit my young brother in hospital.

Then by chance, while walking through the hallway between hospital wards to visit my young brother when wards were now open for 'Patient Visitors', I stumbled upon the interview where for the first time, I witnessed my male parent reduced to a simpleton under a barrage of questions and accusations, the intensity of which left him inarticulate and a chattering imbecile. Rivers of sweat poured down his face. He had removed his hat, crumpled it into a shapeless object and tucked it away under one of his sweaty armpits. From the foregoing, suffice it to say my upbringing at the farm, together with that of my other brothers, was by no means a walk in the park, but a struggle to survive under an authoritarian regime on the watch of a bully.

As soon as my father settled at his new farm, he wasted no time in getting down to work. He would wake up at the crack of dawn daily and continued working on his land until dusk, chopping down and digging up roots of trees and practically turning virgin forests into fields where crops could be grown. He was physically fit and rarely complained of feeling tired. His three wives, sisters, and older children like Misheck Raphael, Kaston Roland and Faith would be found working with him throughout the day in the digging up of tree roots. Even I, at the young age of just six or seven years, was soon often included in the allocations of the more difficult assignments at the farm. It was punishing work for me and these unfortunate people who were not as strong as Father was; and thus, suffered immensely.

None of us would dare complain openly about his ill treatment of us from fear of being beaten up or being ridiculed or humiliated, sometimes in the presence of total strangers. Three of four years after settling at the farm, father almost always expressed disquiet about his eldest son, Misheck's (Raphael's) negative attitude to work. He would complain loudly that the latter was lazy, and he sought to flush this weakness out of my older brother by constantly nagging and beating him. Curiously, when quarrels between Misheck (Raphael) and father broke out, Kaston Roland was invariably included in the punishments my father meted out to the former. Tense situations frequently broke out between Misheck and my father. Misheck would eventually flee into the safety of the woods. Kaston had no choice but to run together with his older stepbrother from fear that father might turn on him and beat him up as well if he stayed behind. They would spend days on end sleeping in the woods around the farm or in the mouths of caves on the slopes of the mountain. My father did not care about the dangers or comforts of his children after they had run away from his ill treatment of them. After a brawl with him, which was all too often at night, we ran off from home during a heavy rainfall. He did not care to look for us and persuade us to return home where it was warm and dry. Even if you spent days sleeping in the bushes, he did not care about your safety. It was none of his concern whether you were eating while you were away or not.

Consequently, nearly all my father's sons, including me, were developing into sad-faced youths as we grew up at his mercy. His mindlessness was unbelievable. His focus was on ensuring that there was enough manpower working the land on his farm and he did not care about the welfare of the people working on his land. Consequently, instead of developing in us a love of the benefits that accrue from a dignity of labour, we all ended up hating farming and everything that was associated with it.

Despite my middle childhood years of between six and eight years of age, Father was of the view that I was old enough to be assigned more difficult jobs on the farm. As there were no other little boys of the same age as myself in the farm compound, I carried out most of these jobs on my own. Dairy cows in the cattle pen needed to be milked daily in the morning before the whole herd was released to go and graze. I had previously watched my older brothers perform this rather difficult and primitive task on a few occasions. I have used the word 'primitive' deliberately because I want to convey the sense that the practice of milking cows in modern dairies is totally different from the 'modus operandi' we used in the underdeveloped environments that were part of my childhood.

My older brothers were therefore needed to join the rest of the adult teams working in more challenging tasks on the farm, so father passed the baton of milking the dairy cows on to me. Little boys Irrigation (Wilfred) and nephew Last (Bernard) sometimes stood around offering me whatever help they could give. However, I was finally accountable for ensuring that all the cows that were calving had been milked to avoid calves suffering from bloated stomachs due to receiving too much milk from their parent mothers. As you would imagine, the job of milking cows was not quite like a walk in the park for a little boy of my age. Before long, I discovered that the process of milking the dairy cows called upon me to have a large reservoir of patience and resilience besides my being required to be able to cope with the different temperaments of the cows. With practice, I discovered that on a given day, one cow would calmly and stand still while I tied its hind legs together with a string made of animal hide. The reason for tying the animal's hind legs tightly was so that it did not move about unnecessarily while I squeezed the milk with my fingers from its tits into a tin or metal pail that I would have placed on the ground directly under the cow's udder.

A more versatile and experienced milkman in those primitive circumstances would hold the tin between his thighs and tactfully milk the cow squeezing the cow's tits with both his hands until the cow's udder was emptied of its rich creamy contents. Then the cow would have its hind legs freed and be allowed to go. The process would be totally different with a cow possessing a mercurial temperament. The new cow and its moods would cause me problems from the very start. It would absolutely refuse to stand still while I tied its hind legs together tightly. The same cow would pretend to calm down, as it were, in response to my energetic persuasion using all the tricks in the book, for example, whistling softly while I rubbed its backside smoothly with my right palm etc. Suddenly the cow would give me a nasty kick on the shin with one of its hind legs, causing me to freeze in one spot, bent double, holding my knee and squealing with pain. Moments later and after the pain had dissipated, I would have another go at the creature and surprisingly succeeding in getting the elusive procedure restarted. But halfway through the milking, the cow would lose its temper again and start hopping along due to its hind legs being tightly tied together. As it moved about, the cow would inevitably knock over the pail that was probably half full of milk, spilling the contents onto the muddy ground. How very frustrating! This result necessitated restarting the process until the job was done. Fifteen dairy cows in the cattle pen needed to be milked and I had no way of knowing their different moods from one day to the next.

A confusion of guinea fowl ('hanga' in Shona) and conspiracies of ravens ('horwe' in Shona) inhabited the long grass and shrubs at the edge of one of Father's field of maize. This field zigzagged for up to two miles along the bottom of the eastern side of Makumimai Mountain. The birds were truly a pain in the neck for farmers on most mornings and evenings of the planting season. As if the birds had been given information by somebody telling them that maize seeds planted in the field had started germinating, scores of these birds would emerge from the undergrowth and descend on the fields now carpeted with the green leaves of thousands of germinating maize seeds. On gaining entry to the field, they caused absolute havoc by not only pecking at and destroying the small green plants using their pointed beaks. The birds also used their talons to scratch and remove the soil around the young plants until they reached the original maize seeds that had been planted in the soil. Then they uprooted the seeds destroying the plants altogether or picking them up and swallowing them. These destructive habits of the birds resulted in reduced harvests for the farmers. My father would not have his maize seedlings destroyed by guinea fowl while we the little ones were there to prevent such events.

While the rest of the adults and the older children were occupied in performing the more difficult work in the fields, e.g. weeding, ploughing with spans of oxen, digging up roots of old tree stumps, trees that that had been chopped down, ('magobo') by Father in his efforts to turn forests into arable land, younger children like my young brother Irrigation (Wilfred), Last (Bernard) and me were assigned the responsibility to scare the birds away both shortly before sunrise and in the evenings every day. Each of us was allocated a certain guarding position along the edge of the field – which we were expected to look after – first thing in the morning and in the earlier part of the evening. In my case for example, I did not just stand in one place and shout at the birds to go away. Instead, I held aloft in front of me an old or used twenty-litre metal oil container. Then as I walked up and down the path at the edge of the field, I would repeatedly strike the surface of the circular prism with a wooden stick. The repeated strikes produced sharp metallic gongs which I accompanied with my rhythmic calls or singing as I paced forwards and backwards within the space allocated to me. I want you to imagine the discordant metallic sounds the three of us produced at the same time when we struck the empty tins with sticks and walked forwards and backwards within our allocated areas of work! If any among the three of us was found to have let the dishonourable birds enter the field and destroyed the young plants, Father would be livid with anger leading to obvious consequences. Without exception, such offences always led to the offender earning painful beatings or sharp rebukes.

I was performing my guard duties at the edge of the field one morning when Father suddenly pitched up at my station. I greeted him but he only made a grunted response. He never ever warned you in advance about his inspection visits. Inviting me to come with him as he commenced his inspection, he walked slowly with his hands folded behind his back, checking to make sure the hated birds had not destroyed the young maise plants. Satisfied that everything was in order, he stammered instructions to the effect that I return to my spot and continue with the work I was doing. There was no mention of credit or praise for the good work I was doing. He had started walking towards Last (Bernard)'s spot when he suddenly stopped in his tracks. Turning round, he seemed to have remembered to mumble a parting shot which turned out to be a warning, "I'll not have my maize plants destroyed by these guinea fowl and ravens. Just let them get in and you know what'll happen to you, do you understand me, Kingi?" Circumspect not to say too many things before that frightful man who really had not a shred of interest in my wellbeing, I answered, "Yes, Father." I do not think he bothered to listen to my response because a moment or two later he was striding surprisingly angrily towards the next stage of his inspections. Skipping my nephew Last who was dutifully positioned next to my patch of the field, Father reached my young brother Irrigation (Wilfred)'s guard post.

Irrigation reluctantly accepted Father's invitation to come with him as he, more alert and suspicious than me or our nephew Last as usual, was uncertain what Father's intentions were. Readying himself for the unexpected, he walked about four metres behind Father when the inspection process at that end of the field started. The drama that followed took place in my full view although I was about five hundred metres away. Irrigation (Wilfred) himself filled me in with some of the comic details later. Unbeknown to my young brother, the silly birds had surreptitiously invaded his patch of the field he guarded after he left to go home at the end of his duties at nightfall on the previous day. Now, we were not in the habit of checking the order of things in the field when we resumed duty on the next day. The assumption was that everything was in order; there was nothing to worry about, taking it for granted that the birds we scared off did not move about at night, we assumed that they would not enter the fields under cover of darkness. On the contrary, when we left to go home in the evening the day before, the hateful birds had emerged from the thick bushes and entered the field on Irrigation's patch of the field and penetrated deeper into the interior of the wide end of the maize field. As they did so, they left a trail of destruction behind them. Many plants had been uprooted and destroyed. Having had their fill uninterrupted by us who always walked about banging old oil metal containers, the birds would have flown out of the field, even in that light darkness, flapping their wings in delight and contentment.

With a keen eye for order, father quickly picked up that something was not right as soon as the inspection started. So did my young brother Irrigation, who became alarmed by his own discovery and the impending consequences at the end of the inspection. Visibly angered by the discovery of damage the birds had wreaked, father continued with the inspection, his eyes reaching out wide ahead of him and he, pointing at some of the dead little green plants which had ruthlessly been pulled up by their very roots and lay shrivelled and limp on the moist floor of the field. Father mumbled under his breath, "Irrigation, have a look. Oh, my God, see all this, just have a look. Where were you when all this happened? Is this what I mean when I ask you to come here and scare these birds away? Look, all the young maize plants have gone – heh! Just have a look. Nothing left in the whole of this area!"

My father's hand gestures showed a wide area in front of him. Carrying on with his soliloquy without turning around, he was unaware that Irrigation was no longer walking behind him. In the first two minutes of the inspection starting, Irrigation quietly made an about turn, took off at speed, and sprinted for cover at high velocity towards the thorny thickets at the bottom of the mountain slopes, two hundred metres away. From where I stood, approximately five hundred metres away, I saw Wilfred literally want to take flight like a jet at full throttle on the runway prior to becoming airborne. He ran so quickly I could hardly detect the scissors or pendulum movement of his tiny legs. Considering his burst of speed to reach safety, I thought to myself 'heaven knows why a small cloud of dust did not form behind him as he ran'. Safely hidden in the thickness of the bushes, Irrigation told me later, he looked back at the scene in the field, but still with his heart thumping like mad.

Father was still walking ahead and making loud comments about the extent of damage the birds had incurred, the man completely oblivious his own bird had flown several minutes previously. Observing that event unfolding from a distance, I nearly laughed out aloud. Finally, stopping in his tracks and swerving round with a sweep of his big hands to escalate his conversation with Irrigation to the next level, his target was nowhere to be seen. Father had hoped to close his massive palms around Irrigation's thin arms and give him his just reward. Discovering that the errant child had fizzled into thin air, he furiously thundered, "My God dammit this! So, I've been talking to myself all along, haven't I?" Shouting at the mountain where he was certain Irrigation was safely hidden from him, he thundered once more, "Hey you, hokoyo wena (watch out, you) Irrigation! You'd better stay put where you're hiding for a long time, damn you! If I'd caught you, I was going to teach you a lesson. Bloody bastard, you musvuchanyoko (swear word signalling anger)!"

Father's loud voice boomed, reverberating in the slopes and caverns of the adjacent mountain, causing a flight of frightened little birds in tall trees at the edge of the field to erupt and scatter in different directions, flapping their wings vigorously.

I was only a shouting distance from Irrigation's patch of the field, so I benefitted from not only observing him dash like a hare for cover. I had also sufficiently eavesdropped the entire proceedings in which father vocalised his displeasure at what had happened. His shouting and threats of vengeance at the end of his monologue rang out clearly like a metal bell summoning congregants in the local community to come to a church service on a serene Sunday morning. Not only that.

Although I had enjoyed watching the event unfold, providing me with some entertainment, the whole episode also left me trembling with fear. After a hurried chat with nephew Last (Bernard), in which he asked the latter to combine his patch and that belonging to Irrigation in chasing away the birds, he walked across the field and re-joined a bigger group of adults who were weeding a crop of maize in another part of the farm. As for my young brother Irrigation (Wilfred), how he would spend his 'free day' hidden in the woods without having to be constantly tied down with work, would be left to his own devices. Conversely, it also meant he was temporarily banned from sharing the lunch meal with the rest of us at the farm. Luckily though, Mother had devised secret ways of sneaking food and fresh water to her children whenever they ran off into the bushes to seek safety from father's brutal beatings or mercurial tempers. I was a victim of these countless episodes as I grew up at the farm. This type of lifestyle, the sort of cat and mouse relationship between father and everyone around him were a common occurrence at the farm. Irrigation's incident was not peculiar to him alone.

The same could happen to me, any of my older brothers, any of his sisters or his wives. Despite some of us having used surrounding forests as our bedrooms, sometimes on dark, wet, or cold nights, we were lucky in that there were no dangerous carnivorous wild animals in the area my father had acquired as his farm. Otherwise, due to the frequency with which some of us spent nights outdoors of the farm homestead following tiffs with father, I am certain that some of us would have been included in statistics of victims of those night prowlers. Also, it is a mystery that none of us were ever reported to have been bitten or indeed swallowed by snakes. Yet the surroundings of our homestead were inhabited by a range of dangerous and poisonous reptiles including 'black mambas', pythons and puff adders. These snakes are mobile and search for their food mostly at night. We were also lucky in that we did not have predator-animals like lions, hyenas, or leopards in our area. Stories from folklore say that with the enactment of the Land Apportionment of 1930 when Rhodesia was divided into European and African Areas, such dangerous animals used to roam free; but that they were all rounded up from our area, put into cages and transported to animal conservancies, hundreds of miles away to the north of us in the Zambezi River valley, so that they would not be left to feast on poor black Africans as they lived in those overcrowded tribal trust lands! If that had not been done, heaven knows what evil fate might have befallen us if on one dark night one of these man-eating animals or creepy crawlies found you sleeping in their path! Wet and warm summers had their perils too.

After quarrelling with father and succeeding in fleeing his fiery temper, the convenience of hiding in the bush meant you would have to be prepared to bear the brunt of being feasted upon by swarms of mosquitoes which bit you persistently all night long. These were serious challenges for young people like us who aspired and cherished to enjoy a better quality of life. Little boys of our age on neighbouring farms seemed to live happier and more comfortably than ourselves.

Next in line was the baboon-and-monkey-scaring-off duties in autumn (the harvest season around March, April and May). The exception this time around was that the new duties involved a different set of animals: baboons and monkeys. Irrigation, Last and I were again placed at strategic positions along the edge of the same maize field to scare away baboons and monkeys from entering the field and stealing the maize crop. My nephew, Last (Bernard), occupied his own position which subsequently became known affectionately as 'Last's Hill' (Chikomo cha Last). Irrigation and I had our own guard spots with corresponding 'Hill' significations. These 'Hill' stations still exist to this day at my father's farm, more than sixty years later. The ripening of the maize crop making the cobs ready for picking or harvesting was a great attraction to a band of marauding baboons and monkeys who suddenly arrived and inhabited the large trees on the mountain side overlooking the maize fields below. These near humans appeared quite intelligent who could easily tell that there were no human beings to chase them away should they decide to enter the fields and have fun feasting on the maize cobs. Satisfied that the coast was clear, they would quietly sneak into the fields, pluck the maize cobs off the stalks, and peel the leaves off the cobs in the same way we humans do. The behaviour of the monkeys, the baboons' comrades-in-arms, was no different from their friends. If you suddenly arrived and caught these animals in the act of stealing maize cobs from the field, they would literally gallop or sprint out of the field, taking cobs of maize with them back into the trees uphill, where they would munch their stolen booty, innocently looking at you from on high in the overhanging tree boughs.

Contrary to the habits of birds I have just described a little while ago, these ladies and gentlemen were perfectly capable of raiding the maize fields at any time in broad daylight. The cunning and more daring of our subhuman counterparts could even enter the fields of maize in the darkness of night! However, if there were people about on guard, the baboons and monkeys would not descend the mountain slopes to enter the maize fields. Any humans, including adults and children, terrified them out of their wits. Effective security of our crops against these marauders was the remedy of continually striking an old and empty twenty-litre metal container of oil with a dry wooden stick. As in scaring off guinea fowl and ravens, you would be required to be continuously mobile. You would hold the old empty oil container aloft which you repeatedly struck, walking back and forth like a yo-yo. The three of us were positioned at between three to four hundred metre intervals along the edge of the field. The loud, repeated bangs on the surfaces of the empty oil tins by all of us separately at different rhythms were effective methods of keeping the marauders at bay.

But the repeated beatings of the empty oil tins produced a discordant cacophony of gongs which in the end not only ignited headaches in us. The loud metallic gangs often made me feel hopelessly giddy on an empty stomach. One area of concern unfortunately we could not complain about was that once we left home in the morning to commence our guard duties, no food was brought to us from home. Father appears to have ruled that no food or water should be sent to us on guard duties at the field. Once we left home to start our guard duties early in the morning, it was as if we ceased to exist. It was therefore nothing unusual for us to spend all day without food or fresh water at our guard positions, so wide gaps in fresh supplies of both food and water often made me fall sleep at my post. This habit of falling asleep at work had unfortunate consequences for me. Some of the male baboons were quite cunning. Noticing that I had fallen asleep and falling back on their terrorist subterfuges, they would lead their friends into the field from my end of the field and plunder it while I was snoring!

Typical of the workaholic he was, father allocated the various jobs to be carried out on the following day to all of us before we went to bed. His orders were that by the time the sun kissed the eastern horizon, everybody should already be occupied at their assigned task. All adults including my Granny had fields or plots of their own to patrol, as allocated to them by Father. These persons could rightly say those plots or fields belonged to them. On certain days of the week, father expected them to attend to their own plots as individuals. Otherwise, most of the time, Father expected all the family to work as a large group, together with him to do jobs like weeding the larger plots which he said belonged to him. Otherwise, the rule of thumb was that communal planting of seed crops, weeding or harvesting was to be done on a rotational basis with individual's field(s) being attended to communally when their turn came. It did not matter whether people worked in the fields individually or as a group. The rule at the farm was that work in the fields should continue uninterrupted by any unnecessary stoppages all morning until the lunch break, the time of which he alone decided upon. A most unusual thing about my father was that he did not have a wristwatch or a clock to mark exactly when work in the fields started or ended. However, for some reason and without fail, he religiously depended on two large passenger aeroplanes which flew past thousands of feet above our farm on every weekday in the searing and sweltering heat of the early afternoon. The large passenger jets hissed, rumbled, and whistled past us overhead at about the same time every weekday.

For some unexplained assumption, my father strongly believed the passengers aboard those birds of the sky were well-to-do

'Europeans' who regularly travelled between Johannesburg – wherever that was – and Salisbury (now Harare), somewhere far away farther to the north of the purchase areas in our neighbourhood. As far as I knew, none of the adults in the field, including my father himself, had ever been to Salisbury (Harare) or Johannesburg in South Africa before. So, nobody could even second guess what places my father would be referring to whenever he mentioned them.

The one simple fact everybody knew or had heard about was that 'Europeans' lived in clean places called towns and cities while most black people lived in dirty and deprived small-scale farms and 'reserve' areas. In that confused scenario, my father would announce convincingly, "It's dinner time everyone. Mothers and you girls, hurry up back home to cook some food for us. Let me see everyone back in your weeding portions at half past two sharp, do you understand me everyone?" He would say these words looking wistfully heavenwards as the large jets whooshed and rumbled overhead. According to a strange understanding, a special knowledge he alone possessed, the large passenger jets he used as his time gauge to release everybody on his assumed beginning of the lunch break, were heading to Salisbury (Harare) where they would land in time for the wealthy 'Europeans' to start eating their lunch. My father would mention the name Europeans giving it an air of superiority over all humans living on earth. He seemed to have resigned himself to the idea that the right to live lives free of despair or to enjoy good living belonged to one race, the Europeans Only. On that note, he would also declare the one-hour lunch break started. Then our mothers and the rest of the female members of the crowd would dash back to the homestead, passing through the nearby woodland to fetch bits of firewood with which to cook lunch. We younger boys would run to the river to swim, freshen up and do bits of our own laundry as well.

On one such extended but unauthorised lunch break, Irrigation, Last and I were the last to turn up for work after the approximately one-and-a-half-hour lunch break had expired. The large group of adults had all returned to the field and were already deeply engrossed in allocated patches of furrows pulling weeds and loosening the soil around maize plants with their hoes. We had delayed returning to the fields for afternoon duties by almost half an hour owing to the fun and games which quietly ate into our time as we swam in one large pool further down the river. Father was bound to express his displeasure about this. Stopping his own weeding temporarily, he stretched himself upright and asked with an angry voice, "Kingi, where have you all been to arrive at this time?" He asked the question looking directly at me because I was the oldest of the small knot of three frightened boys. "We were down at the river father, washing our bodies," was our chorused response given in trembling voices, and with a loud grating voice, he growled, "What did all of you say, heh? Is it true you were washing your bodies for the last one-and-a-half hours? Now tell me, did you become Europeans?" When father blurted out that question, the rest of the odd dozen or so men and women weeding and pulling tufts of grass and throwing them beside their portions of the field, laughed quietly together. Giggling quietly in unison, the large group of men and women engaged in weeding made sure father did not hear them laughing. The work at hand in the fields was serious business and there was no time for idle banter. The impression conveyed by my father here was that he had even lost his soul and surrendered himself to the idea that cleanliness was a privilege enjoyed by Europeans Only and that it did not matter whether Africans went about their businesses or carried out their duties with their bodies unbathed!

Before we could say anything in response to his pointed question, he cut in, "C'mon, pick up your hoes, you naughty brats and start work on your own furrows at the edge of the field until you catch up with everybody else. Put your backs into it, Goddammit you boys – or you'll get it thick from me, do you understand me all of you, especially you, Kingi?" Another chorused 'Yes father!' ensued as we hurriedly picked up our hoes and started working as hard as never before. On that day he held us back weeding in the field of maize together with him until it was so dark that we could hardly see each other as we walked back home for the evening.

# Chapter 5

## Family visitors to my father's farm and how they helped to shape my destiny

Growing up at the farm, I noticed that we rarely had visitors, if any. Father was not particularly intrigued by suggestions for his wives, sisters, or any of his children to travel away from the farm on friendly visits to the families we had left behind in the Nharira Tribal Trust Lands on both sides of our families. He looked supremely elated at seeing the huge body of residents on the farm continuously tied down with working and working non-stop at the various tasks that he assigned. Curiously, he forgot that those of his children as well as even the adults who worked so hard at his farm also needed opportunities to play hard exploited in equal measure, thus promoting our balanced growth and development. In this part of the narrative, I will venture to present observations that I made as I grew up regarding how the human spirit refuses to be denied the ability to express itself freely and how it compensates for those missed opportunities to socialise and to integrate with others in the local community and outside it. Contacts with neighbours occurred automatically arising from an indigenous traditional practice called 'nhimbe'. In this collaborative work system, local farmers came together to work towards a common goal, for example, building of relationships, diffusion and resolution of community conflicts and tensions. The 'nhimbes' were a regular occurrence in the crop-growing as well as in the harvesting seasons. In the absence of these social arrangements, our neighbour farmers or their wives made cursory visits or dropped in for courtesy calls to our farm as they passed by. The visitors exchanged titbits with our parents as they worked in their fields before the callers went on their way. Boys of roughly the same age as myself or those who were slightly older from neighbouring farms often made brief appearances at our farm to deliver messages from their parents to ours.

The children I am talking about were of about the same age as myself. They included Gilbert Chiwandire and/or his young brother Godfrey Chiwandire; Kingston Tagarira, Lucian Tagarira and David Tagarira; Eric Jemwa and Moses Dzvova and his young brother Andrew Dzvova. During their brief visits to our farm, we would steal some chances to interact with these boy visitors; but their visits were not for long periods. They soon left to return to their homes because my father's lack of the soft touch and his inability to engage in small talk with younger children terrified them.

His reputation of ill-treating us, his strict behaviour code and generally the way he was known to abuse his wives had unfortunately gained him a fair amount of notoriety that had spread like a wildfire as far afield as all the 'reserves' four or five miles to the north of our farming community. From my father's side of the family, his numerous cousins still living in Nharira Tribal Trust Lands dropped in occasionally to visit us at the farm, spending a night or two before they returned to their homes. Sometimes, they visited at Father's invitation, arriving in small groups with their spouses, depending on the nature of events at the farm. My uncles Tafireyi, Dende and Gwature almost always attended these once-a-year functions at the farm. Uncle Dende and Gwature would always stay behind for a few more days after the 'Jakwara' while the rest of the visitors trooped back to their homes in Nharira Tribal Trust Lands. These two were charming old men. Uncle Gwature was not only open-minded, but he also had a unique ability for storytelling. He would freely engage with us in conversations in which he proved he was an inexhaustible supply of new information to us about the untold story of the Rozvi tribe of the Moyo/Dhewa Bvumavaranda clan. Conversely, my father had no time to talk to us about these things, so his cousins like Tafirei, Gwature and Dende, who were generous enough to quench our thirst for more knowledge about our tribal origins, were more likeable to us. At the end of the winter season when 'rapoko' ears in barns had dried up well enough, they would be emptied on to a prepared open space in the middle of the farm homestead.

Following harvesting in May of each year, the rapoko would be allowed three to four months to thoroughly dry up, stored in large V-shaped barns or structures whose wider circular side faced upwards so that the winter sun would beat down on the 'rapoko' ears filled inside. Then on a chosen date in July or August, a big 'rapoko'-threshing event called 'Jakwara' was held to break up the rapoko ears, that is, to loosen the grain from the straw to which it was attached. It was to such communal events or activities at the farm father invited all local farmers and their wives, people from the nearby 'Reserves' and his relatives from Nharira Tribal Trust Lands to attend. Rapoko-threshing was usually carried out by men using what were called flails or 'mhuro' in local Shona. These flails were obtained from 'miunze' trees which grew in abundance on the lower slopes of the Makumi Mai mountain nearby.

A day before the 'Jakwara', father would visit the mountain slopes to cut and collect heaps of the flails which I or any of his children would help to carry down to the homestead in readiness for the threshing procedure on the following day. 'Jakwaras' carried with them some significance in that they were viewed as a celebration of the spirits' generosity in providing the rains which led to the farmers harvesting big yields from their farming activities, particularly involving 'rapoko'. To mark their significance, 'Jakwara' parties included much beer-drinking by both men and women, drum-playing, singing and dancing. At some of these parties, farmers with old hunting rifles would have them dusted off and specially loaded for firing into the air while female folk ululated as men gyrated or rolled on the ground in imitation of hunters returning home laden with trophies, they had killed on their successful hunting expeditions. It was such a feast watching the 'Jakwara' event. The 'Jakwara' was largely an adults-only event due to the massive amount of alcohol that that was consumed there. So, the day of the 'Jakwara' at the farm was a big bonus for me and the rest of the children. We were not involved one bit at the event itself nor were we required to do any work in the fields on that day. It was therefore a full day off for us if we were not on duty to mind the cattle. If I was not on the roster to tend to the herd of cattle, then I would hang about in hiding from a carefully chosen strategic position, a reasonable distance from the rapoko-threshing spot. Hidden in our chosen spots around the homestead, we children watched the adults enjoy the fun of these rare gatherings where they sang, danced around the heaps of rapoko ears and threshed them, heaving down the 'threshers' in unison until those heaps were reduced to pulp.

On numerous occasions during the threshing ritual, threshers had short breaks during which they sat in small groups and consumed large amounts of the locally brewed beer. Later, small groups of men and women staggered drunkenly in a bee line towards nearby bushes at the edge of the farm compound to empty their bladders. On reaching safe and secure distances, women would quickly slump to the ground with their long dresses spread around them and start relieving themselves loudly, a clear indication some of these women did not bother wearing any underclothes. Afterwards, they would just get back on their feet and walk gaily back into the homestead to mingle with the rest of the threshers. As for the men, once they found a safe spot to relieve themselves, they remained standing, quickly unzipped the fliers of their trousers, and opened out in splashes without bothering whether anybody was watching or not. These men also did not even seem to wear any underpants because, after emptying their bladders, they promptly zipped up their mostly oversize pairs of shorts or overalls and rushed back to partake of more alcohol prior to resuming the threshing routine. One gentleman who hobbled away from the threshing site was so desperate that he could not hold it in much longer because the bushes which were frequented by other menfolk at the edge of the farm compound were too far for him. Instead, he chose to empty the contents of his bladder right into a bush with thick and fleshy green leaves under which I was unfortunately hidden to observe the goings-on at the 'Jakwara' threshing venue. He nearly urinated into my face. I was left with no choice but to quickly duck to one side lest I got drenched from that man's fast stream of steaming shower of urine. I nearly said to him, "Mate, please mind there's somebody who's temporarily the owner of this bush." After he had left the site and shuffled back into the farm compound I noticed, I was crouching in a pool of smelly urine. I had no choice but to secretly relocate to another hiding place so that I could carry on with my observations.

Uncle Rodrick Tinarwo Mudyara, father's young brother and his only male sibling in a family of seven, was a special and important visitor to me at the farm. I, together with the rest of Father's male children, looked forward to his visits with considerable anticipation. His visits often coincided with some of the religious festivals, for example, Easter or Christmas. Quite often too, he also suddenly pitched up at some of the 'Jakwaras' or on any one of the longer public holidays such as 'Rhodes and Founders' (now Heroes and Forces' Days). These occasions used to be celebrated in July of every year. I was a little boy in 1953 or 1954 when he turned up at the farm with his beautiful young wife, Lucy, who spoke a language that all the farm residents were unfamiliar with. It was not quite IsiNdebele. I later learnt the language was 'Venda' which is widely spoken by the Venda People who live along the Limpopo River, but on the South African side of the river. However, in just a few days' interaction with our Shona-speaking womenfolk, Aunt Lucy had picked up a smattering of the local dialect, making it easy for her to communicate with other people at the farm. The visitors also had a little girl, their daughter and first child named Chipo ('Sipho). Aunt Lucy and her daughter 'Sipho' communicated more in a mixture of 'Afrikaans' (an official language in the Republic of South Africa then), and a local native dialect called 'Venda'. While we could pick only just a few of the words in 'Venda', Afrikaans was alien and sounded completely incommunicable as the words reeled off their tongues and none of them meant anything to us.

Upon arriving at the farm, she promptly began playing with us. 'Sipho' mixed easily with the rest of us. Like a piece of bread that is immersed in a cupful of tea, she had mastered a sizeable vocabulary of the Shona dialect, enabling her to speak fluently with us in our language by the time her parents decided to end the visit and return to Beit Bridge where they had come. Our visitors had travelled from a town called Beit Bridge, a Rhodesian (Zimbabwean) border town far away on the northern side of the Limpopo River. All these bits of information were Greek to most of us, especially, Irrigation, my nephew Last and myself, as schooling was still something that would happen to us in a distant and unknown future. Anyway, we were availed with information later, saying that Uncle Rodrick was employed in a very important job that had connections with weather forecasts.

During the period when Uncle Rodrick made his visits, he was stationed at Beit Bridge Aerodrome. Every time he visited the farm, Uncle Rodrick always included in his luggage goodies for us little children at the farm. The 'goodies' included many colourful and metal toy motor cars which were inscribed "Dinky's" on the bottom of each one of them. In addition, he never forgot to bring with him bags or packets of sweets, toffees, and chocolates. He personally took pleasure in sharing out or distributing these goodies among the children himself, immediately upon his arrival. However, what was even more exciting and added to the pleasure and amazement of all the little boys and even grown up boys like Misheck, Kaston and Douglas Ruhukwa, (a cousin/brother who had started living with us at the farm but more about this later), Uncle Rodrick always brought with him dozens of new tennis balls and many rubber balloons in yellow, blue, or green colours. Reader, I leave you to imagine the fun and excitement Uncle Rodrick ignited in us, growing up blissfully in this otherwise dormant, provincial, and splendid isolation of the farm. Uncle Rodrick loved talking to children.

One Saturday morning following Uncle Rodrick's arrival at the farm on the night before, he asked all the school-going children to gather at a clear spot in the middle of the farm compound. He emerged from Granny VaChemedza's hut where he had been sitting chatting with his elderly mother and his older brother, my father. Reaching where we were quietly sitting, his right hand clutched a big of sweets, each wrapped in transparent plastic paper, he began addressing us: "Hullo everyone. I hope you're all happy and getting on well at school. I have some sweets for all of you here (pointing)." We looked at him fixedly as he spoke.

"But before I hand out these sweets, I want you to tell me what jobs you want to do when you grow up and finish school. There'll be no right or wrong answers, do you all understand? I want to be able to find out how well you can express yourselves. For any answer you give me, you will earn a sweet or two. Come on, who is going to start?"

We sat there huddled together, scratching our heads and searching from our limited fantasies. Then, as it were, switched on like electric bulbs, we chanted in a disorderly fashion, "Me! Me! Me! Uncle Me!" "Let me see who I'll pick first. You all seem to have interesting answers," Uncle said, his eyes sweeping over the tiny anxious faces on the floor below him. He picked my young brother Irrigation (Wilfred) who said, "Uncle, I want to be a driver of these aeroplanes which fly past us here every day!" (General laughter from the audience sitting around him).

"Ah, that's very good, Irrigation", Uncle retorted, "but you'll have to have an airport or aerodrome built somewhere near here where your aeroplanes will land and take off. Here you're (giving him) two sweets for your effort for the answer you gave me … Right, let's see who's next. I think it's you Kingston (pointing at me) who called out 'Me' after Irrigation." I took a deep breath and announced, "I want to be a headmaster." It was the only job I could think of that appeared to be smart and I thought it paid a lot of money. The 'headmaster' I had heard about was a Mr Mamvura. He lived in a smart house and had a shiny new three-speed 'Raleigh' bicycle which was the envy of all the teachers at Maronda Mashanu School. "Ah, that's quite ambitious of you, Kingston. Maybe you want to think of becoming a teacher first before you climb up to your big job as a headteacher or headmaster. Yeah, teaching is a good job. I nearly became a teacher myself before I changed my mind to do the job, I'm in now."

I also earned two colourful sweets, one red and the other yellow, in plastic wrapping. After removing the sweets from the plastic wrapping, I started licking the sweets one at a time with the tip of my tongue. With the sweets getting smaller, I threw them into my mouth and sucked them, swallowing the sweet juice – such a pleasurable experience. The conversation with Uncle Rodrick carried on until everyone in the group had given him different answers which, however, showed him the narrow scope of their fantasies; but I am sure he was aware that he was sharing information with mere children whose perceptions about the realities around them were still developing.

Before he left us to re-join the group of elders back in his mother's hut, while we licked and sucked the juicy rivulets of the sweets liquid that had run down and formed circles round our hands and fingers, he quipped; "Very well children. I've heard what each of you has said about your future jobs when you've finished school. What I can say for now is that there are more sweets where those sweets came from. I will bring you more sweets when I come round again next time. For now, I want you to work hard at school, pass your tests, get into good jobs and be able to buy more of the sweets yourselves rather than me bringing them over for you. Does that make sense, everyone?" We all chorused, "Yes, Uncle."

He then walked back into a hut where the other adults were gathered and talking in a disorganised fashion. When I started school at Maronda Mashanu School in January 1957, the only concrete image I had of a motor vehicle had been formed from the "Dinky's" metal motor car toys that Uncle Rodrick used to bring with him as gifts for us on each of his frequent visits to the farm. Turning our fantasies into reality, he suddenly arrived at the farm in the middle of one dark night of Easter 1957 driving a real car and not a toy one! You cannot believe that father's farm was only ten kilometres (approximately six miles) away from the small rural town of Enkeldoorn (now Chivhu); yet we were rarely, if ever, allowed visits to that town to acquaint ourselves with objects of urban life and civilisation like cars.

Locked away in a remote corner of the purchase area community, miles away from the dusty feeder road that was hardly used by motor vehicles, none of us had ever had the chance to see a real motor car within touching distance. Add to this was the fact that Father maintained such a tight hold on us, within the work programmes at the farm that we were forced to comply with. Therefore, there was no chance given to any of us to be allowed a brief visit to Enkeldoorn (Chivhu). Such allowances might have afforded us opportunities to view cars and also buses and lorries as they travelled up and down the busy Salisbury (now Harare) to Fort Victoria (now Masvingo) Highway. I must admit, the town of Enkeldoorn was still then a small urban growth point with features of ramshackle buildings that characterise modern day 'spaghetti' western films. However, let it be said also that this farming town was on a busy highway that linked Salisbury (now Harare) and Fort Victoria (now Masvingo) and Beit Bridge. Loads of road haulage, buses and passenger vehicular traffic was already using this busy highway in both directions by the late 1950s. A contradiction with father's world view regarding our own visits away from the farm was that while welcoming and entertaining visitors at the farm was acceptable to him, reverse visits by us anywhere outside the perimeter of the Maronda Mashanu community were simply not tolerated. Father was convinced that his manpower resources, which included all his children and adults alike should be exploited to the utmost on continuous work at the farm which kept them sufficiently and seriously occupied.

In that respect, visits to the local town even for a short time to engage in window shopping or travel on buses to visit extended family to places in other rural areas were a waste of valuable time, as that was a luxury Father could not afford. The indefinite ban on leisure visits or travel abroad on buses to visit friends and family also applied to all his wives and sisters. Anyway, to return to my thread of the story about Uncle Rodrick suddenly arriving at the farm driving a real car: here was the concreteness of a proper automobile arriving in our midst at the farm homestead.

Making it more surreal was that this was happening at an unusual hour of the night, hours after everyone had retired to bed. As the car moved slowly along a grassy path, which I cannot describe exactly as a road because there was none, the depressed rumble of the vehicle's engine could be heard after it had passed Jemwa's Farm, a little over three kilometres away. As the first time ever a motor vehicle had travelled in these parts, there was no proper road to reach the farm after branching off the gravel road to Maronda Mashanu School and on to Manyene Tribal Trust Lands. To navigate his way after passing Tagarira's Farm, Uncle Rodrick was frequently forced to vacate his driving seat and, leaving the engine running and headlights on full beam, and he then had to walk short distances to and from the front of the car beating a path through waist high tall grass and moving rocks out of the way so that his car would have passage without the delicate parts below his engine getting damaged. If he had not taken those precautions, he would never have made it to the farm, which in fact was only about a kilometre and a half away.

Meanwhile, enveloped by a thick darkness at the farm home-stead, it appeared as if the sun was rising on the horizon from whence the car came. Trundling along and rocking sideways un-steadily as the vehicle traversed the rough and uneven ground, Uncle Rodrick's headlights flashed on treetops and lit up the sky like sparks of lightning. Uncle Rodrick twisted and turned the steering wheel of his car to stay on course along a zigzagging path. His headlights also momentarily fell on the mountain slopes to his left with a daylight incandescence never seen in these parts before. He was probably two hundred yards away from behind a bend when his headlights brought the rooftops of the huts at the farm homestead into their reach. Noting that he had finally reached his destination, he instantaneously blew his car horn. The sharp piercing sound of a military-type trumpeting of his horn cut through the pitch black night, the way a red-hot knife-blade slices across a block of frozen butter. It was pandemonium when slowly but methodically, Uncle Rodrick made a grand entry into the centre of the farm compound. His horn still blaring out and his headlights burning, brightly turning the entire homestead into a daylight wonder in the middle of the dark night. My dog 'Simbanechako' leapt up and down, barking wildly and wagging his tail feverishly as the car entered the open space in the middle of the compound. Two cats which had quietly purred as they lay in wait to catch a rat or mouse for their evening meal, suddenly sprang to their feet and scurried for cover into their burrows under the barns at the edge of the homestead. I was one of a small group of half-dressed boys, who had rudely been roused from our much – deserved sleep following a full day of hard work on the farm. We stood in front of a hut with a roof that had had half of the grass thatch ripped up and blown off by a passing whirlwind the afternoon before. Father had promised to have the damage repaired on the next day.

From where I stood beside a clutch of other small boys as Uncle's fantasy car arrived in the hullabaloo, I caught sight of a flight of frightened doves rapidly and energetically flapping their wings as they fled from their nests perched high up in the safety of the tall trees overhanging the huts roofs on my left. The sudden flood of light at this unearthly hour of the night, accompanied by the continuous blaring of the horn was clearly a threat to their safety. The great noise and the bright light were enough cause for the birds to fly away to heaven knows where, at the speed of an arrow. Everybody, including naked children still dazed and confused from their disturbed sleep, some writhing and twirling their thin hands around their mother's legs and whimpering impatiently with their bright little eyes peeping from the backs of their mothers, had come out of their huts. All the bemused people were fixed in their standing positions, gaping at this night spectacle without making any sound.

They looked amazed beyond belief and yet some of their amazement was tinged with fear. They were mesmerised by the wonder of it all while others were completely overwhelmed by the arrival of this mysterious invention of science right under their noses. For nearly all of us at the farm, this was a first of its kind we had ever seen: we had never witnessed anything like this before. Uncle Rodrick had arrived. As soon as father recognised that the driver of the car was his young brother, he rushed forward. Uncle Rodrick struggled to stand upright on jumping out of the car.

Father welcomed him with a bear-hug, mumbling in broken thought patterns, "Ah, oh, VaRozvi vakapera nenda (I swear by the Rozvi people who perished due to the bites of lice) Rodrick, is it true, my mother's own son arrives in this home driving a car? From your car headlights, all the people who live in this group of small farms must have seen you arriving here. Oh my God! What can I say, you've made me feel not only proud, my young brother, but also a cut above the rest of the poor people in this community!"

Meanwhile, all the women erupted into rapturous ululating while we simultaneously whistled and clapped our hands, all of us in total disbelief.

None of the children, except perhaps a few of the adults, had ever seen a car from such close range. Its headlights still burning; the vehicle, parked right there in its majesty in the middle of the courtyard, was the mother of all wonders. The spectacle left us all completely speechless. Uncle Rodrick had arrived for his visit at the farm driving his car at midnight.

Shortly before sunrise, my father who was a traditionalist woke up everyone in the farm compound announcing that an important ritual needed to be performed in tribute to Uncle Rodrick's purchase of a motor vehicle. The arrival of the motorcar in the farm compound was an occurrence that had never happened in the history of his family, so the spirits of our ancestors, who we believed always guided and protected the family, needed to be thanked. With everybody, adults and children gathered around the car, father took a whole pot containing two gallons of freshly brewed African beer. Before he did anything, he called everybody to listen while he offered homage to our departed ancestors. Failure to observe that practice could have resulted in misfortune, such as a road traffic accident, befalling Uncle Rodrick as he drove his motor car around.

Then lifting the pot of beer and holding it aloft over the car, he called out, "To all our Rozvi ancestors, it's me Timothy Tazvinga your son. It is rare that we wake you up so early to talk to you. I know you can see me doing this from somewhere in the clouds or in the hills and that you are listening to me while I speak."

Emptying the contents of the pot over the car which formed several beery rivulets, the liquid dripped down all around the car to the ground, making the shining windows dirty and converting the original black colour of the vehicle to a funny mixture of black and faded grey patches. Meanwhile father continued, "This car was bought by my young brother Rodrick Tinarwo for use by himself and ourselves as well. The effort to save enough money to buy the car was not his alone. I am sure you helped him to do this. The purchase of the first car ever in this family has made us feel very proud. Please help him to drive it safely and prevent him from getting involved in road accidents. In addressing you in this way, we are not offering any prayers to you, but we are connecting with you to thank you and ask you to continue giving us more blessings."

His ritualistic incantations were punctuated by women's rapturous ululating and the clapping and whistling of all the men and boys. Following the beer-pouring ritual that same morning, Uncle Rodrick was up by seven o'clock. With the beery markings still showing on the car, he gave small groups of us a taste of the good life in turns, by driving each group down the half-a-mile road to Chiwandire Farm and back to the farm homestead. It was my first time ever to take a ride in a car. The five-minute experience was exhilarating and completely out of this world. That was quite the opposite of the ox-drawn scotch-cart rides that we were accustomed to, that were thoroughly uncomfortable and that frequently made you want to throw up.

The last group of joyriders included Uncle Rodrick's own elderly mother, Granny VaChemedza who at around eighty years of age, had also never travelled inside a motor car. Asked to enter the car and sit on the front passenger seat beside the driver, her son, she went in facing backwards and placed her knees on the passenger seat and threw her arms around the back of the front passenger seat. Our Granny's inexperience produced howls of laughter from the crowd standing around the car. It was true, of course, that none of us were any better than her. Perhaps except for my father, all of us in the farm compound were equally as flabbergasted and inexperienced on the use of these modern gadgets as she was. However, common sense prevailed and older women standing nearby, including my mother, finally assisted Granny to sit in the car seat correctly and off the group went on their spin. Soon they would return to the homestead with all the passengers grinning like the cat that has found the cream when they disembarked from the car.

Big Mother (Maiguru) Jessica, Father's first wife, had people from her own family dropping in to see her and her children at the farm from time to time. For the five years or so of her life at the farm after arriving from Nharira Tribal Trust Lands, I have no recollection of her leaving to pay casual visits to her home of origin at Muroore Village in Nharira. I am sure she would have loved to do so if Father had permitted it. As she did not enjoy the privilege of indulging in such luxury, the Rwodzi family, mostly her brothers, were frequent visitors. She also had one or two sisters who were close to her, apart from nephews and cousins who visited her, and helped her with work in the fields that Father had allocated to her. The Rwodzi family were very pleasant people. When some of her brothers chose to stay on at the farm for a few days, they were open-minded and democratic. They did not just confine themselves to interacting with their nephew (Muzukuru) Misheck. There was the recognition that Misheck (Raphael) had stepbrothers because their sister's husband (and son-in-law) had married more than one wife. Whenever Stepmother Jessica's brothers visited, they encouraged brotherly co-existence between Misheck and all of us from the other house(s). They chatted with all of us while we sat with them round a fire at the 'padare' in the evenings. That is a designated place at the edge of every Shona homestead where men and boys relax in the evenings while womenfolk and girls attend to chores in huts or kitchens.

The last time I remember seeing the largest group of Big Mother (Maiguru) Jessica's family of adult men and women descend on the farm as a large group was in 1958 to celebrate her 'memorial' (kurohwa kweguva). Sadly, she had passed on in the middle of 1956 due to childbirth complications. At about seven years old, I was still a little boy. I only started attending school in 1957. That sad event of her passing on was my first time to experience death in the family at the farm. The whole farm compound was in deep mourning for about three days. To this day, I have a vivid memory of that sad event casting a blanket of sorrow over both adults and children at the farm.

The same rigid rules and restrictions which forbade Stepmother (Maiguru) Jessica from exercising her right to freely visit her family of origin when she wished also applied to my own mother Leah, father's wife number two. Mother hailed from the Muguto family who lived at Masasa Village, Nharira Tribal Trust Lands. I will also place on record here that for the roughly eleven years I lived with my mother at the farm, I do not recollect seeing her voluntarily leave the farm to pay homage or make friendly visits to her family at Nharira. Instead, I remember the numerous and unceremonious departures when Mother went back to her family in sudden and hasty retreats to seek protection from her family, following her endless feuds with father. Many of my mother's quick getaways were made out of the need to seek protection from her family of origin after father had assaulted her for some reason. Mother loved her husband and she had very high expectations for all her children, so notwithstanding the high levels of abuse and lack of respect father displayed towards her as a wife and the mother of his numerous children. Mother would always return to her family at the farm after elders had intervened to ease the tensions in her relationship with my father. Of her two brothers, Uncles (Sekuru) Bertwell and (Sekuru) Leonard Muguto, Uncle (Sekuru) Leonard was the more frequent visitor at the farm. Uncle Leonard had previously worked together with Father, also as senior messenger at the Native District Commissioner's Offices (The Range) years before father resigned his post to take up farming.

These two gentlemen were quite familiar with each other's whims and witticisms. Snippets of accounts by those who knew them in their heyday back then (including inputs by my own mother) confirmed that the European Native Commissioner had built up so much trust and confidence in the two gentlemen in the minds of their 'white' bosses at 'The Range' that they were frequently sent out on two or three weeks of 'patrol' duties in the remotest parts of the Tribal Trust Lands where they were charged with checking that everything was in order, that the villagers were abiding by the law, and that nobody was plotting to start trouble or disturb the peace. When the two gentlemen were away on these 'patrol' duties assigned to them by their 'white' boss, reports say that the two men arrogated to themselves the powers of the Native District Commissioner and engaged in an assortment of nefarious activities which made them popular in and around the villages for all the wrong reasons. Legend has it that they engaged in all sorts of mischief, including extorting free alcohol from villagers, engaging in amorous relationships with women some of whom were married, starting fights at beer-drinking parties and generally being a nuisance and disturbing the peace in the community they were mandated to protect.

In their role as messengers at 'The Range', reports say that father was believed to be superior in terms of rankings; but he went on to marry my mother who was Uncle Leonard's sister. In so doing and according to Shona culture, father had literally demoted himself by marrying my uncle's sister, becoming Uncle Leonard's 'junior' in terms of Shona customs and protocol. Due to Father subsequently resigning his senior messenger job to go into farming years later and relocating fifty miles away to Maronda Mashanu African Purchase Area, Uncle Leonard would often arrive at the farm unannounced. He often made his appearances at the farm dressed up in his prim and proper 'messenger' regalia, that is, shining brown boots, freshly ironed ten-ounce khaki jacket over a pair of well ironed ten-ounce shorts, wide brown leather belt with S-shaped steel buckle and a brown wide-brim hat with a red cloth around it, one side of the wide-brim hat tipped or flapped upward against the hood of the hat. It was like Uncle Leonard had been sent by the 'DC' to come and collect my father for one misdeed or another. Yet he appeared to be simply visiting us socially. Sitting and chatting with our mother in her hut on some afternoons, Uncle Leonard's sudden unannounced arrival would be signalled by the metallic crackling of a loose rear wheel mudguard, whereupon on dismounting, he instantly leaned against the exterior wall of mother's round hovel, whistling and humming a tune to himself at the same time. I do not know how he was able to carry out both these activities simultaneously. All my brothers and I could not fathom how he managed this magnanimous feat.

After wiping beads of perspiration off his face, holding the wide-brimmed hat in his left hand, he would put his hat back on his head and enter Mother's kitchen without even knocking on the door. Uncle Leonard was a boisterous, bashful, and self-opinionated talker. He was the kind of person who wanted his presence and self-assertiveness to be noted as soon as he arrived. If we happened to be inside the homestead when he arrived, he expected us, all his nephews and nieces, to immediately stop doing the jobs we were doing and rush towards him, gather around him, greet him, and ask about his health before he sat down to exchange greetings with the rest of the adults in the homestead. According to him, this was a rule to be observed in accordance with his laws. If we slipped up, he claimed it signified bad manners on our part, resulting in him often complaining about it to Mother. At other times, he would take matters in his own hands. As usual, without warning; Uncle Leonard would present himself at the farm unexpectedly, just before lunch when Mother was busy cooking our lunch meal in her hut.

One day, Father had just granted us the usual much-awaited lunch break from our various places of work and we then walked back to the homestead to eat our lunch. When Uncle Leonard Arrived at the homestead ahead of us earlier that afternoon; no one was there to crowd around him and offer him the obsequious greetings he expected. When we entered the home to eat our lunch, we were surprised to hear his stentorian voice booming from Mother's hut. Brother and sister were obviously engaged in a conversation about something to do with their other siblings, so we thought. Seeing me and Irrigation (Wilfred) enter our mother's hut expressly with the intention to greet him and for our mother to serve us our lunch meal, Uncle Leonard abruptly stopped the conversation he was having with mother. His face became livid with anger because we had not rushed to crowd around him in; in accordance with his oft-stated directive. He charged at us angrily, "You Kingi and Rugisheni (Lawrence and Wilfred), are you deaf or something? Where were you when I arrived in your father's home more than twenty minutes ago? Didn't somebody tell you I had arrived, heh? Answer me, you naughty boys!"

Mother tried to remonstrate with her brother, offering to explain the reason for our absence when he had arrived earlier. My mother's attempts to provide that explanation were completely ignored by Uncle Leonard who sprang to his feet and stormed out of the hut, leaving us beside ourselves with fear and confusion. He immediately returned to Mother's hut hissing with fury like a puff adder. His right hand wielded a two-foot spanking stick, 'shamhu' in the local Shona dialect, freshly tugged from a 'mutondo' plant growing in the small bush behind Mother's hut. Giving us no warning, he lunged at us and quickly clasped our four thin wrists in his grubby left hand which had fingers that resembled a bunch of bananas. He started beating us all over: backs, bums and around the calves of our legs, "Learn this lesson today, you naughty Timothy's children. When your Uncle Leonard Muguto arrives in your home, you must immediately stop everything you're doing and welcome him respectfully by offering your greetings, do you understand me Kingi and Rugisheni (Lawrence and Wilfred)? What did I just say?"

Without allowing us the chance to repeat the words he had just uttered, he continued beating us. After beating us for about three minutes, he started breathing heavily from his exertions. Taking advantage of the widening gaps between his stops and starts, we repeated some of his instructions in halting expressions. We were hot from the pain of his countless lashes. Then he released our wrists from his vice grip, the flimsy skins around which had begun to come off as we leapt up and jumped about yelling for mercy and forgiveness during the beating. We ran out of the hut leaving brother and sister on the threshold of a quarrel over Uncle Leonard's harsh treatment of his nephews. We were made to understand that Father had sneaked back into the homestead to eat his lunch at the peak of our predicament with Uncle Leonard.

As we ran out of Mother's hut to go and sit in the shade of a guava tree at the edge of the homestead, we noticed Father quietly sitting on the ledge that formed the superstructure of Granny's maize barn. We were surprised that he had not bothered to intervene, to fight in our corner, so to speak. Keeping to himself, he pretended that what had happened was none of his business and that it was a matter between my mother and her brother. It left us wondering how our own father would let outsiders come into his homestead and start disciplining his own children without him raising a finger.

To round off on this sad saga about Uncle Leonard Muguto's unannounced visits to our father's farm and how he was such a terror to me and my other siblings, I venture to ask you, reader, to compare this man's visits with Uncle Rodrick's, who always unfailingly went out of his way to bring goodies with him for us on every visit. On every one of his few days visiting the farm, he went out of his way to interact with us, individually and collectively, on how we were coping with work at school and at the farm. In the years after started school, Uncle Rodrick would stop to find out how I was getting on with my schoolwork. He would pleasantly encourage me to work hard, achieve and make progress in my schoolwork. I had started school in 1957 and I remember him giving me a pat on the back when he heard I was progressing well in my first year at school. The sum of all that was that all of us looked forward to Uncle Rodrick's visits, and we wished he could come more often. From my little story about him, it was clear that Uncle Leonard was the very antithesis of

Uncle Rodrick. Irrigation and I agreed that we wished that Uncle Leonard's unwelcome visits would stop altogether as we seemed to receive nothing from them but pain and frustration. We were unanimous in agreeing that Uncle Leonard was no different from our own Father. To us, both these two men were cruel, hard to please, harsh in their treatment of other people and distant from us, as they never made any attempt to communicate with us, either individually or in groups. They both seemed continually determined to make life for us as utterly unpleasant and inconvenient as possible. As Uncle Leonard was our own mother's direct brother, we found it a hard conclusion to reach, but were united in our belief that Uncle Leonard was singularly hateful to us.

Then there was Aunt (Mainini) Jennifer Chigonyati. She was the lastborn in my mother's family and the youngest of her female siblings. Her husband, Mr Chigonyati, had a small landholding in the Manyene Tribal Trust Lands, about fifteen kilometres to the north of our farm. Mr Chigonyati was employed in a modest job as a General Cleaner or Groundsman at Enkeldoorn Tennis Club, a 'Europeans Only' utility. He lived in one-bedroom servant's quarters located out of sight behind the tennis club buildings. In her numerous journeys on foot between Manyene Tribal Trust Lands – nearly twenty-seven kilometres – to visit her husband, Aunt Jennifer often stopped at our farm, which was on her route, to pay homage to her sister and to see us as well. At weekends when Enkeldoorn Tennis Club became busy with local white farmers and miners visiting their families for entertainment and to play tennis, Mr Chigonyati also filled in as a 'Kitchen Hand' at the club, a role in which he served tea and other refreshments to club members, some of whom came not to play tennis but to interact or socialise with kindred spirits while they drank tea or sat on easy chairs on a large, covered veranda, watching couples or doubles play tennis on the courts. Uncle Chigonyati and his wife arranged their meetings at Father's farm in such a way that it would reduce Aunt Jennifer's walking distance between Manyene Tribal Trust Lands and Enkeldoorn (Chivhu), which was around forty odd miles. On a Tuesday or Wednesday, Mr Chigonyati would cycle the ten kilometres from Enkeldoorn to our farm. He would collect his wife who might have been visiting my mother for a few days. Carrying his wife on the bicycle carrier back to Manyene Tribal Trust Lands, thirty miles distant from my father's farm, was a tricky business if Aunt Jennifer had heavy luggage.

But battle-hardened from life's harsh experiences, Uncle Chigonyati was familiar with the ways of handling these challenges. Aunt Chigonyati would sit on the bicycle carrier facing one side with both her legs dangling to the ground. If she had any luggage, which women always carry, she would carry it on top of her head with one hand while the other hand firmly held onto the bottom of the saddle to avoid falling off the bicycle once. When the journey from our farm to Manyene Tribal Trust Lands started, Mr Chigonyati would walking beside the bicycle holding both the handles firmly. On reaching ground where it sloped downward, he would perform a balancing act whereby he stepped on the left pedal with his left foot. Then tactfully maintaining balance and keeping his eyes ahead, he would slide his right leg over the cross bar that links the handlebar and the saddle (for men's bicycles then) while both hands firmly held the handles and his right foot reached out to step on the right pedal. That action is more challenging when the luggage on the bicycle carrier is heavier.

As I grew up at the farm and learnt how to ride a bicycle, I was frequently sent to the local grinding-mill five or six miles away carrying two buckets of maize seeds on Father's bicycle carrier to be ground into maize meal for our porridge and 'sadza' (thick porridge). Mr Chigonyati started his arduous twenty-kilometre bicycle trip with his wife back to Manyene Tribal Trust Lands, mounting and dismounting the vehicle countless times along the way until he reached their destination. Life was clearly an uphill struggle for my uncle. When he arrived at the farm to collect his wife on those brief visits, his formerly white shirt appeared to have transformed into a yellowish grey colour under his armpits, due to the rivers of perspiration that flowed down his back, chest and sides of his chest during his frequent sixty to seventy mile round trips of back-breaking riding on his bicycle between the town of Enkeldorn and Manyene tribal trust lands; but despite Aunt Jennifer's generous help with the back-breaking work in mothers maize, rapoko, groundnuts and rice fields every time she visited, Father would always turn down Mother's requests to return her sister's visits, even for just one day. Therefore Mother did not have the privilege of knowing where exactly her sister lived in the Manyene Tribal Trust Lands. The best she could do whenever we asked her where sister's home was, was to half-heartedly point in the direction she had gone when she had last seen her depart with her husband.

However, for reasons I cannot explain, Mother seemed to relate exceptionally well with her other young sister, Mrs Eliver Ruhukwa (nee Muguto). In comparison with the sisterly chemistry between Mother and her other sisters, Mrs Chandiwana and Mrs Chigonyati. the relationship between her and Aunt (Mainini) Eliver was in a class by itself. It would be utterly imprudent of me to state that Aunt Eliver was my mother's favourite sister. Yet the reality was blatantly there for all to see. The closeness and warmth of feeling between these two female persons stuck out like a sore thumb.

As we grew up, the information we became familiar with concerning Aunt Eliver was that she had suddenly lost her husband, the late Uncle Philemon Ruhukwa, when their one and only son, Douglas, was still a mere infant. Even as a little boy before the mid-1950s, I began noticing the unusual frequency with which Aunt Eliver visited the farm. There was a reason for this, however; details of which I will attempt to provide below. Before I elaborate on Aunt Eliver's visits, I will state here and now that her visits contrasted sharply with those of her brother and sibling, Uncle Leonard Muguto, which I have already described at some length.

After her husband died, when Aunt Eliver was still a young woman with the world at her feet, there was no way she would rot away and wallow in self-pity. If she could do something about it, it was unthinkable to be ravaged by the poverty and suffering that was gripping all the native 'reserves' of the time. Like all sensible people she then decided to improve her livelihood by looking for jobs in the towns and cities that had mushroomed in Southern Rhodesia, Aunt Eliver reportedly took her son Douglas, then a tiny little boy, along with her, when she ventured into the unknown. As a sales employee, initially stationed in Bulawayo and later relocating to Salisbury (now Harare), Aunt Eliver began experiencing childcare difficulties. Her son, Douglas Ruhukwa, was growing up rapidly and had probably just started school then, somewhere in Harari (Mbare) Township, Salisbury (Harare).

Information gleaned from my older brother Roland confirms that on one of her visits to Maronda Mashanu around 1953 or thereabouts, she came to an understanding with my mother and father for Douglas to move over to the farm at Maronda Mashanu and start his schooling at the local rural school, joining the rest of a team of boys, some of whom were roughly the same age as himself, e.g. Misheck (Raphael) and Kaston (Roland). The team grew even bigger at one stage when another cousin from Father's side of the family, Reginald Dzenga, briefly lived at the farm. Mother agreed to provide Douglas with his childcare needs while his mother went to work; first in Bulawayo and then in Salisbury, which freed her from the anxiety and unnecessary worry about her child's welfare and safety while she was at work. Assured that her son was safely installed in the custody of her older sister, Aunt Eliver returned to Salisbury (Harare).

Presumably, Cousin Douglas was still a young boy when he came to live with us on the farm. Father was singularly delighted not simply because he was a visitor but more by the fact there was a welcome addition to his manpower needs at the farm. As I was still a little boy myself, I do not have any information as to whether when Cousin Douglas Ruhukwa began living with us at the farm, he had already started schooling in Salisbury or not.

The information given to me by my older brother Kaston (Roland) is that Cousin Douglas was quickly enrolled to attend school at Maronda Mashanu Primary School in 1953 or thereabouts. Within a short time of starting school at Maronda Mashanu

School, he is on record as having wasted no time in displaying that he possessed exceptional ability in his schoolwork as well as the fact that he needed little or no assistance for him to pass assessment tests. So, other than the brief testimony provided by my older brother, Roland Kaston, I have no reliable information as to whether Cousin Douglas's enrolment was to start school as a fresher or to carry on to the next class when he started school in Salisbury (Harare).

However, although my formal education would only begin four or five years later, I have a photographic recollection of seeing Cousin Douglas depart from the farm every morning in the company of his male counterparts to attend classes at Maronda Mashanu School. They would arrive back home as a group after school in the afternoons, whereupon they promptly changed their school uniforms into shreds of tattered work clothes. Father wasted no time in assigning them various tasks around the farm where they were kept occupied until well after dusk. Then they would return to the farm homestead, eat the evening meal, and immediately went to bed, exhausted from the combination of attendance at school and work on the farm in the latter part of the afternoon. It was a truly energy-sapping routine for these growing minds.

After installing Cousin Douglas at the farm, Aunt Eliver, thenceforth, increased the frequency of her visits, arriving back at the farm once every three months or so. On each of her visits, she would arrive laden with a large khaki carrier bag containing an assortment of fascinating 'goodies' for all of us. She never forgot to bring nice trinkets for her sister, too, including earrings, bracelets, women's clothes and so on. Grocery items she always included in her bag included up to a dozen of freshly baked 'Lobels' bread (bread baked at Lobels Bakery), two or even three four-pound packets of refined sugar, large packets of 'Tanganda' tea leaves, 'Stork' margarine, large tins of fruit jam and tins of condensed milk. These items of food were known to be consumed only in homes of the well-to-do or those members in families who belonged to a certain social status. In addition, she also included in her collection of goodies such items as bars of green 'Sunlight' laundry soap (which we ended up also using as 'bath' soap) and pots of 'Blue Seal' Vaseline. From her previous visits she had noticed some of us complaining chesty coughs and sneezes. However, in the absence of rural health centres or clinics at the time in the local community and with father's tight grip on movements away from the farm for the simple reason to obtain medicines, say, at Enkeldoorn (Chivhu) General Hospital six miles away, we suffered quietly. In these circumstances of hardship, Mother was at a loss to know what she could do to ease our discomforts. In subsequent visits, Aunt Eliver would always remember to include small bottles of cough medicines, packets of 'Aspro' tablets and other painkillers, all of them 'across the counter' medications available from pharmacies and general dealers' shops. Aunt Eliver would hand these items to Mother asking her to hide them somewhere on standby for administration to us and herself too in the event that the flu virus attacked the family. Mother's wardrobe also vastly improved, as her sister brought her an assortment of women's attire every time she arrived on visits.

Whenever she fished out the clothes from her bag to show and give them to Mother, there was this distinctly perfumed aroma of goodness that oozed from the fabrics, filling the air in the room. Such sweet fragrance amidst the rugged aridness of the rural backdrop! During the few days Aunt Eliver was visiting at the farm, our eating habits changed dramatically, resulting in incremental health and happiness on our part. What I cherished most about her visits was that our breakfasts, when she was around, were virtual banquets in my mother's 'house.' Remember, there were several other houses at the farm homestead. Then we ate extremely large pieces of jammed or buttered bread, washed down with steaming mugs of sweet milky tea that was so hot you were in danger of having your tongue and lips scalded if you drank it too quickly. For us, enjoying these rare comforts and luxuries gave us a sample of the good life.

Aunt Eliver's visits aside, the million-dollar question nobody would dare ask my male parent was: Was it not a wonder that the only person at the farm who appeared to enjoy the seemingly natural right to the frivolous partaking of tea on each day of the year was nobody else but my father? Yes, he would have his hot morning tea at about the same time every day, no matter where or with whom he was working with, on the farm. If, for example, two of us boys had been working with him since early in the morning on a piece of land, for example, turning the soil with a span of four oxen pulling a metal plough and both his hands firmly held the piece of farming equipment, his youngest wife, Marumbidza, would suddenly arrive at around eight thirty a.m. holding aloft a tray carrying a hot pot of tea and other tea things in it, neatly covered with a wire netting cloth. On noting his wife's arrival with a side glance, he would beckon us – one of us leading the oxen in front and the other driving the span from the side – to suspend the ploughing and take a short break, standing in our tracks with the animals huffing and puffing while he sat down at the spot where the tray had been placed and started eating his breakfast. This was his 'tea-break' and not ours, so he would not invite us to share the tea with him. Up to ten or fifteen minutes later following his ritual, he would join us where the span of oxen still stood together, with me and my young brother tending them, and we would resume work on the furrow as if nothing had happened. This mindlessness and lack of consideration for the comforts of others was mindboggling, to say the least. It did not seem to concern my father whether we shouldn't also partake of some refreshments or taken note of the fact that we had not eaten or drunk anything as he had. That question of his selfishness was never put to my father by anyone, ever, from fear of being sharply rebuked or physically abused, even! Such topics for discussion with my father were taboo.

# Chapter 6

# The uniqueness of Christmas Day at the family farm

Uncle Rodrick's and Aunt Eliver's casual appearances at the farm and the many joys these events brought helped to brighten our lives. The one occasion everyone at the farm looked forward to with great anticipation every year was Christmas Day. It was the only day in the year when every Tom, Dick and Harry was allowed the indulgence to eat a breakfast meal in father's presence without fear of being publicly rebuked. My father viewed the unusual privilege of drinking tea and eating buttered or jammed bread or cake at the farm as one that was to be enjoyed only by a selected group of people with him occupying pole position. When that event took place, everybody was expected to participate in what amounted to a communal event. My mother Rheya (Leah), renowned for brewing good strong tea for large groups of people, was often the favoured one of father's three wives, charged with the task of brewing the tea in a large three-legged cast iron twenty-litre pot. My father's large family, and everybody at the farm, including the two elderly grannies, would assemble at a chosen spot on an open space in the centre of the homestead. Having secretly done his Christmas shopping in Enkeldoorn (Chivhu) town on Christmas Eve, this was the one day in the year when my father played the unusual role of 'Father Christmas.' Surprisingly, he did not disappoint on the matter of giving Christmas gifts: everyone received something, never mind what it was. When he had fetched the bag of 'goodies' by himself from a secret location in a room specially reserved for his use in a barn where it would have securely been hidden, he would rise from a chair conveniently positioned on a raised portion of the ground.

Clearing his voice once or twice, he would embark on the process of distributing his Christmas presents, attaching sarcastic comments as he did so:

"Er-r", he would pause a bit, looking around importantly. When everybody was quietly sitting and not shuffling their feet, he would continue with his self-appointed task, bending down to rummage in the bag. His right hand would emerge, clutching an item he alone recognised and then he would call out, "Jessica, (his first wife) "Mujivha wako uyo-o! Asi handidi kuti uzonyanya kupindira kana ndichiranga Misheck! Urikundinzwa here?" tossing the item at her with careless abandon. ("Jessica, here you're, there is your dress! But please stop this nonsense of interfering when I am disciplining Misheck. Do you understand me?") Without waiting to see if Stepma (Maiguru) Jessica had received her present, he would bend quickly to dip his hand back in the sack, peering doubtfully and grinding his teeth as he did so, and he would continue, "Eh-er-er, Rheya (that was my mother Leah), Mujivha wako uyo-o!" ('Leah, there's your dress!') As the hurled item was in mid-flight to the recipient, Father Christmas would quip with a touch of irony, "Rheya, ndini chete ndinogona kukutengera hembe dzakanaka, kwete dzimwe hama dzako dzinouya pano dzichindivhairira." ("Leah, here's your costume! It's only me who can buy you clothes of good quality, not some of your relatives who come into this homestead and start showing off!"). If my mother's sister had visited from Salisbury (Harare) for the festive occasion and was present in the audience, father did not make these scornful comments, careful not to offend my mother's relatives or her visitors.

Next in line would be his third wife, Marumbidza, who would also receive the same type of gift as the senior wives, without any differentiation. Thereafter he followed no order of handing out his presents. He simply fished them out of the bag one item after the other and randomly called out the names of the children yet to be presented with a gift. Little boys like Irrigation, Last and I received the same type of gift each which usually was an XXXL shirt. Father preferred to call that type of shirt a 'Jumper'. I clearly remember one of these occasions when it was my turn to receive a long-awaited Christmas gift. On fishing out the present from the sack and recognising I was the recipient, he called out, "Kingi, Ooo-o! (Tossing the item) Jamba rako iro! Asi humambara hwese hwekurega mombe dzichipinda muminda yevaridzi ngahupere. Zvikaramba zvoitika, gore rinouya hapana chipo paKirisimasi. Urikundinzwa here, Kingi-i?" (King, there's your Jumper! But this nonsense about letting cattle stray into other people's fields must end. If I get more of these things happening in the new year, I promise you, there'll be no present for you come next Christmas! Do you understand me, Kingi-i?) with a touch of anger.

Father would go and on until the job of handing out Christmas presents was done and dusted, each of his handouts being accompanied by a scornful remark. I would discover before long that my Christmas present was a hugely oversize khaki shirt with short sleeves that nearly reached down to my wrists. As it was, growing up blissfully in rural areas in my middle childhood years, the wearing of pairs of shorts and pants for little boys seven to eight years of age was something to look forward to in the future. It was unheard of in the environment I grew up in for boys of my age to be seen wearing underpants or shorts. Due to the large number of children that needed to be provided for, father could simply not afford such luxuries for little men like me, so the oversize shirts given to me, Irrigation (Wilfred) and Last (nephew Bernard) as our presents for Christmas were also considered sufficient to cover our clothing needs for the rest of the following year. In short, we would be expected to use our Christmas 'Jumpers' as our shirts and shorts for most of the forthcoming new year!

After the ritual of dishing out presents was over, all the adults and children queued up to receive mugs of literally boiling milky tea and 'half-brick' thick pieces of buttered or jammed bread which we munched quietly as we sat in rows, with our legs stretched forward, against the red brick walls of round hovels, our parents' 'kitchens'. Immediately after that, I would be found running around the yard or playing with my colleagues in the sandy and dusty open space completely barefoot, but proudly showing off in my new oversize 'Jumper'; with its short sleeves reaching down to my wrists and the tail of the large and ill-fitting garment literally sweeping the floor behind me! Unbeknown to me and in my Christmas joy and bliss about the present I had received, I had no way of knowing that I was making a bonny exhibition of myself when later that morning I sped down the road to stop a herd of cattle that was straying into a field of ripening maize. That my Vaseline, shaven and shorn baseball bat of a head glistened incongruously in the bright Christmas sunshine was not causing people to admire me one bit. Instead, Irrigation and Last informed me later that the image I portrayed as I ran down the road in my ill-fitting garment made me the object of downright laughter. By then, I had begun developing a sense of self and these negative remarks about my ridiculous appearance seriously punctured my self-image. What saved the day was the recognition that father had married three wives. Never mind a fourth one who in a very short time appeared to have fizzled into the void by unceremoniously returning to her parents' home in Manyene Tribal Trust Lands.

Marrying three wives had its responsibilities. It was even a bit over the top for my father who was a struggling native farmer. Already his brood of offspring had grown too large, and he was still counting on having more children. If so, there was no chance this man could afford the expense of buying enough fitting clothes for all his wives and children. However, if one of Aunt Eliver's visits happened to coincide with the Christmas festive season, it added more glamour and excitement to those of us in my mother's family. From her previous visits, Aunt Eliver or 'Mainini Mai Dougie' as we used to call her affectionately – Douglas's Mother – would remember that her sister's little boys were always presented with oversize shirts that were invariably torn and tattered each time we ran to welcome her on her visits. There was nothing to write home about concerning our appearances in these ill-fitting rags. To be honest, life was hard for us. Limited by her own restricted means of earning a living and having to look after her son back in Salisbury (Harare), she could only do so much and no more in assisting to resolve the issues of the clothing we had to face.

Aunt Eliver sought to ameliorate our situation by bringing with her on her next visits loads of good quality second-hand shirts and shorts which she obtained at giveaway prices from 'Charity Shops' in Salisbury (Harare). I will now divert a little from the thread of my story by fast-tracking to a little incident arising from my air-brushed appearance two or so years later when I started school at Maronda Mashanu. The local churchgoers and their children almost always appeared at church services wearing their 'Sunday best'. That seemed to be the standard expectation. One Sunday morning, after Aunt Eliver had returned to Salisbury (Harare) at the end of one of her visits, I decided on my own to walk over to Maronda Mashanu School, five kilometres away, to attend a church service that was held for local parishioners in one of the classrooms. I wore a freshly laundered and pressed white shirt and a pair of well-fitting English grey shorts. Using one of the 'Lux Bath Soap' tablets Aunt Eliver had brought for Mother, I had had a good bath. I had also cut my fingernails and brushed my teeth. Although I was barefoot, I looked squeaky clean, smug, clever and well turned out in my outfit. Hardly any of the adults and children from our farm homestead had 'Sunday best' clothes to wear to church, so rarely ever did anyone from our farm appear at these church gatherings on Sundays. It was therefore the first time ever that members of the congregation had set their eyes on a child from our farm looking so smart and smelling of goodness! Those of us from Farm No. 7 were generally looked down upon as a family who had very little solid substance in the Maronda Mashanu community, despite our luck in having a father who owned a farm! That was supposed to mean that we would have more land to grow crops on than most members of the community who lived in the infertile and overcrowded 'Reserves' or communal areas. Unfortunately, the opposite was true.

Be that as it may, my unexpected appearance at the Sunday Church Service at Maronda Mashanu School that day, looking so fresh and smart, turned heads. It especially attracted the attention of a small group of little girls who were my classmates in Standard 1 (year or Grade 3). The girls had walked from the 'Dhobha' communal area, four to five miles away from the school, in the company of their parents and adult relatives. Lest I offend them, I shall deliberately avoid mentioning the actual names of the 'little girls' in this account because I believe some of them are still alive. I also would hate to reveal their identities as I expect they may be respectably married, although presumably beyond recognition today, in their appearance, due to the vagaries of old age.

While people milled about at the end of the two-hour church service conducted by a church deacon, talking and greeting each other before they dispersed to their homes, the knot of girls continually ran around me in rings, clapping their hands and laughing excitedly as I stood at the edge of the open space in front of the large classroom where the church service had been conducted. I have mentioned that people in the community had a very low opinion of my family. Add to this the fact that my father was famous for all the wrong reasons, so with this tarnished and tainted background, who was I suddenly to turn up at church in these nice-smelling, swashbuckling clothes? I realised that without the frills I was wearing, I was a nonentity and that none of these little girls would dream of wanting to stand anywhere near me, let alone talk to me.

I was about nine to ten years old when I made my appearance at the church service. At that stage of my late childhood, I was already striving to establish some sort of identity and recognition of myself and my family. Indeed, as I was walking away at the start of my journey back home, that bunch of curious little girls ran up to me. Catching up with me and blocking my path shrieking and chirping like little birds, they competed with each other in asking me questions and persistently formed rings around me, "Kingston, wait there. Can we walk with you? Tell us, where did you get these clothes from? (One literally pulling at the sleeve of my shirt) Did Mr Mudyara (my father) buy them for you? You look too smart in your shirt and shorts. Are you going to give them to us?"

Sensing the sarcasm and irony in their questions, I decided not to give away too much information and quietly informed them that my parents had bought the clothes for me. I made a hasty detour around them as they giggled childishly and chirped away like female birds in season, I blanked them out and continued on my journey back to the farm. Realising that I had no interest in talking to them, the girls sprinted back to their parents who had begun calling them to return to them in a muddled chorus at the tops of their voices so that they would start the walk back to their homes across the small stream to the 'reserves'. In a nutshell, the account I have described about Aunt Eliver's string of visits to our farm is only but a bird's eye view; a summary of events that took place over a period spanning six years or thereabouts.

We cherished Aunt Eliver's warm, caring, and motherly qualities. In possession of robust and no-nonsense character traits; of all those who visited us from my mother's side of the family, she was the only one who was not terrified by father's fearsome persona. She was the only other visitor from my mother's side of the family who could puncture his pride, stand up to my father's obliqueness of character and attitude, thereby demystifying the myths he had of himself of possessing royal blood: that he was descended from a Rozvi deity who must always be feared!

Sometimes, suddenly arriving at the farm, she would discover that Mother and Father were not on speaking terms, that a wall of tension between them over a previous dispute needed to be knocked down.

Aunt Eliver would engage with father playfully as a sister-in-law but albeit fearlessly and diplomatically. She convinced him to understand that differences of opinion between spouses were not always resolved through the use of violence. To those young people like me who had started on the long journey to stamp my existence in this world amidst the suffocating dreariness of my farm upbringing, Aunt Eliver ushered into my life and the lives of my mother, brothers, and sisters a new promise and a breath of fresh air. The huge amounts of food and drink that we had at the family banquets held in my mother's house each time she showed up at the farm, the bundles of new and old clothes she supplied to Mother, my brothers, and sisters and all her philanthropic actions, too many to itemise, had a civilising influence on us. While her visits lasted, we were happy. We virtually lived in the lap of luxury that, if it weren't for Aunt Eliver, none of us would have ever known at the time. Aunt Eliver Ruhukwa (nee Muguto) unwittingly afforded us the rare opportunity to sample the taste of the good life, contrasted against the many constraints of our grim existence.

To compensate for the hours allegedly 'wasted' while they were at school, father made sure that his children put in significant amounts of farm work in the mornings before they left home to attend school. That meant him often waking the boys up to start work at the farm at around three a.m. If the boys failed to complete the tasks he set, he often stopped the boys from going to school altogether, resulting in numerous missed lessons which had a knock on effect on how they performed at school. In due course, the difficulties I encountered with father over the issue of non-attendance at school were comparatively of less magnitude in terms of the level of hardship that was brought to bear on me. However, I am informed my older brothers Misheck (Raphael), Kaston (Roland) and cousin brother, that Douglas Ruhukwa literally suffered. Father completely ignored complaints he received from school about the boys' poor attendance record and how this was affecting their class work. Instead, he would accuse the school authorities of interfering with the rights and authority he enjoyed as a parent over his children.

Similar restrictions were applied to his boys after the school timetable ended at three p.m. Yet father expected us back at the farm promptly so that we would put in a fair amount of farm work before nightfall. However, schooling was not just about attending lessons. Other things were happening in the school calendar. For example, the school authorities would hold us back at school for an hour or so after three p.m. for us to participate in co-curricular activities, such as football training, physical training, choir practice, athletics, scouting, baseball and others. On set days, teachers with senior classes like Standard 2 (Grade 4) and Standard 3 (Grade 5) would hold back their classes for an hour after school ended, for a perfectly legitimate reason. The extra lessons we had then were meant to help those who were lagging behind with their schoolwork so that they could pass their assessment tests at the end of the year.

Regrettably, these arrangements by the school were not considered by my father as having any importance. The result was that he was always at cross purposes with the fine intentions of the school. In his view, the six hours we spent at school being taught by teachers was more than adequate for our learning. Therefore, he did not see any reason why we should waste any more time at school after the school timetable had expired. Neither did Father embrace the significance of 'extra lessons,' nor would he grasp the educational value that we would benefit from taking part with others in 'co-curricular' activities. These terms were absolute Greek to him.

Just to remind you, Cousin Douglas Ruhukwa had been living with us at the farm since his mother, my Aunt Eliver, had entrusted him to his aunt, my mother, in around the year 1953. I need hardly remind you that when Douglas started attending school at Maronda Mashanu School, he showed great potential as a talented pupil; but barely two or three years after that and with all the disturbances as well as the stifling environment at the farm, a pattern of bad performance results in Cousin Douglas's classwork, as well as that of his counterparts Misheck (Raphael) and Kaston (Roland) began to emerge. On the strength of the background I have given, this was not surprising.

Their home environment was not supporting them to achieve success in their schoolwork. They were missing most of their lessons at school, due to punishments inflicted by Father for what were merely misdemeanours of one sort or another. Efforts were put in place by their teachers to help them catch up with their missed schoolwork by getting them to attend extra tuition lessons after school hours. Because of my father's negative attitude to additional assistance being given to the boys to catch up with missed lessons, the strategies put in place by their teachers failed to produce the intended result; and their problems with Father, regarding regular attendance at school, continued unabated.

Their lifestyle, often spending nights on end in the woods following quarrels with Father, had an adverse effect on the boys' emotional and cognitive wellbeing. At the end of the third year after my cousin started school at Maronda Mashanu School, he reportedly flunked his end-of-year tests. So also did Misheck and Kaston. In those years, failing to pass tests at the end of the year in primary school necessitated repeating your class in the following year.

It is important to put on record here that despite the child abuse, ill treatment and virtual slave labour demands father imposed on us his children, testimony given by my own mother before she passed on years ago was that he singularly spared Cousin Douglas Ruhukwa the rod. Perhaps that was because he realised that Douglas was not his child on whom he could routinely administer corporal punishment. Father was therefore reported to have hardly ever touched Cousin Douglas Ruhukwa with a stick or a belt for the entire period he stayed with us on the farm. However, that did not mean that he was spared a loud telling-off when Father was convinced that he had erred. In equal measure to the way he treated his own children, Cousin Douglas was also on the receiving end of father's harshness of temper, thunderous voice, and the brutality with which he dealt with his own children. These aspects were believed to have completely terrified Cousin Douglas Ruhukwa. This occurred in 1955 or thereabouts and little Douglas Ruhukwa was then around ten to twelve years of age. Hence, whenever explosions occurred causing Misheck and Kaston to run off into the safety of the bushes, Cousin Douglas is reported to have also run off into the woods, together with his colleagues, for fear that if he stayed behind, my father (VaMudyara) would shift his attention onto him and vent his anger on him, with grave consequences. Thus, the trio would share the comforts and safety offered by the bushes for days, during which time, they would also miss lessons at school. These were terrible experiences for young growing minds to endure. The boys would eventually sneak back into the homestead after father's temper had been calmed down by the passage of time. People do say that time is the best healer.

On her next Christmas visit just after those 'failed' test results had been announced, Aunt Eliver was reportedly quite dismayed by her son's performance at school. She had been well aware of the potential that he carried, so, she realised that the end-of-year school results did not reflect the son she knew. Mother also expressed disquiet to her sister about her son's results at school; exhorting her to understand that Cousin Douglas and his colleagues, Kaston (Roland) and Misheck (Raphael), who had similarly failed their tests, should not be blamed for the poor quality schoolwork they had produced, as their restrictive and difficult home environment was the reason why they had failed their tests.

The bad results were caused by failure to support them in their learning pursuits, due to circumstances prevailing at home. My cousin brother Douglas had unsuspectingly been caught up in the crossfire. He had been in the clutches of the evil and restrictive regime on the farm. Mother was left with no choice but to request her sister to immediately withdraw her son from the farm and Maronda Mashanu School, to ensure that his academic potential was not irretrievably damaged. Mother requested for urgent arrangements to be made for Cousin Douglas Ruhukwa to be placed in a suitable school setting in Salisbury (now Harare) that was less disruptive and more supportive of his learning capabilities. I picked up snippets of the conversation between my mother and her younger sister that ran as follows:

"... Douglas loved going to school, my sister. I'm told he was doing well in class. He showed lots of potential when he started school here. ..."

"... Oh yes, some of his school reports I saw confirmed that. I wonder what happened along the way."

"… Simple my sister. The blame is on the horrible conditions at this farm. Half the time the time, the boys are missing lessons at school due to too many work commitments the boss at this farm gives them."

"… And what of these reports I hear of the boys spending nights sleeping in the …"

"… The bush; true. Their father frequently quarrels with his own children. So, when Kaston (Roland) and Misheck (Raphael) run off to seek shelter in the woods, Douglas has no choice but to join his colleagues, fearing that …"

"… Oh my God, that his uncle might turn round and vent his anger on the poor boy?" …

"… Yes, so, after spending the night in the bush, the boys cannot come back into the farm compound on the following morning to prepare to go to school."

"… Did this happen often? …"

"… Countless times. I'm not surprised their schoolwork was affected. They missed far too many of their lessons at school."

"… That's sad, my sister" …

"… Yeah, those bad school results are testimony of what's going on here. In Douglas's case and for the sake of his academic future, I suggest …"

"… that I take him with me back to Salisbury (Harare) straight away and …" "… Please place him in a school and home environment which will help him to learn and attend all his lessons. (Wringing her hands) If we can do anything to help Douglas's education, let's do so now. I'd hate anyone to blame me for denying our boy the educational opportunities that he deserves."

"… You know, my sister, Douglas's stay here would have worked out nicely for him and myself. But from what you have told me and the bad results of his at the end of this year, I have no choice but to remove my boy from your custody without further delay. Thank you very much for the childcare role you played on my behalf for the past few years."

These were my formative years and the accounts I have given took place when I was beginning to make sense of the world around me. Some things I understood, others I did not. For that reason, memories become blurred with the passage of time and the exactness of dates becomes an issue. Mother however thought the event of Cousin Douglas Ruhukwa's return to Salisbury was at the end of 1955, another full year before yours truly started going to school. Though still a little boy then myself, I still have fresh memories of the cloud of sorrow that descended on my mother's household as my cousin and his mother prepared to leave the farm and begin the six mile walk to Enkeldoorn (now Chivhu) to catch one of the buses that plied the ninety-six mile route, so we heard, to Salisbury. During his remarkably short stay with us that was packed with many happy as well as sad recollections, Cousin Douglas Ruhukwa had become one of us, a soulmate, and a kindred spirit who it was going to be difficult, if not impossible, to detach from us. We would miss him dearly. I literally shed tears of sorrow as cousin brother Douglas Ruhukwa finally bid everyone farewell to return to Salisbury (Harare) with his mother.

From then on, Aunt Eliver's visits to the farm became markedly more and more irregular. She did not stop coming to the farm completely but the intervals between her few visits became so wide that I am on record as constantly asking Mother, "Please tell me, Mother, when will Aunt Eliver visit us again so that we can eat buttered and jammed half-brick slices of bread and drink loads of tea in this house?" Looking into the distance, Mother would chuckle quietly to herself, poking the smouldering log of wood in front of her. After taking her time to think of the best possible answer she could give me, she would only finally speak to me reassuringly, "My son, Kingi, don't worry yourself so much. Your Aunt Eliver still loves all of you here very much. I'm quite sure she'll visit again soon once she finds it convenient to do so."

In the aftermath of cousin brother Douglas Ruhukwa being retrieved from the farm to return to Salisbury (Harare), the only home my other brothers Misheck (Raphael) and Kaston (Roland) knew was nowhere else but Farm No. 7, Maronda Mashanu Native Purchase Area. They had no choice but to stick it out at the farm for the next three years, having to repeat their Standard 1 (Grade 3) in 1956. After Cousin Douglas Ruhukwa's had been packed off back to a better and more supportive learning environment in Salisbury (Harare), his counterparts forged ahead in utterly inhospitable conditions and successfully completed Standard 3 (Grade 5) in 1958.

A few days after Christmas in 1958, there was a major fall-out in the relationship between my father and his firstborn son, Misheck (Raphael). They had always lived a cat and dog's life and the events that unfolded this time around were not unexpected. As usual, the argument pertained to work tasks set by father either being half done or not even being started at all because father was in the habit of giving fabulously long lists of assignments to be completed in one day. The quarrel resulted in the two boys, Misheck and my older brother Kaston, spending two consecutive weeks sleeping in the bushes around the farm. Father breathed fire and, threatening vengeance, he declared that he did not want to catch sight of them in the homestead, so I was one of those who assisted Mother secretively pass food and drink onto my brothers while they were hidden in the woods. Having started school in 1957, I was in Sub-Standard B (Grade 2) at the end of 1958. I had first-hand experience of the nasty things that happened to my brothers. It was immensely disconcerting emotionally. The local rural primary school offered education up to Standard 3 (Grade 5) only then, so seeing no future in their educational prospects with all the bad things happening around them and in the absence of any concrete plans by Father regarding how they would proceed with their education the following year, they were forced by the intensity and hardship of their circumstances to do something about it on their own, otherwise their lives were doomed.

They both expressed their wish to seek to complete their primary school education by staying with Uncle Rodrick who was then stationed at Thornhill Airforce Base, Gwelo (Gweru), approximately ninety miles away from Enkeldoorn (Chivhu). For some reason, Uncle Rodrick had not come to spend the festive season at the farm that year. Perhaps if he had, the future of my brothers' education in Gwelo would have been discussed and their travel properly arranged. In the absence of a clear programme of action, I clearly remember the duo bidding Mother farewell in the bush and secretly leaving the farm to walk to Enkeldoorn (Chivhu), ten kilometres away.

Setting out on that adventure to Gwelo with not a penny of travel money jingling in their pockets, my brothers' journey to reach destination is a story whose gory details I had best leave out of these pages. Very briefly, Roland (Kaston) made me understand that they walked the distance for the bulk of that awful journey and for the remainder, they were offered freerides, thanks to the kindness of some of the haulage lorry drivers.

# Chapter 7

# Exploiting opportunities to earn pocket money and engaging in other childish forms of entertainment

Elsewhere above, I have hinted that father did not set aside any time for his children to enjoy any form of entertainment. It was all work, work, and work in the fields at the farm. He strictly prohibited us from making any visits to the households of the extended family during weekends, school vacations or public holidays. These circumstances remained the stuff of our life at the farm long after my older brothers' unceremonious departure for Gwelo (Gweru) at the end of 1958. It was a straightjacketed existence. We remained, as it were, permanently condemned like prisoners to a life of nothing else but penury, hard graft in the farm fields for most of the time when we were not at school. That left us with no social life to speak of. The almost total absence of opportunities to mix with others of our age in my middle childhood years must have far-reaching consequences to people like me in their formative years; yet the human spirit is an irrepressible force: it will always find ways to express itself even when other dark forces attempt to throttle it. If it cannot freely express itself, then opportunities will almost always unwittingly avail themselves, making it possible for our individualities to express themselves. In silent protest against my father's unwritten law that prohibited any of his family, including his hapless wives, ever to be found indulging in any leisurely activities outside the confines of the farm, Saturdays or Sundays often provided little boys like me with opportunities to poke holes into that prohibition law.

By dint of good fortune, work around the farm was considerably reduced following the harvesting season. Interestingly and correspondingly also, father himself became laid back at this time and he did not adhere as strictly as before in checking whether we were at the locations of work he had assigned to us on the night before. Quite often, at these times of plenty also, my father became negligent and inconsistent in his use of time and adherence to his behaviour patterns, focusing more on spending whole days at beer-drinking parties, miles away in the nearby 'tribal trust lands.' On return to the farm late at night in a state of stupor, he promptly jumped into his bed singing tuneless songs without ever finding out whether any tasks set had been completed or not. My two young colleagues and I exploited father's seasonal weaknesses of character to maximum advantage. Our nearest town, Enkeldoorn, was barely ten miles away. Under no circumstances were any of us allowed to be found walking about in it. "There's enough work to keep all of you busy at this farm, all the way from January to December, without any of you wasting time walking about aimlessly in the 'damn' town!", my father would assert, stamping his right foot on the ground.

On some Saturdays or Sundays, father was in the habit of waking up well after the sun had climbed quite a distance into the morning sky. So, we took a cue from the generosity of his new habit which made it possible for either me, my young brother, Irrigation by himself or both of us, to craftily slip out of the farm unnoticed and head to Enkeldoorn (Chivhu). Even if he had struggled to wake up and shake off his drunken stupor of the night before, there were more chances that the fellow would still not possibly catch sight of us sneaking out of the farm as he frequently complained of nursing terrific hangovers that gave him throbbing headaches. All the same, we took great care that he did not catch sight of us leaving the farm to go and have some fun in the town. Taking care that none of the people in the neighbouring purchase area farms who were familiar with us saw us walking along the gravel road everybody used to reach the town, we would joyfully dash like little hares along winding pathways through the sparse bushland on the white man Mr Kerry Schultz's Farm and all the way until we reached the exclusively 'Europeans Only' Tennis Club, under a mile, west of the fledgling town of Enkeldoorn (Chivhu). Uncle Chigonyati on my mother's side of the family was in paid employment at the tennis club as a Labourer or Cleaner, what you would politely call a 'General Hand' in today's lingo. However, at weekends, the atmosphere at the tennis club assumed a new vibrancy. It became quite busy resulting from several Europeans with land holdings in surrounding areas of the small town, coming to do their grocery shopping in town as well as to meet with their other folks. Many of them ended up at the tennis club where they interacted with their friends and enjoyed a spot of tennis on the courts. At such times, my uncle doubled up as a 'Tea Boy' or 'Refreshments Boy.' One should note, however, that the same person was a grown up man with a wife and children somewhere at his rural home! Here was a fellow who had to plod on with his life somewhere and it was not the right time for him to start arguing about the semantics of his job titles.

On his off days in the middle of the week, Uncle Chigonyati sometimes diverted from his bicycle journey to Manyene, nearly twenty-five miles farther north of my father's farm. On his journey back to Enkeldoorn (Chivhu) after visiting his family for a few days, he would briefly stop and pay homage to my parents. Before he left our farm to continue with his journey, he patted all of us little boys on the shoulders, feverishly bidding everybody goodbye.

Balancing himself back on his bicycle, Uncle Chigonyati playfully invited all those of us little boys who stood by as he commenced his bicycle ride to come and visits him at his workplace in Enkeldoorn (Chivhu), especially at weekends. If chances arose for us to visit him at his workplace in Enkeldoorn on some weekends, he would talk to his bosses to see if we could earn a bit of pocket money in the form of tips for being 'ball boys.' Standing beside his bicycle, with both his hands firmly placed on the bicycle handles before his journey back to Enkeldoorn (Chivhu) started, he said: "Look here boys, I love to see children like you having a little bit of fun. I'm unhappy with your lifestyle here, locked up at this farm, as it were. Just imagine, Enkeldoorn is only about eight to ten miles from here. Why don't you visit me where I work during weekends? I would gladly welcome you. Then perhaps I can talk to my bosses so you can earn a bit of pocket money for yourselves from catching tennis balls that have fallen out of tennis courts and giving them back to European adult tennis players. Some of the club members might also give you good 'tips money' for your efforts. I'm sure your father does not mind letting you off farm work for a bit, maybe one or two of you at a time, hey! What do you think?"

After wiping sweat off his knitted brow, Uncle Chigonyati would suddenly throw his right leg over the crossbar and vigorously pedal the bicycle out of the courtyard, leaving us gazing after him as we had thought that his conversation with us had not been concluded. He had inserted a question at the end of his last little speech, but he did not wait to get our input on the question. Father was not present during that conversation. He was probably busy on some part of the fields, somewhere on the farm. We knew perfectly well that if such a request was put to that old 'geezer' by one of us, he would reject it outright. It was common knowledge he would dismiss the idea completely out of hand. He would not want to hear about it in at all. Henceforth, thereafter, our repeated but secret expeditions to Enkeldoorn (Chivhu) during some selected weekends in the off-farming season were hatched out and they developed into a pattern. However, it remained a closely guarded secret that was known about only by my young brother Irrigation, my nephew Last and myself.

Our roles as 'ball boys' therefore marked the beginning, the very first time we had ever been within arms' reach of people of other races, especially Europeans from England, who we found to be pleasant, kind and more tolerant and accommodating in their attitudes. At my age of about nine years, the only European I knew was Mr Kerry Schultz, our white next door neighbour; but we would rarely ever see him; and on the golden days when he appeared on the opposite side of his huge perimeter fence, he would be at a distance, either walking about three hundred yards away from us, with a double bore shotgun slung on his shoulders; or he would be riding on a massive horse which soon impatiently galloped off towards the opposite side of its owner's perimeter fence as if frightened by our fixed gazes.

We never ever got the chance to speak to this man who we sometimes heard him address his hordes of African herd 'boys' in the hateful medium called 'Chilapalapa', a pidgin form of communication. So, except for the few patrons at the club who spoke a language called Afrikaans, many of those who spoke clear English indicated a readiness to engage in conversation with us despite the not-so-clean, ragged and ill-fitting clothes we always appeared in and our bare feet because none of us had any shoes or trainers. All our lessons at school, including even our native 'Shona', were taught in the English language, so we deliberately ignored some of the non-English speaking European club members or their visitors who insisted on wanting to speak to us in 'Chilapalapa'; because we wanted to practise our listening and speaking skills in the Queen's language that our teachers were using to teach us at school. 'Chilapalapa' was a kind of derogatory or hybrid mix of language involving use of borrowed words from IsiNdebele and the then little-known 'Kalanga' dialect. Many European employers on farms, mines and residential properties in towns were then in the deliberate habit of using that inferior medium to communicate with their mostly lowly educated African employees.

Use of the medium generally gave the impression that the persons being spoken to by Europeans were of a lower grade in terms of status and that Europeans were the more superior beings. As our consciences were slowly awakening due to the education we were receiving at school, we hated the negative messages that were conveyed using 'Chilapalapa'. I took the lead in conversing only with those of our hosts gathered at the tennis club who chose to speak to us using the English language in its unblemished form. Many tennis club members, especially those of English origin, tipped us so generously for our efforts that we ended up not bothering our parents for money to buy replacement exercise books when the old ones were full with classwork at school. Being the more grown up of the little knot of 'native' ball boys who put in appearances at the tennis club during weekends, one of Uncle Chigonyati's bosses made it very clear to me that the facility was for use by Europeans Only, so try as I might, I was never allowed the chance to take part in the actual playing of the game. It was still too early for me to ask why persons of colour, all of whom lived in the location two or so miles away from the tennis club, did also not use the same facility as everybody else I saw there. However, in hindsight, I have to say that by the time I finished my middle primary education at my local rural school, I had become familiarised with terms used in playing the game of tennis such as, for example, 'deuce', 'advantage', 'backhand', 'backspin', 'doubles', 'love', 'singles', 'serve', 'volley' and so on.

Sadly, most African rural primary schools, even those that were government-funded in urban areas then, did not have facilities for having sporting games played on site such as tennis, golf, hockey, cricket etc. Consequently, tennis-playing as a sport remained a specialty for the European side of the education system in Rhodesia then and was not part of the sporting curriculum in the Native Department of Education at the time. I would therefore never get the chance to apply the wealth of vocabulary about tennis-playing I gained at Enkeldoorn (Chivhu) Tennis Club as I progressed with my education.

In my middle-to-late-childhood, I got to know that a Thursday of every week – so-called 'Chisi' – was a traditional holiday in our local Shona community. I understand that it is still so to this day. It was regarded as a holiday in that no productive work was allowed in the fields in honour of the spirits who were believed to cause the rains to fall, thus enabling crops to grow. Being a 'free' day, so to speak, Thursday held the same status as a Sunday. In my middle-to-late-childhood years, if I were not on the duty roster to herd cattle on that day, real excitement came from my taking part in walks around the farm, climbing up the mountain and taking part in an assortment of games and entertainment. There was a part located south of the farm, behind the mountain which we used to call 'kuseri' (a place behind). Hardly anyone ever visited that part of the farm unless they were accompanied by another person. In an area of approximately fifteen hectares, there existed an atmosphere of eerie serenity which always hung over the area. Walking there on your own, the only sounds you would hear would be the shuffling of your feet as you moved through the tall grass or the different sounds of bird song. Stories from some of the elders said that at the time when European settlers arrived in Zimbabwe in 1890, right up until the changes in the law pertaining to land ownership in the 1930s, Headman Maromo and his people used to occupy and live in this part of father's farm and on the surrounding tracts of land.

With the founding of Maronda Mashanu Christian community by Father Arthur Shearly Cripps at around 1910 and later the Native Purchase Area just before the start of the Second World War (1940), Headman Maromo and all his people were moved to the 'Dzvova and Mutasa Reserve' areas, farther north-north-east of our farm. When the Maromo people were forcibly moved, arising from the changes in law pertaining to land occupation for Rhodesian Africans in 1930, they left behind cemeteries with hundreds of graves. Some of these ancestral burial sites had become shrines where traditional rituals were performed once every year; but all those holy places were left behind by the forced movement of the people to other locations far away. If you wanted to walk about in that place or were looking after a herd of cattle there with any feeling that you were secure, the best thing would be to do it in the company of someone else. Even then, the silence pervading that area often made your hair stand on end. The scariness of the area was also made worse by old stories by unnamed people from neighbouring farms to our south-east who were alleged to have gone round saying they had spotted a pack of white adult lions prowling about at the bottom of the mountain next to Kerry's huge fence. We do not know whether such stories held any truth or were mere fabrications. Whatever they were, they only added to making the place scarier.

Throwing all caution to the wind and ignoring what we believed were fantasies deliberately meant to inspire the fear of God in us, my young brother Irrigation (Wilfred), my nephew

Last (Bernard) and I would sometimes be found jumping about playfully in that part of the farm as we looked after huge herds of cattle. Standing in a small group, we would gaze curiously at the headstones mounted on hundreds of those graves, all of them without inscriptions on them. You could literally lean on the serenity that forever hung over the area. The only sounds you heard would be the distant chirping of birds in huge trees growing in the bottom slopes of the mountain. Grazing our cattle in that part of the farm, we would hurriedly drive our animals away from that area and return to the more user-friendly side of the farm before sunset. From the spin, it was alleged that sunset was the time when the lions in the fantasy story were spotted! Other than stories about lions that our grannies had told us, I had never seen them alive and pacing up and down before, and I did not relish the misfortune of meeting with them for the first time! Therefore, we would therefore hurriedly drive our cattle away from that part of the farm, turning our heads continuously to check that no strange man-eating animals were following us.

We enjoyed further relief on some Thursday afternoons when my two colleagues and I were not on the duty roster to herd cattle. Somehow, out of some quirky curiosity, we would visit the 'kuseri' place again in the vein hope we might find those mythical lions sunbathing among the graves in the massive cemetery, while the spirits of dead people conversed with them! We never made such a discovery of course although we ventured into such expeditions with a great deal of trepidation. By all accounts, it seemed to me that the story about lions was totally unfounded and possibly a figment of somebody's imagination. We would hurriedly leave the deafening silence of that area.

Surprisingly, we remained undaunted, resulting in our boyish squeals of fun and laughter as we gambolled and clambered up and down low tree branches in the small forest that formed the boundary between father's farm and our next-door neighbour in the south. Then our new-found feeling of freedom would find us squeezing through the two-strand dangled barbed wire fence with most of its wooden poles fallen to the ground between our farm and Mr Chiwanza's Farm. Just after squeezing our entry through the fence, we would pluck and eat 'hute' (plum-like fruits) from a grove of the plants which grew in the marshy area. The Chiwanza's were an elderly but very pleasant couple. The husband, who allegedly was a nephew of my family by marrying a distant aunt, always made us laugh with his barbed jokes he made about other people each time he came to our farm on occasions of a 'nhimbe', a 'Jakwara' or just to an ordinary beer-drinking party with other adults. We quietly swept past the Chiwanza's homestead, moving on to the next farm. Now, a whole forest of 'mizhanje' (wild loquat) trees grew just outside that farm's homestead. The old couple lived with a little niece who was maybe the same age as my nephew Last (Bernard) and Irrigation (Wilfred). But as anybody would guess, girls grow faster than boys physically. For inexplicable reasons, we did not have these types of wild plants growing in our farm, so once the unnamed old couple recognised us, the wife was not fussy about our picking the brown and juicy fruit which, when ripened, dropped off from the branches and was strewn on the bottom of the trees. The little niece would sneak away from her Granny's and Grandpa's house, two hundred yards away on the edge of the homestead and join our group under the tree during which there was plenty of laughter and shouting as we picked the fruit.

Then to our bewilderment and surprise, the niece often excitedly climbed up some of the huge trees and shook the branches of the trees hanging low with fruit so that we could pick it. By a cruel twist of fate on one of those days, the girl called out to me from somewhere up in the tree to come and stand directly beneath one of the tree branches she stood with her legs apart, and she intended to shake so that the ripe fig-like 'mazhanje' fruit would drop to the ground below in a flurry. I had not expected to witness the event that followed. I looked up in the tree where the lass stood on a branch with her legs wide apart as she asked directly above me if that was the right branch for her to shake so that the ripe fruit would drop to the ground where I stood. I glimpsed at her for a moment in time and noticed that the young girl had no knickers under her skimpy skirt. She was just a tiny little girl whose adolescence was still yet to arrive. So, in that split second, I had noted her pubic area was still plain and as yet uncovered with the black thatch. Nothing had prepared me to handle the details about the young girl's private part that registered in my mind, so I quickly looked away by way of protecting her dignity. Steadfastly continuing to look away, I politely called out to her to climb back down, telling her we had had our fill of the fruit and it was time for us to leave. The incident appalled me to the core as my knowledge of gender differences between male and female humans was still small and only just developing. I was probably just over ten years old when this incident happened. The only genital areas I was familiar with at that time were only those of my little colleagues who were about three years younger than me. A boy older than me would have smacked his lips with excitement. Instead, I felt deeply embarrassed. Neither did I experience that overwhelming feeling of lust, nor did I even have the courage to tell my colleagues what I had seen as we walked back home.

Once more, on another sunny Thursday afternoon during the off-farming-season after our dinner, the three of us decided to go on a maiden climb to the summit of Mount Makumimai which towered over our farm homestead. Apart from previous small expeditions into the lower slopes to look for firewood, collect 'miunze' fibres or rein in oxen which would have run away from being put in the yoke, none of us had ever quite climbed Makumimai Mountain and reached its summit. In the same fashion as the stories pertaining to the 'kuseri' (or at the back) bit about that geographical feature. It would appear that only a few adults, if any, had ever reached the summit of Makumimai Mountain, thereby rendering the mystery about that part of the mountain open to widespread speculation. Wild rumours said that one could find all sorts of things at the top of the mountain: It was said that the top of the mountain had a pool of sugary water beneath it. Others said that if you were lucky on reaching the summit on a quiet day, you might find angels riding on white horses.

Some of the myths were even more frightening, such as the story that If you went up there on your own, the spirits who were believed to inhabit the summit of the mountain would catch you and hand you over to the pack of white lions they kept as their guard dogs. On and on went the fantasies. It was not our intention to prove any of these fantasies true or false. We simply wanted to quench our childish curiosity; and reach the summit of the mountain, period. 'Makumimai' means tens of hundreds. Folklore has it that during the Matabele raids of the 1820s against the Shona tribes, the Maromo people lived in the lands surrounding Makumimai Mountain. Another eighty to ninety years would have passed before Father Shearly Cripps arrived to establish the Maronda Mashanu community.

On being raided by the AmaNdebele warriors, Headman Maromo's people would have been rounded up like a herd of cattle from the pieces of land they were working on at the bottom of the mountain. Then women, children and the elderly would be herded, literally frogmarched, up the steep gradient and into the hollow caves found in the middle slopes, overlooking both our side of the mountain and the 'kuseri' I have already briefly described; while the men engaged in pitched battles to fight back against the AmaNdebele warriors at the bottom of the mountain. Climbing up the slopes facing Tagarira Farm, we fearfully peered into the black stillness of some of these caverns. Their flimsily lit entrances revealed gruesome objects. Clearly observable from the darkened orifices facing Tagarira Farm were several human skulls and bits of broken skeletons strewn on their dark entrance floors as they receded into the pitch black and spooky interior of the caves. The human bones had turned a whitish grey colour from the ravages of weather and time. The Matabele raids were reported to have taken place around two hundred years previously. They were linked directly with the skulls and broken skeletons that we had seen in the caves. But the spectacle of these human remains was frightening. The tens of skulls differed from each other showing that they had belonged to people of different ages, faced the front of the cave entrances. If you continued examining these horrible-looking skulls and peered through their hollow eye sockets, teeth still lined up and still stuck in dangling or loosely hung jaws, you might suspect that the human beings whose minds had once inhabited those fleshless bones would suddenly begin asking you questions as to what you were looking at. Folklore says these human remains were part of the hundreds of the Maromo people who had perished on the slopes of Makumimai Mountains in wave upon wave of attacks by the Matabele warriors, having been unwittingly entrapped and starved to death in those dark enclosures. Blocked from escape by the enemy soldiers farther down below, their own soldiers could not fetch food and water for their people packed in the assumed safety of the caves like sardines. It is said that when the AmaNdebele warriors arrived, they would literally set up camp around the whole mountain base for weeks, thus starving the enemy and cutting water supplies to the escapees on the slopes higher up the mountain. The existence of so many human skulls and skeletons on the mouths and darkened passages of the caverns often made me wonder how so many people could have perished in such places. It was indeed a dreary picture of desolation. The sights were simply terrifying. Part of our motive in undertaking the mountain climbing expedition arisen from our childish craze to find out who among us would beat the others in reaching the summit first. The frightful images we had viewed in the cavern on the slopes in the southeast of the farm had forced us to abandon using that route to reach the top of the mountain.

We resumed the task of trying to reach the summit of the mountain using a beaten track we had watched our older brothers use in the northern end of the mountain, although the gradient in using that route was steeper. Besides, the route was covered by many soft boulders which protruded obtrusively along your path, and you could unexpectedly topple to the ground as you held onto them in the process of working your way upwards to reach your destination at the top, an estimated four hundred metres from the base of the mountain. Being the older of my two colleagues who presumably had stronger bones and better muscle manipulation, I huffed and puffed my way up, powering up and zigzagging along a meandering route that diverted endlessly round rocky outcrops until I finally reached the summit of the mountain first. Nephew

Last (Bernard) and Irrigation (Wilfred) displayed considerable tenacity for youngsters of their age. They were not too far behind me during the climb. Soon, they caught up with me at the top of the mountain, sweating profusely and completely out of breath from the arduous effort of climbing up the mountain behind me. Resting for a while and looking around, we agreed that the summit of the mountain was indeed flat. The absolute serenity that pervaded the mountain top that we had reached gripped us almost immediately. Except for the distant call of the 'titihoya' bird from among a clump of tall 'mitobwe' trees one hundred yards away. One was seized with the urge to lean on the silence and absolute peace that reigned at that spot. In terms of space, the ground we had reached covered an area of approximately three hectares. In the hot afternoon sunshine. The putrid smell of wild boars – renowned for their mobility at night only – signified that they were present in hiding in a hole somewhere underground not far from where we were. The ground had a few scattered rocks with barren patches of ground in between, which were covered with tufts of dry grass. The few stunted thorn trees growing up her were not as massive as the ones growing on the lower slopes of the mountain.

Demystifying the myths people had thrown around, we did not find any white horses grazing here with winged angels riding on them. We soon convinced ourselves that such crazy ideas may only have existed in the fertile minds of the fantasy storytellers. For me though, the excitement was in discovering that my young brother Irrigation (Wilfred), my nephew Last (Bernard) and I had reached the highest part of the world around us. I had never looked at the world from such a dizzying height before. Perched at the summit of the mountain, as it were, we literally had the world at our feet. I had never observed my surroundings with such a bird's eye view. From where we stood, the stunning views simply blew your mind away. They were so very beautiful and breathtaking as they stretched interminably into the limitless misty blue horizon. From our elevated position, it was possible that on a cloudless day, one could see the entire landscape spread out below the mountain. I was personally struck by the immensity, the topography of the rural hinterland stretching into the boundless distance for miles around. Farther northwards, I saw the rough outlines of the Nyevhe Hills, approximately ten kilometres away. I could also make out the little dots of the villagers' huts at the bottom of the hills; snakes of blue smoke billowed from their thatched roofs. Farther west of Nyevhe Hills was the expansive blue sky that seemed to meet in a friendly greeting with land on the shimmering and distant horizon. Slightly to the east of my reference point, the clump of tall eucalyptus trees growing between Chief Nyoka's homestead and Bwanya Farm, approximately three kilometres farther to the east, were clearly detectable.

From our strategic position, the tall gum trees in the hot afternoon sun appeared bent westwards on their stems in a sort of crude and prayerful response to the cool breeze that was blowing from their east to drive away the baking mid-afternoon temperatures. I trained my eye to a feature in the foreground. Oh my God, it was Maronda Mashanu Primary School itself, approximately five kilometres away, but seeming within touching distance as we viewed it from a higher elevation. It was perhaps several hundred feet below us. Yes, I could pick out our classroom blocks and Mr Machingambi's old Ford pickup truck parked right in front of his house at the teachers' quarters behind the classroom buildings. The tall eucalyptus trees in the north of the school towards Mutasa 'Lines' also came into sharp focus. "And look at the tall trees, Irrigation", I whispered to my young brother, "they are definitely swinging back and forth to the tune of the music played by the wind that is sweeping into our faces!" Indeed, before the end of my exclamation, some of the tree branches visibly bristled and swayed in the swirling wind.

Of course, considering the five-kilometre distance from where we stood to Maronda Mashanu School, the only sound missing as far as we were concerned was the buzzing and swishing of the trees as the wind rustled and blew through their branches. Moving on in a south-south-easterly direction was the vast expanse of landscape, sparsely populated by a crag here, rocky outcrop at Father Cripps' Hills behind which were Chari and Mamvura Farms and a mixture of bare land patches and thin forests stretching as far as the eye could see to Marisira and Masendu Farms.

The evergreen treetops of the aged eucalyptus trees at 'The Range', Native District Commissioner's Offices, maybe twelve miles away southeast, were clearly observable from our observation point. Nearer us but backed up by a broken horizon against which Ziriro Farm is set was the Mashonganyika Farm. Clearly visible in front of their homestead were the greyish brown fields in which they had grown a maize crop in the last growing season. In the south, a carpet of treetops, presumably of the same height, obscured our vision. It indicated a flat piece of land dominated by a dense forest. Finally, looking in the west, the prince of the sky was still in charge. The simmering red sphere had still about five metres to fall before it bade us farewell and slid behind a brownish blue haze on the western horizon. The wide landscape comprised mostly European farms who largely practised animal husbandry. All the way to the distant west would be about twenty-five miles until you reached the blue-hued range of Mhondoro Hills. Between us and those blue mountains in the far west was a rugged mixture of thick forests and expansive grasslands. Not far from the high point whence we perched to view the world, as it were, the wider landscape from below the western base of the mountain was Kerry's farm in the foreground. For the first time, we saw where the white man 'Murungu', our next door neighbour, lived. We could see Kerry's residence far in the west from where we stood. However, reaching it on foot was not as easy as we would have imagined. Adults who had previously walked to Kerry's homestead had hinted it was four miles from our farm. They were probably correct in their assumption. Beside the large white farmhouse with a green tiled roof was a windmill which we saw clearly turning in the wind and swivelling back and forth at an angle of maybe sixty degrees. Farther north of Kerry's farmhouse for roughly three miles was a dense stretch of forest. After that forest, a plateau was gradually revealed, that exposing moving images of haulage lorries, buses and passenger vehicles passing each other in opposite directions at high speed. "Look at all that traffic passing each other. That must be the Salisbury (Harare) to Fort Victoria (Masvingo) Highway that passes just by Kerry's farm and through our town Enkeldoorn (Chivhu)!" I quietly observed to my two colleagues; and my nephew Last (Bernard) concurred, "People say the highway you mentioned passes just by Kerry's house." 'This is hard to believe', I thought to myself, 'I think I live in the back of the woods, cut away from modern civilisation, yet vehicles I see once in a blue moon in our hidden part of the world are only four miles away from us as the crow flies'. So, the heavy rumbling, buzzing, and clattering that reach us at the farm on quiet mornings and evenings or after it has rained is the sound of traffic on that road, isn't it?

I was overwhelmed by a disarming sense of the large number of vehicles on that highway. I had never seen anything like it in the whole of my childhood. It continued to irk me as time went on: The bits of tarred road I have just seen from the top of the mountain, together with my younger colleagues, were only four odd miles from our farm as a bird flew. Yet none of us in our mid-to-late childhoods had been prevented by all sorts of restrictions from visiting the highway and viewing the passing traffic! but that highway was within touching distance of our farm! Something was wrong somewhere, I said to myself. A year or so previously, Uncle Rodrick had surprised us all by arriving at the farm driving a real car for the first time and he surprised us out of our skins. The real car he drove was nothing like the toy wire cars we were used to making and 'driving' around in the sandy pathways as part of our entertainment. Yet a highway with so many real different types of vehicles lay just under our noses, just four or five miles westwards across the forests and grasslands on the white man Kerry's farm.

It took nearly all of my impressionable years before I could acknowledge the full import of my own sense of confinement, thus hideously infiltrating me with a kind of claustrophobic agoraphobia, which gave me an inescapable feeling of being in prison. To hell with these restrictions, I swore quietly to myself. Something must give. Tired of sight-seeing from our beauty-spot, we descended the mountain slopes and went back to the stifling gloominess of our monstrous existence at the bottom.

Even at my young age of ten years then, I began vowing that one day I would pull myself out of the clutches of the misery and isolation that imprisoned me at the 'dump' of a farm, perhaps never to return! The hard work I was always forced to do; the fact that I was not afforded opportunities to play and mix freely with other children of my age group in the neighbourhood. All these factors found me, on one hand, feeling disoriented and occasionally even lost. On the other hand, instead of me developing a positive work ethic and an appreciation of farming, I began to develop a passionate hatred of farming!

I have already described the nature of Mr Schultz's six-strand barbed wire fence. The message that perimeter fence carried was simple: his farm was private property, so he was totally against 'natives' or local people from across his farm to the east, entering his farm for any reason. In short, trespassers caught on his farm risked being arrested or he would use his own means to punish any trespassers found on his property. However, during the off-farming season and with childish abandon and a touch of carelessness, my two colleagues and I were united in ignoring the warnings against trespassers found in Kerry's farm. The problem was compounded by the fact that not many wild fruit trees grew on our side of the farm. Perhaps this resulted from a massive cutting down of trees that took place when father, on settling at the farm, turned virgin forests into arable land to grow farm crops. With this situation, when we were desperate for wild fruit, there were virtual forests of wild fruit trees growing next door to us. We dared visit these virgin forests although we knew of the danger of trespassing into the white man's land. Our usual or favourite point of entry into the prohibited area was the 'kuseri' place, behind the mountain, but at the back of the farm but on Kerry's side of the farm and the 'sacred' area at the bottom. Before daring to enter, I would always check from a distance first, making certain that neither Kerry himself nor any of his dozens of herdsmen was watching us as we illegally spilled over into the white man's property. Once certain the coast was clear, we would crawl through under the first strand of barbed wire fence. All of us were of slim build, so we could squeeze through the barbed wire strands with remarkable ease. One of us pulled apart the first and second strands of wire fence or the second and third strands of wire fence, leaving a gap wide enough to push your frame through and lift your leg over without the barbs tearing your clothes or causing you a nasty skin laceration. As soon as all of us had safely been admitted, we would move adroitly like an army passing through enemy country. We picked any chance fruit that we came across until we reached an area deep in the interior of the white man's land where literally forests of the wild fruit variety of plants grew together.

The range of wild fruit at our disposal in those 'virgin' forests included 'matufu', 'matamba', matohwe', 'nhunguru', 'tsubvu', 'tsvoritoto', 'tsvanzva' and others; typical of the types of wild fruit one would find in a Zimbabwean forest. In a year when the rains had fallen well, the boughs of these plants would be bowed down heavily, like woman with child, from the abundance and proliferation of ripe, juicy, sweet fruit. In short, we would enjoy the feast, picking and eating these priceless gifts of nature.

Lurking at the back of my mind though would be the fear of being caught in the brazen act of stealing from the white man's land! I have to say that when we went on these fruit-collecting adventures, half the time we would recklessly forego our dinners at home as the 'Gardens of Eden' would provide sufficiently for all our masticatory needs. It would be foolhardy, if not pointless altogether, returning home for dinner when mother nature had put on hold the ravages of hunger on us and adequately filled our stomachs with all the nutrition, we needed. Enjoying our stolen bounty, we usually overlooked making noise or shouting, both of which had the potential of attracting attention.

We had thrown into our bags the last bits of 'nhunguru' (plum-like) fruit and were on the point of leaving our 'Garden of Eden' when Irrigation (Wilfred), holding his ears with turned palms listening, suddenly said, "Please wait, boys. Can you hear what I can hear?" We had grown to know Irrigation as the cleverer and

142

most mentally alert of the three of us. He always quickly sensed any approaching danger to our safety. True; listening carefully, the combined rumble and splutter of an approaching engine struggling to navigate the rough terrain somewhere behind the rise of land two miles away was unmistakeable. Immediately, a four-wheel all-terrain red vehicle came into full view from around the edge of a thicket of twiggy and leafless thorn trees. The afternoon sun shimmered against the red colour of the vehicle as it evidently raced in our direction along rugged and uneven ground. The old white male driver of the motor scooter wore a large sandy tan cowboy hat. Bobbing up and down as he struggled to remain in his driving seat.

Huddled beside him were two very large black 'German Shepherd' dogs, both so massive in their appearance that they resembled tropical gorillas. The two dogs resembled a type of bloodhound which, at their master's bidding, had a reputation of attacking and clinging to their catch just like the common bulldog will cling to a four-footed animal it has caught in a hunting expedition. Gripped with sudden fear, I thought I also detected that the white man clutched a big double bore shot gun with its back resting on the floor of the all-terrain vehicle, with the muzzle of the gun pointing skywards. 'My God', I thought quietly but very quickly to myself, 'we are in the kind of trouble nobody in the adjacent African Purchase Area has ever witnessed.' Without further ado I shouted, "Murungu, vakomana!" (The European, boys!) and all hell broke loose. Our honeymoon had to come to an immediate end, so we cast the bags we had slung over our shoulders into the nearby bushes on the spur of the moment. As if somebody had fired a starting gun, all of us burst into speed to escape the impending doom, dashing for cover into the canopy of huge trees in the immediate environment. Unsure of our security from the canines and with a rush of adrenaline in our circulatory systems, we proceeded farther and up the lower slopes of the mountain, each of us pursuing his own path and direction.

Powered by the sensation of fear with my heart pumping wildly under my breast, I ran so fast up the steep gradient with the aim to reach the barbed wire fence on top of the mountain. Despite traversing a very steep part of the incline, fear of those dogs gave me strength and I utilised it to maximum advantage. I leapt over boulders and rocky outcrops. A Klipspringer would have found me a keen and serious competitor. Every few moments I could hear the yelping of Kerry's dogs which he obviously had released to catch any one of us or the three of us. Continuously working my way up and moving my legs back and forth rapidly, I felt that the hounds could not have been too far behind me. I knew their savage yells indicated either they were on my track or that of my young brother or nephew, both of whom were engaged in their own getaways. I quietly wished them success in eluding the canines. Meanwhile, I could hear the dogs supposedly crashing and plunging through the small bushes under the darkened canopy of massive fig trees on the lower slopes of the mountain, their loud, eager yells making the whole mountain side clamorous with their sound as they searched for us. At times I felt airborne as I flew past tree trunks and edged round large balanced rocks.

My hope was revived when I suddenly reached Kerry's six-strand boundary barbed wire fence near the summit of the mountain. Just before I slumped on the ground to quickly slide under the bottom strand to safety on the opposite side of the fence, I heard Kerry's dogs huffing and puffing in repeated gasps and wild barking somewhere on the lower slopes of the mountain. Their barking reverberated in the adjacent caverns as they searched for us frantically, albeit unsystematically, in the bushes at the bottom of the mountain. Stopping to listen and peeping timidly from behind a huge rocky outcrop on my father's side of the fence, the dogs' savage intonations grew more and more distant.

From my place of relative safety behind the rock, I realised with satisfaction that the dogs had spectacularly failed to gain on me. They had probably lost the plot and were confused. Tired from my burst of speed up the mountain, I breathed heavily and spasmodically; but I felt safe and secure and that I had beaten the dogs in the mad race. The overfed dogs were too big to cope with the energy required to climb the steep slope if they dared follow my scent at high speed. As for Mr Kerry Schultz himself, he was an older man, so he would not bother to follow us in the mad chase up the mountain. Also, I hoped Last (Bernard), and Irrigation (Wilfred) had been as successful as I had in eluding capture. Then from somewhere below, I heard Mr Schultz shout to the winds using the bastardised 'Chilapalapa' lingua franca in a husky, smoke-damaged voice, "Hey wena Piccaninis! Hipi enafuna lapha purazi kamina?" (Hey, you African small boys! What do you want; What are you doing on my farm?). Without getting any responses from anybody but the barking sounds of his dogs, he closed the conversation with a final remark which was a warning, "Pela ngizakubona futi lapha, ngizakubulalani mina or lo inja lena kuruma stereki, enazwile wena, Piccaninis! Hamba lo khaya kawena and shala konalapha!" (If I find you in my farm again, I'll kill you or I'll get these dogs to bite you all over. Go back to your homes and stay there, do you hear me, little boys?)

Half an hour later, the three of us regrouped on the mountain top and congratulated each other for the narrow escape. Peering into the little clearing below from where we stood in a proud cluster, we saw the 'white man' had packed his dogs back into the vehicle and had quietly started on the return journey to his farmhouse four or so miles away to the southwest. His motor scooter trundled on the uneven and rough terrain. As his vehicle approached the rise, there was a sudden gust of wind and his cowboy hat almost flew off his head, so he firmly held on to it with one hand while the other manoeuvred the vehicle. It had been a day full of adventure, excitement and near disaster. We descended the mountain of mysterious stories on our side of the six-strand barbed wire fence to return home. Before we reached home, we passed through the dry and windswept fields to check if our mice-traps had caught any mice. The incident I have related in the foregoing dovetails neatly with the next instalment where I continue with the theme that the human spirit will often find a way of expressing itself and compensate for missed opportunities despite efforts by other forces to bottle it up, place controls on it or restrict it.

Through summers where I was pinned down in work, work, and work at the farm, I will repeat it here for emphasis's sake that the first ten years of my life as a child at the farm were very difficult for me although I benefitted from acquisition of a discipline of labour. However, by way of a strange compensation, shafts of welcome relief lit up my life and that of other children in my environment. Most of our lives were happier in the off-farming seasons between May and September of those unhappy years. For me therefore, winters and springs provided opportunities to make up for the time we lost on learning and having fun. Some of these opportunities that enabled me to learn or to have fun presented themselves due to our carefully planned incidents. Others occurred by coincidence or completely by accident. By a strange coincidence, it was in these off-farming seasons father arranged to spend several days and nights on distant visits alone in the Nharira Tribal Trust Lands. I have already mentioned it above; visits to maintain relationships with the extended family seemed to be a privilege he alone enjoyed.

I do not want to belabour this point. In keeping with the old saying that 'When the cat is away, the mice will play', we welcomed and relished my father's absences from the farm with plenty of joy. As soon as he left on his jaunts and it became public knowledge that he would be away for an extended amount of time, which seemed to be the norm, we would quickly inform the children of our neighbour farms that the coast was clear and that they were free to visit us and play with us untrammelled by my father's fierce presence. Alternatively, we arranged to visit their homes.

I actively took part in playing a variety of games with groups of children who visited us at our farm or those with whom I met when we visited their homes. One of the games was 'nhodo' which we played in mixed groups of boys and girls. In this game we sat cross-legged in a circle forking small objects, either small stones or seeds, from a hole in the centre of the circle. The individual players would tactfully return the same objects into the hole one by one by throwing bits of the same objects into the air, looking at them as they fell and receiving them simultaneously as one forked out more objects from the hole with your hooked fingers. It was such fun to watch. 'Tsoro' was another game which both boys and girls play together although it involved male child participants mostly. It was instrumental in promoting our critical thinking, mental co-ordination, and numeracy among other qualities. 'Tsoro' equated to modern games like the game of 'Draughts'. Then there was swimming from which I derived considerable enjoyment if we swam in natural pools along the river which were not infested with crocodiles and snakes. This was one game where boys and girls did not mix for obvious reasons. But I would team up with groups of boys of my age from neighbouring farms to go swimming. Fortunately for us, there were no crocodiles in the one and only Chiputya River which passed between us and Father Cripps' shrine over the riverbank across it. The Chiwandire Farm, ours and the Pfumojena Farm were in the upper reaches of the river where it was too shallow for crocodiles to live in. But we often heard that crocodiles would be found along the river as it became bigger and wider as the Chiputya River reached its confluence with the much larger Munyati River, twenty or thirty miles farther down.

On several occasions, though, we would abort our swimming activities on discovering that the pools we were using had large and poisonous river snakes living in the undergrowth along the riverbank. As I swam with my friends in one of the pools one day, I noticed a large green reptile slither from the grass at the edge of the pool and enter the water. Collecting small rocks from nearby bushes in our birthday suits, we pelted the unwelcome visitor with the missiles and killed it. But surprise, surprise. Thinking we had removed one threat to our safety by crushing the head of the first snake to smithereens, a second and even larger green snake, who probably was a partner of the snake we had killed, appeared from the other side of the pool and began swimming powerfully towards us, its bullet-head above the water. Picking up our clothes which we had left carelessly scattered on the dry side of the pool in a great hurry, we sprinted away from the pool amid a mixture of fear and childish glee in just our birthday suits. We escaped into the sparse forest just above the river valley, where we wore our clothes back on before emerging into the clearing to walk back to the farm homestead.

One other game which I actively participated in, together with other boys and girls was 'mudzerendende', a sliding game in which we used slimy stems and branches of a tree called 'munhanzva'.' Minhanzva' trees grew wild in large numbers on the slopes of small hills or mountains like Makumimai Mountain on my father's farm. The game was more enjoyable when carried out on the steeper surfaces of the open rock hillside. We derived loads of fun from this game by repeatedly climbing back to the top of the rock carrying fresh branches of the 'munhanzva' tree and sliding down, sitting on a well-arranged piece of the 'munhanzva' tree which grew in such abundance at the bottom of the mountain slopes in our farm. Sliding down rock sides was such terrific fun as there was fun and joy in repeating the slides. Overall, the sky was the limit regarding the games and activities we could engage in as children, to light up our otherwise dull and monotonous lives.

Now, before the onset of my adolescence, there was the critical matter of my curiosity regarding the sexual maturation of girls or even that of boys that occupied me ceaselessly. It was strictly a personal and very private matter which had slowly begun to gnaw my psyche. Curiously, none of my male visitor playmates seemed prepared to share with me the differences that they may have noticed in the geographical appearance of their sisters' sub-navel regions. Generally, the subject of male/female genitalia was taboo in our family, so it was never openly discussed, even among us. Father would never talk to us about anything, particularly not that issue. My young brother Irrigation and nephew Last, were my juniors in age by nearly three years, so I ruled them out as possible sources of information on this sensitive subject. As I was growing older, it dawned on me out of shame that there was no way my own mother could talk to me about those things.

Feeling lonely sometimes, it worried me that I lacked adult guidance on male and female maturational development and that

I was therefore growing up completely ignorant about it, randomly picking up bits of information on these matters by hook and crook from rumours, as I went along. Fortunately, I was still very much a little boy and such things as 'wet dreams' or growth of hair under my armpits or in my sub-navel region had not yet started. I do not know what chemistry was going on inside my system, but at eight or nine years of age, it boggled my mind I had no idea about the precise nature of these differences until one afternoon at our large farm homestead.

There came a day when a mixed group of boys and girls, most of them about the same age group as the children who lived in our farm compound, arrived from other homes in the Maronda Mashanu African farming community; to play with us that day. I noticed that some of the girls who arrived in the group were not only slightly older but also that I did not recognise them. I later learnt that due to it being school holidays, some of the children I did not recognise were visitors at the homes of our neighbour farmers. They had therefore joined up with the younger girls we knew to come and play with us. Now, it's hard to imagine that a fifteen-year-old girl today would play 'Hide and Seek', but that is what ended up happening on that glorious afternoon. I do not remember the specific details of the 'Hide and Seek' variant, but I imagine anyone finding the person who was 'It' stayed hidden in a secluded place until everyone else had found them; and the last to join the chortling throng becomes the 'It' for the next round of the game.

When my turn to hide came, and being a small boy in stature then, I hid in a dark corner of a veranda behind a large brick farmhouse my father had built two years previously. From where I hid, I had a full view of the orchard with an assortment of plants in it. Most of the plants' branches had shed their leaves because it was wintertime and most of the plants in the orchard did not have any fruit on them, as it was their off-season period. However, a large banana plant with luscious green leaves was within touching distance from where I hid. It was around three p.m. Being winter, the sun was going down fast. It would be darker soon where I was standing, chuckling to myself. 'It's going to be hard for them to find me here', I thought. Barely three minutes later, I heard the 'pat-pat-pat' and shuffling of feet, as someone presumably wearing a pair of cheap 'Bata' slippers but walking in a hurry appeared. From behind a far corner of the brick veranda column to my left, a fifteen year-old girl who I did not recognise rushed and stood to the right of the banana plant close to where I was hiding. Turning round abruptly and completely oblivious of my hidden presence, I heard her announce beneath her breath, "Oh, my God, I'm bursting for a wee! I need a wee badly!"

There and then with her feet astride, she bent over and grabbed the bottom hem of her skirt, simultaneously pulling down what looked like an oversize pair of knickers right down to a point well below her knees. Promptly holding up the hem of her flared skirt with her hooked fingers, she pulled it right up to her waist and squatted on her knees instantly, revealing a rectangular patch of jet-black hairy thatch below her abdomen. Wasting no time, the innocent girl began urinating on the ground in a loud hissing stream that issued forth from a dark orifice hidden by dark hairs. In my bliss, I gazed at that spectacle in complete consternation.

Again, as in the recent other incident, involving a much younger girl, nothing had prepared me for what I saw that day. I am proud to make the confession that perhaps due to my age of innocence, I was able to practise enough self-control; nor did I freak out or did I slump onto the floor in a fit of excitement or anxiety. Finished in a matter of a minute and clearly relieved, the girl sprang to her feet. She quickly pulled her pants up and adjusted them before she pulled her skirt back down. Looking about furtively, to be quite sure no one had invaded her privacy, she nervously stepped away and disappeared round the corner as promptly as she had originally emerged.

To this day I have often wondered who that girl was. I was pretty sure she was not one of the girls from our farming community I was familiar with. Whoever she was, I have often wondered if she realised the effect, she had on my young, uninitiated and developing imagination. Still, the situation was not without some degree of eroticism, although one that was remarkably tempered by my age of innocence. I guess a boy much older than me would have smacked ed his lips, obviously in a different response to the 'manna from heaven'. As an outcome of this rather unsavoury encounter with that hapless female adolescent, I henceforth took less and less interest in 'Hide and Seek' games involving mixed groups of boys and girls from other farms in the area; although there was nothing wrong with the game itself.

To summarise this part of my account, participating in that game – innocently as I had done on occasions prior to the incident I have narrated – provided me with challenges which affected my ability to navigate my surroundings. In later life, I would use the skills I acquired from these simple forms of play to participate effectively in carrying out research for my advanced degree studies and other life's adventures.

# Chapter 8

# I start formal education at the local rural primary school

Towards the end of 1955, I remember Mother and Father disagreeing and having heated exchanges in their conversation about when I should start attending the local primary school. If Mother had had her way in the decision-making process, she would have packed me off to school in the new school term starting in January 1956 when she felt I was mentally fit to start learning at school. "King's eight years old now and his start of school is long overdue," she said. Having the final say in these matters, my father would not have it, especially when such an opinion was proffered by my mother. However, fighting to advance her argument, she pointed out that boys of about the same age as myself from farms in the neighbourhood like Gilbert Chiwandire and Kingston Tagarira had already started school; but this point did not sit well with my father. He strongly opposed it basing his thinking on my stunted physical appearance. Shouting orders at me, he commanded, "Come over here, Kingi. I want your mother to see what I am talking about: stand over there before us with both your hands beside your body. I want you to stretch your right arm and throw all of it over your head and let's see if you can touch your left ear." Try as I could, I failed dismally to reach my left ear. It was such a primitive readiness for learning test which had no grounding in science. But my father clung on to that test with such a passion that his argument carried the day. "Do you see what I mean, Leah? I've always told you that I'm the decision-maker in this home and I'm always right. King starts school when he is ready and if I am satisfied, he is physically fit to start school. Those are my orders!"

My start of formal schooling was therefore held back by another full year until January 1957. Uncle Rodrick had been over at the farm for Christmas festivities in 1956. Before he left to return to Gwelo (Gweru) thereafter, he left word with father insisting that I should start school at the beginning of 1957. My father always paid attention to any advice given to him by his young brother. If Uncle Rodrick had not intervened, my father might have let me continue working at the farm until perhaps when I was ten, eleven or twelve years old. My father might not even have been the slightest bit worried if I had not started school at all, as then I would add to the manpower working on his farm. Because of my slow physical development and the primitive yardstick used by my father to measure my 'readiness for learning', I only started formal schooling when I was nine years old instead of the standard practice of seven years, which was when those of my age group started school then. This time around, it appeared that my readiness for school was not measured using the outdated eligibility test my father preferred. For me, starting school was long overdue yet the prospect of joining my older brothers when they left home to go to school every morning electrified me.

Once Christmas celebrations were over, the beginning of 1957 started with my mother's experience of trauma over having to see to it that I was ready to start school. For days long before schools re-opened on a date that January, she would sleep late at night crushing groundnuts to fill up to two buckets of unshelled groundnuts. On a chosen date, she would wake up at the crack of dawn, balance the load of shelled groundnuts on her head and walk all the way to a service centre named 'Dhobha' – approximately five miles to the north of our farm – where there was a small general dealer's shop and a grinding-mill. On her way to the service centre, her route would take her through villages in Mutasa, Dzvova and Chiwandire communal lands. It was a circuitous route, but she had no choice because there was no shorter route to reach the service centre at 'Dhobha'. On reaching her destination, she engaged in a type of barter transaction with the shopkeeper in the general dealer's shop. She exchanged her two buckets of unshelled groundnuts for maybe a new pair of khaki shorts and a new short sleeved khaki shirt for me. Depending on the effectiveness of her bargaining powers, she might also obtain a few extra small items like a packet of salt, laundry soap, rolls of cotton thread and some needles. At the completion of her transaction, she would embark on her reverse trip, travelling light this time around as the heavier load would have been replaced by a smaller bundle of clothes. Then she arrived back home later in the afternoon, looking the worse for wear because she would have had nothing to eat for most of that day.

Letting me try my new school clothes on, she would smile with contentment and pat me on the shoulder when she noted that the clothes fitted me like a glove. Even if the little shop would have had pairs of shoes in stock, Mother would not have been able to afford a pair for me. Thank God, back in the day, the school did not demand the wearing of school shoes as part of the uniform. For goodness's sake, it was not yet the tradition for children in our rural setting to go to school wearing shoes. On the first morning I left home to go to school, I was smartly suited in my new school clothes. I felt on top of the world as I walked in a large group of other older children from our homestead. The group included my older brothers Misheck (Raphael), Kaston (Roland), stepsister Faith, Aunties Jasmine, and Lucia. The latter two in were already overgrown girls in their late teens or early twenties. Surprisingly, they were still attending middle primary school which did not matter very much in those days. Two years after I started school, I noticed that some of my male classmates were men who shaved beards off their chins every morning before they went to school!

Comparing rainfall patterns in the years I started school with these years of climate change, it appears as if rains used to fall more heavily in the Maronda Mashanu area than they currently do. In the months of January and February, the Chiputya River between my father's farm and Pfumojena Farm was always in flood, due to the incessant rains at that time of the year. For several days of the first few weeks of the year I started school, Aunt Jasmine has had to carry me on her back to cross the river to go to Maronda Mashanu School, two miles after passing by Pfumojena Farm.

Aunt Lucia helped to transport me across on the reverse journey back home from school in the afternoon. Then the flooding would have subsided and the levels of waterflow in the river would also have lowered. Both my two aunts were very kind and helpful. On the night prior to my first day at school, there had been a heavy downpour in the upper reaches of the river. So, although the river was in flood but had not broken its banks, the current was quite swift and strong. Small children like me would have easily been swept off our feet and carried down in the burbling, swirling waves that reached Aunt Jasmine's waist with me clutched on her back as she waded across to reach the opposite bank of the wide and fast flowing river. Today, seventy years later since I started schooling, the same Chiputya River no longer exists. It probably still flows below the dry and sandy riverbed, due to changing climatic patterns on the one hand and the poor farming practices of bordering farms over time which have led to massive soil erosion.

Starting school in the late 1950s, Maronda Mashanu School was administered by the Anglican Church authorities at Daramombe Mission, approximately fifty miles away in the Nharira Tribal Trust Lands. Without exact statistics to hand, I can only guess that when I started school at Maronda Mashanu, that little rural primary school would have been in existence for around forty years, i.e., considering the fact that a pioneering Anglican Church missionary, Father Arthur Shirley Cripps, founded the school in the first dozen years of the 1900s. Having himself arrived from Great Britain, this man of the cloth had founded Maronda Mashanu – then a motley collection of villages under the supervision of headmen – in 1907 following a brief stop at All Saints or also known as 'Wreningham Mission', as parishioners sometimes called it. Ten miles north of Maronda Mashanu, it already existed as an Anglican Church mission station when Father Cripps arrived there from the UK, en route to the City of Salisbury, Rhodesia. Combining his Christian missionary work with his quest also to give the local community some degree of literacy, it was not long before he started out on his own initiative and founded the Maronda Mashanu School.

The reverend priest had done that out of appreciating the importance of providing at least a basic education in numeracy and literacy among the children of his congregants, nearly all of whom could not read and write. Christianity had spread in Rhodesia (Zimbabwe) under various religious denominations following the arrival of Europeans in that part of the world at the end of the 1800s. For the reason chiefly to civilise the local communities, many church-run schools like Maronda Mashanu had started operating mainly in rural areas. This was a feature all over Rhodesia at that time. The bulk of the schools offered a rudimentary education amounting to the achievement of scarcely more than the lower primary school up to Standard 3 (now Grade 5). Young people who wanted to take their education to the next higher level, that is, upper primary school up to Standard 6 (now Grade 7) had two choices. Either they attended boarding school in a few places far away, like Daramombe Mission or St Augustine's Penhalonga near Umtali (now Mutare). (The latter option depended on whether their parents could afford to pay the high boarding and tuition fees charged at these schools). Or the children's dreams of attaining a higher level of education would abruptly come to an ignominious conclusion. That meant such unfortunate children's only option would be to seek employment opportunities as labourers in mines, farm workers, herd 'boys', garden 'boys', cooks and kitchen 'boys' etc in surrounding large-scale European farms and mines which had mushroomed following the promulgation of the Land Apportionment Act of 1930. It was very frustrating for many young African children who could not proceed with their education beyond lower primary school up to Standard 3 (Grade 5). Their quest to attain higher levels of education was restricted by circumstances they had no control over.

Returning to the matter of my own father's relationship with his children, the few times that he invariably chose to speak with us were those occasions, sometimes late at night, when he returned home in a drunken stupor from beer-drinking outings. Then he would start bragging about how intelligent his young brother, Uncle Rodrick, was and how his own children's heads were full of water and that we were all dunderheads! All his bragging about his brother, and his failure to put in not a single word of praise for his own children's efforts at the farm or at school, made us all feel unvalued, unimportant, and worthless. That did not augur well for what we hoped to achieve in life. Going on and on, he always reminded us that his young brother had successfully completed his education up to Standard 6 (Grade 7) and that he had even attempted studying to acquire both the South African Matriculation Certificate and training as a primary school teacher at the then much talked about Roman Catholic Kutama Mission in Zvimba District.

However, although my father had paid one hundred British pounds in fees for Uncle Rodrick to complete his teacher training course, Uncle had decided to quit his course preferring to take up the job he then had as a Meteorologist or Weather Forecaster. In the few times the two brothers quarrelled, my father would always get his way by reminding his young brother about the one hundred British pounds he had paid for his education! It seemed as if Uncle Rodrick owed my father some money which needed to be paid back in one form or another. Anyway, whatever the nature of Uncle Rodrick's job was, for me and the rest of my colleagues at the farm, it looked attractive, a smart and well-paying job. In all his appearances at the farm, he always looked smartly turned out, usually wearing either a black or navy-blue blazer, matching black or brown pairs of shoes and grey trousers. In their friendlier conversations, Uncle Rodrick would frequently slip into the use of the English language which he spoke fluently. Father would respond in like manner in a lower quality and unrefined manner, considering that he had only attained a Standard 2 (Grade 4) level of education. At the end of 1956, Uncle Rodrick brought father an extraordinarily unique Christmas present: a portable wireless radio. Wow, a radio from which one could hear people speak and music play! What a wonderful gift that was!

It was the first time such an object had ever been seen, not only at our farm but also at other farms in the neighbourhood. Powered by a twelve Volt battery which was bigger than the radio itself, the receiver crackled, cheeped, and hissed in stops and starts as Uncle Rodrick showed father how to tune it. When the radio received wave lengths, people's voices and mostly classical music issued forth from that object. The wireless aerial, a long piece of copper wire tied at the top end of a stick shooting up more than fifteen feet above the father's homestead's thatched roof, was quite a sight to behold. Occupying pride of place on top of the roof, that aerial put us in a class by ourselves.

The first item to be observed by any visitors from local farms, that aerial became the talk of the neighbourhood, placing father several cuts above other struggling farmers in the community socio-economically! Here was a wonder of all wonders: the wonderful invention of science had a knock on effect on father's outlook to life. The new sounds he was picking up from the radio began softening his hard, dry character. On a day he was in a happier mood, which was occurring more regularly than before, lunch break for all would be brought forward by at least half an hour. However, take note: the early release for everybody to go for the extended lunch-beak was not necessarily a comfort meant for us to enjoy but to enable him to rush back to the farmhouse where he would relax in his lounge chair awaiting his lunch meal and listening to the BBC World Service news bulletins at one p.m. At that time, radio had not quite arrived in Southern Rhodesia (Zimbabwe), so all news bulletins to Southern Rhodesia (Zimbabwe) and the rest of the Federation of the two Rhodesia's – that is, Northern Rhodesia (now Zambia) and Southern Rhodesia (now Zimbabwe) and Nyasaland (now Malawi) – were beamed from one BBC station in Lusaka, Northern Rhodesia (now Zambia). At that time, African Nationalists in the three countries which made up the Federation of Rhodesia and Nyasaland had begun agitating for changes in laws which segregated and discriminated against African peoples and for independence to be granted to each of the three territories from Great Britain.

The likes of illustrious names of African political leaders, very active during the Federation of Rhodesia and Nyasaland, such as Joshua Nkomo, Kenneth Kaunda, Hastings Kamuzu Banda,

Ndabaningi Sithole, James Chikerema, Leopold Takawira, etc., were frequently mentioned in the news bulletins. Being an ordinary rural farmer with limited education, father could not quite comprehend the complexity of the issues these 'townee fellows' were raising. Yet he wanted to keep himself updated with what was going on even if he was unclear what the argument was all about. He therefore took time off and adopted the habit of listening to the radio broadcasts during most lunch hours. He also rarely missed the BBC six p.m. news bulletin that was broadcast in English from the Lusaka Studio in Northern Rhodesia (now Zambia).

All in all, Uncle Rodrick did not just inspire me by his towering presence and the many good things he did so that his older brother would stand out among other farmers in the area. Uncle Rodrick became not only my role model but also the springboard of all my ambitions. Here I was on the brink of starting an education career endowed with bright prospects for a future full of success and achievement. I was starting school at a time the Native Education Department in Rhodesia only provided funding for the needs of a few African children who were attending government schools in towns and cities. Otherwise, the then Rhodesian government had virtually nothing to do with the education of children attending the bulk of church-run schools in African communal areas. Schools like Maronda Mashanu only benefitted from the Department of Native Education by way of small amounts of 'grants-in-aid' money which was given to church-run schools to assist them with the payment of teachers' salaries. These church-run schools received no other financial aid from the government. After teachers had been paid their salaries, there was absolutely no money left to contribute towards the building of better classroom structures or the purchase of such critical needs as school equipment in the form of classroom furniture and learning materials.

Consistent with the situation at most, if not all, church-run primary schools throughout the tribal trust lands in Rhodesia (Zimbabwe) then, a pitifully small number of teachers on the staff at Maronda Mashanu School had received training for the role of teaching. Starting school in 1957 at Maronda Mashanu as I did and going through the first four years of my education at this institution, I found it a motley collection of classroom buildings that were at various stages of dilapidation. The three or four classroom blocks at the school appeared to have been built by people who were in a hurry and who did not have the slightest idea about the beauty of presentation when putting up building structures of a school. The classroom blocks looked simply ugly and unattractive to young people like me with a huge thirst for an academic education. Whoever were the builders contracted to build the classroom structures, they had used large concrete bricks by carelessly lumping brick and mortar together and in places just piling bricks on top of each other without checking uprightness of the built structures. As a result, the walls were bent in many places, with some of the concrete bricks jutting out precariously; and entire sections of walls might collapse at any time into a shapeless pile on the ground. The excessively wide classroom entrances, which had no door frames or doors, allowed stray cattle from surrounding villages to find their way into the classrooms at night.

Arriving at school on most mornings, my classmates and I would begin the school day by driving these herds of cattle from our classrooms before we embarked on removing their moist and porridge-like cow droppings that would be strewn on the floor where we would sit during lessons. While there were large window spaces in the classroom walls, these spaces had neither window frames nor windowpanes in them. Until I finished Standard 1 (Grade 3), my classmates and I either sat or squatted on dirty, dusty and uncemented classroom floors because these structures did not have any furniture in them besides just the teacher's rickety chair and wobbly home-made table. By the end of lessons at lunchtime for those of us in Sub-Standard A and B (Grades 1 and 2) and Standard 1 (Grade 3), the dust and grime that covered our seats and stuck to our clothes made us look like long forgotten scarecrows at the end of the harvesting season.

I find it incomprehensible that in these dire conditions of learning, it became possible to be able to read and write by the end of my second year of starting school. Textbooks and stationery were in horrifically short supply. For my Grade 1 (Sub-Standard A) lessons, we had no writing materials for our writing practice; so we depended in large measure on scrawling in the sand with our bare fingers, imitating the teacher by writing in the air or writing on cardboard slates with old and broken pieces of chalk. Most of the time, we shared the use of cardboard slates in groups because there were simply not enough of them for us to use as individuals or to share in pairs. The situation was pathetic fights often broke out as we competed to have first access to the few cardboard slates available. Textbook supply throughout my first four years at Maronda Mashanu School was completely shambolic. The few old, soiled and tattered textbooks available were shared by up to six pupils leading to regular friction and fights between pupils resulting in lessons frequently being disrupted as teachers were forced to devote more of their teaching time to classroom behaviour management. It was appalling. This was an extremely unhelpful learning environment for anyone to find himself or herself in. There were thirty of us in my Sub-Standard A (Grade 1 or year 1) class of 1957, most of whom came from the villages in Mutasa, Dzvova, Chiwandire and Nyevhe 'reserves' or 'lines'. Less than a quarter of us in that mixed class of boys and girls came from the African Purchase Area farms, most of which were situated upwards of three to seven miles north, south and south-west of the school.

The farthest of the few Native Purchase Area farms north of the school were the Bwanya, Mhandu, Mutsvangiri and Mutongerwa farms, upwards of five to seven miles from the school. Having spent our childhoods with our parents at the farms and in the villages, the adventure of starting school was quite exciting to us. However, it took some time for us to adjust to new routines at school, familiarise ourselves with staff and form new friendships. Once we were familiar with these demands of school life, school itself became a breeze. For my Sub-Standard A (Grade 1) and Sub-Standard B (Grade 2), my teachers were Mrs Mhlanga and Mr Machingambi, respectively.

We were only supposed to know our staff by their surnames, so I never got to know the first names of Mrs Mhlanga and Mr Machingambi. My two teachers had both been trained as lower primary schoolteachers. I can therefore proudly record it here that I acquired my taste and flair for academic education due to the solid foundation that I believe those two teachers invested in me. I have no doubt that investment of able, dedicated, qualified and experienced staff led to most of my cohort being able to read, write and do arithmetic through their excellent teaching: a feat achieved in difficult circumstances spawned by a critical shortage of teaching/learning materials and school equipment.

Mrs Mhlanga was a charming, beautiful, and a very responsible young woman who loved her work as a teacher. She lived with her husband, Mr Mhlanga, who was the local 'Agricultural Extensions Officer' ('Mudhumeni' in local parlance) for both the Maronda Mashanu Native Purchase Area and small landholder farmers in the adjacent 'Reserves'. The Mhlanga's lived on their own small farm among the few African Purchase Area farms north of the school. Mrs Mhlanga cycled to work in the morning and back to her home in the afternoon at the end of the school day. Patience was one of Mrs Mhlanga's personality traits. This quality enabled her to put strategies into her teaching which allowed some of her learners who were not academically gifted to catch up with her faster learners. Even if we had serious shortages of teaching/learning materials that I have already been on about, she herself was resourceful and full of creativity; aspects which enhanced her ability to facilitate our learning.

I was in her group of fast learners, and she assured all the learners that all those in my group were assigned more challenging work to keep us busy. In view of the general untidiness of our classrooms due to the way they had been constructed, Mrs Mhlanga preferred to teach her lessons outside her classroom, provided it was not raining, or too cold or windy. They used mobile blackboards in those days, so it was a matter of getting two clever boys who would lift and carry the board and aisle and set them up at a chosen spot outside. Because I always completed the work Mrs

Mhlanga gave us as a class, I was one of her favourite pupils. For that reason, I do not recall her ever shouting at me, twisting my ears or applying corporal punishment on me for anything I had done wrong. Instead, she provided me with plenty of motivation by showering me with praise and getting my classmates to clap hands for me whenever I performed exceptionally well in my schoolwork.

My next lower primary school teacher was a Mr Machingambi. He was a married man who lived with his wife and two sons in one of the staff houses, within shouting distance behind the classroom blocks. Although I remember Runyararo, one of his two sons, memory fails me as to whether he was old enough to attend school. What I clearly recall is that this young man was not attending lessons with me or the others in my group. Mr Machingambi spoke in a Karanga dialect and there was a rumour saying that he came from the Gutu District of the then Fort Victoria (now Masvingo) Province in Zimbabwe. He was not a fan of pupils who were naughty. Whenever he lost his temper during lessons, he would often swear by his Granny, "Iwe, iwe, zvokwadi naMbuya vangu vokwaGutu, ndinokurova zvogwadza!" ("Hey, you! Honestly, by my grandmother, I'll give you a painful beating!") Or, if one of us persisted in showing disrespect towards him or other pupils, he would shout hysterically, "Iwe chikomana, uri chana chokwaani iwe?" ("Hey, you, little boy, which family is teaching you such bad manners?")

Mr Machingambi's status as one of the few qualified teachers on the staff at the time conferred on him relative respectability and dignity compared with several other teachers on the staff who were known to be untrained for their teaching roles. Many pupils liked him and regarded him highly as an effective teacher. He was probably in his early thirties when he taught me and my classmates in Sub-Standard B (Grade 2). Outside the classroom, he was active as a sportsman, a quality which enabled him to play a leading role in the co-curricular life of the school. Age was not a barrier to Mr Machingambi. In the after-school sporting timetable, he played alongside the bigger boys in the senior school football team, performing wonders as a front right winger. In athletics, he would roll up his long khaki trousers and compete with some of the ablest of pupils to run the two hundred and twenty yards or the four hundred- and forty-yards track events during which he often outperformed most of them.

The only pupil he could not beat in these field events was a certain Mark Mudonhi, an older and more mature pupil, who was such a sprinter he reportedly could run and catch rabbits and deer with his bare hands while out hunting in the forests. If by any chance any of my classmates in 1957/1958 are lucky enough to be reading these pages, they will be reminded that Mark Mudonhi was in a league of his own as a local celebrity speedster when I attended primary school at Maronda Mashanu School. If any of my classmates from 1957/58 are still alive and able to be reading these pages, they will also remember our teachers, Mrs Mhlanga and Mr Machingambi, for their effective use of the phonic method in their teaching of literacy. I am convinced their clever and repeated use of this teaching method during my formative years was instrumental in helping me and others in my cohort to master the English Alphabet and subsequently helping to facilitate my ability to read and write within a comparatively short time. Considering that teaching and learning materials were woefully deficient, the task for the teachers of my first two years of schooling was by no means an easy one.

At the beginning of 1959, a Mr Dhodho arrived at Maronda Mashanu School on transfer from an undisclosed school. He was allocated to my Standard 1 (Grade 3) class. Rumoured to be an untrained teacher, accompanying reports said that he had acquired considerable experience in the teaching field and as an achiever of good test results. My 1959 class still contained many of those pupils with whom I had started school two years previously. If my memory serves me well, a few pupils joined us on transfer from other schools for one reason or another. Mr Dhodho may have lacked formal qualifications as a teacher, but he quickly adapted to the demands of his new situation. He achieved fame for his enthusiasm and devotion to the discharge of his duties, both in the classroom and in the co-curricular life of the school. Despite his lack of training as a teacher, he did everything within his means to build on the solid foundation that Mrs Mhlanga and Mr Machingambi had laid in the first two years of my education. Mr Dhodho was hard to beat as a physical training (now called Physical Education) teacher and football coach. When I was in Standard 2 (Grade 4) the following year, I was included in his physical training school team of thirty boys who were randomly selected to take part in Inter-School PT Competitions involving up to six primary schools in the Manyene and Maronda Mashanu areas. The competitions took place over ten weeks at a central venue, usually St Mark's Primary School in Manyene Tribal Trust Lands, some eighteen kilometres north of our school. It would be my first time of taking part in competitive sports as a pupil in a group of other children. In a separate meeting with our trainer, we resolved to achieve victory in the competition. Mr Dhodho laid out a comprehensive and rigorous training programme, requesting us to strictly abide by it if our school were to stand a chance of winning the competition.

At that time, there was one school in the grouping of schools that had won the coveted trophy every year for the previous five years. Our objective was to beat that school. Mr Dhodho therefore ordered that all of us in the team should report for an hour's physical training drills at the school before the commencement of the normal school timetable, every morning Monday to Friday, starting at seven a.m. Nearly all of us lived between three and six miles away from the school. In the rural setting we were in, there were destined to be complications in complying with the demands of such a rigid timetable. Besides, other social determinants arising from the support (or lack of it) rendered by the different home environments, could impact the extent to which we would be expected to comply with these near-military training arrangements.

At precisely six forty-five a.m. on each day of the PT practice period – which was unusually early for a rural environment – Mr Dhodho would mount and stand upright on a waist high desk or teacher's classroom table placed somewhere in the sports field at the school. Then he would start blowing a metal whistle that he kept tied on a string around his neck. The whistle shrieked so loudly that it could be heard miles away in the morning serenity of the countryside. Any of us who arrived late for training would earn countless straps on our bums. Mr Dhodho would usually administer the beatings using a thick hard-to-break skipping rope or indeed, at times, a sjambok. If you were for example a mile away from the training venue and you heard the deafening shrill of that dreadful whistle, you ran like a hare to avoid the flogging that was usually administered in the full glare of your team-mates. I resented such an eventuality and sought to prevent it happening to me at all costs. I was surprisingly lucky in that, for once, my father was supportive of these PT training arrangements. He avoided giving me assignments at the farm which had to be completed before I went to school in the morning. I was therefore always punctual for the early morning drills and thus avoided the humiliation of being thrashed in the full presence of my friends and associates in the team.

At the end of the scheduled training period, my team participated in the competitions and returned to the school raising aloft the coveted trophy. We had won. It was my first time I had felt a sense of pride in achieving a goal. In addition, I was imbued with the feeling that diligence and persistence in whatever you do will pay off in the end.

The year 1960 stands out in my mind for two reasons: the younger of my two sisters, Winnie (Phyllis) was born, and Mr Mamvura was my teacher for most of that year. He was deeply involved in promoting the religious ethos of the school and its links with the local community, so when he was occupied elsewhere in these matters, a Mr Chiguvare – who lived in the community – covered his lessons. We never got to know exactly whether Mr Mamvura was a trained teacher or not. It was strongly rumoured, though, that he had attended St Augustine's Penhalonga to complete his upper primary school up to Standard 6 (Grade 7). Thereafter, he may have trained as a policeman at Domboshava. I would not be surprised by his alleged training as a police constable as being true because he was physically well-built. When he stood up to start walking, he was straight as a rod.

Mr Mamvura lived at a small holding he owned approximately two miles away south from the school. He either walked to school or at other times, he turned up for his duties riding a shiny 'Raleigh' men's bicycle. Halfway through the morning school timetable, Mrs Mamvura also frequently arrived in the school pedalling a ladies' 'Rudge' bicycle. She would use that vehicle to bring Mr Mamvura a pot of hot milky tea in a well-covered basket. Mr Mamvura would drink the steaming cups of tea in large gulps of the sweetened liquid which we could clearly hear him swallow as he sat or stood teaching the first lessons after the morning breaks. I have already hinted on the huge contributions made by Mrs Mhlanga and Mr Machingambi in setting me off on my long journey as a reader, writer, and researcher.

Mr Mamvura is credited with reinforcing the skills I had acquired in my first three years of schooling. He had his unique way of coping with the acute shortage of teaching/learning materials across the full range of the school curriculum. Learning aids were simply unavailable to assist us in getting to grips with the demands of learning abstract concepts in arithmetic such as 'Ratio and Proportion', Percentages, Subtraction where you discovered you could not subtract a bigger number from a smaller number and you said to yourself, 'It can't be' then you engaged in 'equal addition' etc. Every one of Mr Mamvura's arithmetic lessons was triggered off at the start with mental arithmetic drills in the form of either quick oral or written exercises at the back of our exercise books. Or he would launch his arithmetic lessons with multiplication table drills of 3, 4, 6, 7, 8, 9, 11 and 12 each number multiplied by up to a maximum of twelve times. He wanted us to think very quickly during the brainstorming exercises. To assist us, each number timetable was beautifully written out with whatever black markers (hard to obtain in those dark days!) on khaki manila sheets and displayed on the inside walls of the classroom for all of us to study and internalise. Regularly and without warning, he would take the sheets down and embark on an exercise where he randomly asked individuals to recite the 'multiplication' or 'division' tables to the whole class. Any errors, omissions or forgetfulness were mercilessly rewarded with loud telling offs or strokes of the skipping rope on palms.

By the end of Standard 2 (Grade 4), my classmates and I could literally sing off-hand the multiplication and division tables of numbers three up to twelve. Mr Mamvura also attended dutifully to other processes of addition and subtraction, but his stress was more on our mastery of the multiplication and division tables. He would always remind us that arithmetic (mathematics) was a 'tool' subject and that we were going to need the constant use of our skills in that area and across other disciplines of our lives. He would never get tired of telling us, "When you get to the end of your school career, some of you will become teachers, nurses, and builders. Others will be carpenters or leaders in all these big companies which make things. If you find yourselves in any of these professions and you discover you can't do them because of your weaknesses in arithmetic (mathematics), you will be ashamed of yourselves." On the matter of literacy development, the supply of classroom textbooks in English and Shona had reasonably improved by my Standard 2 (Grade 4) class. In English language, at least two pupils shared a reader which also contained a series of language and comprehension exercises at the end of each chapter. But library books or supplementary readers remained critically in short supply; yet Mr Mamvura constantly encouraged us to read whatever reading material we could lay our hands on; to increase our literary ability. That included any litter or shreds of old newspapers whirlwinds in the dry season deposited in the environs of the school. As I walked back home after school, I would be found running after and picking up any bits of old and torn newspapers that I found flying about after chance whirlwinds which were a frequent feature in the dry season. Much to my horror, when I opened some of these dusty old bits of ripped up newspapers for the purpose of reading the text they contained, I would discover to my horror and consternation that the dry but unsightly, brownish yellow and smelly discolouration's on them were human excrement! Some unknown persons somewhere, maybe faraway from our school, would have innocently used the bits of paper I had just picked up to wipe their bottoms after relieving themselves! You can bet that I very quickly let go of the soiled litter and continued with my search for cleaner supplementary reading materials. It was like trying to catch the wind. I realised that pursuing the elusive dream could be quite a messy affair.

Now and then in the dry season, whirlwinds passed by and ripped off whole sections of our thatched classroom roofs. The damaged roofs needed to be mended. Furthermore, the six-strand and thatched perimeter fence around our nearly two-hectare school garden often developed holes in the thatch and so it needed regular maintenance to prevent village cattle roaming about from entering it and devouring our garden crops growing in the allotments or the several 'beds' which school children shared to learn and to practise the art of good gardening. Repairs of these amenities were the responsibility of the community. Our school was among thousands of other little church-run schools scattered throughout African Reserve Areas and the government did not give any financial assistance whatsoever in the way the school funded the costs of repairs to damages incurred on their properties.

In these eventualities, the school had been empowered by the parents' body to ask boy pupils to bring along with them from their home's items such as thin wooden poles 'mbariro' and types of string or fibre that were obtainable from thin tree bark 'makavi'. Girls would occasionally be asked to bring with them to school bundles of grass and empty old five or ten litre metal containers which they used to draw water from the nearby river and water the school garden. Registers were kept and called out showing which pupils had complied with the requests and which ones had not.

It was on these occasions when the animal nature in some of our younger and untrained teachers manifested itself. Contradictory to his reputation as the less demonstrative and friendliest among the male staff, the evil in Mr Chiguvare revealed itself on such occasions. Staff would therefore single him out to mete out particularly harsh and brutal punishment on the hapless and unsuspecting pupils who, usually through no fault of their own, would have failed to bring the requested items with them to school. I do not want to speculate what may have been happening in the European section of the education system then, but it is fair to submit here that flogging was rampant across most schools in the Rhodesian African education system in Rhodesia at the time. Legislation literally banning all forms of corporal punishment in African schools was a development still to come some fifteen to twenty years later.

On one of those days when I was in Grade 4 (Standard 2), I was unlucky enough to be included in a list of little boys who had not complied with the request to bring from home small wooden poles to school to mend the damaged roof of a classroom block. Mr Chiguvare stood in a clearing well in front of the long queue of about thirty of us. A two-seater classroom bench had been placed somewhere in front of the queue as a flogging frame. Other male members of staff ensured that we moved little by little along the queue as we quietly waited to go for the flogging in turns. My turn soon came, but I hesitated to step forward. I was terrified. My heart thumped like thunder below my breast. One of the male teachers nudged me on the left shoulder to move on. Instead of stepping forward, I hopped on my legs like a little bird: I was gripped with so much fear I could hardly move my lower limbs. Like a lamb to the slaughter. I finally got the strength to walk over to the frame. Mr Chiguvare stood a yard or so looking at me rather pityingly. I noticed he was sweating profusely through the armpits of his white shirt around both of which big circular blobs of sweat formed, presumably from the continuous exertion of his laborious undertaking. He bawled at me with a rough voice to lie lengthwise face down on the frame with legs dangling downwards behind me. Waiting for the flogging to commence, I shook like a reed in a fast-flowing stream. Towering above, my tormentor swore loudly, ensuring that his muttering would register within the group of frightened onlookers, warning them that a similar punishment awaited them next time if they did not cooperate with the lawful requests given by the school: "Kingston, you'll not repeat this behaviour of not obeying school requests and instructions, do you understand?" He tossed the question with a husky, angry voice suggesting I had offended him rather than the school. I mumbled a response in the affirmative, "Yes, Sir!"

Simultaneously, the first stroke of the thin wooden pole – a fresh one he had randomly selected from a heap nearby my colleagues in the audience had brought from their homes – descended on my buttocks like a tonne of bricks. The stinging pain that rifled through the whole of my body made me squeal as I squirmed and rolled from side to side on top of the flogging frame. Ordering me to remain still, his right hand that was grasping the hateful instrument heaved skywards and it came down on my bum, literally setting it on fire from the fiery pain I felt. I shrieked and hopelessly grovelled for forgiveness as the third, fourth and fifth strokes rained on me in rapid succession. I could hear murmurings of both despair and disapproval from an unidentified section of the audience.

I could not move my limbs although he asked me to get off the frame at the end of his task. I felt paralysed as if a bulldozer had been driven over me and I was stuck to that abominable frame pancake-like. A group of six older boys from within the audience were asked to carry me off the frame and they placed me in the shade of a 'musasa' tree, a few yards away from the shocked crowd of onlookers witnessing this degree of evil being perpetrated on budding youth. I suffered this consequence all because I had committed the cardinal sin of failing to respond to a request made by the school. Two hours later and my pain having gone down considerably, I was fit enough to be able to walk off the school grounds and head straight back home. But I was limping visibly in my right leg because of the swelling I had sustained on my bum. My mother informed my father about my horrific and life-threatening experience at school that afternoon, "Timothy, please look at the swelling and cuts on the skin around Kingston's bum. Something happened at school. It does not look good for such a little boy. We let him attend lessons at school to be taught and not to be hurt. You might have to visit the school and have a chat with the headmaster. What do you think?"

Instead, my father spurned my mother's request, remaining utterly unmoved by the incident itself given to him by my mother or to intervene as a parent. He did not bother to check the extent of my swellings or whether the beatings had broken my skin or generally to find out how I felt. His uncaring was defeating, to say the least. He would not even admit that I had suffered the horrible experience at school because of him. On returning from school on the day before, he had set me to work on tasks at the farm until well after dark, making it impossible for me to go into the bush to look for the items wanted back at school on the following morning. For expressing no concern or fear for my wellbeing like any normal parent would, I could not understand his mindset which did not allow him to interrogate the circumstances that had led to the nasty experience I was exposed to at school that afternoon. I was a little boy of about nine or ten years of age when I was the recipient of that most hateful experience.

Before I go on to tell you about my final year at Maronda Mashanu School in 1961, it would be remiss of me if I do not describe an incident that I feel was a serious threat to my continued existence. It occurred in the last few months of 1960, when I narrowly escaped being bitten to death by a large snake. If fate had given way to the unexpected, yours truly would have immediately become history and you would not have had the luck you are probably enjoying in reading these pages. It was a Friday afternoon, so there being no sporting activities at the end of lessons, I promptly walked back home. Arriving back at the farm, I found father sat sitting outside on the wooden superstructure directly opposite Mother's granary. He was putting the finishing touches to pieces of wood he was turning into hoe handles. Like all the womenfolk at that time of the day, Mother was tidying up in her hut and making sure the new-born infant Winnie (Phyllis) was comfortable after having had a nappy-change. Spotting me arriving back home between stolen side-glances, father shouted short, sharp instructions to the effect that I should quickly change my school uniform and be ready to go look after the herd of cattle as soon as I had finished eating my dinner. My school bag slung on my shoulder, I walked straight into Mother's hut and greeted her. It was hot and sticky in Mother's smoke-filled kitchen. Buckets of sweat were pouring down her face when she faintly responded to my greeting, telling me she was struggling to get moist logs of wood in the fire to burn. I quickly walked out of my mother's hut and headed straight to a 'bedroom' allocated to her by father in the large brick farmhouse behind her hut. Those of us who were her children also kept our clothes in that room, so my purpose was expressly to change from my smart school uniform into the ripped shreds that were my 'work clothes'. Thereafter, I would have to quickly return to eat the food Mother had cooked and placed on the side for me before I commenced the afternoon chores Father had instructed me to do a few minutes before.

Two years before that, father had constructed a large five to six bed dwelling. In designing the building, he had allocated a separate bedroom for each of his three wives. From the main entrance door, all the bedrooms were arranged in a row along a passage that led to a big lounge. My Mother's room was in the middle, i.e., second along the passage from the main entrance door. Stepmother Marumbidza's room was the third and last along the row. I entered the large house with careless abandon and, leaving the main entrance door slightly ajar, headed straight to my mother's room where we, her children, also kept some of our own clothes and other small items.

After changing into my work clothes, whistling to myself and without suspecting anything sinister or out of the ordinary to happen, I walked out of Mother's room, whistling a quiet tune to myself. I intended to report back to Mother's hut and eat something solid quickly before I embarked on the work at the farm father had wanted me to do that afternoon. Casting my eyes towards the exit door approximately six metres ahead of me, I saw a huge black snake trying to squeeze itself through the narrow gap in the door I had left not quite closed. The snake also saw me instantaneously. My sudden appearance on the scene, even if I was at a distance, appeared to have panicked my visitor. Then it began wriggling its muscly and shiny black body faster with the purpose of bringing the whole of its full length indoors through the narrow slit between the door and the door post. I had already had sight of these types of snakes from a distance while herding cattle. But they would quickly slither away into the bush or grass and that would be it and I would not bother them. This one was the largest 'black mamba' I had ever seen try to enter a house where humans lived. The rotund portion of its body that I had chanced to see was the size of a man's thigh.

To say I was gripped with fear is putting it mildly. In the split second of my indecision caused by surprise, I instinctively walked backwards, looking at the snake with a fixed gaze. When father finished building the large farmhouse and it was ready for people at the farm homestead to start using it, Mother and her other colleagues/wives had hardened and smoothened the floors of the whole house using home-made wooden flat platforms called 'zvikuvauro' in the local language. So due to the smoothness of these floors right up the hallway to the main entrance door, I noticed the snake's bottom rings struggling to get a grip, but it was making some progress in its effort to gravitate in my direction.

Remembering that I stood directly opposite Mother's room on my left, I barged into it with my left shoulder and simultaneously sidled into the interior of the room the way frightened reptiles out in the bush suddenly scuttle back into their burrows when strangers arrive in their territory unexpectedly. On gaining entry, I immediately slammed the wooden home-made door shut and squatted behind it making sure that no amount of force exerted from outside would have open been able to open it. In making the home-made door, father had joined together wooden planks which he nailed down with cross planks that left chinks or gaps in the wood through which it was possible to observe objects or people as they passed by on the outside.

A short while after I had slammed the door shut, I noted that the creature of death had arrived by the whooshing and scratching it produced as it moved. The 'black mamba' was right there under my nose outside the door. The whole of its body pitch black in colour and with its bleary eyes shining, it briefly stopped by the door behind which I squatted, flicking its forked tongue in and out of its mouth in front of its bullet-shaped head as if it were trying to guess whether I had made my escape through that closed entrance. If that snake had ears with which to hear, I feared it might soon pick up the hammering of my heart that was going on under my ribs. Seeming to give up the idea of ramming the door with its fierce-looking head, it moved on down the passage, its full length passing the door behind which I sat with the muffled rumbling and hissing of a big airline jet taxiing off the runway to offload its passengers at 'arrivals'. 'Black mambas' give off a powerful odour wherever they are, causing swarms of flies to buzz around or along the full length of their bodies. In times of drought when they cannot catch rodents and reptiles like lizards as prey, the snakes turn to these dirty insects which they catch and swallow in to assuage their hunger.

As the snake passed by where I secretly squatted, the unmistakeable smell of somebody who had farted resulting from a bloated stomach wafted through the door cracks into my nostrils, giving me an overwhelming punch of nausea. I almost threw up. Stepmother Marumbidza's own bedroom door was closed and padlocked, so it did not bother checking here. With me gazing after it in total disbelief, the poisonous snake turned left at the end of the passage. It carried on farther to the left, passing beneath the easy chair father loved to relax on while listening to the BBC News bulletins from the squeaky, old-fashioned wireless radio that Uncle Rodrick had given him as a Christmas present four years before.

Arriving at a dark space in the far corner of the lounge beyond Father's favourite chair, the snake carefully coiled itself up into a triangular cone of a mountain. It left its ugly head jutting out of the mountain summit, pivoting round in its hinge, and ominously suggesting that it was ready to strike to kill at the slightest provocation. By my rough calculation, I guessed the snake was seven metres from where I was a prisoner of fear. If that happened; having noticed its struggles and clumsiness on the smoothened floor while in motion, I was convinced that if it tried to reach me, I could beat it for speed to reach the exit door six metres away. Trusting my instincts and throwing all care to the wind in the grip of a new determination, I yanked open the door of my temporary shelter and bolted from the room at supersonic speed. Slipping through the main entrance door and breathing the fresh air of the outdoors, I ran shouting at the top of my voice, "Snake! Snake! There's a big 'black mamba' right on the floor of the large farmhouse! It almost bit me. I'm lucky to be alive! Big snake in there!"

Caught unawares by my shouting and calling out while he was deeply engrossed in his little project of making a hoe handle as he sat on the superstructure of the granary directly opposite my mother's hut, father could not quite make head or tail of what I was on about, "Hey, Kingi, calm down! There's no need for all that shouting. What's the matter?" he said. I had to feverishly repeat my message using both my hands, waving wildly in the air above my head.

Granny VaChemedza, my father's own elderly mother, heard the commotion in the courtyard from within her hut and emerged at the same time my father had picked up a pounding rod 'mutswi' with the intention to enter the main house, wrestle with and kill the snake. His mother remonstrated with him, telling him that if the snake was truly a 'black mamba' and the large size I had described, then he risked being bitten to death by that large reptileHis best bet was to seek assistance from some of the local farmers on how best to deal with the snake. A local farmer, Mr Marisira, had been known for years to have been issued a licence by the Native District Commissioner to keep and use a shotgun. In the whole of the local African farming community, he was the only one in possession of such a licence. the purpose of which was primarily to hunt down and kill troublesome wild pigs and deer that were renowned for straying into farmers' fields at night and eating the crops, thereby reducing yields. Father firmly shut the main entrance door of the large farmhouse. Meanwhile I was dispatched with an urgent message to Mr Marisira to bring his gun for the purpose of killing the snake. Snakes are despicable and nobody likes them, especially when they come into our homes. By three a.m., well before the sun disappeared behind the tall and leafy trees in the west of our homestead, Mr Marisira arrived with his gun, with me in tow. He climbed to the top of the farmhouse using a creaky home-made wooden ladder. The roof being thatched, he had to remove a portion of the grass so that he could spot the exact location of the snake on the floor metres below. He identified the location of the unwanted animal. With a reputation in the local community as an experienced marksman, shooting at a snake on the floor of the lounge a few metres from his position on the roof was an easy task for him. Both the two bullets he used to do the job were on target with the second one ripping the head of the snake into shreds. Father and Mr Marisira hauled the dead reptile out of the farmhouse. On measuring it when they reached outside, they found it was about four metres long. They carried it on long wooden sticks and placed it in a hollow anthill at the edge of the homestead. Then they placed an old motor car rubber tyre on the snake before piling heaps of dry wooden poles on it as additional fuel. The bonfire lasted two hours and the snake was burnt to ashes. Thus a particularly distasteful and unwelcome visitor was destroyed at the farm. If I had been unlucky enough as to allow that snake to sink its poisonous fangs into my flesh, I would probably be a mere statistic, by now. I owe my life to nothing else but sheer good fortune.

Surprisingly, 1961 started off on a very bright note for me. It was to be my last year of school attendance at Maronda Mashanu Primary School. My Standard 3 (Grade 5) class received a young brand-new teacher, Mr Reginald Tsimba. Speaking with a Chimanyika accent, rumour confirmed that he hailed from Rusape area of what was then Manyikaland (now Manicaland). My class still retained most of my classmates I had started school with in 1957. If my memory still serves me, some of the original list of pupils in that class included Augustine Mhandu, Victor Diura, Ennia Chiwandire, Vengai Hundi, Virimayi Masendu and Sylvia Chiwandire. I can't remember the others. Along the way in Standard 1 (year 3) and Standard 2 (year or Grade 4), my original cohort caught up with my stepsister Faith Mudyara, Henry Diura, Harris Mamvura, Mark Mudonhi and Chomumwe Zinwamhanga (I hope I've got his surname right. If my memory is right, Chomumwe was later christened 'Livingstone'). In Standard 2 (Grade 4), two girls, Susan Bwanya and Zvakarimwa (later christened Florence) Bwanya and Nunurayi Tembo joined our class on transfer from another school. My Standard 3 (Grade 5) in 1961 was therefore a mixed bag of pupils of various ages. A sizeable number of the boy pupils were men who shaved their beards. Some of the big girls could have easily suckled infants, if given a chance. This was so because several of the older pupils had either started school late or were slow learners who had failed tests in their old classes once, twice, or even three times. The system of primary school education at the time demanded that all those who failed their end-of-year tests had to repeat their classes. Automatic promotion was unheard of, and it only became an innovation years later.

My Standard 3 (year 5 or Grade 5) teacher, Mr Tsimba, had successfully completed his two-year Primary Teachers' Higher teacher training course at St Augustine's Teacher Training College at the end of 1960. Being a church-administered teacher training college, the Anglican Church head office in Salisbury (Harare) deployed Mr Tsimba directly to one of their rural mission primary schools that were desperately in need of staff in possession of qualifications to teach in upper primary school, i.e., from Standard 3 (Grade 5) up to Standard 6 (Grade 7). He was therefore the first of teachers in possession of his esteemed teachers' qualification to be placed at Maronda Mashanu School. Fresh from teacher training college, Mr Tsimba was bristling with many new and refreshing teaching methodologies. On the learning of the English language, I recall him placing heavy stress on the mastery of grammar, i.e., the rules of the language. In that respect he was adamant that should know our tenses, word order in sentences and correct punctuation. He never tired in giving us language activities, which exhausted the four types of language learning, that is, reading, writing, speaking, and listening. Calligraphy, the art of writing and shaping letters, was in those days a subject with a fixed spot on the school timetable. Our new teacher was the proud owner of the gift of handwriting. He therefore went to great lengths in ensuring that we shaped our letters correctly on the written page. He greatly improved on our writing in cursive. Before Mr Tsimba arrived to take up our class for his teaching duties, most of us had been practising writing in cursive with limited success since being introduced to it in Standards One (Grade 3) and Standard 2 (Grade 4). Mr Tsimba's own writing in cursive, whether on the class blackboard or on paper in our books, was in a class by itself. It was beautiful to look at. Slanted forward in uniform pattern, the upward and downward strokes of his letters combined with the downward loops of such letters as y, g, f, and j were simply a work of art to admire. Sixty years later, I still have vestiges of the writing skills he drummed into us when he was our Standard 3 (Grade 5) teacher.

As I have already explained in an earlier instalment, Maronda Mashanu School was church-run. So, our parents were required to make small payments by way of contributing towards the cost of procuring the writing materials we used, e.g., exercise books, rulers, pencils, rubbers, etc. The church sourced these resources, heaven knows where, delivered the stocks in bulk and left the headteacher to look after them as well as administer how they were disbursed. For example, whenever I wanted any of these items, I visited the headteacher's office to purchase them before I returned to my classroom. In Standard 3 (Grade 5), Mr Tsimba's success in teaching us 'writing' lessons was by dint of the large amounts of written work he gave his classes in the subject. For that reason, our thirty-six-page exercise books filled up with written work very quickly. That necessitated us to buy replacement exercise books without delay. Now poor little boys like me never ever kept any money, even a coin as small as a 'tickey' (three pence), in our pockets to buy a new exercise book. If you did not have the tickey, Mr Tsimba was in the habit of sending you back home four to five miles away in the middle of the school timetable to fetch the money from your parents. After trotting non-stop in the sizzling morning heat, I arrived back at home on one school day at eleven a.m. to collect the 'tickey' for another writing exercise book. My mother, who I saw first, did not have that kind of money anywhere in her hut, so she referred me to my male parent who was engrossed in digging a new water well, about five hundred yards outside the farm homestead. I thought to myself that father was not quite the best person to approach with these sorts of requests because of his fearsome and unfriendly personality. Anyway, I had no choice but to present myself before him because Mr Tsimba expected me to report back at school before the lunch break at one p.m. Arriving at the site where he apparently looked too busy to be disturbed, I noted he had already dug a large circular manhole wherein he stood at a shoulder-high depth.

Whenever he bent down to use the pick or the shovel, he literally disappeared in that hole until he stretched up again. A very large freshly dug pile of red soil was beside the manhole. Father added to the heap of soil by ladling out shovelfuls of soil which he threw one shovelful at a time, onto the larger heap. Seeing me arrive, he stopped the work he was doing. He wiped sweat off his furrowed brow with the back of his right hand and asked with a husky voice without even a preface, "Er-r, zvaita sei? Urikudei pano nenguva dzino apo unofanira kunge urikuchikoro, heh?" (Er-r, what has happened? What do you want here when you are supposed to be at school?).

I replied politely but with fear to his questions, telling him about my need for a new exercise book which had a price tag of a three-penny coin, a 'tickey,' as its price. Then he grunted back at me roughly, "What do you write in those exercise books that you seem to be in the habit of buying so frequently, heh? During my schooldays, I never filled any of my exercise books.

You're a spoilt child. That's the problem with you, Kingi! Learn to write less work in your exercise books, do you understand? You know very well I don't have money to spare on such things as exercise books."

I was going to tell him that my teacher gave us plenty of work that needed writing in exercise books; but ignoring me completely, he rifled through the right pocket of an old, grubby, and ripped pair of khaki shorts that he wore to see if he could find any coins in there. The hand he pulled out of his pocket clutched a 'tickey' in his clammy fingers the size of a healthy crop of bananas, all of which were covered in red dirty soil. Father chose not to hand the coin to me. Instead, he hurled it at me, five metres away from where he stood, telling me to go back to school promptly and to tell the new-fangled teacher not to continue with the habit of sending me back home whenever my exercise book was full! Then, without bothering to find out whether the coin had reached me or not, he resumed the digging and shovelling from the bottom of the floor of the hole he was standing in. He mumbled remarks in which he ordered me to go back to school quickly besides reminding me to report back at the farm straight after school because there were many tasks he wanted to be completed before sunset. Missing his target, the small coin he had thrown landed and promptly disappeared in the pile of red, powder-like sandy soil three metres away from the manhole where my father was working. Trusting my instincts. it took me another fifteen to twenty anxious minutes of arduous searching in searing heat for the small coin, digging and scratching with my fingers and kneeling in those dusty red soils to retrieve it. The dirty brown and red texture of the sand soiled my smart school uniformed appearance. I thanked the gods in heaven when I eventually found the coin. I arrived back in the school premises just before the 'lunchbreak', but I was unhappy and miserable due to my appearance and how my father had hauled me over the coals just for the sake of my obtaining a 'tickey' from him.

Mr Tsimba was indeed the first of my primary school teachers to involve his class in small group activities where we shared ideas through discussion and reported back to the whole class. That was how he consolidated learning, a teaching practice which was unheard of at the time but only became fashionable a few years later. My groups always chose me not to lead our group discussions but as a rapporteur or minute-taker who would produce a summary and report back to the whole class. By year five in primary school, I had already acquired a degree of fluency in the use of English language, so I did not have any qualms about reporting back to the whole class on my groups' discussions. It became my pastime, and I derived a lot of fun and enjoyment from giving presentations and feedbacks on group discussions to the whole class.

I gloried in the approbation whenever the whole class clapped their hands at the end of my presentations. My public speaking skills were honed at that early stage of my school career. Mr Tsimba's classroom displays were among the best in the whole school. All of them would be originated by him and none of them were borrowed from some audio-visual services place in Salisbury. During lunch breaks, other teachers in the school would pop into his classroom to admire and copy some of these apparatus for use in their own classrooms. Back in Standard 1 (Grade 3) and Standard 2 (Grade 4), Mr Mamvura and a bit of Mr Dhodho had introduced us to writing in ink using penholders. Widely used at higher levels of primary school education then, there were accessories such as nibs, penholders and inkwells and blotting paper that went with the whole business of learning to write using ink. Ball point pens were unheard of when I attended my primary school. They were only to become an invention of science and a phenomenon of the future in later years. Any haphazardness using these items in writing lessons resulted in making your work look thoroughly messy and untidy. Mr Tsimba kept a tight rein on our practice of calligraphy. In those days, there were paraphernalia such as ink, inkwells, nibs, blotting paper and penholders that were in use in the 'Rhodesian' school system then. He reinforced our skills of writing using ink by resorting to every detail he could muster to get us to do the right things. He would therefore throw up his hands with rage if, after his explanations, we became slipshod, haphazard and spilled ink from the 'wells', little china pots which we slipped into small holes along the top surface of the writing desks. I was slow in coping with the efficient use of the 'blotting paper'. One day, after using up the standard rectangular bit of blotting paper he issued to each of us at the beginning of the writing lesson, I had no choice but to use an old piece of chalk I found lying near my feet on the floor. My teacher kept a ruler in one of the drawers of his table. Noticing the large blob of ink spread out on a page of my writing book, worsened by my reckless use of the old piece of chalk to suck up some of the ink, he rapped me several times on the knuckles of my right hand, using the edge of that hated ruler. I was in pain for most of that day's schoolwork. By the following morning, all was forgotten; the pain had fizzled into thin air. I carried on with my lessons as if nothing had happened on the day before.

Due to his outstanding performance as a young teacher, Mr Tsimba was soon promoted to the position of headmaster of the school within the first eight months of starting his career as a teacher. Notwithstanding, he continued with his normal load as a fulltime classroom teacher. Working closely with a Reverend Father Fenwick who was based at Daramombe Mission, funds were sourced from a donor in the UK through Head Office of the Anglican Church in Salisbury (Harare) to assist in the structural development of the school. Long before Mr Tsimba's promotion to headmaster, local parents had agreed to contribute some money each towards a fund they called the 'Building Fund'. A big parents' meeting had been held where it was agreed each parent would pay two shillings per child at the beginning of each term. Father was one of the culprits who had refused to attend the meeting. I remember these payments towards the 'Building Fund' causing quite an uproar with people like father when their children were sent back home by appointed parents' representatives due to their parents lagging with their payments. Father was also one of the miscreants in this quarrel because he had a whole 'school' of children from his home attending school, so paying the required amounts was proving burdensome for him. Luckily for him at the time, the Grain Marketing Board sent him a big cheque in payment for the bags of maize and 'rapoko' he had delivered to them at the end of the last harvest. Otherwise, we would have carried on losing lessons by continually being sent back home for not being paid up with the 'Building Fund'.

By the end of 1961, two new blocks housing four classrooms with zinc roofs over them had been constructed and already in use. When schools re-opened for the third term in September 1961, Mr Tsimba's Standard 3 (Grade 5) class in which I was a pupil was the first to take lessons in a spanking new classroom with sparkling new desks and benches. Despite his elevated position as headmaster of the school, Mr Tsimba led by example by not exempting himself from carrying out co-curricular duties which the rest of the teachers did. He played an active role in co-curricular life of the school. I was in his 'Boy Scouts' team of boys., Before he arrived in our community at the start of the year, 'Scouting' had never been heard about in the history of the school nor in the whole district, including the Manyene Tribal Trust Lands. Through the scouting movement and motto 'Be Prepared' that Mr Reginald Tsimba introduced to us, we learnt many survival skills including the tying of different types of knots, mountain climbing, construction of temporary bridges across rivers in flood, raising and lowering of flags, constructing SOS (Save Our Souls) signs on the ground, going camping, etc. To this day, sixty-two years later, whenever I tie objects together using a reef-knot, I always remember Mr Tsimba's 'right over left and left over right', to signify a knot which will not undo.

'Baseball' was another sporting innovation Mr Tsimba introduced by way of an addition to the list of co-curricular activities at the school. He did not just teach us the modus operandi of playing the game; he also actively participated in playing the game with us. The game had similar characteristics to those of the modern game of cricket. Mr Tsimba's game of baseball variant involved using a tennis ball and the handle of a pickaxe as a baseball bat. A group of boys in the team stood five yards apart in a big circle and one of us stood about ten yards inside the circle directly facing the person holding the 'baseball' bat. Being my turn to hit the ball after the tennis ball had been thrown, I remember striking the tennis ball and letting it fly high over the circle of my team-mates. As it flew to the edge of the sports field, I would run like made round the circle as many times as I could and only stopped behind one of the boys in the circle when the ball was retrieved. The new player, one whose turn it would be to hit the ball would be the boy behind whom I stopped. It was so much fun playing this game. The catch was in the player connecting the tennis ball with the baseball bat. Those who missed hitting the ball automatically left the game to sit down at a designated space. Playing the game of baseball was so much fun for me at my impressionable age; as well as learning all these exotic forms of enjoyment. I was also in Mr Tsimba's School Choir. I believe he was the first teacher at Maronda Mashanu to introduce us to singing in a choir using 'Tonic Solfa' or the so-called 'Staff Notation'. I remember him making a big effort to familiarise his choir with the initial 'doh-reh-mi-fah-soh-la-ti-doh' and visa-versa to test our voice boxes for singing purposes. Is it not a wonder that at Standard 3 (Grade 5) of my primary education in the splendid isolation of the backwaters of a small rural school, I became familiar with such musical terms as 'semibreve', crochet, minim, soprano, alto, tenor, bass, andante, adagio, crescendo, etc'? We did all the choir practices in Mr Tsimba's class which would have the classroom furniture re-arranged prior to choir practice, to allow his choir to be formed in the shape of a horseshoe. Standing in front of his choir made up of around thirty or forty of us, he would conduct it with both his hands waving them in sweeping movements or waving them up and down depending on the notes he had drummed into us during practice. I was one of a group of boys who sang 'tenor' in the School Choir of 1961 which for the first time, in a long interval, lifted a magnificent and much coveted trophy that was competed for by up to ten primary schools at a big Inter-Schools Choir Contest held once-a-year at Chamukwenjera Township in Manyene Tribal

Trust Lands. Our winning of the huge illustrious trophy at the inter-school choir contest made the school famous. Its popularity spread far and wide.

The nearest local European farmer, Mr Kerry Schultz, rarely got himself mixed up with events in African areas, even if he lived only five miles from Maronda Mashanu School as the bird flew. Nevertheless, word of the school's success at the singing competition reached him through some of his farm workers who had spent the weekend with their families in nearby Mutasa and Dzvova and Chiwandire Villages. Some of these men had children who attended Maronda Mashanu School.

He would have telephoned the headteacher to offer his hearty congratulations out of a feeling of good neighbourliness; but the school did not have a fixed landline telephone. Instead, Mr Schultz sent a message to the headteacher by word of mouth with one of the 'boys', one of the servants who herded his cattle, to say he would personally drive over through Enkeldoorn on a nominated date and time (there being no shortcut, which was the only route he could use) to fulfil what he felt was his obligation. Mr Schultz did not disappoint. True to his word and on the appointed date and time, Mr Schultz arrived at the school at around one forty-five p.m. driving a covered Land Rover in the company of one of his senior foremen. Approximately three hundred pupils and the entire staff of ten teachers were waiting for Mr Schultz's visit.

It was probably that white man's first time to drive along the nine mile gravel feeder road from Enkeldoorn to visit us. The four-mile road from his farmhouse to Enkeldoorn (Chivhu) town was fully macadamised. Promptly on his arrival at the school, Mr Schultz made a brief congratulatory address (surprisingly in good, fluent English and not some half-baked 'Chilaphalapha') In that short speech, he extolled the merits of hard work and achieving success in competitions. Without further ado, he asked if clean, cold fresh water in two fifty-litre drums could be fetched. Clean water was quickly fetched and brought over from a spring well not far from the school premises by a group of some of our bigger and more mature boy pupils.

Meanwhile, Mr Schultz quietly conversed with the headmaster and Mr Mamvura while also an aide who had accompanied Mr Schultz unloaded, from the back of the Land Rover, a crate carrying six bottles of standard two-litre bottles of 'Schweppes Orange Crush'. He also unloaded khaki carrier bags containing dozens of loaves of bread and countless scores of freshly baked buns and countless bags of 'Valencia' oranges. Water now available, one group of lady teachers began slicing the loaves of bread into large pieces while another group emptied up to six of the undiluted orange crush bottles into the drums of water, part of which contents had been poured out to leave room for the orange crush. Pupils and staff alike lined up to collect portions of the drinks and hunks of bread pieces and buns. There was so much food and drink that despite pupils returning to obtain second or third helpings, the gathering failed to finish it all. Mr Schultz sneaked away, accompanied by his Foreman, when the banqueting was at its peak.

Some of the little boys and girls had never seen such an abundance of food before. They engaged in a feeding frenzy, feverishly at first but lugubriously in the end, until their stomachs looked so distended that it looked as if they had swallowed footballs. Struggling to walk back to their homes in the nearby reserves later that afternoon, each of the children clutched an unpeeled orange in their hands. It was a day that would be remembered for a long time in the history of the school.

My Standard 3 (Grade 5) education had come to an end on a very high note indeed. In the end of the year test results which were announced to the congregation of mainly parents after the Sunday Service by the headmaster, I had not done badly either. That sharp-shooter, Zvakarimwa (then christened Florence) Bwanya had beaten me for the top spot. I had shared second position with another wonder-boy Nunurayi Tembo who was also known for his prowess as an athlete. In recent months, his classwork had improved by leaps and bounds. When Uncle Rodrick visited the farm at Christmas in 1961, he was pleased with how I had distinguished myself at school. Before he left to return to

Gwelo (Gweru) after the Christmas holidays, he left word with my father that, now that my older brothers Raphael and Roland had both successfully completed their Standard 6 (Grade 7) at the end of 1961 while living with him in Gwelo (Gweru), it was now my turn to go and stay with him and his family at the start of the school term in January 1962.

Reader, please place yourself in my position and imagine my excitement at finally having the golden opportunity to leave the stifling confines of my life at the farm to enjoy the chance of pursuing my education for the first time, not in a small provincial town but in the comfort of a big place called a city! I had never been filled with so much happiness before. It was like winning a passport to go on a tour of heaven.

# Chapter 9

# Maiden bus and train journey to Gwelo (Gweru)

Three days before schools re-opened for Term I in January 1962, my mother told me I was going to travel to Gwelo (Gweru) alone on the following day. She said she had already bought new clothes and a few other personal items which she was going to pack into an old medium-sized suitcase Aunt Jasmine had kindly donated for my use on the journey. Aunt Jasmine had reportedly used the same suitcase in previous years when she attended as a boarder at 'Wanezi or was it Mwenezi (?) Girls Handcraft School,' somewhere in either Fort Victoria (Masvingo) Province or Matabeleland South. I was still too young to know about the geographical exactness of these places. Inspecting the suitcase that night when Mother had temporarily left her hut to fetch something outside, I felt happy to be the proud owner of a suitcase in which I would carry my luggage. However, the happiness did not include the sickening feeling the unattractive suitcase gave me. Its outside appearance was bespattered with stains from what might have been blobs of raindrops or cheap brown paint. Its original grey colour had irretrievably faded into an ugly mixture of yellowish brown and black.

Mother woke up at cock's crow the following morning. She heated plenty of water in a metal twenty-litre metal container. Waking me up at five a.m. that morning, she asked me to bathe and be ready by eight a.m. when she and I would start the ten-kilometre journey on foot to the bus terminus at the African Location in Enkeldoorn (Chivhu). She said after putting me on one of the buses that travelled to Umvuma (Mvuma) and seeing me off, she would find her way on foot back to the farm. When my mother gave me a virtual breakdown of her programme of activities for the day, she spoke quietly and sombrely. I may have been just about eleven years of age then, but I was old enough to read an undercurrent of unhappiness in my mother's tone. From about the age of five years old, I had noted that my parents persistently lived a cat's and dog's life.

For a strange and inexplicable reason, it always was my father who instigated the quarrels. Completely oblivious of us, their children being present or otherwise, they argued all the time about one thing or the other, with my mother always getting the worst end of the stick by being physically abused by my father. Alongside a litany of other negatives, chief among them my hatred for farming which my father had perhaps unwittingly promoted, overall, the whole situation made me feel unhappy. Against such a background, growing up at the farm was synonymous with misery for me. Granted, I was excited by the opportunity that had arisen for me to continue my education in another location.

As would have been expected in view of my mixed emotions, I also strongly associated leaving the farm at the beginning of 1962 to attend higher primary school far away in Gwelo (Gweru) as a form of escape from the wrenching sadness that made up the general atmosphere pervading the farm compound.

I really should have loved farming, but the negative outcomes from eleven years of deprivation and suffering far outweighed any prospects of ever achieving positive gains from a future life on the land. Following a quick breakfast of 'rapoko' porridge and a large piece of buttered home-baked wholewheat bread washed down by a steaming mug of milky tea, Father quietly walked into Mother's hut and sat on a chair with his back against the mantelpiece on which lay neat piles of polished and shining clay pots. I sat on an elongated low bench near the exit door. The low bench was made of mounted soil along part of the inner wall of the hut. Father was in a calm and stable mood that morning, so the choice of where I sat did not for the first time give me a hint that I should prepare myself for a quick getaway should an explosion suddenly occur. That morning was different from other occasions. Moments after Mother had pulled out of the fire two logs of wood from which clouds of smoke billowed and made us cough and our eyes itchy and tearful:

Sitting on a highchair that was especially positioned for him somewhere inside the hut, but facing the hut's main entrance, Father cleared his throat and started his little farewell speech thus: "Kingston, my son, it's your turn today to leave this farm and go off to Gwelo (Gweru) where you will live with your Uncle Rodrick, while you also attend school. There's plenty of work that always needs doing here, so if I had my way, I would have preferred you to finish your school at the local school so that you could always help with farm work during those times when you will not be attending classes. Unfortunately, they don't have the higher classes there that you want to attend. Anyway, I hope you will continue working hard at your new school in Gwelo (Gweru) and pass your tests. Whatever you do, always remember that I will not tolerate any reports of your being lazy from your uncle. As I speak to you, the Spirits of the VaRozvi (Rozvi) ancestors are listening from wherever they are hidden. They will continue to guide you and bring you good fortune in most of the things you will do. Most importantly, and I'll repeat this, this is your home (stamping the floor with his gum-booted foot) and you belong here. Have a sense of belonging and be proud that you belong to this farm. Whenever schools shut for the holidays, please let your uncle release you quickly and travel back here so that you can help with all of the farm work that needs doing here. Travel well, my son." Then making a little snort, standing up unceremoniously and without talking to anybody, he walked out of the farm compound carrying a hoe on his right shoulder.

It was the first time I had ever heard him speak to me so calmly and with a voice that was friendly and low in volume. Even then, a few threats of possible beatings if he could reach out and get hold of me in Gwelo (Gweru) were hidden in his speech. I also noted a note of sadness and regret that in my leaving to embark on another level of my educational career, he was also losing manpower to help him work the land so that he would have bigger harvests.

After bidding farewell to the few people who were still within the farm compound before they all disappeared to their various stations in the fields, Mother and I started on our long walk to the bus station in Enkeldoorn. Mother balanced on her head the old suitcase which, packed with bits of my clothes and a few other things that had been added in there, looked so fat and disfigured that it was like a python that had swallowed an overgrown deer. My young brother Irrigation (Wilfred) walked beside me holding my hand, his fiery eyes teary, a sign he was going to miss me after I had vanished into the void of extended absence. At Jemwa's Farm two miles away, Irrigation (Wilfred) gave me a pat on the back, his eyes welling up with tears, and bid me farewell before he started on his reverse little trip back to the farm. As Irrigation found his way down the rocky path, I also had this strong feeling I was going to miss my young brother and tears started rolling down my cheeks, too. Reaching the bus station at the African Location in Enkeldoorn (Chivhu), there was a bigger crowd gathered at that spot than I ever seen before.

Well, Mother said schools were re-opening in a few days, so people were travelling a lot up and down the country. Adults mixed with large numbers of school children who were gathered in disorganised groups all over the place. A mixture of men, women and children vendors crisscrossed the place, selling their wares to waiting passengers. The items they sold included boiled groundnuts, cooked or roasted cobs of mealies, a range of wild fruit, e.g., 'matamba', 'hute', 'figs' and an assortment of oily and fatty edibles some of which made you want to vomit just by the look of them. The vendors carried their items in either baskets or small trays held aloft in their hands or slung round their necks. A few buses that had arrived earlier from their routes appeared parked and their bus crews were nowhere to be seen. Buses were arriving one at a time after long intervals, so many people milled about waiting for buses which never seemed to come. The waiting passengers constantly craned their necks to see if any buses were turning into the T-Junction at the 'Madhanga' Cattle Sale pens by the Salisbury to Fort Victoria Highway to follow the gravel road leading to the bus terminus where they anxiously awaited. In the absence of public notices to inform travellers of the departure and arrival times for the various bus companies, all the waiting passengers could do was to second guess when the buses they wanted to catch would arrive. One adult female passenger standing not far from where Mother and I stood waiting for the bus to arrive was heard mumbling to herself in exasperation, "Bus come! Please come!" After quietly enquiring from another waiting passenger standing near us about the bus to Umvuma (Mvuma), she was politely informed that one bus travelling from Buhera to my destination would soon arrive. We continued waiting.

Meanwhile, a little distance behind where we stood, someone had just passed wind. A powerful stench of raw human manure sailed into our nostrils. We turned round to see a crowd of people move away, hands clutching their noses and feet shuffling, from a male adult who himself had started hobbling with a slight limp in his left leg towards the public toilets two hundred metres farther away from the crowd. A swarm of flies followed him. The hapless fellow had obviously lost control of his digestive system. I pitied him. By eleven thirty a.m., my bus to Umvuma (Mvuma) had still had not arrived. Another passenger volunteered information to Mother that my bus should reach Umvuma (Mvuma) Bus Station by one p.m. latest for me to be able to connect with the train from Fort Victoria, leaving Umvuma (Mvuma) to start its journey to Gwelo (Gweru) at precisely one thirty p.m.

The informant made it clear that the train did not wait for latecomers. The bus's lateness in arriving combined with the chaos we found at the bus station gave my confidence a nasty knock. You see, I had never travelled on a bus or train before. In that situation, you do not want to be greeted by any degree of disorder. My heart began to thump beneath my breast. But Mother assured me things would go well. By then a crowd of people waiting to catch the one bus I was waiting for had grown bigger. It finally pitched up with great fanfare at eleven fifty a.m. As the bus driver slowed down to stop with screeching brakes, he blew his horn several times while the conductor, standing two steps up at the door of the bus with the metal door swinging back and forth shouted in a hoarse voice, "Those for Umvuma, let's go! Umvuma, Umvuma, Umvuma! All those for Umvuma, please get on board! The bus leaves once we have finished loading. Umvuma, Umvuma, Umvuma!" Reader, please imagine the scramble that occurs when hordes of people have anxiously been waiting for just one bus and when that bus suddenly arrives, they are unsure whether they will succeed in boarding it after their long wait. The scenario became a free for all. Everybody sprang into action. Some headed for the bus door while others rushed to hand in their suitcases to another bus tout who had already mounted the steps at the back of the bus to receive the cases and store them on the carrier on top of the bus.

In those years, queues were an unknown phenomenon, so when emergency situations arose, it was survival of the fittest as people followed no particular modus operandi. I was lucky to have my mother with me when the bus suddenly arrived, telling me to get into the bus while she lifted the suitcase to hand it over to the bus tout standing three or four steps up the ladder behind the bus, I joined the mad rush of the throng who were headed for the door of the bus. There was considerable pushing, pulling and thudding. Using the athletic skill I had acquired at school by then and being small boy in stature, I literally rode on the heads and shoulders of the crowd, which surged forward towards the bus entrance like huge waves of the sea during a storm. By the time my mother handed my suitcase to the bus tout who placed it securely on the bus carrier, I had also succeeded in gaining entrance into the bus. I was one of the first few passengers not just to enter the bus but also to find somewhere to sit. I secured a seat by a window which I slid open for a whiff of fresh air. I badly needed that after my ordeal to enter that bus. Mother came round to the open window where I conversed with her, standing outside beneath the window while the bus engine idled and more passengers came aboard.

I thanked my mother for accompanying me to the bus terminus and for her help with installing the suitcase on top of the bus carrier. I said to her that I did not know how I would have coped on my own without her assistance. The bus conductor announced from the front of the bus that he would issue tickets after the bus had started its journey. Mother gave me ten shillings ($1.00) which was more than adequate. I had learnt that for that bus trip to Umvuma (Mvuma), I needed two shillings and six pence (twenty-five cents); and I would need three shillings and six pence (thirty-five cents) for the train fare from Umvuma (Muma) to Gwelo (Gweru). It would leave me with a handsome balance of four shillings as change, and Mother said I could use some of that to buy refreshments at Umvuma (Mvuma) while waiting for the train to arrive from Fort Victoria. My bus eventually left Enkeldoorn (Chivhu) at twelve fifteen p.m. which some of the passengers felt was a bit too late because the trip to our destination would take at least an hour. Once the bus driver started the engine and rammed the accelerator loudly, he produced three or four ear-shattering blasts of the horn of the bus. I shot my thin arm through the open window and bid my mother goodbye. Unsteady on her feet, she looked as if she was going to start crying. The rickety old bus edged out of the bus station at the start of its journey to Umvuma (Mvuma).

Mother, who had recovered her composure, waved back at me feverishly and called out wishing me a safe journey, "Uve nerwendo rwusina tsaona, Mwanangu, Kingi! Uzotinyorerawo tsamba kana wasvika kuGwelo. Tichakusuwa." In short, she was saying "Travel safely, my son, Kingston! Also write to us when you reach Gwelo. We shall definitely miss you." She was saying these parting remarks as the bus swayed side to side and slowly navigated the corrugations and uneven surface of the gravel road a mile to the 'Madhanga' T-Junction at the Cattle Sales stalls, with clouds of silvery dust trailing it. Soon it would enter the wide macadamised Salisbury (Harare) to Fort Victoria (Masvingo) Highway, flit past Enkeldoorn (Chivhu) town centre and proceed with its journey to Umvuma (Mvuma). Groaning, juddering but powering on during the thirty-two-mile journey, the old DAF engine bus made it to Umvuma (Mvuma) Bus Station at one fifteen p.m. said the few passengers who were wearing shiny wrist watches. When the brakes of the old bus screeched and brought it to a jerky halt, those who were familiar with the geography of the bus station reported that they had looked through the bus windows as the bus arrived and could confirm that the steam train from Fort Victoria (Masvingo) had already arrived and was parked at the train station, about five hundred metres away.

Peering through the bus windows, those passengers who were already standing, and were familiar with the goings-on, said they had spotted groups of passengers boarding the train. Having never seen a real train or travelled in one before, I did not have the foggiest idea what they were talking about.

The urgency for us to get out of that bus all at once became more heightened than the chaos of boarding it that I had experienced just over an hour previously. Everybody was in a great hurry to leave the bus. I noticed a few clever boys with experience of bus travel kick the 'emergency exit' doors on the back and off-side of the bus and leap out of the vehicle one after the other. For me and the rest of the passengers who were squashed near the front of the bus, the pushing, thudding and brutal force that ensued were simply unbelievable. Thinking about this event in retrospect, I am still surprised that I emerged from it all without breaking a limb or having my ribs crushed. It was probably still about six minutes before the steam train departed Umvuma (Mvuma) Train Station on its journey to Gwelo (Gweru), so time was of the essence. Every bit of that time still available had to be utilised to maximum advantage.

As soon as I set my feet on the ground after alighting from the bus, I rushed to join a mixed knot of children and adults who, with their faces looking up, stood beside the bus, feverishly pleading with the bus conductor to hand them their suitcases from the carrier on top of the bus. When the bus conductor eventually came and stood over at the side of the bus where we eagerly awaited, I called out to him pointing, "Conductor, please, mine is right here above me. Next to your left leg!" I could clearly see my old suitcase among a batch of others securely placed along the edge of the bus carrier. "Which one did you say? This one here?" the bus conductor shouted his questions from the top of the bus, pointing and waiting for me to confirm within that split second. "Yes, can I have my case, please! I am late for the train!" I answered in a shrilly voice. Lifting the suitcase by its lid which curiously did not fit exactly, and it lay half-opened, the conductor held it aloft and dangled it down the side of the bus. I held out both hands, standing on tiptoe to receive it, but that could not be. I was too short; the suitcase was too high up for me. Meanwhile the clock was ticking. Swearing under his breath, the conductor had had to squat on one knee on top of the bus and reach further down. He continued to dangle the suitcase with the intensity of the weight on the weak lid. The tension and weight were simply too much for the old cardboard material that had been used when the suitcase was manufactured. The lid that the conductor hooked his fingers in suddenly gave way and ripped up. Exposed for the public to see were all the contents of the suitcase which dropped in a shower to the ground, leaving me and the conductor holding just the fragments of the original container.

How embarrassing it all was! Some of the innocent bystanders stood there clearly enjoying my embarrassment and feeling of discomfiture. But I said to myself, "Never mind, my dear friend. Life has got to go on." I only had maybe three minutes on hand before my train left, so throwing aside old useless fragments from the remainder of the suitcase, I knelt on the ground and quickly grabbed what I could lay my hands on of the clothes Mother had bought me. Among the bits of essentials that I laid my hands on, I remembered to include my Standard 3 (Grade 5) Report from the pile of disorganised rubble. I left most of the junk strewn on the ground beside the bus, including bits of food items Mother had stuffed into the suitcase making it look so fat and heavy. That was why the lid had split when the bus conductor was handing it down to me from the carrier on top of the bus. Anyway, that was it. I broke into a mad sprint towards the train which I could see about five hundred yards away. The steam train blew its last whistle, an unusually piercing sound that frightened me, as I dashed like a hare to reach the train station and get on board. I was pretty running much on adrenaline. At that moment of my desperation, I derived a feeling of comfort in numbers when I noticed scores of other people were in the same predicament as me. We were all racing against time to catch the train.

Carrying my clothes in my bare hands, some of them dangling from the ill-arranged bundle in my hands. Some of the clothes flapped against my legs and almost tripped me as I sprinted along the outside of the line of passenger coaches, desperately looking for an entrance through which I could hop onto the train. The doors of the passenger carriages were shutting, bells were ringing, and the steam engine had started hissing, puffing, and chuffing when I miraculously squeezed through the closing doors of one of the coaches. Phew! Another few seconds too late and I would have missed that train. I was a total stranger in these parts and if I had missed that train, where would I have spent the night? I was completely out of breath and sweating all over; but I felt happy that I had succeeded in catching that train although the embarrassing and shameful event at Umvuma (Mvuma) Bus Station still mortified me.

I resolved to put the nasty sequence of events at that spot behind me and to concentrate my mind on the journey that still lay ahead of me. Sweat was pouring down my face when I took a seat beside an adult female passenger in one of the several 'Economy Class' passenger carriages. I clutched the remainder of my possessions in my bare hands. The kind lady quickly noticed something was amiss with my frazzled appearance. She offered me an old paper bag which she said she could spare me. I stuffed what remained of my clothes in it. I thanked her for her kindness.

As I looked through the window as the black steam engine powered ahead, and noticed that whenever it reached a bend, the massive metal bars adjoined to its huge steel wheels jerking backwards and forwards in rapid succession. Counting, I also noticed the engine was pulling up to twenty-five passenger and cargo carriages. It was a long train stretching up to almost half-a-mile. The train stopped at smaller stations every fifteen miles for a few minutes before it resumed its journey. The longest it stopped was at a stop called 'Lalapanzi', almost halfway between Umvuma (Mvuma) and Gwelo (Gweru). It stopped here for about fifteen minutes. At that station, the steam engine was removed from the line-up of carriages it had carried from Umvuma (Mvuma). The steam engine shunted past the passenger carriages twice seeming to be picking up more cargo carriages which were loaded with wooden logs and other items that I could not identify. The smell of the thick black smoke that billowed through a wide funnel affixed to the top of the railway engine as it passed by the window where I sat gave me a strong sensation of wanting to vomit. But I fought back the disgusting feeling. The journey to Gwelo (Gweru) resumed after they had put the steam engine back in front of all the carriages which, as I observed later, had a longer line of passenger coaches and cargo carriages in tow. But it did not struggle with its load as we then seemed to be going downward. At around four p.m., I began to fret about Mother. I guessed that by then she had already arrived back at the farm after seeing me off at Enkeldoorn (Chivhu) Bus Station. I missed her already. Besides those few thoughts crossing my mind and the few absent-minded observations I made as the train chugged towards its destination, my first journey by train was laid back and uneventful. The train arrived at Gwelo (Gweru) Train Station at four forty-five p.m. on the dot. A big clock face in front of one of the buildings along the railway platform confirmed the time. Passengers on the train filed out. I noticed several had relatives and friends crowded on the platform waiting to receive and welcome them. As soon as they recognised their visitors among the disembarking passengers, they ran wildly with arms outstretched to give them welcome bearhugs. Looking around nervously, I was satisfied that no one was waiting to welcome me. I did not know anybody around there and for a while I was lost for options. I had a vague memory from letters that father used to receive from Uncle Rodrick with an address which said 'RRAF, Thornhill, Gwelo'. Not far from where I was, I saw a building with 'Enquiries' inscribed on top of its entrance door.

A man in that office, wearing a white shirt, black tie and a black cap, informed me that the 'Thornhill' place I was asking about was near the last train station into Gwelo (Gweru) from Umvuma (Mvuma) which was called 'Guinea Fowl'. It had been our last stop before we reached Gwelo (Gweru) Train Station. He suggested that maybe I should have got off the train at that stop. He did not know that that was my maiden train journey to Gwelo (Gweru). I did not want to waste my time explaining all that to him. I still had four shillings of change in my pocket from the ten shillings Mother had given me at Enkeldoorn (Chivhu) Bus Station. I did not know whether the cash I had was enough to cover the taxi fare there, if I took a taxi to go back to Guinea Fowl, as suggested by the man in the 'Enquiries' office. He said Guinea Fowl Station was about five miles away along the railway line, so as it was still daylight, I decided I would have to find my way back there on foot. I only had a small paper bag, so I was travelling light. Without wasting time, I embarked on my five-mile walk back to 'Guinea Fowl' Station. I walked briskly on a gravel path along the railway line and reached my destination just before six p.m. Uncle Rodrick was well-known in the area by virtue of the unique nature of his job as a Weather Forecaster. Not many Africans were so privileged as to be employed in such white-collar jobs in those days.

My few enquiries and directions offered by kind people eventually led me to his house in the 'African Section' of the Royal Rhodesian Air Force compound at Thornhill, Gwelo (Gweru). I announced my arrival at Uncle's house when it was already dark because the sun had set. He said he had waited for me at 'Guinea Fowl Station' but had given up waiting seeing I had not come off the train when it stopped. Uncle Rodrick probably did not remember that days before I embarked on my journey to Gwelo (Gweru), he may have overlooked writing a letter to or telephoning my father telling him I should get off the train when it reached 'Guinea Fowl train station'. I had never travelled to Gwelo (Gweru) by train before, so there was no way I would have known about that on this maiden journey; nor that he would be waiting to meet me and collect me from there! While Uncle Rodrick had stepped outside the house to talk to a Mr Made, his neighbour, I was chatting with the rest of his family in the lounge of the house, including his wife, Aunt Lucy, who had visited the farm on the Christmas before; as well as all my cousins from Matabeleland and parts of the Midlands. I began addressing them as best I could although my IsiNdebele was somewhat intelligible at first. I had come from Mashonaland where Shona was the medium of communication, not IsiNdebele.

My uncle's in-laws did not speak one of the native languages, 'Shona', largely spoken in the northern half of Rhodesia (Zimbabwe), so in my first few days of arriving at Thornhill Air Base, there was little to no communication between me and them, as at that time, I was mainly Shona-speaking with a sprinkling of fluent English. Yet both 'uGogo' and 'uBabamkhulu' were a pleasant couple who were welcoming and anxious to engage in conversation with me.

Suddenly, amid the conversation I was having with Aunt Lucy and everybody else, there was a very loud noise like nothing I had ever heard before. It was the earth-shattering loud roaring of an air force jet that filled the whole atmosphere of the house and seemed to shake its walls to its foundations. While I trembled with fear and felt insecure, the loud noise did not seem to have the same effect on everybody else. Not even a twinge! Aunt (or Mainini) Lucy, who quickly noticed the noise had unsettled me – although it had now died away into the night after a minute or two – calmed me down and said to me reassuringly, "Sorry, King. I see you're shaking with fear! Don't be frightened. (I was to be christened 'Lawrence' later in the year). You will come to no harm. Maybe you need to know that you have now arrived at Thornhill Airbase. It will not be anything like at the farm, though. This house is within the grounds of a military airbase, Kingston. The noise you've just heard came from a military jet taking off the runway less than a mile from these houses. It will be noisy in the first few days as you've just heard. But you'll get used to these noises because on every Thursday night, the air force pilots have what they call 'night fly'. That is when they practise at night taking off and landing the military jet aeroplanes at this base." I had indeed arrived at Gwelo (Gweru). 'Thanks to the warm welcome accorded to me by the eerie, rumbling, and ear-splitting noise of the air force jet, a little while before'.

# Chapter 10

# My full year's stay in Gwelo (Gweru): A combination of happy and unhappy experiences

Making comparisons with the rural setting in which the whole of my childhood was nurtured, Gwelo (Gweru) was completely new territory to me. Then I was a teenager whose prospects for the future were tinged with a curious mixture of certainty as well as fear regarding how the new set of circumstances would give impetus to my long-term objective to achieve educational success and live a life of comfort in my adulthood.

Uncle Rodrick was not in the military. Yet, here we were, his family home was within the same grounds as the soldiers' compound. However, by virtue of the uniqueness and distinction of his job title at Thornhill Air Base as a Weatherman, he and his colleague (a Mr Made) had been allocated standard married men's government houses on a separate site of the 'African Barracks Section' of Thornhill Royal Rhodesian Air Force Base in Gwelo (Gweru). European air force men and women personnel had their own separate compound, a few hundred yards to the east of the African section. African families at Thornhill Air Base did not have a school or schools in the neighbourhood where their children could attend school. Ironically, Thornhill Primary School, just a couple of a hundred yards away east, in the 'European section', already existed on site. Also, there was Guinea Fowl School less than two miles along the Thornhill to Umvuma (Mvuma) road. Nearby, about two or so miles outside the fenced-off military compound in Riverside, Athlone and Windsor Park suburbs were primary schools we from the African Compound at Thornhill Air Base could have easily attended if the laws had permitted it. With discriminatory laws in force, which was not to be. All the school in the suburbs I have listed were in areas designated as 'Whites Only' areas. Under no circumstances in terms of the racial segregation laws in Rhodesia (Zimbabwe) of that time, could black children be enrolled in schools located in white areas. The immediate choice left to black children whose soldier-parents were accommodated at Thornhill Air Force Base Camp was to live with their grandparents far away in the tribal trust lands where they would be expected to utilise the schooling opportunities that existed there. Alternatively, those children who had the stamina and stoic endurance would have had to walk one-way trips of up to six or seven miles each way to reach the few government-funded or church-run primary schools in the African locations of Ascot, Mambo, Senga and Monomotapa.

All the African townships listed above were in the west of Gwelo's (Gweru's) central business district, which was upwards of seven miles away from Thornhill Air Base Camp. As I have already provided details of in an earlier chapter, my older brothers Misheck (Raphael) and Roland (Kaston), lived with Uncle Rodrick and had to attend upper primary school from 1959 through to 1961. These two men had to grin and bear the hardship of walking daily between Thornhill Airbase and the African locations in Gwelo (Gweru), a round trip of up to fourteen miles on every school day. The quest for them to acquire at least a Standard 6 (Grade 7) level of education necessitated the need for them to walk literally hundreds upon hundreds of miles to achieve that goal! My older brother, Roland (Kaston) who is still alive at the time I am writing this book, says he does not want to talk too much about the extreme levels of hardship he and his older brother Misheck (Raphael) endured to complete their primary school education in Gweru.

Despite the hardships they had to endure, he remains deeply grateful at the golden opportunity Uncle Rodrick availed to them to obtain at least an upper primary level of education. He believes that without this legacy invested in them; and sixty-five years later, he would not be enjoying the benefits he currently has. At the same time, he confesses that it is hard to forget how generally uncaring Uncle Rodrick was about their quality of life, how they were always hungry because there was hardly ever enough to eat at home. On the other hand, there was this persistence Uncle Rodrick had in which he demanded with a certain passion that the two 'boys' should promptly arrive back from their seven mile walk after school and that they should then work in the garden – which was in fact a large field! – until it was dark. Also, their weekends were completely tied up with work in that dreadful garden from five a.m. until seven p.m., allowing them no time to socialise or do any of their schoolwork privately in their room where they slept on a cement floor for three years. "Zvakange zvakaoma," he observes, "asi zvakapfuura nenguva iyoyo, munin'ina." ("It was hard, and we went through hell, my young brother,") he observes, "but it's all water under the bridge now. Life goes on.") I was probably exceptionally lucky to be spared the dreadful suffering my older brothers Misheck (Raphael) and Kaston (Roland) went through. At the very least, the two of them could afford to share their discomforts and lift each other's spirits when faced with having to make difficult choices. I cannot fathom how I would have coped with all that, on my own.

When Uncle Rodrick gave the green light for me to come over from the farm and live with him as a replacement for Misheck (Raphael) and Kaston (Roland) who had left Gwelo (Gweru), I am sure he was aware of more favourable developments that were expected, which would allow me to avoid having to walk fourteen miles round trips alone, to attend school in the African locations west of the city and back to Thornhill daily. I simply could not imagine myself surviving the exposure to such an ordeal. At the start of the new school term of 1962, I was one of the few guinea-pig pupils who started learning in a 'pilot school for Africans' that had reluctantly been allowed to begin operating at Thornhill Air Base in Gwelo (Gweru) by the Ministry of Defence, working in collaboration with the Department of Native Education. If the experiment proved feasible, similar arrangements would be repeated at all military air base stations across towns and cities in Southern Rhodesia.

Mind you, these were still the 'Federation of Rhodesia and Nyasaland' days. These developments followed years of fervent appeals and representations to the powers that be in the colonial administration by senior African personnel in the then Royal Rhodesian Air Force for better educational opportunities to be provided for the children of their married men and women at air force base stations where they lived and worked. Those who made these appeals wanted to enjoy the same benefits being provided for their counterparts in the European sections of the air base stations. The achievement to start a pioneer school for African children at Thornhill Air Base was a significant milestone in the quest for racial equality in a society which was rigidly segregated according to the colour of one's skin. The immediate benefit that accrued to me was that whereas my older brothers, to all intents and purposes, had to walk up to seven miles one way every school day to attend school far away in the African locations, my own school was literally a stone's throw from Uncle Rodrick's house.

My new school at Thornhill was deliberately named 'Thornhill African Primary School' to distinguish it from the 'whites only' primary school that already existed in the same neighbourhood. Our classroom blocks had originally been residential barracks for unmarried African male air force trainees or recruits. Arising from the authority given to start a school for African children at Thornhill Airbase, the recruits had been relocated to barrack blocks in another part of the compound, thus giving way to the conversion and refurbishment of their old barracks into classrooms for our use.

The 'married quarters' section of the compound had many young families with a considerable number of school-going children, so the school enrolment was oversubscribed from the commencement of the school. All our teachers, from the headteacher downwards, were fully qualified for their teaching roles. However, as the school was sited in a military establishment, all staff were always required to carry out their duties in full air force uniform. The navy-blue uniforms made them look very smart indeed. On some occasions they were presented in full camouflage fatigues during lessons, thus making it appear as if we the children were undergoing military training! Both our male and female teachers were automatically placed at the minimum higher rank of 'sergeant' on joining the staff. This meant that the 'privates', 'corporals' and 'lance corporals – all of whom were of a lower rank to that of sergeant – saluted our teachers every time these soldiers of a lower rank came into the presence of any of our teachers. Having been given just basic training in this 'greetings' procedure, all our teachers stood at attention and saluted the head teacher who himself held the higher rank of 'Staff sergeant'. We were by no means air force trainees ourselves. But as an intrinsic part of our learning, it was interesting observing the code of military discipline at work and how the different rank holders accentuated their positions in the pecking order.

My Thornhill Air Base School was fully funded by the Department of Native Education. It was also rumoured that the Ministry of Defence threw bits of its budget into the funding of the school. Judging by the abundance of teaching and learning materials in the school just two months after the school started, it was hard to believe the school had been in existence for such a short time. All our classrooms from Sub-Standard A (Grade 1) to Standard 4 (Grade 6) had been equipped with sparkling new furniture from the very start. Each of us had a desk and a chair to ourselves. There were plenty of writing materials in each classroom, including exercise books marked 'OHMS' on the front cover, pencils, rulers, penholders, nibs, ink and inkwells, ink blotters, drawing books, crayons, rubbers – all these items at absolutely no cost to us. All of us had textbooks to ourselves right across the subjects in the school curriculum. There were library books galore. And would you believe this? School Fees were two shillings and sixpence (2s 6p or 25p) at the beginning of each year! That practically amounted to going to school for free. In the co-curricular area, our teachers led us in a wide range of sporting activities including football, athletics, netball for girls, tug-of-war, and so on. Approximately two hectares of land separated the army compound from Uncle Rodrick's and Mr Made's houses. Previously, air force recruits used to carry out some of their drills on that spot.

Then it had been converted into our sports field where we did physical raining, athletics and played football. As we were situated in a military environment, I developed a great deal of interest in physical exercises, so I was in a group of boys who voluntarily teamed up with groups of the army recruits when they went jogging in the mornings during the week. I also joined these groups of men occasionally when they went to take dips in the icy cold water of a pool behind their barracks in the middle of winter! At Maronda Mashanu School, I had been more of a spectator who enjoyed observing other boys play football while I cheered them on from outside the football pitch. The tables were turned at Thornhill African Primary School. Here I participated in plenty of football-playing in which I gave the spherical and leathery object countless kicks and punches on the front right flank. Those in my sides at the time and are privileged to read this account will remember that most of my passes or servings – done with military precision (sic) – to the front runners almost always resulted in scores for my team.

Uncle Rodrick was not different from my father on the matter of how I should be occupied at home after school. It would appear he had borrowed the template from his older male sibling. Just like Father, he expected me to report back at home as soon as the school timetable ended. Just like my father, he was not too happy about excuses associated with my involvement in co-curricular activities at school. There was a big garden area at the back of the house. I would not even call it a garden. It was a vast three-hectare piece of land with red loam soils, so instead of reading my library book or taking time off to do homework given by my teacher, Uncle Rodrick insisted I should, according to him, be occupied more meaningfully in that field. I would therefore promptly change into my work clothes after school whereupon I would embark on doing one task or another including watering beds of vegetables, weeding, digging up or loosening up soil using a mattock and a hoe in readiness to make new vegetable beds. Other tasks included transplanting and planting seedlings of either rape, cabbage or tomato crops, compost making, making fresh sweet potato ridges, after which I went on to plant sweet potato stems by vegetative reproduction. Except perhaps for the job of watering where I used a hosepipe, nearly all the other jobs were intensely difficult, back-breaking, time-consuming and energy-sapping. There was always some type of work to be done. Insisting I was old enough to generate the line-up of tasks that I should do every day, he said I should not wait for him to prompt me on what to do. On Saturdays, he exchanged duties at his workplace with Mr Made who lived at a house next door.

On the weekends he was off duty, Uncle Rodrick would wake me up early in the morning and he would work with me in the 'field' until about two p.m. Occasionally, he allowed me mid-morning breaks for me to eat and drink something before resuming work. Regularly, we would forego these breaks. On such occasions, it bothered me that my uncle assumed I was as hardy and resilient as he was, so it did not seem to occur to him I was a young boy who should be spared time to eat and drink to build up some energy in me so I could continue working with him in the field. During the week and after school, Uncle insisted that I continue working in what he called the 'garden' but was really a large 'field' until well after seven p.m. The most uncomfortable thing about this bit was that most of the time, I worked all on my own in that field with nobody to talk to or exchange banter with.

The suffocating lonesomeness that pervaded me on these occasions often made me feel like a ship lost upon the vast expanse of the sea, making me feel quite exhausted in the end. Besides hoeing, digging or weeding in the field at the back of Uncle Rodrick's house at Thornhill, he also expected me to play a part in the cleaning of the house and the preparation of meals.

Uncle Rodrick's wife, Aunt Lucy, was almost like a visitor in her own home. She would put in brief appearances, but she hardly lived with Uncle Rodrick because she spent most of her absence at her parents' home somewhere in Matabeleland at an area called Nyamandlovu. In time, I noticed she returned to stay for short periods with all her children before they all packed up again and returned to Matabeleland where I guessed her older children, my cousin's sisters, attended school. When they arrived at Thornhill in January 1962, the house was full. Besides Uncle Rodrick and his wife, all their children thus far were at home, including Chipo (who everyone except me was calling 'Sipho'), Margaret, Moses and Praxedes. In residence also were Grandad and Granny (the latter of whom the children called 'Gogo'). They were Aunt Lucy's parents who spoke very little Shona and communicated mostly in the IsiNdebele dialect. My cousin's sister Praxedes was still a tiny little girl, approaching three years old. Her milk teeth were falling out. Chipo and Margaret were still small girls who could not yet be of a great deal of 'hands on' assistance to help Aunt Lucy with cleaning and other tidying up work around the house. Moses was maybe two years older than Praxedes. That left me to combine work in the 'garden' with assistance with cleaning of the house. Fortunately, the house was not a big place. It was a four-roomed house, but the tidying up work in it included kneeling on the concrete floors and scrubbing them, using damp cloths and water.

After that, I applied 'Sunbeam' floor polish to the floors before I gave them a sheen using a brush with hard teeth and dry pieces of cloth. If the product was good, the hard work was satisfying. Uncle Rodrick's and his colleague Mr Made's houses were standard, solid, and well-built government dwellings. But they seemed to be the only properties in that government complex which were not wired with electricity. Yet in the tens of homes belonging to air force personnel less than three hundred yards away, they had electric lighting at night and the housewives in those homes cooked meals for their families using electric stoves; and inside the senior air force personnel 'Mess' utility just by the air force 'married quarters' nearby, it was brightly lit with electric lighting as soon as it got dark in the evenings. I could not understand the logic by the government in denying Uncle Rodrick and his colleague and workmate, Mr Made, a supply of electricity to their family homes.

When night fell, the area where Uncle's and Mr Made's homes were sited was the only one upon which a blanket of darkness descended with the air force camp nearby swathed in a sea of electric lighting. In the absence of electric power in Uncle Rodrick's house, it was therefore my responsibility day in day out, to ensure that some of the logs of wood heaped outside the house had been chopped up into small strips which would fit into the large 'Welcome Dover' firewood stove on which food for the family was cooked and water for bathing was heated.

Within about a week of my arriving at Thornhill Air Base, Grandpa and 'Gogo' packed their bags and left to return to their home somewhere in Matabeleland North. Except my little cousin sister Praxedes who was still too young to have started school, they took their other grandchildren, i.e., Sipho, Moses and Margaret with them. Schools having re-opened for term 1 that year, I would like to believe that my older cousins left together with their grandparents so that they would resume attendance at a school in that part of the world. In another fortnight or so, Aunt Lucy herself was off to join the rest of her family in Nyamandlovu, taking with her youngest daughter, Praxedes. In the few weeks I had lived with her, Aunt Lucy displayed a motherly attitude towards me. I was sure she liked me. I missed her and all her children after they all suddenly seemed to have fizzled into thin air.

With Aunt Lucy gone for what seemed to be forever, that left me – a twelve-year-old boy – with the task of juggling my time between maintaining the work commitments in the field and making sure that the neatness of the house was kept up to scratch besides attending to my schoolwork. Also, Uncle Rodrick needed food to be cooked for him. His clothes, especially his khaki trousers and shirts which he always wore to work, needed to be washed and ironed.

That was a tough call for me but thrown at the deep end, I had no choice but to swim with determination, doing the best that I could under the circumstances. Six months later, Uncle Rodrick maintained a strict and overbearing regime about my working in the field. His eating habits were erratic. Sometimes he ate the food I prepared for him. At others, he just ignored it. I discovered that he ate some of his meals at the Air Force Mess where meals were prepared and served to senior air force personnel, together with refreshments which included alcoholic drinks. He spent most of his evenings at that venue, hobnobbing and rubbing shoulders with his mates among the senior army personnel who lived in the 'married quarters' of the compound. He was not that fussy about the washing and ironing of his laundry, preferring quietly to re-iron some of his clothes if he felt the pressing of his clothes that I had done was a sloppy job. Yes, he was strict, and he demanded absolute compliance with routines, but he was not as harsh as my father. I have no recollection of him giving me a beating, not even one day, for the twelve months I lived with him in Gwelo (Gweru). Of course, he would loudly tell me off if my actions did not meet the standards he expected.

After two p.m. on Saturdays (and on Sundays all day), I was a free agent. Then I was free to roam the air force playing fields and socialise with some of my schoolmates. If on some afternoon there was a rugby game involving 'whites only' teams from either Bulawayo or Salisbury (Harare) in the European section of the air base, the 'white' game organisers were not fussy about my friends, and I could go over to their games venue and watch their team(s) play from the grassy terraces at the edge of the ground. These frequent visits enabled me to begin noticing that the European section of Thornhill Air Base had far better and more advanced facilities than the next-to-nothing or inferior quality facilities on offer at the African side of the air base in terms of sporting facilities, housing for their officers and the privacy they enjoyed.

On some afternoons when playing games in the sports field had exhausted us, my friends and I would wander in the bushes then surrounding the air force base and engage in what I can only describe as naughty youthful escapades. One day as the three of us sat on one of these quiet spots in the bush, one of the boys who was visibly older than the two of us in the group, offered to let us see his penis. Although I objected to this at first, I re-member being impressed by its massive size and the lad's ability to make it grow bigger or smaller, seemingly at will. My other friend and I declined his follow-up invitation later to gaze at his male reproductive organ once more. I have to say the thing was a large and unsightly object, though.

As I grew up at the farm, Father never had time to speak to any of his male children on matters in connection with our reproductive organs, preferring to leave health and welfare issues to Mother or another unknown person. Thus, whenever matters of moment came up for discussion among those in my age group, I noted with dismay that my sexual maturation was lagging way behind. Any persistence by my colleagues in pursuing to discuss sexual matters disgusted or embarrassed me. Caught up in these scenarios, I would often quietly stand up and walk away. That has been the quintessential me to this very day.

Elsewhere, I have vowed never ever in my life to adopt any of my uncle's negative character of miserliness. I had previously showered him with praise when he brought us 'goodies' in the form of toy cars, balloons, and sweets whenever he visited us at the farm in Enkeldoorn. But when I started staying with him and lived with him day in and day out, I discovered that he was peculiarly strict and firm to the point of stinginess about how he spent his money. His miserliness made one want to throw up at the best of times. I could not be quite sure why or where that particular character trait had its source. Often, I suspected it came about due to his meagre earnings which presumably did not allow him sufficient leeway to be generous with his giveaways. For the full twelve months I lived with him in Gwelo (Gweru), there was not a single day he volunteered to part with the loose change anyone could hear jingling in his pocket and kindly give some of it to me when I attended Thornhill School.

One Sunday morning in August 1962, his family, and in-laws, were back for a brief visit at Thornhill. Uncle sent me on his bicycle to a bakery in Gwelo (Gweru) city centre to buy three loaves of freshly baked bread. The bread was to be consumed by the whole family at breakfast that morning, so I had to hurry up and return to Thornhill as soon as possible. We were still using the imperial system in those days and the pricing of some of the items in shops resulted in customers receiving change in loose coins like shillings, pennies, and farthings. A 'farthing' was equivalent to something like a quarter of a cent in today's money in Zimbabwe. It was a very small coin, but it had value. Among the change given to me after purchasing the bread was the small farthing coin.

As luck would have it, the farthing within the change in my pocket must have passed through a small hole in the bottom of my pocket and dropped to the ground while I was riding the bicycle back home to Thornhill. Uncle Rodrick was by no means amused by the loss of the coin. Receiving the rest of the change, he asked me, with his teeth grinding, to leave the bicycle leaned against the wall outside the house, and there and then to walk back to the City of Gwelo (Gweru) – five miles away – along the path I had used and search everywhere on the ground until I recovered the missing coin. I did as per the orders of the 'penny pincher'. I didn't have any luck perhaps because the silly coin might have dropped and been buried in the sand or rolled somewhere in the undergrowth beside the path I used.

It was well after midday when I returned home looking tired and feeling miserable and hungry. Uncle was staunchly unforgiving, even when I apologised profoundly for the accidental loss of that quarter of a penny! I had committed a grave error, according to him, so my punishment would consist in having no food for the whole of the daylight hours of that day until supper later in the evening! Uncle Roderick truly did have money-supply challenges though. Most of the time, there was hardly enough money even to buy firewood that we needed as fuel to cook our food and to heat water for our baths in the outside toilet and shower room.

To cope with that challenge, Uncle Rodrick would regularly drive out of Gwelo (Gweru) late in the darkness of the night with me sitting in the rear passenger seat of his car. He would drive for up to thirty miles along the Gwelo (Gweru) to Umvuma highway. On reaching a certain milestone and noticing huge trees or thick bushes in the glimmering light of the night on the side of the road, he would stop and make a U-turn. Leaving the car parked on the highway and carrying an axe pulled from somewhere in the boot of the vehicle, we trespassed onto farms belonging to Europeans and under cover of darkness fetched logs of firewood which we would carry across the barbed wire fence along the edge of the highway and load them into the boot of the car as well as in one portion of the rear seats.

Loaded with 'free' firewood, obviously pinched from an unsuspecting farm owner's land, Uncle would calmly start the car and drive back to Thornhill. We went to fetch our stolen booty quite a few times during the dry season. One day on our way back to Thornhill from one these adventures, the car suddenly ran out of petrol. We were still twenty miles away from Thornhill. But the nearest petrol station was somewhere towards Guinea Fowl, five miles down the same road we were in. The time was nine thirty p.m. and petrol stations were known to close their tanks for business at ten p.m. To this day, it still boggles the mind how he was such an experienced driver could have dared drive his car up to thirty miles out of Gwelo (Gweru) with the fuel gauge needle on the dashboard steadfastly pointing below 'E', i.e., less than the Reserve Tank!

Here was a tricky situation that we found ourselves in: the car, laden with stolen firewood, was parked off the road along a busy highway because it had run out of fuel. My uncle vowed that there was no way he was going to leave his car parked in the dark by the roadside while both of us went to search for fuel. He therefore decided he would remain sitting in the car for its security while I dashed down the road to get some petrol. Gosh, I thought to myself, with all that darkness around me and walking all by myself? Handing me the jerrycan he had fetched from somewhere under the firewood in the boot of the car, Uncle rummaged in his pocket and produced a coin, the worth of which I could not quite see because it was quite dark. Handing it to me, he said, "You'll have to wake up, Lawrence. I'm not too sure, but the petrol station must be something like five miles away from here. Please go and get us some petrol for the car. Start running down the road now, otherwise you'll find the petrol station closed for the night." Dropping the coin deep in one of the pockets of my shorts, and jerry can in my hand, I raced down the dark left edge of the macadamised road. Sometimes I was guided to stay on course by the flashing headlights of vehicles which 'vroomed' and wheezed past me in both directions.

Nearly an hour later, I reached the petrol station which, thank God, was still open. The petrol attendant expressed surprise when I said I needed petrol for only two shillings! I walked back to the car carrying certainly less than a fifth of the five-litre jerry can's capacity. My route back to the car was mostly darker as my vision was unaided by the absence of other vehicles' beams because traffic had become thinner due to it being late at night. I eventually arrived back at the spot where Uncle waited for my return. After he had put the petrol in the tank, it was not easy getting the engine to start running again. Several of his attempts to start the engine failed dismally. He said the vehicle had developed an 'airlock' due to his having driven it on a nearly empty tank. After several attempts during which the engine coughed and spluttered, it eventually started running smoothly again. We arrived back at Thornhill well past midnight.

Contrary to the negative observations I have conveyed about my uncle, I am still convinced that deep down in his heart of hearts, he was a Christian as well as a committed Roman Catholic for that matter. He certainly had more humane qualities that overrode the picture I have projected about him above. His attendance at church on Sundays was irregular. Yet when he felt like wanting to go to church, he would simply get up, have a bath, dress up and soon he was off to church service at the Roman Catholic Cathedral in Gweru city centre. He always drove his car to church. Waking up on some of those Sundays in a happier frame of mind, Uncle Rodrick sometimes invited me to come with him.

Would you believe it that it was his example of attending church services on Sundays, though irregularly, that subsequently led to my being baptised in the Roman Catholic Church? Although I had attended Maronda Mashanu School – an Anglican Church-run school – from Sub-Standard A (Grade or year 1) to Standard 3 (year or Grade 5), I left the farm to go to Gwelo (Gweru) before

I became a Christian. Both my parents had been converted to Christianity as Methodists before they got married or before they subsequently moved to Maronda Mashanu Native Purchase Lands. There was no Methodist Church anywhere in the Maronda Mashanu area, so they did not attend any of the church services that were held at Maronda Mashanu School every Sunday. Consequently, the model of my parents, or at least one of them, of leaving home to attend church service on a Sunday was missing throughout my entire childhood. Once I started catechism lessons in Gwelo (Gweru) with Uncle Rodrick's encouragement, I no longer waited for him to give me a lift in his car for me to attend Mass on Sundays. I adopted the habit of walking on my own most Sundays from Thornhill Air Base to Gwelo city centre and back after church services, a round trip of roughly some eight kilometres. By August 1962, I had been baptised into the Roman Catholic Church and christened 'Lawrence,' dropping forthwith the name, 'Kingston', that had been given to me at birth. I adopted the Christian name 'Lawrence' by recommendation from Uncle Rodrick.

The one and only Parents and Prize-Giving function at Thornhill African Primary School was held on the first Friday of December in 1962. Schools had just closed for the end of term and Christmas holidays. Uncle Rodrick attended that school function in his capacity as representative of my parents in Enkeldoorn (Chivhu). He was delighted by my end-of-year test results in which I took first position in my Standard 4 (Grade 6) class. Time flies like a bird in flight. With schools closed for the Christmas holidays, the time had arrived for me to travel back to Enkeldoorn (Chivhu) and spend the six-week long school break helping my father at the farm. Uncle Rodrick had stopped me going to Enkeldoorn in the August school holidays of that year citing difficulties finding the bus-fare money for my round trip. I had been away from the farm for eight months. Reports that had been received from the farm said that my father had not been amused by my failure to turn up at the farm during August school holidays as he had wished. Indications were that even for the upcoming Christmas school holidays, Uncle Rodrick was going to find it hard to raise the bus-fare I needed to travel to Enkeldoorn (Chivhu). One morning, over a week after schools had closed for the Christmas holidays, Uncle woke up and cut twenty cabbages from a large crop that I had grown in the large garden at the back of the house.

After pricing them by inscribing the sale price on the base of each cabbage according to his perception of their size and quality, he shoved them all into a large bag. I lifted the heavy bag and placed it in the car. Before I had had a shower or eaten any breakfast, Uncle hurriedly asked me to jump into the car. When I asked if he could give me a chance to tidy up and eat something, he became quite harsh and impatient, asserting there was no time for that sort of thing. While travelling in the car, he informed me that he was taking me and the cabbages to a spot just by the entrance to the African section of Gwelo (Gweru) General Hospital. He was going to leave me at the said spot to sell the cabbages to members of the public leaving to go home after visiting their sick relatives in hospital wards. Arriving at the hospital entrance area which he seemed to have already identified, Uncle located a strategic position by a large tree from where he said the cabbages would attract customers. I emptied the cabbages on the green grass and spread the empty bag on the space available in front of me, displaying the cabbages in neat rows and showing the prices Uncle had marked on each of them. Before he drove away. He emphasised that under no circumstances should I leave them unattended and insisted that all the cabbages must sell so that I could travel to Enkeldoorn (Chivhu) for Christmas. Leaving abruptly, he left me with not even a penny with which to buy food or drinks. By the looks of it, I concluded I was going to starve that day. True to my fears, I spent the whole of that day without eating or drinking anything.

One vendor sitting a little distance from me and selling a mixture of vegetables and root crops helped me with a large cup of plain cold water at about lunchtime. At about three thirty p.m., a huge belt of cumulonimbus clouds suddenly formed, obscuring the sun and darkening the sky above Gweru General Hospital. That abrupt change of weather followed a hot and humid morning with no wind blowing whatsoever to ameliorate the searing heat. Before long, it was as if someone had turned on the rain taps in the sky. The skies opened, and heavy rain started falling, accompanied by flashes of lightning, rolling bouts of thunder, and driving winds that came from a northerly direction. Regarding my merchandise, none of the three-shilling cabbages had sold. Of the one shilling and six pence ones, only two had attracted buyers who walked over to view them. Soon my potential customers left with their hands in the air in exasperation as they left, complaining that my cabbages were too expensive. Before the rain started falling, my sale items remained neatly displayed to attract buyers. Seeing the sudden change in the weather, my counterparts who had a few bundles each of rape, tomatoes and carrots quickly wrapped up their wares in the empty bags on which they had displayed them.

Then as huge drops of rain began falling, my vendor colleagues dashed with their items for cover in the veranda, several yards away by the entrance into the hospital. I would have done the same, but I had twenty cabbages which I could not possibly load into the empty bag within the short time before the downpour started. Besides, I also considered that the bag of cabbages, if I had succeeded in loading it which was unlikely, would simply be too heavy for me to carry with me for cover from the impending storm. Just when I had opted to leave everything behind and dash for cover, a voice at the back of my head reminded me of Uncle Rodrick's stern warning never to leave the cabbages unattended. It was still dry under the big leafy tree although the rate at which rain started falling was rapidly increasing. I quickly sat down feeling confused and frightened, my back firmly against the bottom of the tree trunk. Meanwhile the rainfall intensified. Waves of strong wind began to blow from somewhere behind the hospital buildings overhead. They threatened to lift whole portions of the roofs and hurl them onto the ground. Soon the winds transported with them not raindrops but a thick shower of hailstones which instantly filled all the small galleys and potholes around. I was mercilessly pelted on the head and body by these missiles as the wind howled, hissed, and roared like the hidden scene at a busy airport for the best part of a full hour.

The intermittent lightning flashes which were punctuated by deafening bursts of thunder left me utterly frightened out of my wits and thoroughly confused. As the rain carried on gushing down, I noticed that a brook with a fast-moving current had formed on lower ground just below where I sat. The brook rapidly transformed into a furious stream which soon burst its banks. Some of the filthy water, carrying an assortment of cargo, overflowed to where my cabbages lay. I quickly reached out with both my clammy hands to maintain possession of the cabbages which had prices marked on them. I was not fast enough. Five of the large cabbages were swooped upon by one massive splash of a wave. I watched helplessly as my possessions trundled one behind the other down the corrugated ripples of the fast-flowing stream that would eventually empty its contents into River Gwelo (Gweru) in the small valley below. Little by little, the storm lessened in intensity. It became less intense and stopped completely at four twenty-five p.m. according to the large clock-face on top of the entrance into the general hospital. I was in an utterly hopeless condition.

Thank God, I had survived the eye of the storm, but I was completely drenched, soaked through the clothes I wore right down to my bare bones. Mysteriously though and to my surprise, Uncle Rodrick arrived at the spot he had dumped me earlier in the morning. The tyres of his motor car squelched in the mud as his engine stopped running. I noticed he had company in that car. I wondered who that man was. Looking again more carefully before they both climbed out of the car, I discovered the mysterious passenger travelling in the car with Uncle was my father! I had last seen him eight months previously. His sudden appearance in Gwelo (Gweru) – and his finding me in my predicament then – filled me with more than just surprise, but certainly wonder and foreboding as well.

Fragments of the story told to me later by someone at the house was that father had unexpectedly turned up at Thornhill to the surprise of everybody shortly before the storm; all of which occurred after he had arrived and was safely indoors. He had been lucky not to get caught in that horrible storm. Father had travelled on an unannounced visit from Enkeldoorn (Chivhu) to pay his homage to Uncle Rodrick and his wife Lucy, following the birth of Vincent, my little cousin/brother, a month or so previously. He was heard saying that since his arrival he had seen all of Uncle Rodrick's family at the house and wondered where I was in all the rain that had fallen. Uncle Rodrick was heard to have responded saying he had sent me to do a job somewhere. An hour after the storm had subsided, Uncle Rodrick was reported to have informed his older brother that he was driving to that place to collect me. Father is alleged to have said he did not mind coming in the car with him. Arriving at the spot where Uncle Rodrick had left me in the morning, they found me still sitting down feeling uncomfortable in my wet clothes which still dripped from my recent experience.

The last time I had seen my father was during the April–May school holidays when I travelled to Enkeldoorn (Chivhu). The incident I am describing was in December 1962. Seeing him suddenly arrive in the car, together with his young brother, one would have expected me to spring to my feet, run and greet him excitedly considering I had last seen him around eight months previously. It did not quite happen like that because of the miserable condition I was in. Drawing closer in the car and seeing what state I was in, father immediately expressed shock and dismay at the spectacle he beheld. Without beating about the bush, he complained bitterly and loudly about what he said was Uncle's ill treatment of his child.

Renowned for his short fuse, the quarrel with his young brother was ignited. The two men had to help me to get back on my feet in between heated exchanges between the two blood brothers. After Uncle had collected the remaining sale items and packed the bag in the boot, we all sat in the car and Uncle drove back to Thornhill with both the two men shouting at each other. It was a shouting match. Back home at Thornhill, the quarrelling continued with me the bone of contention. Aunt Lucy had returned to Thornhill from another of her extended absences two months previously to give birth to Vincent. She attempted to remonstrate with both Father and her husband to stop the shouting and the arguing. Uncle Rodrick told her firmly to keep out of the wrangling because the issue they were arguing about was between him and his older brother. Even I felt the urge to hold out the olive branch between the two men, but I held back, feeling that I was too small to place myself between two angry, brawling men. The shouting went on into the night with accusations and counter accusations being traded between them. Their shameless shouting unavoidably woke up the baby who had quietly been asleep in the bedroom next door. I heard the suckling infant bawl out several times to the chagrin of Aunt Lucy. Poor little child, Vincent could not catch any sleep with all that shouting, use of bad language and banging of doors.

In her frantically effeminate intervention, Aunt Lucy had expected her husband to end the point-scoring by simply making a statement that showed remorse for what the older of the contestants believed his young brother had done wrong. Unfortunately, nothing of the sort happened. After ten thirty p.m., Father made a knee-jerk decision. He was not putting up at his young brother's house that night and he was going to leave with me to go and sleep elsewhere. Uncle Rodrick repeatedly pleaded with his older brother to reconsider his decision to leave in the darkness of night as it was against custom and un-African to just to leave without proper farewells. But his pleas fell on deaf ears. Father peremptorily ordered me to hurriedly pack the few belongings I had in a small paper bag. He did not allow me the chance to bid proper and dignified farewells to Uncle Rodrick and Aunt Lucy.

Father and I left Thornhill Air Base and walked in pitch darkness to an address in Senga African Location within Gwelo (Gweru) where we arrived well past midnight. We spent the rest of that night at the home of a Mr Diura who my father knew from

Maronda Mashanu tribal trust lands. We caught a long-distance bus at the main bus terminus in Gwelo (Gweru) – now named Kudzanayi Bus Terminus – early the following morning and we travelled to Enkeldoorn (Chivhu).

In his rushed and ill-judged decision to literally snatch me back from Uncle Rodrick's care, my father failed to think about the wider ramifications, the limitations he had imposed, might have, unwittingly, reduced the chances I had of proceeding with my education in Gwelo (Gweru) in the coming year. In my view, he hurriedly decided to solve a problem by creating another problem; forgetting that Uncle Rodrick, at that time was the lifeblood of our family, without whose support and sustenance, all our educational pursuits would come to a standstill. That single action alone on that fateful night had wide-ranging consequences, the details of which I will reveal in the next chapter.

My stay with Uncle Rodrick for the previous full year, which largely had been successful save for a few welfare pinpricks here and there, had been brought to an abrupt and unceremonious conclusion. It was an end without any agreement regarding the way forward for my education at the beginning of the new school year in 1963. Due to the unresolved tension in the relationship between the two brothers, Uncle Rodrick did not show up at the farm in Enkeldoorn (Chivhu) for Christmas festivities in 1962, which was completely out of habit and character for him. It had never happened for many years I could remember as a child.

# Chapter 11

## My first visit to Salisbury (Harare) ever and the wild goose chase it turned out to be

The first term of the school year in 1963 was commencing in about week, yet I had no indication as to where I was going to attend school for my Standard 5 year (Grade 7).

After Father and I had arrived back in Enkeldoorn from Gwelo on the bus weeks before Christmas, he appeared to be pleased with my work contributions on the farm, but he did not seem interested in talking about my prospects of attending school in Gwelo after his disagreement with Uncle Rodrick. As time was running out, I plucked up enough courage one evening and brought up the subject of my schooling for discussion. From the sentiments he expressed and the fact that Uncle Rodrick had not turned up at the farm for Christmas, it was clear they still had not patched up their differences. He was convinced that I would not be readily welcome if I travelled back to Gwelo (Gweru) without my uncle's permission. In short, he was not too sure what would happen to my schooling when the new term was to start in a few days' time.

Two days later, Father said he had given the matter some thought. He believed that my older brothers Raphael and Roland had by then found employment and had started working in Salisbury (Harare). My older brothers had not been in touch with him since they relocated to Salisbury after completing their education in Gweru at the end of 1961. If they had found employment, he was not sure of the jobs they were employed in or where they lived in that great city. Convinced that my old brothers had begun working somewhere in Salisbury (Harare), he suggested it was my older brothers' turn to take over the task of assisting with the education of their younger brothers and sisters from Uncle Rodrick. Of course, being a rural person himself all his life, he would be unaware of the complications my brothers might encounter in getting me to enrol as a pupil in any of the urban government primary schools. Without any form of communication between Father and my older brothers, he organised some bus-fare money and I was immediately put on the next bus to Salisbury (Harare).

Besides father's fallout with his young brother at the end of 1962, father's own relationship with my mother seemed to have broken down. When I returned to the farm with father from Gweru, I discovered that Mother had packed her bags and moved from the farm and was staying with the family of one of her brothers far away in the Nharira Tribal Trust Lands. In her continued absence, I and my younger brothers Irrigation (Wilfred) and Wonder (Gibson) and my two sisters Shupikai (Lilian) and Winnie (Phyllis – who then was just about two years old) – enjoyed one of the dullest Christmas festivities ever in December 1962.

At the time, I set out to travel to Salisbury (Harare) at the start of 1963, Mother and Father had already had a long separation in which it was rumoured that there was no hope of salvaging their marriage. Nobody could give me the details of what the rift between them was all about. Their fallout had happened during my seven-month absence at school in Gwelo (Gweru). I remembered that exactly a year previously, she had seen me off to Umvuma (Mvuma) by bus at Enkeldoorn (Chivhu) Bus Station. This time around, my younger brother Irrigation (Wilfred), who had grown up physically and become more mature and cleverer, accompanied me to the bus station. I waved him goodbye as the 'Mudiwa Bhiri Bus' left on its long journey to Salisbury. Then it was widely believed to be ninety-seven miles away from Enkeldoorn (Chivhu), using the strip road on the old route from Enkeldoorn (Chivhu) to Salisbury (Harare).

After passing Kerry's farm on the overloaded bus and about three miles thereafter, the road suddenly veered off to the left and followed a route due west and passed by a place called 'Pa Dhirihora', marked off by towering walls of an abandoned and crumbling tobacco barn within a large clump of tall eucalyptus trees. The trees growing wild and uncared for suggested a large commercial farm. It was formerly a residential property presumably once owned by a rich 'white' farmer. He probably had left for an alternative location many years before because the soils at that farm were not giving him the amount of tobacco he had anticipated. The old strip road carried on westwards for approximately twenty miles. Then just before reaching the bluish range of Mhondoro Hills, the road took a sharp turn to the right and followed a northerly stretch for thirty miles and reached a place called 'Featherstone'. The bus did not stop there. It carried on for another forty miles, crossed Umfuli (Mupfure) River bridge and immediately arrived it at 'Beatrice' where it stopped, nearly three hours since it had left Enkeldoorn (Chivhu).

There were a few old shops in front of which the driver parked the bus. Tired-looking passengers disembarked to stretch their legs and to buy refreshments. The bus seemed to stop at Beatrice forever. It was up to two hours later when the driver and his conductor emerged from dirty and tumbling down dwellings hidden behind trees near the bus stop. The pair looked visibly inebriated obviously from drinking alcohol or some toxic substance. The conductor loudly ordered passengers standing on the ground outside the bus to get back on board besides rudely asking passengers who had boarded the bus at that station to pay their fares. His general conduct and negative attitude towards service users were quite rough and disrespectful, making it appear as if they had committed an offence in choosing the bus company for their journey from Enkeldoorn (Chivhu) to Salisbury (Harare). Meanwhile, as the old and rickety 'DAF' engine bus raced towards Salisbury, roughly some thirty miles ahead, it occasionally swayed dangerously sideways, an indication that the driver was not in full control of his vehicle. However, thank God, we safely reached our destination at four p.m. precisely.

This was my first visit ever to Salisbury. 'Harari Musika Bus Station' was the largest I had even seen. The Enkeldoorn (Chivhu) and Umvuma (Mvuma) bus stations that I have already talked about were nothing compared to the station I had reached. At the time our bus arrived, many buses belonging to other bus companies were also arriving and entering the large bus station from their various routes. A few others were leaving. After alighting from the buses, crowds of people crisscrossed each other, seeming to go nowhere. I did not know any one of these people. They were all total strangers who seemed to be in such a hurry. I was not sure if any one of them would have the time to stop and speak with me. Time waits for no man or woman and the sun was about to set shortly; before I knew where I would sleep for the night. When I realised that Father had put me on this journey without precise details regarding my older brothers' physical addresses in that massive place, my heart began beating furiously. In that seething mass of humanity and standing against a tall concrete electricity pole, I felt like an atom lost upon the vast expanse of the cruel sea. However, a little distance away from where I stood, I saw a lone policeman who appeared to be on his beat. He walked slowly and checked around to ensure that order prevailed. I rushed up to him and put him in the picture about my situation. I asked him if he could be of any kind of assistance to me. The police constable politely listened to me as I spoke. Speaking slowly, he made a statement and asked,

"Young boy, we are in a location called Harari now. Do you have any relative or family who lives here whose address you know?"

I hesitated at first before I blurted out, "Yes, Sir."

At that opportune moment, I remembered that when I was searching for something in Mother's hut on the day before I left the farm to go to Salisbury, I inadvertently came across an old letter Aunt Eliver had written to her sister years previously. When Aunt Eliver was unable to visit her sister at the farm, as she often was in later years, she would instead write to her sister. On all her letters, she always wrote House No – as her residential address in Mbare, Harari. As if I was half-guessing my (the then) predicament would come up, I said to myself, 'This piece of paper might become handy in future' and I folded the old letter and slid it into my folded Standard 4 (Grade 6) School Report.

To offer confirmation to the policeman's request, I searched quickly for that old letter in the paper bag I held in my hands.

Finding it, I thrust it into the policeman's hands who calmly nodded after studying it. Handing the letter back to me, he asked me to come with him. We walked to a building some three yards away inside of which were many offices. On entering one of these offices, the policeman explained my predicament to the office attendant after which the police constable left, leaving me with the man. Further details were sought from me about how related I was to Eliver Muguto, and I explained while he jotted the information down on a piece of notepaper. While quietly sitting on a bench outside the office, I was suddenly jolted into life on hearing the details I had provided being announced on the public address system on loudspeakers that, to this day, remain placed on tall steel pylons all over Harari (Mbare):

"Attention please, all residents of Harari, attention! We have a young boy who has arrived here at Harari Musika Bus Terminus on a bus from Enkeldoorn (Chivhu). His name is Kingston Mudyara. He says he has an aunt going by the name Eliver Muguto who lives at No – here in Harari. If those boy's relative is receiving this message, please report to the Salisbury (Harare) Municipal Offices by the main Musika Bus Terminus and collect this boy. I repeat, if Eliver Muguto of No – Harari can hear me, please report to these offices as soon as you can to collect Kingston Mudyara who has travelled from Enkeldoorn (Chivhu). Thank you."

Somebody's attention was certainly captured by the blaring and piercing sound of the reverberating announcements. When the announcement on the public address system was made, Aunt Eliver happened to be at home. She could not have missed the announcement. To Harare residents who are familiar with the sound, the high volume through the loudspeakers is ear-shattering to say the least. Stopping everything she was doing, she hired a taxi and in less than thirty minutes, she arrived and collected me, tears streaming down her face, "Maiwe mwanangu-u Kingi, wauyawoka. Zvino dai pangapasina ivo vanodaidzira ava, waigoita seiko? Zvisineyi, waita rombo rakanaka ndanzwa vachidaidzira kusvika kwako pano. Chipinda mumota tiende kumba, mwanangu." ("Oh, my son Kingi, you're also here in Harari (Mbare) at last. If it were not for these announcements through the hailers, what were you going to do? Anyway, you were lucky I picked up the announcement of your arrival here through the loudspeakers. Get in the taxi now my son and we'll go to the house where I live.") It was about a five-minute drive from Harari (Mbare) Musika Bus Terminus to her home in the 'National' section of the township.

As soon as we reached her home, she prepared a sumptuous hot meal which I ate hungrily because I was starving, having eaten nothing all day. I spent the following three days staying with her at her home while she contacted my older brothers and told them I was in town. Aunt Eliver worked as a Sales Lady at a big department store in the heart of the city. She said it would be easy for her to nip along during one of her lunch breaks to the General Post Office in Kingsway (now Julius Nyerere Way) where both my older brothers were employed in the postal section of the general post office and update them about my arrival besides requesting them to arrange to collect me from her address in Harari (Mbare). That happened almost immediately and within another day or so, my older brother, Roland Kaston, picked me up from Aunt Eliver's residential address.

It soon became apparent that when I turned up in Salisbury in January 1963, my older brother Roland (Kaston) had recently secured employment, having spent most of the previous year as a loafer, looking for a job in Salisbury (Harare). He had completed his Standard 6 (Grade 7) education in Gwelo (Gweru) in 1961. With a mere Standard 6 (Grade 7) qualification, jobs were not easy to come by. The reports went on to say he was unemployed for most of 1962 and only finally got a job in the last few months of that year. Collecting me from Aunt Eliver's home, older brother Roland (Kaston) travelled with me on one of the numerous Salisbury (Harare) United buses to an address, in Old Highfield.

He and older brother Raphael were living together, sharing a rented medium size lounge of a four-bedroomed house. Several other unmarried men rented adjoining rooms as lodgers. The room they rented served as their bedroom, their living room as well as their kitchen all rolled into one. I remember us using one tiny space of that room for cooking. All the cooking utensils were neatly kept in that corner. The house was not wired with electricity, so we used a portable 'primus stove' to cook all our meals or to heat small amounts of water. The 'primus stove' was a funny contraction in which you poured paraffin into a little drum at its bottom. Then you had to pump hard into the drum at the bottom of the primus stove.

Soon you would need the use of a little metal needle (a pricker?) to clear an air passage near the top of the stove where a blue hissing flame appeared to tell you your cooking could now commence. My older brothers had a three-quarter size bed which they shared while I peacefully slept on the cement uncarpeted floor. There was a single door wardrobe. Other than these items, there was no room for anything else. As you can guess, it was already overcrowded with two of my older brothers and myself as a recent addition. We used cold showers to wash our bodies, with the shower room and toilet facilities located together in an outbuilding, ten to fifteen yards from the main building. To provide lighting, we used candles which quickly ran out, so my older brothers kept bundles of them in stock.

With no electricity in the houses as well as along the streets and roads the whole of Highfield became quite dark at night, appropriately earning it the nickname 'Dark City' by its residents. The schools re-opened for Term I in January 1963. Brother Roland took several 'days off' to assist me get enrolled as a Standard 5 pupil in one of the government primary schools in Highfield nearer where I lived with my brothers. However, all our repeated visits to Mbizi School, Chengu School and Kuwangira School came up against the same snag: I needed to produce a document called a 'D7' which would confirm that I was a child of parents who had a property registered under the African Services Department which dealt with the welfare and registration of 'natives' in Salisbury (Harare) Municipality.

On production of the document and with my name appearing in the list of children of the named parents, I was swiftly be enrolled as a bona fide pupil and immediately started lessons. I did not bother visiting Tsungayi School, Mutasa School or Nyandoro School as these schools were too far from Old Highfield where I lived with my brothers. However, I recall making repeat visits and spending whole days with hordes of other home seekers sprawled on the lawns in front of the reception offices of Chengu School and Kuwangira School hoping that the heads of these schools would respond to our plight. My hope was that the headmasters might feel pity on me and admit me despite the rules. The headmaster at Kuwangira School then nearly yielded to my request to be admitted in a Standard 5 class at his school when I showed him my colourful Standard 4 report with floods of tears streaming down my cheeks. However, in the end, he admitted that it was not him refusing to admit me but that his hands were tied due to the rules from the Department of Native Education at Ambassador House in the city centre! Handing me back my Standard 4 end-of-year school report, he said if there was a different way of doing things, he might have given me a place at the school that I desperately needed, "As it is, there's very little I can do to help you, young boy. You see, all of us must follow the rules which require us to admit in our schools only those seeking places with the required documents."

Having lost all hope of ever finding a school to continue with my education in Highfield Township, I, as a twelve-year-old boy walked out of his office feeling utterly depressed. I nearly decided to go to the nearby Mukuvisi River, look for a deep pool and drown myself in it. Meanwhile, time was moving on and lessons in classes were being taught in earnest without me. Walking aimlessly past some of the classroom blocks during lesson time, I could hear teachers teaching and peals of laughter from happy children in classrooms who seemed to be enjoying their lessons. The intensity of my frustration increased, reaching a point towards the end of February of that year when I stopped visits to Mbizi, Chengu or Kuwangira Schools altogether because all my efforts to find a place for the Standard 5 (year 7) had proven fruitless. My brothers would spend all day at work while I spent all day in their rented room wallowing in self-pity, engulfed by a stifling feeling that the unfortunate event in Gwelo (Gweru) at the end of the year before might have doomed my blossoming educational career.

It was utterly boring for an adolescent like me to spend all day twiddling my thumbs, surrounded by a vacuum while nearly all my agemates in surrounding homes went to school. Refusing to continue facing the wall of frustration and bitterness that faced me, I requested my brother Roland to arrange some bus-fare money so that I could travel back to Enkeldoorn (Chivhu) with a view of reviving my fortunes by getting my father to normalise his relationship with Uncle Rodrick. It was my last hope that if that happened, I would be able to claim back my Standard 5 place at Thornhill African Primary School in Gwelo. I strongly believed that a place was still available for me. As matters became clearer later, the hope I had of returning to Thornhill African Primary School for my Standard 5 (Grade 7) turned out to be false. Leaving Salisbury (Harare) a disappointed and frustrated boy, I returned to Enkeldoorn (Chivhu) at the beginning of March 1963.

Without going into details, Father informed me that that Uncle Rodrick had contacted him when I was in Salisbury (Harare). Better still, my uncle resumed his visits to the farm at Easter of that year. He found me a very unhappy young person because I was not able to go to school, spending most of the time twiddling my fingers, unsure of what the future held in store for me. For the first time in a very long time, I heard my father speak with a touch of compassion, "I am sorry Kingi" (he insisted on calling me 'Kingi'). Although that name had been dropped when I was baptised in the Catholic Church and adopted 'Lawrence' as my new Christian name seven months previously. That was when I began to understand that it is hard to teach an old dog new tricks. It became clear that he understood that the quarrel between him and his brother had led to the misfortune of my being kept out of school. At the same time, having never lived in Salisbury

232

(Harare), he could not understand why I could not find a place to continue with my education in Salisbury (Harare); until I explained the challenges I had encountered in finding a place to do my Standard 5 (Grade 7) and he then understood what I was up against. Uncle Rodrick, as before, came over to the farm in Enkeldoorn (Chivhu) for Easter celebrations that year.

On being updated about my predicament, he blamed my older brothers in Harare for not doing enough to get me into a school in Salisbury (Harare) so I could continue with my education. Of course, he did not have enough patience to understand what went on regarding my admission into government schools in African townships. As far as he was concerned, I had lost valuable learning time already, due to no fault of my own. After a thorough review of the disruption caused to my education and an exchange of apologies between him and his older brother, Uncle Rodrick finally agreed that I should return to Gwelo (Gweru) the following May and "I'll do my best, Lawrence, to help you get back into school. However, I cannot guarantee that you will get a place at the school in the group you started in is still available."

He went on to let me know that the school my cohort had started at the Air Force base no longer existed in the same space we had left it at the end of the previous year. Nobody explained to me what had transpired, which led to my former school being moved to a different site and changing its name completely. I remembered that we existed in the military compound as a school on the strength of an experiment. A few weeks before we broke off for the Christmas vacation in 1962, the Governor-General of the Federation of Rhodesia and Nyasaland, a Lord Dalhousie, had been on a tour of the whole of Thornhill Airbase complex, including the African Compound the old and vacated barracks which we had used as classrooms for the whole of 1962. The special guest was accompanied on that tour by a high-powered delegation of senior education officials from the Department of Native Education. In the same delegation was also a coterie of very senior army officers. All the senior officials in the said delegation were Europeans. The pilot scheme to allow a school for black pupils to operate in a 'whites only' area was probably declared not fit for purpose; hence the immediate changes that occurred without any clarification being given. Irrigation (Wilfred) and Last (Bernard), who had replaced me at Thornhill for their Standard 4 (Grade 6) at the beginning of 1963, were attending the same school, but it had been moved with a new name and was then operating under new management at a different site near 'Guinea Fowl,' approximately three miles away farther east of Thornhill!

Uncle Rodrick either had or did not have the full details regarding what had happened to my old school. Instead, he was reticent and would not immediately disclose to me where I would attend my Standard 5 (year 7) when I returned to Gwelo (Gweru), together with Wilfred and Bernard in May 1963. Wondering what the immediate future held in store for me, I was like a festering wound, anxious and deeply worried about the uncertainties of my situation.

# Chapter 12

# Standard 5 (year 7) at Dhonga farm 'boarding' school

I arrived back in Gwelo (Gweru) in May 1963, together with my young brother Irrigation (Wilfred) and nephew Last (Bernard) whose turn it was to attend Standard 4 (Grade 6), while staying with Uncle Rodrick at Thornhill. In truth, when I travelled with the two boys on that journey, they were returning to Gwelo (Gweru) for the re-opening of schools in term two after spending their April-May school holidays at the farm in Enkeldoorn (Chivhu). The reception Uncle Rodrick gave me was very cold. He was aware of the date when I and the boys were arriving, but he did not await our arrival and pick me us up by car from Guinea Fowl train station. Anyway, all of us knew where home was at Thornhill, so we found our way to the house on foot. Fortunately for me, I was travelling light. The few shreds of clothing I had were in an old but clean 'Compound D' fertiliser bag. Arriving at the house just after sunset, the place was deserted, locked up and in darkness. His wife and children were not at home. I suspected they were away in Nyamandlovu as usual. We could not tell where Uncle was, although I guessed he might be meeting his mates and having some drinks at the local 'Mess.' The 'Mess' was only about three hundred yards from where we stood but we resolved not to go looking for him. I was aware he did not like people from the house or visitors popping in at the 'Mess' enquiring after him.

He hobbled back home drunk, well after ten p.m. and expressed no regrets whatsoever at finding the two boys and myself sitting on an old creaky wooden bench in the darkness of the veranda. Opening the main entrance door, he let us in without talking to us. Uncle went straight to bed and left us to sort our bedding out. We were all familiar with the geography of that house, so it did not bother me, nor the two little boys. We had no worries about food either because earlier that afternoon, we had eaten a substantial hot meal in a cheap restaurant at Umvuma (Mvuma) while waiting to connect with the steam train from Fort Victoria. (Masvingo).

The following morning, Uncle Rodrick woke up at four thirty a.m. That was not an unusual hour for him to wake up. His duties at Thornhill Airforce Base commenced early so that by eight a.m., he would have completed all the weather checks and submitted his reports about the weather conditions in Gwelo (Gweru) on a big machine called a 'teleprinter.' That machine, he said, would convey his reports to a place somewhere in Salisbury (Harare) for database capture and statistical analysis by between seven a.m. and nine a.m. Before Uncle left home, he banged on the metal door of the spare bedroom where Bernard, Wilfred and I were sleeping. He shouted orders for us to wake up straightaway and start doing some work in the big vegetable garden behind the house. We woke up promptly and started carrying out work in the large field at the back of the house Uncle had assigned to us. He returned home on his bicycle at or around nine thirty a.m. and found all of us at work in the large field. He walked up to the spot I was working.

Before I could even exchange morning greetings with him, he harshly told me to stop the work I was doing and, in ten minutes, be ready to leave and come with him in the car to the bus station. You see, there had been no chance for us to talk since the boys and I arrived on the day before. I became anxious and worried that he would probably sending me back to Enkeldoorn (Chivhu). He said very little, and I couldn't be sure of anything. His whole conduct towards me since I had arrived back in Gwelo (Gweru) remained an enigma. So, I started to pack the shreds of my mostly ragged clothes in the old 'Compound D' fertiliser bag as if it was an emergency evacuation. Without being given as much as a chance to wash off the red soil on my hands and feet and a chance to eat something solid, I was bundled into the back-passenger seat of the car where I sat with my old fertiliser bag beside me. Since the incident at Umvuma (Mvuma) Bus Station the year before when the old suitcase I had accidentally ripped up when the bus conductor was handing it to me, that suitcase had never been replaced. Getting older brother Roland to buy me another suitcase when I spent two months with him in Salisbury (Harare) was simply too big as he was apparently struggling to make ends meet.

Mother was no longer with father at the farm and my older brother Roland Kaston was literally struggling in Salisbury (Harare) because his earnings were so low. Nobody could afford to buy me another suitcase. It gave me a terrible feeling travelling around with the few items of clothing I called mine stuffed in an old fertiliser bag.

Uncle Rodrick drove his car to Gwelo (Gweru) Bus Station without saying a word to me. On reaching our destination where there were a few buses, he stopped the car with a screeching of brakes. The rubbery smell of burning tyres as they ground into the tarmac filled the car interior. I almost bumped my head against the passenger seat in front of me as the car stopped with a jolt. After he impatiently turned off the car engine, he flung open the driver's door and jumped out of his seat first. Then he went round the back of the car and suddenly flung open the rear passenger door on the near side where I sat. He virtually shouted, speaking very quickly, "There's a bus that stops here. I can't remember the bus service's name. You will have to ask from others waiting for the same bus here. When it arrives, I don't know what time it arrives, board that bus and it will take you to a place called 'Donga' in Selukwe (Shurugwi). It's a farm board- ing school. That's where you're going to attend your Standard 5 as well as Standard 6. Now, get out of the car please, Lawrence, and hurry up because I want to rush back to work!"

Although Uncle had said something about my attending school somewhere, I could not squeeze any thrill or excitement out of it perhaps due to the low spirits and the generally unimpressive condition I was in. I miserably eased myself out of his vehicle clutching my small old fertiliser bag. Mind you, I had not been allowed any time to clean up, bid the other fellows in the garden goodbye, or eat or drink anything before I left Thornhill. I therefore appeared in seriously bad shape, to say the least. My uncle hurried back into his car, slammed shut the driver's door shut and promptly started the engine. Uncle was going to drive off without as much a chance to bid me 'Bon voyage' when I called out to him hysterically, using the little energy I could muster although I had left home without eating anything, not even a little breakfast, "Uncle! Uncle, Pleeease! Ple-ase! I-I- um, I don't have any bus-fare money! I don't even know what it costs to reach this school you mentioned. And what about the payment of school fees? Father at the farm gave me no money!"

With his engine still running, he flung open his car door again and standing beside that door, he shoved his right hand into the right pocket of his trousers. Upon retrieving his hand which clutched some coins, he opened his palm and seeming to count with two fingers of his left hand, he suddenly tossed several of the loose coins to the spot where I stood saying, "There's your bus-fare! In future, ask your brothers in Salisbury (Harare) to give you bus-fare money. About fees, I don't know about that. Write to your brothers Roland and Misheck in Salisbury (Harare) when you reach Donga School and ask them to send you the fees the school will require!" Then he jumped back into the car, banged shut the driver's door and departed with the rear left tyres of his car screeching loudly on the tarmac before the car picked up speed and disappeared behind the buildings. The coins he had thrown at me had hit the ground and rolled off, scattering in different directions, leaving me the big job to pitifully round them up. Two innocent bystanders who witnessed the incident of my being dumped at the bus station helped me to pick up the coins. On counting the coins together with me, we discovered Uncle had only left three shillings and a tickey (roughly thirty-two cents) yet the bus-fare to the said school was three shillings and sixpence (approximately thirty-five cents). Besides leaving me with insufficient bus-fare, he had also not bothered to leave me even a small allowance as 'pocket money' for food. "My goodness me, what am I going to do?" So, I conversed with my inner self, thoroughly at a loss. Look, I was only twelve years old at the time, but I began to feel I was being persecuted for an offence or offences I was unaware of. A total stranger, a boy slightly older than me, Enos Mhlanga was the name of the boy he later told me, was one of the bystanders who helped me pick up the loose coins Uncle Rodrick had tossed at me. He introduced himself to me in IsiNdebele dialect because he was from somewhere in Matabeleland and he was going to the same school that I wanted to reach. My full year in Gwelo (Gweru) had armed me with a smattering of that language. Looking visibly concerned worried about the scene he had witnessed, he asked, "Who's he to you, the man who just dropped you here?" I replied politely without showing a readiness to reveal too many of my family details to a person I had just met, "He's my uncle, my father's young brother." Then he went on, "But you're closely related. If he's family like you have said, why does he treat one of his own so unkindly, so roughly?"

Keeping most of the thoughts to myself and avoiding saying too much to a person I did not know well about, Enos Mhlanga voluntarily offered to pay for my bus-fare to 'Dhonga School'. The bus was due to arrive at the station in another hour, so he invited me to come with him into one of several cheap restaurants facing the bus station. He bought me six large freshly baked buns and a cold bottle of 'Fanta' and asked me to sit on one of the four chairs around a table in the restaurant and eat the food he had bought. As I ate the food, Enos Mhlanga provided me more information about 'Dhonga' School telling me the school where my uncle was sending me was not a 'school' in the proper sense of the schools he and I knew. 'Dhonga' was a type of 'boarding' school where I was going to pay for both my school and boarding fees by working as a labourer in the mainly tobacco fields of a large commercial farm from seven a.m. until twelve p.m. and attend school from one p.m. until six p.m. Enos was not too sure about the teaching qualifications the headteacher held. As far as he knew, having already spent the whole of the previous first term at the school, all the teachers on the staff had not received any training as teachers!

Reader, I will spare you the bulk of the gory details of my experiences at 'Donga School' where I spent seven months of child labour and unadulterated educational abuse, cut away from all links with my family and the civilised world. The last time I saw and heard of Uncle Rodrick that year was in the incident that I have described of him dropping me off at Gwelo (Gweru) Bus Station. My older brother Roland could not get in touch with me because no one had furnished him with information about my whereabouts after I left Salisbury (Harare) at the end of February that year. There was hardly any communication, whether by letter or telephone, between Uncle Rodrick and my older brothers since they had moved to Salisbury at the end of 1961.

In short, 'Donga' was the most difficult and the worst school that I ever attended. In retrospect, I wonder whether the 'white man' farm owner of the 'school', a Mr John Plagis, had authority from the Department for Native Education for the school to operate the way it did. Or he was running that school privately, making use of child labourers like me and other pupils, over two hundred of us, to supplement his manpower requirements at his large commercial farm and thereby lining his pockets. I would not be surprised if we were victims of child abuse that went on quietly on many white-owned large commercial farms. Some of these farmers had connections with people in high places in the colonial government at the time, so they had plenty of protection against prosecution. The new low that I reached while at 'Dhonga School' was like a dark cloud which passes overhead blocking the sun. It made me persevere more in the hope that sooner rather than later, the sun would come out again after the cloud had passed.

In September of 1963, I wrote a letter to my older brother, Roland, in Salisbury (Harare). Somehow, I had retained his work address since leaving Salisbury (Harare) in February of that same year. In that letter, I described the difficulties of life I had faced since I had arrived back in Gwelo (Gweru) the previous May. I provided him details of the hard conditions of my schooling as a child labourer at a big tobacco farm owned by a European farmer. I requested if he could kindly buy me the things I needed most: a suitcase, a blanket, a pair of black shoes a black pair of trousers and a white short sleeved shirt. I had a hunch this was a bit too long a list for a man whom I knew earned around thirteen pounds per month. But I said, if he could afford it, I would appreciate very much if he could also send me a bit of whatever he could afford in the way of cash. There was no response to the letter I had sent to my brother Roland for the next three months. I began to fear that perhaps he had changed jobs or that my letter may have got lost. One very hot afternoon, two weeks before the end of that third term, the headteacher popped into our classroom. He announced I had a parcel awaiting collection at the Farm Shop! Me? Of all people me to receive a parcel sent through registered mail system. It could not be true. Nothing of the sort had ever happened to me before. It seemed hardly unlikely. This would be my first time to receive anything registered through the post office in Selukwe (Shurugwi) from anybody outside of this dump called 'Dhonga School'! Dashing to the little shop just after we had returned from work in the tobacco fields on the next day, I discovered to my greatest joy the parcel received by post had come from my older brother, Roland. So, the letter that I assumed had been misplaced in the post or got lost had reached him.

Checking the contents of the parcel and reading the letter he had enclosed with it; I noticed my brother responded to all my requests. Also enclosed was a tidy sum of two pounds ten shillings in a sealed envelope that contained his covering letter. The amount of money brother Roland had sent me was quite a large sum of money in those days. As the school term was breaking for the Christmas holidays in a matter of a few weeks, my brother asked me to reserve some of the money he had sent to cover my bus-fare from Selukwe (Shurugwi) to Gwelo (Gweru). Asking me to rule out going back directly to Enkeldoorn (Chivhu) when schools closed for the Christmas holidays, he suggested the remainder of the money should go towards the fare on the overnight train journey from Gwelo (Gweru) to Salisbury (Harare). My brother said he had made further enquiries during the year and that, contrary to what had happened at the start of that year, there were other opportunities that could be utilised for me to complete my primary school education in Salisbury (Harare) and not at 'Dhonga School'.

When I finished reading my brother's letter, I felt elated. I was completely overwhelmed with happiness. Tears of joy flowed down my cheeks. Instead of stopping by at the farm in Enkeldoorn after schools were shut for the Christmas holidays in 1963, my brother had sent me enough money to travel straight to Salisbury from Donga Farm Boarding School. My brother had instructed that I spend the festive season of Christmas that year with him in Salisbury. I travelled from the school together with other 'boarder' pupils on the bus to Gwelo (Gweru).

Since Uncle Rodrick had literally dumped me at the bus station in Gwelo (Gweru) eight months previously so that I could board a bus to Dhonga Farm School, I had had no contact with him. He even had even ignored a letter I had sent to him in July of that year asking him politely if he could kindly send me bus-fare money so that I would either report to Thornhill, Gwelo or go to the farm in Enkeldoorn (Chivhu) for the three-week August-September school holidays. If my relationship with Uncle Rodrick then had been still warm and amicable, it is certainly true I would have dropped in at Thornhill to say 'hullo' to him and his family if they were about. I had the whole afternoon to spare. Instead, I aimlessly wandered around Gwelo (Gweru) Railway Station for the whole afternoon and early evening, waiting for the passenger steam train from Bulawayo which would only arrive later that evening to stop and pick up passengers on its journey to Salisbury (Harare). Sitting on a wooden bench at the train station as I waited for the train early that evening, many thoughts flitted through my mind. I reflected on my progress through life thus far and I came up with a mixture of observations. From childhood, my parents had brought me up in the best way they knew, my father as a hard and strict disciplinarian and my mother with her loving and tender care. They had done what they could against the narrow and stifling deprivations of a thirsting environment. Then came the likes of Uncle Rodrick and Aunt Eliver whose frequent appearances at the farm as I grew up, bringing with them an array of presents for us all, food and sweets; goodies that thrilled us beyond belief and filled us with so much joy, a feeling of great enthusiasm and expectation. Their much-awaited visits showed us that our deprived circumstances at the farm were not cast in stone and that there was a better life somewhere; that, like everybody else who did not necessarily need to be rich or have a lot of money, we could also enjoy the comforts and conveniences that life could offer.

In my restricted view as an adolescent, Uncle Rodrick may have behaved funnily towards me at the end of 1962, but without that man, who I really liked with a certain passion, I would have remained forever condemned in the dull and suffocating obscurity of the farm, unable to proceed beyond the level of Standard 3 (Grade 5) education which I had acquired at Maronda Mashanu School at Enkeldoorn (Chivhu) two years previously. My short-lived apprenticeship under Uncle Rodrick in Gwelo (Gweru) had been a rare stroke of luck and escape route for which I shall remain eternally grateful. Then came the God-sent young boy, Enos Mhlanga, who had come into my life at the then Gwelo (Gweru) Bus Station like a bolt from the blue. I understand that the bus station in Gweru central business district has now been renamed 'Kudzanayi Bus Station'. If that boy, Enos Mhlanga, who I had never met before and was therefore a total stranger to me, had not been present when Uncle Rodrick literally dumped me at the bus station on that fateful day, I bet you, only heaven knows whether my journey to 'Donga Farm School' and my general welfare at that 'school' for the following eight months would have been like. Last but not the least to filter into my mind was my own blood brother, Roland Kaston. I was travelling to Salisbury (Harare) from Selukwe (Shurugwi) at his expense. Knowing how measly his monthly earnings were, the hapless man probably sacrificed the whole of his salary to buy me a full kit of clothes, a blanket, and a suitcase that I desperately needed to replace the old fertiliser bag that I used to keep and carry the bits of my personal belongings around in. By moving me back to Salisbury (Harare), my brother had, with one huge feat, saved me the ravages and corrosion that resulted from deliberate actions of child abuse and slave labour that were being perpetrated by the 'white' farm owner of 'Donga Farm Boarding School'. I vowed I would always remember my brother's kindness.

I was roused back into consciousness by the steam engine which chugged into the train station on its arrival just half an hour before midnight. Then I connected with that night passenger train travelling from Bulawayo to Salisbury (Harare). The train departed from Gwelo (Gweru) Train Station just after midnight, travelled the whole of that morning and reached Salisbury (Harare) Train Station at sunrise, just before seven a.m. My brother was waiting to collect me at the railway station.

# Chapter 13

# My teenage years in Harari (Mbare) Township

I was in my early teenage years in the mid-1960s when I arrived on my maiden visit to the City of Salisbury (Harare). The purpose was for me receive a reasonably well-rounded education while I lived with my older brothers Roland and Raphael before I subsequently escaped into the world of work. As I explained in the previous chapter, I lived with them briefly in Highfield in 1963. Then I had to leave and return to Enkeldoorn (Chivhu) because I could not be enrolled for part of my primary school education at Highfield government schools that I had hoped to receive. Then, following a tumultuous nine-month absence at Donga Farm Boarding School in the Selukwe (Shurugwi) European commercial farming areas, I returned to Salisbury at the beginning of 1964. If you have followed the thread of my story, please call to mind my experiences and some of my childhood observations as a 'ball boy' at Enkeldoorn (Chivhu) Tennis Club at the tail end of the 1950s. The sensibilities that were imprinted on my young and vulnerable mind then were replicated, first when I lived with Uncle Rodrick in Gwelo (Gweru) in 1962. Then a bolder picture of the same bolted into my face when my brothers took turns to take me on familiarisation tours of the Salisbury (Harare) metropolitan area. Those familiarisation tours were an eye-opener.

Over thirty years after the enactment of the nasty Land Apportionment Act in Rhodesia, racial discrimination was discernible and clearly visible everywhere my brothers took me to within Salisbury. There were several places, shops and restaurants within the city centre Africans were denied entry, even during broad daylight. All Africans lived in townships dotted around Salisbury. Deprived of most of the comforts of life, they lived in absolute penury while their European counterparts, who lived in the leafy European 'suburbs' in the city, enjoyed comparatively better-quality lifestyles. To my mind, the townships of Harari (Mbare) and Highfield, where I had the opportunity to live in the 1960s, were to Salisbury (Harare) as Soweto was to Johannesburg during the apartheid era in South Africa.

They were 'dormitories', if I may put it that way, where the black men and women who worked in the Salisbury Central Business District as shop assistants, street sweepers, messengers, cleaners et cetera, making the 'Sunshine City of Salisbury' always look prosperous and sleek, slept and were supposed to spend their non-working part of their waking hours. None of the people of African heritage were allowed to seek entertainment in bars, cinemas, restaurants or theatres in Salisbury's (Harare) central business district. In line with the racial discrimination laws in place, town areas in and around the city centre had been demarcated or set apart for use exclusively for Europeans, a southern African term for whites or people of Caucasian origin. Services and facilities were completely segregated along lines of race or ethnicity.

My motive for coming to Salisbury (Harare) was to attend school, but I could only find enrolment places in the few government schools that had been built in the African townships and not anywhere in the 'white' areas in town. Indeed, until Zimbabwe gained independence in 1980, implementation of these restrictive laws had been tightened by law enforcement agencies to include curfews which were thrown over towns and city centres all over Rhodesia that prohibited the presence of Africans in such places daily between the hours of seven p.m. and seven a.m. the following morning. The curfew by-laws literally ordered that all Africans in or near any city or town centre should pack their few belongings at the prescribed times and return to their homes in the black townships. Curfew law breakers were summarily arrested, fined or sent to jail. Period. A certain Mr Mussett who was a Minister of Internal Affairs in the Rhodesian government of that time was quoted to have said in an interview, "The townships (southern African term for black ghettos) are in European

246

lands designated for African use. They are there to service the European economy."

I have given Harari (Mbare) and Highfield as examples of townships that sprouted all over Rhodesia (Zimbabwe) arising from the black rural-to-urban migration that began in the 1930s. With some of the self-same four-roomed housing structures still standing for more than forty years, especially the earlier ones built in Harari Township, most of these structures looked like tumbledown shacks, decrepit, unimpressive to look at and extremely crowded together. Whatever planning was done before building them left a great deal to be desired. How does one construct a structure for human habitation without running water in the kitchen, with toilet and shower facilities placed in an outbuilding several yards away at the back of the house? Highfield Township had no street lighting whatsoever and those four-roomed structures were not wired with electricity. Hence it was popularly known as 'The Dark City' because of the innumerable crimes that took place in this township in the darkness of night.

Prowling in these townships of Harari or Highfield with my agemates for lack of funds to gain entry at entertainment venues, which happened most of the time, I concluded that townships were all that Salisbury was not. Our townships were simply bursting at the seams due to the high density of the ramshackle structures that were built and the large number of people who were packed into those places. The winding streets were teeming with noisy people of all ages both during the day and at night. Pacing up and down the dusty untarred streets of the 'National' section of Harari (Mbare) – either to visit a playmate in another section of the township or simply prowling in the streets for the sake of it – it was possible to listen to the entire sixty minute 'Top of the Pops' radio programme that was broadcast from Harari Studios of the Zimbabwe Broadcasting Corporation at full blast on those radio and record player combinations from each house as you walked in the streets. You could almost lean on the noise. It was as if the noise from those radios played the role of driving out the angst and frustration from within their midst.

The dirty streets swarmed with children and teenagers like me (then) with nowhere to go and no facilities to occupy us meaningfully. That was why there were so many reports of teenagers and even little children falling victim to cases of substance abuse, among other crimes. It was against the string of stories of children dropping out of school that reached my elder brother Roland and the fact that his low earnings placed him in the category of the population who were below the poverty datum line that he would become more protective of me saying, "Lawrence, we cannot continue suffering like this. I want you to obtain a better education than myself. When you complete your studies, you will get a job that will pay you well. Then we can buy a house in a nice area where you and I can live more comfortably."

My older brother would do everything to protect me from the urban toxicity of our environment. Yet in September of each year in Rhodesia (Zimbabwe), after the frosty weather in June and July when new life seems to begin, the purple Jacaranda and the bright flame trees of the spacious Salisbury (Harare) Gardens seemed much further removed than just the few miles that separated town from townships. On the contrary, though, there were sections, as in any ghetto, where those Africans who had succeeded in climbing the ladder of success against heavy odds lived. Such places in Harari (Mbare) included the 'John Briggs' Cottages/ Flats and the Beatrice Cottages. In Highfield such places included the 'Six Pounds Houses' area and the New Stands behind Old Highfield Clinic. Just outside Mufakose Township was the middle density area of Marimba Park. These were the seemingly pleasant places strategically showcased along main roads to hide the grinding poverty pervading the tumbling down shacks behind them. Rhodesian officials in the Tourism Ministry were known to take the odd foreign visitor to view them pointing out lamely how successful and happy Africans were in white-ruled Rhodesia. But such places were representative only of these isolated parts of the townships and nothing more.

On my return to Salisbury (Harare) at the beginning of 1964, brother Roland's status as an unmarried 'lodger' at a house or houses in African townships in Salisbury (Harare) was still unchanged from what it had been the year before. Of course, the only visible change that had occurred was that towards the end of 1963, he had moved from Highfield Township to Harari (Mbare) Township. Upon my arrival back in Salisbury, brother Roland was one of three unmarried 'lodgers' renting a small kitchen at 52 Peter Start Drive in the 'National' section of Harari (Mbare) Township. The municipal dwelling was an ordinary two- bedroomed core house. It had a medium size lounge and a small kitchen. The registered owner, a kindly pensioner who earned his living by driving cars for a private taxi company to supplement his small pension, occupied the master bedroom together with his cigarette-smoking, middle-aged South African wife and a small child. He also used that same dwelling as his kitchen. His son, a young bachelor who was looking for employment after completing his advanced level examinations at Bernard Muzeki College, occupied the one and only spare bedroom in the main house. The lounge was largely shared between the house owner and his family. At weekends, especially on either Saturday or Sunday afternoons when the house owner was off duty and wanted to have a bit of entertainment in the house, he brought a few bottles of alcohol into the house. He had an old radio/record player combination, the type that dropped one vinyl record from a pile on top at a time, which he kept in his bedroom. Then bringing out this musical piece of equipment, he converted the lounge into a dancehall or an impromptu performance space where loud music was churned out repeatedly from old, scratched seven-inch vinyl records and he danced a sort of jive routine with his wife. On a good day, they all got along with each other like a big happy family. On a bad afternoon when alcohol took hold of both partners, they snapped and snarled at each other like a pack of mongrel female dogs in a slum alley.

Then there was Enock Chiwandire. He came from the main Chiwandire Village in the 'reserves' area behind Dzvova Villages. Enock Chiwandire had been a home-mate and colleague of my older brothers Roland and Raphael while they had grown up and attended school together at Maronda Mashanu School before they went their separate ways but regrouped again as workers in Salisbury. The house owner had allowed them to rent the real 'kitchen' in the house together as a trio. Small as that room was, a three-quarter bed and a two-door wardrobe had fitted neatly in it, leaving absolutely no room for much else. Those of us condemned to do other work in that kitchen used a tiny dark space in one corner of the room to prepare meals. The threat of a fire outbreak from cooking meals under these squashed conditions was palpable. After doing the dishes at the end of meals, I would be telling a lie if I said the cooking utensils were neatly put away, as they were literally piled up in an empty old crate in the only free space that was available, if any, under the three-quarter bed. The entire household shared the toilet/shower room, which was a small outbuilding outside, attached to the main house. Talking of over crowdedness, a headcount of the household, when everybody was in residence, showed eight human beings living in that house. I became aware that there was a general shortage of rental accommodation in Harari (Mbare) Township. But how three of my 'brothers' were given the green light to share one tiny kitchen as 'lodgers' with all their personal belongings was beyond my comprehension. Even before I arrived on the scene to stay with my brother, the three of them in the kitchen were already packed like sardines. With my addition to the number of occupants in the kitchen, sleeping arrangements presented their own complications. To get around that challenge, my brother Roland and stepbrother Raphael shared the three-quarter bed in the kitchen. The owner of the house granted me the privilege to sleep on the cemented floor space somewhere in one corner of the lounge. The nature of Enock Chiwandire's work duties really helped to ease the complication that might have arisen if he, the third lodger, had spent his nights under the same roof with all of us. Enock worked permanently 'nights only' as a waiter/night porter at the plush upmarket Meikles Hotel in the city centre of Salisbury (Harare). His duties started promptly at seven o'clock in the evening and ended at seven o'clock sharp on the following day.

When Enock Chiwandire returned home in the mornings, still smart and well turned out in his grey suit, white shirt and tie despite the exigencies of his all night 'shift' as a waiter/night porter in a busy five-star hotel, he often found me still at the house, preparing to leave for school in another half hour or so. Both Roland and Raphael would have long left home long before at the crack of dawn by bus to report on time at their 'Postman' jobs at the General Post Office in Salisbury (Harare) city centre. Due to their lowly salaries which were just adequate to enable them to pay their rent and do nothing else, hunger and starvation reigned supreme in our 'room' most of the time.

Enock Chiwandire may have been just a lowly paid waiter/ night porter, but whenever he returned home and discovered that I was preparing to leave for school having eaten no breakfast because my brothers had left me no money with which to buy tea things, he would dip into his trouser pockets that jingled with an assortment of coins. This was 'tips' money generously given him by the rich European guests who patronised the expensive hotel he worked at. He would give me a handful of the numerous spare coins jingling in his pockets without a care in the world saying, "Young man, it's not your fault that things are as difficult as they are. Neither is it your brothers' fault, either. What I will not stand for is to see you starve while I live with you under this roof" (pointing at the roof). By the time I left to go to school, I would have already been to and returned from the shops which were nearby, carrying all the tea things we needed, such as bread, teabags, sugar, margarine, paraffin for the primus stove etc; times without number,

Enock Chiwandire would also kindly give me some pocket money to buy items that I urgently needed at school. Whenever my brother Roland sought to pay him back the full amount of money he had given me, Enock Chiwandire flatly refused to accept it, saying that I was no different from any of his blood brothers. That was his pattern and approach to life: kind, easy-going and incredibly generous of spirit. On his return from work, Enock Chiwandire would spend all day asleep on the three-quarter bed in the kitchen, undisturbed by his other co-occupants who would be at work nor by me because I would be at school. Surprisingly and despite the most uncomfortable and inhospitable conditions of our extraordinary lifestyle at the Peter Start Drive address, the three men remained united in their choice to stay at that address for the next eighteen months. These unsavoury conditions of life did not sit well with me as a teenager nursing a burning desire to continue with my education. It was not easy. I had no choice, but to grin and bear it and take the situation in my stride.

Meanwhile, getting me enrolled as a pupil at one of several state primary schools in Harari (Mbare) Township for my Standard 5 (Grade 7) was still not a walk in the park. My brother was confident that I would be enrolled in school eventually and when that happened, I would have to repeat my Standard 5 (Grade 7), as he felt that the quality of education I had received at 'Donga Farm Boarding School' had not been up to scratch.

At that moment, he said we were going to have to face several unfriendly headwinds in our quest to accomplish our objective. Chirodzo, George Stark and Chitsere Government Schools still had European Headteachers who rigidly enforced the stipulated requirements for all new pupils to produce the hateful 'D7 Form,' prior to admission. So, although these schools were nearer where my brother rented a room, I had no choice but to give those schools a wide berth in my enquiries for enrolment. At the same time, the whole question of urban government schools' refusal to admit pupils from outside the municipal area, due to my not being in possession of the dreadful 'D7 Form' had become a political minefield. Topics like these, among others, were being vented at political meetings held privately at night where nationalists agitated for racial equality and removal of all forms of discrimination. In cases like mine and a group of other children facing the difficulty of non-admission to schools, due to our failure to produce the 'D7 Form', senior local politicians privately approached the African Headteachers in government primary schools. The number of African Headteachers in urban state schools versus those of 'white' origin had increased. Several of the new school heads in the townships gave in to pressure to bend the rules and admit us under certain very confidential arrangements. Those who were finally admitted used fake names from their actual family names. I was one of the beneficiaries of these strictly confidential arrangements. Of course, when it came to the official registration lists submitted to the Department of African Education to enable us to write Standard 6 (Grade 7) Examinations, headteachers included our actual names in the lists so that our proper names would be reflected on certificates.

Quite often, the pseudonyms were captured in error and would end up appearing on official documents! Due to the inferior quality of education my brother believed I had received at 'Donga' the year before, the headteacher who finally admitted me placed me back in Standard 5 so I could stand a chance of passing the Standard 6 (Grade 7) examinations in the following year. Once I was admitted into class well into the middle of 1964, things moved very rapidly. I was living with my brother at another address where he rented a single room for our lodgings. That was still in the so-called 'National' area of Harari (Mbare) Township. The Landlady at that address in Zambe Street, as far as I can remember, was quite pleased with my work whenever I brought my homework exercise books home and did some of my work using her large table and chairs in the lounge. She felt my capabilities were not being fully utilised at Nharira Government Primary school where I was enrolled as (an undercover name under which I had been enrolled). She felt that I was perfectly able to produce even better-quality work if I transferred from the school I was at to another bigger and better-run school nearer her home.

She said her son who had completed his Standard 6 (Grade 7) at that school years before had gone on to complete his secondary school at Goromonzi High School, a well-known government high school just outside Salisbury (Harare). On finishing high school, he was employed in a high-paying job at one big multinational company in Bulawayo. The hidden name trick I used to be enrolled at the earlier school was explained to her by my brother. She said that would not be a problem. She was aware that the last European headmaster had recently left the headship of the school and she proposed to personally visit the school she was talking about and speak to the new 'black' headteacher on the matter of my transfer using the name of one of her sons. It all happened very quickly.

The newly appointed African Headteacher at the new school acceded to that conspiratorial disposition. I immediately commenced lessons with my actual name pseudonymised. Care was taken to ensure that on the submission of official name lists of Standard 6 (Grade 7) Examination registrants to the Department of Native Education Offices by the headmaster, my real name and not the fake one would be included. The process was tricky and fraught with danger for the headteacher concerned. However, it seemed to have paid off well by removing the threat of excluding pupils like me from enjoying the benefits accruing from acquiring an education. I finally completed my Standard 6 (Grade 7) and passed the examinations in 1965. I passed my Standard 6 (Grade 7) with grade scores in English, arithmetic (mathematics) and Shona which qualified me to proceed to the local Harare Government Secondary School for my Form 1 (year 7 in the UK).

Henceforth, there were two immediate challenges. There was only one government secondary school in Harari (Mbare) Township at the time enrolling pupils for Form 1. There was no other school with secondary school facilities besides Harare Government Secondary School yet there were six large primary schools in Harari (Mbare) Township, each of which could produce up to ninety Standard 6 (Grade 7) certificate holders at the end of each year. The large primary schools in Harari (Mbare Township) then were, to name them without any order of importance, Chirodzo, Nharira, Shingirai, Chitsere, George Stark and St Peter's Roman Catholic Primary School. The other government primary school in Harari (Mbare) Township, Gwinyai, was built years after I had moved on.

To expect the one and only government secondary school in the huge area to absorb all the large numbers of ex-Standard 6 graduates from over seven large primary schools would be a miracle of mathematics. In practical terms, the only government-funded secondary school in Harari (Mbare) could enrol only maybe up to three classes, thirty students in each, of new Form One (year 7 in the UK) pupils in their school. In grappling with the problem of accommodating all those of us with a quest to start our secondary education where there were fewer schools, the Rhodesian government introduced what those who study Social Policy then dubbed it 'bottlenecking'. It was part of a plan and a political ploy which meant that most of those African pupils who, for one reason or the other, could not enter secondary school would eventually be forced to look for employment in the mushrooming factories in industrial areas in towns or indeed on farms and mines back in the countryside. Or if they could not find jobs as envisaged and insisted on continuing to live in towns and cities which the law had designated 'European areas', then they would stay at home as school dropouts with the associated outcomes of such a situation.

If there had originally been a plan that was inclusive and catered for the interests of all, there would have been more secondary schools in the catchment area to provide for the needs of feeder primary schools in Harari (Mbare) Township alone. This was not so. The next hurdle I had to overcome was that of my continued use of pseudonyms. It was a tricky business as all my manoeuvres or dealings with headteachers were carried out strictly under cover to ensure I continued enjoying the privilege of attending school and to protect the headteachers concerned from losing their jobs.

So, at the start of 1966, the Headteacher of Harare Government Secondary School was still a white man, a Mr –. When my brother persuaded him to have me enrolled at that school without the 'D7' Form, the 'white' headteacher would simply not hear of it. He would not be persuaded to admit me on the strength of my use of a pseudonym. He clearly said he still had a few vacancies available, and my Standard 6 subject grade passes qualified me to be admitted into Form 1 at the school, but the absence of a 'D7' Form would not have me admitted at the school for Form

1. I had no choice in the circumstances but to approach Harare Community Secondary School. Like its other larger and older counterpart 'Highfield Community Secondary School south-west across town, Harare Community Secondary School was a newly established secondary school which had been brought into existence by pressure groups. Some of these groups were backed up and pushed by political motives. The late Josiah Chinamano, initially a trade unionist who became an active Zimbabwe African Peoples' Union (ZAPU) politician in the mid-1960s, played a big role in the founding of these community secondary schools in the two urban conurbations of Highfield and Harari (Mbare). The main objective in starting these secondary schools in towns was to provide opportunities for secondary school education to the many ex-primary school pupils who could not be accommodated in the few government schools, if any, in suburban African townships.

The net effect of starting these 'community schools' was to counteract the 'bottlenecking' that I have briefly discussed above. The political elements of these groups also advocated for the starting of community secondary schools to provide for the education of children who had drifted into towns from rural areas, together with their parents, due to shortage of schools and other inadequacies of life there. Harare Community Secondary School was located on two church-building sites, i.e., Church of Christ and Evangelical Church sites. The teaching/learning facilities in these church school sites could only be classified as 'inferior' compared to what was on offer at the nearby government-funded Harare Secondary School. Our classroom blocks were donated church buildings which were quickly partitioned or refurbished into learning environments. Many of the 'classrooms' did not have the appropriate sizes – as well as the classroom furniture – to accommodate the large size classes of mostly adolescent boy and girl pupils. We had to buy our own textbooks and exercise books and all the learning resources right across the curriculum. This was not an easy burden for the bulk of our parents and custodians like my brother who earned very small salaries.

As far as the then government were concerned, these community schools were illegal; they did not exist in terms of the law, so they did not provide grants to them to mitigate the expense of teachers' salaries and provision of such things as teaching and learning materials, as well as the structural development of such schools. Payment of teachers' salaries was therefore obtained from the school fees each of the pupils paid at the start of each term. The wooden desks, benches and chairs were all products of community effort. Our counterparts across the fence at Harare Government Secondary School did not have all these bottlenecks. Nearly all our teachers including even the headteacher had not been trained as teachers. But many of them possessed General Certificate of Education 'A' Level qualifications from reputable schools in the country like Goromonzi High School, Fletcher High School, St Ignatius College, St Augustine's Secondary School, Kutama High School, etc. Learning materials like blackboard chalk, dusters, board rulers and other critical teaching equipment either did not exist or were almost always in short supply in those illegal schools.

The inferior appearance of my new secondary school often infused me with an inferiority complex that was hard to beat. I would always ask myself questions like: Why is it that it seems the worst end of the stick is reserved for me? Will this dump of a school ever get any better than this? From this scenario, Reader, I leave you to judge or estimate how our choices were constrained by the narrow and restricted learning circumstances that my colleagues and I found ourselves in. My feelings of discomfiture were increased when at the beginning of my Form 1 (year 7) and much in conflict with my expectations, I had what I interpreted to be the misfortune of meeting among the groups of other students walking back home together after lessons a girl named Sarah Chikoto. That was in 1966. I had last attended Standard 3 (year 5) with that girl in 1961 when both of us attended Maronda Mashanu Primary, a small rural school. In other words, Sarah Chikoto and I had attended school together five years previously.

The girl was then a gifted performer in the classroom. Competing with her for the top position in the end-of-year tests our teachers gave us was a constant tug-of-war between me and her. The conundrum of who exactly was better than the other in terms of mental ability remained unresolved until we parted ways, both of us disappearing into the void at the end of our Standard 3 (year 5). That was the highest class any pupil could get to at that small church-run rural school. When we met again in vastly different, if not entirely conflicting circumstances, both of us had undergone huge transformations in our physical development, emotional and psychological make-ups and how we made sense of the world around us.

Some of our changes were obviously patently determined by many other subtle characteristics which shaped our progress through life in the intervening period. Sarah Chikoto and I had met several times on our way to or from school without recognising each other. One day, amidst a noisy group of other students Sarah Chikoto stopped me and said she suspected she knew who I was: "Please correct me if I'm wrong. But I'm sure you're Kingston Mudyara, aren't you? I was in Standard 3 (year 5) with you at Maronda Mashanu Primary School. Mr Tsimba was our teacher, do you remember?"

I have already confessed that my sexual maturation was slow in rising from its slumber, so as it was still to kick in, the twinge that there was something unusual in a girl of fifteen or sixteen years old confronting an adolescent boy like me and talking to me the way she had done never bothered me. The girl's temerity in displaying such photographic memory that stretched into the hinterland of those dark days of my childhood flabbergasted me. I had thought that I was camouflaged in that urban environment, unbeknown to anybody who might have been familiar with my unflattering experiences in the backwaters of my early to middle primary school days. The battle for me at that later stage of my life was to ward off any suggestions of my struggling existence and try to start avenues which, as I fervently hoped, would culminate in my beginning to live well and to enjoy the good things of life. It appeared Sarah Chikoto's progress through life thus far had been smooth and unhindered by the undulations in the paths of our lives since we had parted five years previously. She informed me, "I am now in Form 2 (year 8) at Harari Government Secondary School, Kingston."

I was almost ashamed to tell her I was in Form 1 (year 7), a class lower than hers, having repeated Standard 5 due to my difficulties at Dhonga Farm School in 1963 and that I was attending school at the inferior and discredited Harare Community Secondary School, a motley collection of discoloured church buildings with no proper learning facilities. Their exterior walls had their paint peeling off. The church buildings in no way resembled a school. In contrast, Sarah's progress since we were classmates five years previously appeared to have been unhindered by any hold-ups. Confidently and without beating about the bush, she went on to tell me, "I have had no break from school since you and I finished Standard 3 at Maronda Mashanu five years ago."

She lived with a married relative who, together with his wife, had a large four-bedroomed house in the upmarket 'Beatrice Cottages' section of Harari (Mbare) Township. She had a bedroom to herself in the house. At that time in pre-independence Zimbabwe, Africans were not allowed to live in European areas, in terms of the Land Apportionment Act of 1930. However, a select few of the rich and well-to-do black people in Salisbury would be allowed to build houses and live in such places like 'Beatrice Cottages' in Harari (Mbare), West Wood near Kambuzuma or Marimba Park. It became obvious that Sarah Chikoto's relatives were people who lived not just comfortably but also possessed some influence. They had made it possible for her to be enrolled for Form 1 (year 7) at her current school, even if she probably did not have the bothersome 'D7' Form that had created all sorts of complications for me.

I could not possibly reveal to my former classmate the depressing circumstances pertaining to my home environment and living conditions. In response to her question about where I lived, I carefully avoided being specific and by way of a red herring, I simply pointed embarrassingly in the general direction of Stodart Hall or changed the subject about where I lived altogether.

There was no way I would let that girl know anything about the drab, deplorable and off-putting appearance of the tumbledown shack of a house where I shared a small, ill-fitting kitchen with my brother. Rounding off the conversation to tell me about her hopes, she said, "It seems likely I'm proceeding to complete my General Certificate of Education 'O' Levels at Harari Government Secondary School. After that, it will be down to me to decide whether I should carry on to Upper Sixth or go on to train as a nurse or something like that." Sarah rambled on, bristling with confidence.

I do not know where I got the notion from, but it seemed to me she had been born lucky. The stage seemed already set for that lucky girl to succeed. By all appearances, she appeared to have been born with a silver spoon in her mouth. Back in the days of our attendance at Maronda Mashanu School, it was rumoured that Sarah Chikoto came from a wealthy family. Her father was a Headman who owned businesses at Manyene Shopping Centre. All she needed to do was just to put in a little more effort in her work and she would pass her examinations. Smartly dressed in her trademark school uniform that set all the girls at her school apart from the riffraff at my school next door, Sarah appeared happy and contented. I was not. My circumstances were completely at variance with hers. All the boys and girls at Harari Government Secondary School were distinguishable by the beautiful uniforms they wore which seemed to reflect their positive behaviour patterns and the way society seemed to regard them. It depressed me that my school did not have a uniform policy. The absence of such a policy resulted in most of us appearing at school wearing all sorts of civilian clothes in wide-ranging colours. Some of my girl schoolmates at Harare Community Secondary School reported to school looking like Christmas trees, turning the school into a venue to make fashion statements.

Consequently, there were numerous disciplinary issues arising from romantic dalliances between our younger male staff and girl-students. Where Sarah Chikoto seemed to have had her path already mapped out for her after her Rhodesia Junior Certificate (year 9), I had no prospects to speak about whatever. The community school I was attending did not have GCSE classes. The school had been created as a stopgap measure hurriedly brought into existence by desperate parents and political activists who were assisted by churches.

The objective was to solve a big problem where large numbers of ex-Standard 6 (year 6) pupils like me could not all be accommodated into the one and only Harari Government Secondary School in the area. That explained why unfortunately, my school did not have classes beyond year 9 (Form 2). Time elapsed little by little and, Sarah and I continued with our haphazard meetings. As she was a class higher than me, I detected that she slowly began to look down on me. Our conversations became less vital and witty. Gradually, we seemed to drift apart because there was no common ground in the topics that came up for conversation between us. As I was finishing my Rhodesia Junior Certificate (now Zimbabwe Junior Certificate or year 9), Sarah Chikoto was in year 10 or Form 3 at Harari Government Secondary School where I believe she went on to complete her Cambridge School Certificate. By the time I left the despicable Harari Community Secondary School at the end of 1967, all lines of communication between me and my former primary school classmate had terminated. I am quite sure she went on to do great things in her life.

Despite their operational privations, all my teachers faced the teaching/learning limitations at Harari Community Secondary School courageously. Nearly all of them displayed outstanding dedication to their duties and an unmatched zeal and enthusiasm to promote our learning in very difficult circumstances. I had passed through 'Donga Farm Boarding School' a few years previously where none of my classroom teachers possessed even a single General Certificate of Education 'O' Level Pass, let alone a teacher's qualification. Against the numerous pitfalls they faced in front of the classroom, my cohort of teachers at Harare Community Secondary School were in a class by themselves. I will not forget my geography teacher, Mr Gilmas Kusema, who at Rhodesia Junior Certificate level helped me grasp all about the Solar System.

There was a Mr Wagoneka, an ex-Fletcher High School student who taught me English Language and Literature. If Sir, you are still alive and are privileged to be reading this document, please take note that my ability to use my senses in descriptive writing as well as the generality of my writing skills were bequeathed upon me by you. You were simply amazing in those dire circumstances in which you worked. Then there was a Mr Chifamba who taught us European History of the pre-historic type.

I will never forget his sterling efforts to help us understand about 'Alexander the Great' and how he travelled all the way eastwards from Macedonia to the distant east in Pakistan, defeating all the enemy forces he encountered and left an everlasting legacy in the physical appearance of all Pakistani people that we see to this day. The story of the widely acclaimed conquests of the Roman Armies commanded by the renowned Julius Caesar who 'came, saw and conquered' Britain still rings in my ears. There was a Mr Ruzande, who remembered being in the same cohort with my cousin Brother Douglas Ruhukwa at Fletcher High School in the early 1960s. He taught us history as well. He was very competent. I also will not forget to mention a Mr Gashu who taught us Religious Education. My understanding of the 'Solar System' in geography was engineered by a Mr Kusema who had studied and passed his 'A' Level geography at Goromonzi Government High School.

There were lots of other teachers whose names I now forget, not because they were bad teachers but because it is over sixty years ago since their last interface with me as part of their classes. All those teachers who taught us Latin (Mr Marume and his 'W. W. Eubank'). A Latin textbook by which we ended up calling him, mathematics, Biology, Shona etc were all wonderful people. That wonderful band of brothers – for those teachers were all men – promoted a dignity of labour in me and a great opportunity to learn in very challenging circumstances of deprivation.

My stay with my older brothers at 52 Peter Start Drive in Harare (Mbare) in 1966-67 was facilitated by my fortuitous meeting and acquaintanceship with one, (the late) Charles Mungoshi.

He suddenly arrived by bus from Enkeldoorn (Chivhu) one day where his father owned a small farm holding at Mutoro African Purchase Area near Manyene Tribal Trust Lands. Having recently completed and passed his Cambridge School Certificate Examinations (Form 4 or year 11) at St Augustine's Secondary School, Penhalonga, his purpose for visiting his uncle, my brother's Landlord, was to stay with him for a period while he looked for a job opening in Salisbury (Harare). From my earlier instalment on the geography of the property at 52 Peter Start Drive in Harari (Mbare), you will agree with me that with eight people already in residence at that small house, there was hardly any more space to accommodate another body. But come hell or high water, Charles Mungoshi being 'family', so to speak, would have to be squeezed into the spare bedroom which he shared with his cousin, the Landlord's eldest son Jeffrey, who also happened to be looking for a job. The two men also used the same room to prepare meals which they ate irregularly. When Charles Mungoshi did not go out looking for job openings during the week and at weekends, I would always spot him sit under the shade of one of the few mango trees that grew in the garden outside the house, absorbed either in reading books (novels) of one kind or the other or engaged in non-stop writing.

Warming up to him and talking to him, he discovered I was interested in reading books. Charles was such a pleasant fellow and a book worm himself. He simply adored reading what he termed 'serious literature' novels that belonged to the fiction genre written by Ernest Hemingway. By the end of 1966, I had finished reading all the detective novel titles written by James Hadley Chase, but as I had only started my secondary school education, I read the fast-moving storylines just for the sake of it without differentiating between the various strategies writers use to tell their stories. Charles Mungoshi helped me to understand all about genres. Then he introduced me to writers like William Shakespeare, Charles Dickens, Thomas Hardy, Ernest Hemingway and others whose works he said he had read to prepare himself for his Form 4 or year 11 English Literature examinations at St. Augustine's Secondary School. Noticing I had a deep love of reading, he would release some of the books by Hemingway he had already read for me to read, one at a time. Then when I handed the book back to him after reading it, he would ask me questions to check my comprehension of its contents and to see if I made sense of Hemingway's trajectory in telling the story, etc.

By the time I finished studying for the Rhodesia Junior Certificate at Harare Community Secondary School, surprisingly where we did not have a single Learning Resources Centre (School Library), I had done justice to the following titles by Ernest Hemingway: 'A Farewell To Arms'; 'The Oldman And The Sea'; 'The Sun Also Rises'; 'To Have And Have Not'; 'Islands In The Stream'; 'Death In The Afternoon' and 'For Whom The Bell Tolls'. I am sincerely grateful to Charles Mungoshi's unwitting influence on the development of my reading culture. At the same time, little did I know that his incessant if not altogether laborious writing were his humble beginnings as a short story and novel writer of the future. Not long after he and I parted ways and moved on in our different directions, Charles Mungoshi became a Zimbabwean literary giant in a class of his own. I would meet this gentleman again years later in altered circumstances at the University of Zimbabwe where for a period he was 'Writer-in-Residence.' He was a critical thinker who was seized with this passionate zeal to reflect honestly and sincerely upon the goings-on in the human psyche and how the same was mirrored in society. It is not my wish to record here that Charles Mungoshi was a drunkard because that reference would be unfair to him. At the time I knew him, and that is a long time ago, he only sometimes partook mildly in alcohol drinking for the sake of socialising with others.

His belief at that time was that far too many young African men of his age, young talented people who had finished either their Form 4 (year 11) or Form 6 (A Levels) in Rhodesia (Zimbabwe), were shooting stars who shone brightly. But those shooting stars faded out far too young through over-indulgence in binge drinking and substance misuse. Nevertheless, a parallel view that he also held was that, drunk in moderation, alcohol is one of the few intoxicating substances a writer of newspaper articles, books, poems, etc., can take and continue to produce work of a reasonable standard while still having control over it. In other words, he often observed precariously that the young imbibers' critical faculties were more in danger of being impaired by their excessive drug-taking but not necessarily obliterated by drinking in moderation! On the strength of that reasoning, he was upcoming writer who occasionally experimented with writing short stories in a state of mild stupor or with hangovers of a sort. He would quip: "I find the worse the hangover, the worse the mind seems to crackle!"

Seeing that I was only just a young teenager, Charles never ventured to encourage me to start experimenting with taking the cup that cheers. That was the quintessential Charles Mungoshi for you, long before all these trimmings of celebrity whereby some of you got to know of him, a few years before he passed on only just recently.

For two years between 1965 and 1968, I lived with my older brother at No. 18 Peter Start Drive in Harari (Mbare) Township. That address was, and I believe still is, less than three hundred yards from the iconic 'Stodart Hall', the biggest community centre in Harari (Mbare). My brother rented the spare bedroom of the two-bedroom house that was owned by a quiet Malawian gentleman. Despite his poor wages, Brother Roland always spared me a shilling or two shillings (ten pence or twenty pence) every Saturday afternoon so that I could attend film shows at Stodart Hall. The admission charge was just about ten pence. Very few people, especially the young ones born in the 1980s, cannot truly identify with the history surrounding Stodart Hall in Mbare, Harare. It is one of the grand structures built in the 1950s by the colonial authorities of the former Federation of the two Rhodesia's, i.e., Northern and Southern Rhodesia (Zambia and Zimbabwe) and Nyasaland (Malawi). Even if it was built that long ago, the structure still looks solid and strong. Many young residents of Mbare would probably only associate Stodart Hall with Zim dancehall music gigs, church gatherings and other conferences that are held there. Yet the truth is that since 1980, that same hall has been known to be a place of last vigil for deceased national heroes of the liberation struggle.

It was in that same emblematic building that nationalists secretly met in the early 1960s to plot confrontation with the colonial government. The result of those secret meetings in Stodart Hall turned Harari (Mbare) into a hotbed of political activism and running battles with the law enforcement agencies. Many political leaders were arrested and thrown either into prison or into lengthy detention. Tracing the story back to my days as an adolescent in Harari (Mbare) in the mid-1960s. I attended most, if not all, of the Saturday afternoon film shows in the company of my friend and age-mate Munetsi Magwenzi. My mate was young brother to the then famous Dynamos Football Club goalkeeper Eric Magwenzi both of whom lived with their parents in a house directly opposite ours, but their address was in Daniel Street in the 'National' section of Harari (Mbare) Township. My mate's brother Eric Magwenzi often arranged for Munetsi and I to attend big games between Dynamos and other National Professional Soccer League teams without paying when games were played in Harari (Mbare) at Ground Number 7. Rufaro Stadium did not exist at that time.

Always accompanied by my playmate and urban groover, Munetsi Magwenzi, I watched nearly all of Ian Fleming's Sean Connery acting in films like 'Goldfinger', 'From Russia with Love', 'Dr No', 'On Her Majesty's Secret Service' and 'You Only Live Twice'. We also watched several other non-secret agent films at Stodart Hall. One of them was 'One Million B.C.', a 1940 film production. That was my first film to watch in the fantasy genre where two tribes with different ideologies come together when a volcano erupts in the city. They fight a monster together, saving the lives of the tribal grouping. The vivid images of those giant monsters that caused us to sit on the edges of our seats still haunts me to this day. On those Saturday afternoons my mate Munetsi Magwenzi and I did not attend at Stodart Hall, watching films of one kind or the other, we would usually be found at the adjacent George Hartley Swimming Baths. The admission charge into the swimming complex was only around a shilling (almost equivalent to ten pence) per visit on any given day. The place was popularly known in the Harari (Mbare) community as 'KwaNowero' because of the famous and well-liked Life Saver called 'Noel' who worked at the swimming pool for many years. That venue was directly opposite the house I lived at with my older brother across the street in Peter Start Drive. Then, the swimming bath complex only had a six-foot fence around its rectangular perimeter. So, on a Saturday afternoon even if I didn't have the admission fee to go swimming at George Hartley Swimming Baths nor to watch films at Stodart Hall, it didn't bother me so much.

My older bachelor brother was renting a room in a house at No. 18 Peter Start Drive. From that address which was directly opposite George Hartley Swimming Pool', I had the advantage of being able to watch through the fence (there were no Durawall structures then) as other youths and children took dips into the pools from the shallow end, the deep end or from the diving boards. I enjoyed this view for free through the window of our room facing the swimming baths across the street. Just watching these goings-on as a passive viewer was such a joy; however, it was far better when I physically attended the swimming activities with other boys and girls of my age. To give our swimming sessions a tinkling and exciting sensation, the legendary Thomas Mapfumo and his earlier band 'The Springfields' would then suddenly arrive and be allowed to go into the swimming complex with their full kit of musical instruments. Thomas Mapfumo was in the early stages of his music career then and not as popular as he became ten to fifteen years later when he switched to 'Chimurenga' music. The band would set up their instruments at a space several yards away from the swimming baths.

Then they would belt out tune after tune of pop music while we dipped into the water. In the years I am writing about, Thomas Mapfumo's genre of music featured mostly little more than poorly performed cover versions of tunes by the likes of Elvis Presley,

The Beatles, Otis Redding and other famous overseas pop stars at the time. As time went by, we also got to know that some of these unannounced day time appearances by bands such as Mapfumo's 'The Springfields' and other small upcoming bands at 'KwaNowero' were for the purpose to practise and perfect their talent in preparation for their Saturday night and even Sunday night performances to paying audiences in hotels, night clubs and even in beerhalls, scattered in locations across African townships in Salisbury (Harare).

It has been more than thirty years since I left Salisbury (Harare) to go and work in a small farming town called Chegutu in 1990. I understand that many changes have taken place in relation to the Stodart Hall Complex. I personally associate with the iconic Stodart Hall was an integral part of my adolescent years and young adulthood. However, reports reaching people like me as far afield as the UK suggest that the paint on its walls is peeling off and the complex generally looks run down due to general neglect and poor maintenance by the City of Harare who are the owners. Another of my associates who is still alive and has continued living in Mbare says the place seems to come alive again when a semblance of effort is taken to refurbish Stodart Hall by patching up the many potholes on roads that lead to that place of historical importance.

However, this seems to happen only in preparation to receive the honour of a deceased hero or heroine of the liberation struggle who must stop at that national monument as a place of last vigil before he or she is taken away and buried at the National Heroes Acre in Harare. Despite its current modest appearance, Stodart Hall in Mbare maintains its unique position in its connection with preparations for the 'Second Chimurenga' in Zimbabwe. Besides that, Stodart Hall is also largely connected with the upliftment of music and entertainment talent among Africans who lived in Harari (Mbare) and surrounding townships like Highfield, Mufakose, Warren Park, Mabvuku and Dzivaresekwa. Townships like Chitungwiza, Glen Norah, Glen View, Budiriro and several other new ones did not exist in the years I am writing about.

In the late 1960s through to the mid-1970s, my bosom friend Charles Jambaya and I attended several Saturday all night 'teen-time' gigs – then popularly known as 'Pungwes' – that were laid on in Stodart Hall. I personally attended performances in that venue by the then budding musicians and guitarists like the renowned Manu Kambani (who was a proper Harari (Mbare) product), Thomas Mapfumo (who was then into 'Chimurenga') music, Oliver Mutukudzi (who originated in Highfield but perfected his art at Stodart Hall in Harari), drummer Jethro Shasha (also hailed from Harari (Mbare), etc., etc. to showcase their God-given talents.

The contemporaries who showcased their God-given music talents in Stodart Hall include Jonah Sithole, Biggie Tembo, Leonard Dembo, Leonard Zhakata, Johnny Papas, James Chimombe and several others too many to include in this list. Apart from perhaps the celebrated Thomas Mapfumo and his 'The Blacks Unlimited' music outfit and maybe a handful of similar musicians, many of the Black music giants of those heydays have regrettably passed on. Finally, Stodart Hall in Harari (Mbare) also attracted international artists. I was in Standard 3 (year 5) in the backwaters of Maronda Mashanu Primary School in 1961 when I am told Sir Cliff Richard and his backing band 'The Shadows' performed in Stodart Hall when they toured Southern Rhodesia (Zimbabwe) as an extension of their tour to South Africa. Bob Marley and The Wailers was the reggae megastar and guest musician at Zimbabwe's independence celebrations at Rufaro Stadium in 1980. Then before the international star returned to Jamaica, he performed a noisy and oversubscribed gig which I was not able to attend in the grounds outside Stodart Hall in Mbare. Arrangements for Bob Marley to perform his final show inside the hall had to be cancelled at the last minute when it was discovered that far too many people wanted to attend the show. Packed in the allocated space like sardines in a small tin-can, I am informed there was standing room only and all that the huge crowd who attended could afford to do was just to watch the star do his own thing in front of his fans. It was sad to learn through the media of the passing on of that reggae music icon shortly after his guest appearance at the Zimbabwe independence celebrations in 1980. I will not apologise for going off at a tangent to talk about the significance of Stodart Hall and its environs in my life. I had to say something about that complex in the centre of Harari (Mbare) Township as my teenage growth and development were closely linked with its existence.

Before I proceed, it is prudent of me to make one small diversion and make a special tribute or reconnect with some of the social networks I formed as a student at Harari Community Secondary School. The following names of some of my classmates at Harare Community Secondary School still ring a bell: (the late) Benjamin Ndhlovu, (the late) Anthony Mushipe, (the late) Earnest Shamu, Jonias Tugwete, Jasmine and a gentleman by the name Frank (both whose surnames have slipped my memory). On the same issue, here is a wonder of all wonders: I met Jonias Tugwete fortuitously in the heart of the City of Birmingham, UK, in 2012! That was forty-seven years later since our last meeting as Rhodesia Junior Certificate Classmates at Harari Community Secondary School. The 'rush hour' here in the UK starts at around four p.m. The streets of Birmingham were packed with people rushing up and down to catch buses and trains back home after knocking off work. Following a busy afternoon of shopping, Mr Tugwete calmly sat beside his wife on a bench at a bus stop, awaiting their daughter to pick them up in her car. Would you believe this: I had just got off a train myself from one of the towns around Birmingham called 'Solihull'. I was wending my way through the ever-increasing crowds so that I could catch a tram a kilometre or so away and head home to the town of West Bromwich where I lived. As I hurriedly walked past where the couple quietly sat amongst a group of other rush hour commuters who anxiously waited for their buses to arrive so that they could go home, Jonias recognised me and instantly called out with a loud voice, "Lawrence Moyo! It's nobody else but you, Lawrence!"

Stopping in my tracks, I turned round and recognised him immediately. I also called out simultaneously, "Jonias Tugwete, my friend!" rushing towards him and he rushes towards me, both of us with our arms raised. We embraced in a feverish bear-hug of long lost friends. I was so delighted to meet this man with whom I had last shared a two-seater wooden desk and a bench in Form 2 (year 9) at Harare Community Secondary School in 1967. Jonias believed my appearance had not changed that much which accounted for him finding it easy to pick me out from amongst the throng. Nearly fifty years later, he admitted to my having put on a little bit of weight, but I still maintained my trademark head of long jet-black hair. Despite the unavoidable marks of ageing, I thought the fellow still held himself together and the sound of his voice had not changed one bit. He, the late Anthony Mushipe and I would compete in writing English language compositions some of which Mr Wagoneka would read to the whole class. Jonias Tugwete was also one of the biggest contributors in class-room debates with which Mr Wagoneka stretched our thinking skills and intersubjectivity. Mr Tugwete had a mind of his own. He was fearless and he expressed his thoughts fluently in what we called the 'Queen's language.' In the accidental meeting, Mr Tugwete and his wife were in transit through the UK on their way back to Zimbabwe after visiting one of their children who work and live in the United States. That meeting also made it possible for me to meet Mrs Tugwete for maybe just that once and never again. We have not been in touch since that accidental meeting ten years ago. Bless them.

Refocusing on my welfare at home in Harari (Mbare) and how that impacted on my schoolwork and psychological make up as a young teenager, my custodian and older brother Roland's earn-ings remained disappointingly low. So, he persisted in finding it increasingly challenging to cope with managing the cost of our living expenses. That included his inability to pay the school fees that the authorities of Harare Community Secondary School were charging for my studentship at that school. I have already hinted somewhere that his monthly salary was nothing to write home about. For that reason, I was nearly expelled from school in the middle of the second term of my Form 1 (year 7) for failing to keep up with the payment of my school fees. On reporting for lessons in the morning like everybody else, a parents' representative tasked with the duty to check on pupils who had not paid their fees would send me and others like me back home to collect from our guardians any outstanding school fees payments. That resulted in my missing lessons for nearly three weeks in a row. When it really got to the crunch and I was nearly struck off the class register for continuous absence from school, I approached a Sister Barbara, an Anglican nun who lived in a community of other nuns at 'Runyararo' or 'St Michael's,' an Anglican Church mission station in Barbara Tredgold Circle right in the heart of Harari (Mbare) Township. Being Roman Catholic myself, I had never met her before.

But from enquiries that I quietly made, I had obtained a tip-off from other kind people that she was a powerful, kind and influential religious woman. If I presented my plight to her well, she might feel pity for me and kindly offer to assist with the payment of my fees. Sister Barbara received me warmly when I reported to see her at her 'Runyararo' residence. That was my first ever interview or direct interface with someone from a Eurocentric origin in Salisbury (Harare). She was not a small woman in physical appearance and just her presence of authority filled you with some degree of foreboding. Be that as it was, I presented my case well and I think I was confident in my presentation. Her conversation with me was quick and sharp and she reached her conclusion immediately. "Lawrence, let me thank you for taking the trouble to come and see me about the difficulties your older brother is facing in paying your school fees. I was sorry to hear about that. You said you're Roman Catholic, didn't you?" she asked. I answered in the affirmative. Without wasting time, she went on, "Well, I often get these sorts of requests for assistance from students who belong to my denomination. I belong to the Anglican Church. Have you ever heard of the Church of England, Lawrence?"

I said that I had grown up at Maronda Mashanu, an Anglican Church community that had been founded by Father Shearly

Arthur Cripps, a well-known Anglican Church missionary who had died nearly twenty years previously. Then she continued, "If you were Anglican, Lawrence, I'd have seen what I could do to help you out of your predicament. There's a Father Dale who's the priest-in charge at your local Roman Catholic parish near Stodart Hall. I often meet him whenever we hold liaison meetings for the different religious churches in this township. Have you approached him about this?"

I admitted being familiar with Father Dale at the local St Peter's Catholic Church and that I was often one of the boys who served at his church services on Sundays. I had never approached Father Dale regarding the purpose of my visit to see Sister Barbara. She picked up a pen lying on the desk before her and scribbled on a piece of note paper what looked like a hurriedly written letter. Sticking the note paper into an envelope, she sealed it, breathing heavily, and gave it to me, asking me to hand the sealed envelope to Father Dale. That interview with Sister Barbara ended abruptly but in a business-like fashion.

She bade me farewell and wished me good luck in my search for assistance with the payment of my school fees. I may not have quite obtained the assistance I went to see Sister Barbara about. But I felt that a load had been taken off my shoulders by the mere fact that that a total stranger was prepared to listen to my problem and offer useful suggestions on possible solutions to it. On receiving Sister Barbara's note when I went to see him at his parish office on the following morning, Reverend Father Dale was very sympathetic. Unfortunately, he was not in any position to help me as he himself depended for his upkeep largely on the measly offerings his congregations contributed during the Holy Masses he said on Sundays. Instead, he said he would telephone a Reverend Father Denis Mangan to see if he could help. On checking with Father Dale again two days later, I was informed that Reverend Father Mangan wanted to meet with me at the small school he ran at the Old St. Peter's Roman Catholic Church. No specific date was given. He was a Roman Catholic Jesuit Priest who administered a small private secondary school, that is, it ran a few General Certificate of Education 'O' Level classes of students at the old site of St Peter's Catholic Church in Harari (Mbare). Reverend Father Mangan did not live at the old site of St Peter's Catholic Church but at Prestage House, a Roman Catholic Church priests' residence in Mount Pleasant, Salisbury (Harare). A few days after my first attempt to see him at his school failed, I received a letter from him asking me to meet with him at Prestage House to see if he could help me out of my school fees logjam.

Reverend Father Mangan provided all the detail on how I would travel to reach the priests' residence in Mount Pleasant by bus. To remind you, I had arrived in Salisbury (Harare) for the first time just over three years before. Notwithstanding, I had never ventured to travel to 'whites only' suburbs, so I did not have the foggiest idea where 'Mount Pleasant' in Salisbury (Harare) was. Such low-density areas were designated strictly 'white areas only' in the 1960s and appearances in them by the bulk of us 'blacks', especially youths of my age, were looked down upon as tantamount to trespassing. So, our best option was to stay confined in areas where we were meant to live. The only few areas I knew and had had chances to travel to were African townships like Highfield, Mufakose and Harari (Mbare) itself. I had heard of Mabvuku and Dzivaresekwa Townships. But having had no relatives who lived in those townships, there was no attraction for me to visit those areas at all.

On a set date one morning as instructed by Reverend Father Mangan, I caught a bus from Rezende Street in Salisbury (Harare) City Centre. I did not have prior knowledge that for all Salisbury (Harare) United buses plying the routes between the city centre and all European residential suburbs, the seating arrangements on those buses were segregated. 'Whites' were accorded seats in designated portions of the bus while the other smaller portions on the same buses were for non-whites, which included 'Coloureds' and other people of colour like Asians. Unaware of these seating arrangements when I entered that bus, I innocently sat on a row of seats that were reserved for passengers with a lighter complexion only. That seemed to have annoyed a few of the 'white' passengers who were already occupying nearby seats. Before the African bus driver could continue with his journey along Second Street, one of the white passengers called to the driver to stop the bus moving immediately, pointing a wagging finger at me, and telling him I was sitting in an 'illegal' seat. Both the driver and the beret-clad bus conductor, who had been standing by the steps of the bus entrance looking lost, ran and crowded around me saying I had offended the 'bosses' and should change to a seat reserved for 'blacks' only without wasting any more time. That was in 1966, long before anyone could dream of Rhodesia (Zimbabwe) gaining its independence from Great Britain and attaining sovereign status as a nation state in 1980. I quickly complied with the required seating arrangements and the bus continued its journey to 'Mount Pleasant'. On leaving the bus at a drop off point Reverend Father Mangan had stated I should disembark from the bus; a heavy canopy of black rain clouds had gathered in the sky above me. Before long, it started raining heavily. I did not have an umbrella or an overcoat to protect me from the rain.

Also, come to think of it, I was a complete stranger in that low-density area, one of several suburban residential areas in Salisbury (Harare) which were strictly reserved for Europeans only to live in. Passing by a locked metal gate with a pasted sign that read "Beware of Dogs, Keep Out," the roofs of large houses I could see through the rain were also surrounded by either huge concrete walls or massive leafy trees, a few branches of which spread low over the walls. I realised I was walking about in a low-density area where few people and domestic animals like dogs and cats, if any, could be seen in streets. I had nowhere to hide from the buckets of rain which pounded the ground and poured down from the heavens above me. Curiously, I wondered where everybody else was. I asked myself whether it was only me destined to be caught in that downpour. I seemed to be the only human being alive in these deserted streets and pathways as I walked across 'Upper East Road' to search for the road sign 'Mount Pleasant Drive'.

In less than fifteen minutes, all my clothes were totally soaked, but I continued trudging haggardly along the approximately two-mile long Mount Pleasant Drive. The rain continued pouring down. Just as I passed the north-eastern entrance gate of the University of Rhodesia (Zimbabwe), the rain suddenly and curiously stopped as if some mythical being high up in the heavens had turned the taps off; but I was drenched to the skin.

The clothes I wore stuck to my body, and I was finding it hard to walk. The dull hollow feeling I experienced about myself and my shambolic appearance made me suspect that perhaps I belonged to an extraordinary club of eccentrics who were never destined to achieve success and to enjoy the comforts and conveniences of life due to the nature of their birth! It was a horrible feeling, the kind of cattle fodder fed to those who finally decide to commit suicide. A few yards at the north-eastern end of Mount Pleasant Drive before the road veered to the left and continued towards another satellite town of Mount Peasant called Groomsbridge, the street sign-post inscribed 'Prestage House' came into my full view. I had reached my destination, but at such great cost!

Reverend Father Mangan had been expecting me. He was so sorry I had been caught in the heavy downpour which had just stopped. He was physically a big well-built man, while I was a frail-looking young adolescent. But he rushed to his large in-built wardrobe and pulled out freshly washed and ironed clothes that belonged to him: a large pair of trousers and a large shirt and he gave them to me asking me to use an adjacent room, which was his loo, to change into them. While I changed into these dry but obviously ill-fitting clothes because of their size, he hung out my own clothes to dry on the radiators in another part of his self-contained flat.

Sitting by an electric heater in his lounge, I explained the hardships my older brother was experiencing to pay for my school fees due to his small postman's monthly earnings and that unless somebody came to my rescue immediately, I was going to be expelled from school. Reverend Father Mangan listened quietly as I explained. He said he had consulted with Father Dale, the then Parish Priest at the new St Peter's Catholic Church – a stone's throw from the address where I lived near Stodart Hall in Harari (Mbare) – and he had been told that I was a practising Roman Catholic. Father Dale had also confirmed that for the two years he had known me, I had not only attended Holy Mass regularly but also that I had gone out of my way to serve at some of his Holy Mass celebrations. Reverend Father Mangan lived in a community of other mainly English Jesuit priests at Prestage House. He ordered a steaming hot cup of milky tea and buttered bread to be brought over from their communal kitchen. Sipping the hot tea and taking care that it did not scald me, Reverend Father Mangan spoke with a priestly demeanour, "Lawrence, I'm taking over the payment of your school fees, including your arrears, at Harare Community Secondary School until you finish your Rhodesia Junior Certificate."

I had never been so overwhelmed with happiness and a sense of fulfilment. I nearly leapt to my feet to jump and shout with joy, but I quickly checked myself and realised I was in a priest's home and still clad in over-sized shirt and trousers that belonged to him. All the same, I blurted out a "Thank you so very much, Father" before I continued to sip my hot tea and chew the jammed and buttered half-brick sized piece of bread that one of the kitchen staff had been asked to bring to me. Moments later, I checked to see if my clothes had dried up on the electrical radiators and I discovered they had dried up, so I quickly changed back into them.

Then Reverend Father Mangan wrote a huge cheque payable to Harari (Mbare) Community Secondary School, tore it out of a thick book of blank cheques and handed it to me. Tears flowing down my cheeks, I received the cheque and thanked him from the bottom of my heart for his generosity using the few words I could muster for a deprived but rejuvenated youth. The sum of money on the cheque was inclusive of all my school fees arrears from the beginning of the second school term of that year until I completed Rhodesia Junior Certificate (now Zimbabwe Junior Certificate) in the forthcoming year.

My visit for the interview with Reverend Father Mangan at 'Prestage House' was on a Friday. He did not want me to continue missing out on lessons at school, so he insisted, saying, "You must report back for school on Monday, Lawrence." Instead of taking the bus back into Salisbury (Harare) city centre from the leafy 'white' suburb of Mount Pleasant following my first visit to see Reverend Father Mangan, he generously offered to give me a lift in his VW Beetle on the five-mile journey. That day in July 1966 marked the beginning of my long association with this Man of God and reverend gentleman. Without offering any written guarantees, he promised he would decide on the level of assistance he would offer on how my education would proceed after I completed my Rhodesia Junior Certificate. The money Reverend Father Mangan kindly gave to pay towards my fees was not a loan. He did not want me to repay anything, but he would appreciate it very much if at weekends and during school holidays, I could come out to Prestage House and assist with odd little jobs like pulling up weeds on the vast lawns that surrounded the priests' flats. Or he hoped I did not mind dusting off the thousands of books in the priests' communal library. To ease my travels between Harari (Mbare) and Mount Pleasant, he promised to buy me a new bicycle. In line with his promise in the following week, he drove with me to a shop called 'Fereday and Sons' in Salisbury city centre where he bought me a brand-new 'Raleigh' bicycle. I rode the new bicycle back to the address where I lived with my brother in Harari (Mbare)) while my benefactor drove back to Mount Pleasant.

From having fallen far back in my payment of school fees at my secondary school – which threatened my ultimate expulsion from school– I automatically became the first pupil to be fully paid up in terms of school fees not just for that year in Form 1 but also for the whole of the following year in Form 2 (year 9)! I continued to live with my brother in his one-rented room in Harari (Mbare), but on weekends and during school holidays, I would ride out in the mornings to do odd little jobs at Prestage House in Mount Pleasant, as agreed with Reverend Father Mangan. Then I would return to Harari (Mbare) in the evenings.

My brother insisted that I should not ride the bicycle to and from school lest it fell prey to bicycle thieves. He observed that Reverend Father Mangan had bought the bicycle for a specific purpose which he said we must honour and respect. Henceforth my involvement with the reverend priest's Christian ministry increased. It became more than just doing odd jobs on the lawns surrounding the priests' residence at Prestage House in Mount Pleasant or helping out with tidying up in the large priests' communal library.

Reverend Father Mangan himself was a busy man. Running his small private secondary school in Harari (Mbare) was just a side job for him. Besides being a fulltime priest required to play his part in serving the needs of the Christian community in the Roman Catholic Church Archdiocese of Salisbury (Harare), he was also the national coordinator of a Roman Catholic movement in Rhodesia (Zimbabwe) then called 'Sodality' which was targeted mostly at young Catholic adults. 'Sodality' promoted conscientisation among young male and female Roman Catholics of all races; thus, ensuring that they portrayed good models as practising Christians. As 'Coordinator' his work involved contacting the young adults and discussing issues with them at meetings or conferences. Sometimes, Reverend Father Mangan arranged several days' 'retreats' for small groups of these young people at chosen venues which would culminate with him celebrating Holy Mass for them. To this end, some of his behind-the-scenes-activities included researching and producing documents on his findings and producing handouts, pamphlets and circulars – all of which entailed considerable typing, duplicating and stapling together of papers. He went out of his way to help me to learn the art of typing using his own typewriters. He had three such desk-type machines in his office besides other office equipment like duplicators, binding machines and so on. I quickly became proficient as a typist.

He was surprised at how quickly I got to grips with office administration, which included distributing the work he produced by mail to various contact people at Roman Catholic Churches and schools all over Rhodesia (Zimbabwe). With practice, I ended up doing most of his reprographic work for which he was grateful. Before I started helping Reverend Father Mangan with his reprographic work, it appears that there was a Mr Paul Dunduru who had been his aide and confidante for a long time, but he seemed to have decided to move on. However, Paul continued visiting Reverend Father Mangan, not to do the work he had previously done for him, but to consult with him on matters of a private and confidential nature.

Before long, Mr Dunduru fizzled into thin air and up until I left Zimbabwe in 2002, I never heard of what became of him since I last saw him in 1969 or thereabouts. While I worked with Reverend Father Mangan at Campion House in 1968, I was also afforded the rare opportunity of informally meeting with some important young people. Some of these people had become luminaries, the 'Whose Who' or modern-day celebrities among the upcoming young people in Salisbury (Harare) then whom I would never have had the chance to meet if it were not for my working with and helping Reverend Father Mangan.

The following people were among some of his Sodality Group who met in his office at Campion House for an hour or two after five p.m. once every fortnight: Wilfred Mbanga who worked for a newspaper publication somewhere in Salisbury. He frequently visited Reverend Father Mangan to chat with him on a variety of issues. Speaking with a distinct English accent, revealing that he had gained some of his education from a private school, Mr Mbanga expressed his thoughts clearly in English. Michael Hamilton, the only European young man who also turned up frequently attended Reverend Father Mangan's Campion House Sodality Group meetings. I never got to know where he was employed. Whenever he attended those meetings, Michael made a supreme effort to bring himself down to the same level of understanding as everyone else. He was not one of the pretentious European young men who would assert their personalities needlessly because they were 'white' Rhodesians. Patrick Chingoka displayed impressive leadership skills. The Group Sodality meetings were chaired by either Patrick Chingoka or Wilfred Mbanga. Patrick Chingoka was in a high-profile job as a Court Interpreter or something like that. There was also Benedict Chikwana, a quietly spoken and kindly-looking gentleman. He was then employed as a bank cashier with Barclays Bank at Tanganyika House in Third Street, Salisbury (Harare). As the group always found me doing odd bits of jobs in Reverend Father Mangan's Office every time they reported at Reverend Father Mangan's Office, I became familiar with all of them. I never became a member of their Sodality Group, but it was such a joy interacting with them, either individually or as a group before or after their meetings.

Mr Chikwana and Mr Mbanga particularly liked talking to me whenever they visited Reverend Father Mangan's Campion House Office, with the former always saying I reminded him of his young brother, whoever that was. I cannot remember ever getting the opportunity to meet Mr Chikwana's young brother. Then there was the deep-throated and renowned newsman and broadcaster John Bishop. He was not a member of Reverend Father Mangan's Campion House Sodality Group, but he visited Reverend Father Mangan at Campion House quite a few times to consult with him on matters of topical interest. Then Mr Bishop was a main newsreader at Rhodesia Broadcasting Corporation, having come over from British Broadcasting Corporation in London where he was employed in the same capacity. I remember chatting with him in my simplicity as Reverend Father Mangan's helper and him telling me in his trademark BBC accent that he was enjoying his main news reader stint at the Rhodesian Broadcasting Corporation immensely.

My older brother's bachelorhood ended somewhere in August/ September 1967 when he got married to his beautiful girlfriend, Faith Zifamba. She moved in to live with her husband almost immediately. I continued living with the couple in the one room(s) that they rented within Harari (Mbare). making things rather complicated when it came to sleeping arrangements. The landlords would usually let me sleep in their lounges.

Their firstborn child, a girl named Carol Makawana, was born in the last six months of 1967. I cannot remember the exact date. To begin with and clearly squeezed for space, we were packed like sardines in a can in one tiny 'spare' bedroom or sometimes even a small 'kitchen' that my older brother sometimes obtained as rented accommodation for our lodgings. At the two separate addresses in the 'National' section where Roland and Faith rented a single room each time in those few hectic months, the landlords were kind enough to allow me space on the cement floors of their lounges to sleep on during the night. Then the burden of looking after his growing family became heavier as looking after a wife, one tiny baby and myself did not correspond with his persistently small earnings. In keeping with standard practice, rentals were supposed to be paid in advance. However, for failing to pay his July rent at the end of June 1968, my brother and all his dependants who included me, were evicted at short notice from an address in Harari (Mbare) where we lived. My brother had no choice but to make hurried alternative accommodation arrangements for all of us. He dispatched his wife and little daughter Carol Makawana back to his in-laws, the Bakasas, who lived a short distance away across the vlei. Without a roof over my head, I do not know how I would have got along if I were still attending school.

Fortunately, or unfortunately for me, school was temporarily suspended for the time being, having failed to find a place for Form 3 (year 10 in the UK) at the one and only government secondary school in Harari (Mbare) Township at that time. Instead, I was using my time to travel up and down and help Reverend Father Mangan with his work as Sodality Coordinator. Uncle Toendepi Mudyara Dzenga who was a police constable in the Highfield/ Southerton area of Salisbury (Harare), gladly accepted older brother Roland's request for me to temporarily live with him and his family while my brother re-organised himself. I therefore ended up being whisked away from Harari (Mbare) Township to live with Uncle Toendepi and his family in the 'married quarters' of the new Police Camp behind the New Stands in Old Highfield. My brother Roland also quickly arranged to be temporarily accommodated in the municipal run 'Matapi Hostels', two or three miles from where we lived. These residential quarters catered specifically for the accommodation needs of lowly paid single and married men whose families lived in the 'reserves,' but who were in paid employment in the city centre or nearby industrial sites of Salisbury (Harare).

However, these dwelling places were famous for all the wrong reasons: they were dirty and unsightly to look at, for a start. They were very badly maintained by the local authority. The doors into the residents' rooms virtually did not have any security at all as the locks or padlocks were made of cheap materials that could be broken easily. Consequently, burglaries in the absence of tenants were frequent.

My brother returned from work one day and discovered that his room had been broken into and all his clothes were missing. Supplies of fresh running water were very inconsistent, so communal toilets in these four-floor structures were almost always blocked, a near-permanent feature creating a thick stench that attracted swarms of lies that continually hovered over the area. On returning from their jobs in the evenings, the residents used the open plan cooking areas communally to prepare their meals.

My brother told me that if you wanted to have your meal, you would have to remain in the communal kitchen while your food cooked. Otherwise, left unattended to do other small jobs in your room, other bachelor residents were known to sneak into the communal kitchen, remove your pots with your food nearly ready for serving from the cooking plates and carry them to eat your food in the secrecy of their rooms! I remember urging him not to spend a long time staying in such inhospitable conditions and to organise better accommodation for himself and his family as soon as possible.

Apart from the year 1968 being a game changer to me, I recognise it as a significant shift in the way I may have adopted new habits and lifestyles, some of which remain part of who I am to this day. 1968 also heralded the end of my stay under the courageous custodianship of my older brother in extremely challenging circumstances caused by his low wages. It was the first time in a period of five years that I lived a life without his support. I had depended upon it so much it sounded funny and unusual not having him around.

My two months' stay with the Toendepis in Highfield was also the beginning of my grand entry into uncharted territory, a point at which I officially embarked on thrashing out a path in a desperate search of my own destiny. The twenty-kilometre round trips between Campion House in Fifth Street, Salisbury, (Harare), where Reverend Father Mangan lived then and my new temporary home in Highfield, became quite tiresome and rather heavy-going for me after two months of cycling up and down. Besides, we were having a particularly cold winter in July 1968, and it was proving pretty challenging for me to cycle in frosty weather and on ice-covered cycle tracks and slippery macadamised roads during the 'peak' hours of the morning, through Salisbury's (Harare's) busy streets.

On one very cold morning towards the end of July 1968, I was nearly killed by a huge garbage collecting trucks when the driver suddenly veered to turn into an alley on the left. He could not see me as I was cycling beside the massively large vehicle towards the end of my long riding journey to reach Campion House from Highfield. As I pedalled hard in the morning rush hour traffic, I had nearly passed the vehicle, but the lorry hit me on the rear wheel of the bicycle, the force of which hurled me off the bicycle and I was airborne for a little while before I landed with a nasty bump on the macadamised sidewalk at the left edge of the road. The rear part of the bicycle, including the saddle where I was originally perched, was mangled into an unrecognisable piece of metal and leather. If I had been hit directly by that lorry, I do not think I would be alive today to tell this story. I am therefore incredibly lucky to be here. There was a palpable risk of meeting my death or sustaining life-changing injuries on that fateful day. Reverend Father Mangan – who was summoned by the police to come to the scene of the accident – wasted no time in taking over control and adjusting my movements.

I could not possibly get back together with my older brother in Harari (Mbare). He was still disorganised following his eviction from the room he had rented two or three months earlier. So, Reverend Father Mangan stepped in and moved me from my Uncle Toendepi's family home in Highfield to the Priest's Flat upstairs behind the Sacristy at the Old St Peter's Church, Harari (Mbare) Township. Reverend Father Mangan bought me another brand-new bicycle to replace the old one which had virtually been trashed in the freak accident along Fourth Street in Salisbury (Harare) city centre. The flat was a self-contained dwelling with two single beds which fitted neatly in a large room, a small side kitchen and toilet/shower room facilities.

I shared that flat for four months on and off with a tall kind gentleman called Martin Chikomo until I left to go for teacher training at St. Paul's Teachers' College in January 1969. I didn't know what Mr Chikomo was into, whether he was working somewhere in the city or attending college. He would always leave the flat in the morning and return in the evening well turned out in black or grey suit, milky white shirt, tie and shiny black shoes. Nor do I know what eventually became of Martin Chikomo. In September 1968, Reverend Father Mangan was moved again from Campion House.

He had stayed briefly at Campion House following his transfer from Prestage House. I do not know what the practice is today. In the years I am writing about, Roman Catholic priests were regularly moved about depending on the needs of communities and the supply of priests available to serve those needs. That time around, he was transferred to 'Mazowe Novitiate', a Roman Catholic institution thirty miles out of Salisbury (Harare) along the Old Mazowe Road, deep in the picturesque large-scale farming area of Mazowe Valley. The Novitiate was a rambling old farmhouse with several 'en-suite' bedrooms to accommodate several residents.

Just outside the large house was a beautiful little church which had allegedly been built by the former owners to provide for the spiritual needs of local worshippers who included several 'white' commercial farmers and their workers in the surrounding farming area.

The property and the small hectarage on which the Novitiate was located had formerly been owned by a family who reportedly had links with the British aristocracy. A story that was told said that upon winding up his farming activities in Rhodesia, packing up and subsequently returning with his family to the UK, a certain 'Lord Acton' had given up ownership of the large house and donated it, together with the beautiful little church and the small piece of land on which it was sited to the Roman Catholic Church. Despite the move to Mazowe Novitiate, Reverend Father Mangan remained deeply involved in 'Sodality' work. I was not employed by Reverend Father Mangan for all the work I did for him. However, as he had virtually taken over from my brother as the provider of my general welfare, there was no way he would have left me with no one to take care of me in Salisbury (Harare).

I continued offering him assistance and I frequently travelled with him back and forth between Salisbury (Harare) and Mazowe Novitiate as he coordinated his 'Sodality' activities. In the end, he invited me to go and live with him and the body of other people at Mazowe Novitiate as his assistant. He was the Priest-in Charge at the Novitiate where I was offered sleeping quarters of my own, a large bedroom almost twice the size my older brother Roland rented in Harare (Mbare) Township. It had its own private bathroom and toilet facilities! My bed linen was changed every day for washing and fresh sheets and pillows installed to replace them. For the five months I stayed working with Reverend Father Mangan at Mazowe Novitiate, my sleeping quarters were cleaned, and my laundry was washed and ironed by staff who were employed to do those jobs. I had never lived in a hotel before and here I was sampling the luxury of staying in a five-star hotel, a far cry from the cement-floored rooms I slept in where my brother was a 'lodger' in Harari (Mbare) or Highfield Townships.

For the first time, I experienced no 'Colour Bar' in Rhodesia (Zimbabwe) and shared my meals with the rest of the European clergy in their communal diner. I was exposed to eating four course English meals using implements such as forks and knives, a habit that I was unaccustomed to, so it was a complete novelty to me. Contrary to the bruising experiences that had been my diet in all my childhood and adolescence so far, it was amazing to engage on equal terms in quiet and civilised conversations during meals with all the European clergy without having to suffer any twinge of embarrassment. Everyone went out of their way to help me acclimatise, to make me feel that despite my Africanness, I was their equal and was welcome to participate in their company. On occasions in the evenings, Reverend Father Mangan was invited for meals at households of successful and rich large-scale commercial farmers of British stock in the area.

Anxious that I should be rid of any feelings of inequality or embarrassment in the presence of Europeans, Reverend Father Mangan would take me with him for some of these meals. Unused to having Africans eat together on the same table with them, you could see the hosts become aghast and turn red in the face on seeing Reverend Father Mangan arrive for their meal with him, accompanied by an African. As this was Reverend Father Mangan's way of preaching or advocating for racial integration, the hosts would have no choice but to hurriedly adjust their arrangements to accommodate my presence. I ate meals together with them and contributed actively to the conversations that ensued during the meals. Many of them who were used to interacting only with their lowly educated farm workers in 'Chilapalapa' expressed surprise that after all there were Africans who spoke better English than they did! When they discovered that I had received some education and that I had a touch of sophistication in my use of English language (despite my having obtained my education in low-grade schools only meant for African children), I noticed that they scuttled away back into their burrows, and none dared speak to me in that dreadful 'Chilapalapa' medium they often used to communicate with their farm workers.

Back at Mazowe Novitiate, I would mix with some of the Priests and Brothers, all of them of European origin from either the UK or the Republic of Ireland during the day and evenings in the large airy lounge where we watched TV, listened to mostly classical music and played games, e.g., Scrabble. Reverend Father Mangan was a star at the game of Scrabble. Immediately after lunch, there was a Father Kennedy, an elderly Irish priest who was fond of inviting me to the peace and quiet of the Entertainment Room, a large place which also filled in as the lounge and community library. On reaching this venue, he would reach out and select from among Dvorak's vinyl long playing records. After pulling the record carefully out of its sleeves, he would place it in the record player, asking me to listen carefully to the LP record together with him while it played. Thereafter, he would want me to give him feedback on what I thought about the beauty of Dvorak's symphony music. Walking out of the diner, he would chortle, "Lawrence, come along with me, young man, and listen to this most beautiful and heavenly symphony by Dvorak! It's golden and simply the best we have in these woods for purposes of relaxation." Father Kennedy would rattle away talking to you in very good English, his flickering eyes looking directly at you full on over his spectacles that dangled precariously towards the end of his nose bridge.

Often, I wondered why he ever saw the need for that eyewear at all as the glasses did not seem to perform the task for which he had bought them. Anyway, to go back to the matter of music he wanted me to listen to; a classical music vinyl record can play for ages before you can begin to make head or tail of what is going on. For starters, I had not been brought up on the diet of this type of music and I found that genre of music unexciting and unappealing to my taste, to say the least. I had grown up in the African townships where pop music by The Beatles, Elvis Presley, Cliff Richard and others was played loudly on radio and record player combinations throughout the day. This happened twice or three times with the reverend priest falling fast asleep within the first three minutes of the LP starting to play, so I never got the chance to give him any feedback on my appreciation of (or lack of) Dvorak's music. Seeing him snoring and clearly enjoying his 'siesta', I would quietly sneak out of the room and return either to rest in my own room or walk back to the office where I busied myself for the afternoon with various assignments given to me by Reverend Father Mangan.

Within the first few weeks of my arrival at Mazowe Novitiate, Father Kennedy left to spend two weeks away on a 'retreat' at one of the priests' residences in Salisbury (Harare). When this happened, another priest usually arrived to replace the priest who had gone away so that the timetable and frequency of Holy Mass celebrations in the community would not be affected. A Reverend Father Gregory, (not his real name) a Circular Priest, arrived as a replacement for Father Kennedy. By a queer coincidence, Father Gregory also arrived to do his 'retreat' for two weeks, after which he would return to where he had come from. Father Gregory also loved to play classical music which he said assisted him with his meditation. During his two weeks' retreat, we would find him mostly sitting quietly in the communal lounge listening to the music from the full range of vinyl classical music LPs including Beethoven, Handel, Tchaikovsky, etc. Being the only other person among the clergy at that institution who seemed to be deeply interested in classical music, Father Kennedy went out of his way to ensure that the vinyl record collection was always kept in a particular order he alone knew. After listening to each record, he would carefully return the record into its sleeve without any scratching. Unaware of the punctiliousness with which Father Kennedy cared for the vinyl records, some of the records ended up with ugly scratches across their grooves. Others were inserted into wrong pockets or sleeves or were left in careless heaps on the bookshelves in the communal lounge. At the end of his two-week retreat, Father Gregory returned to Campion House where he was based.

Within a day or so following our visitor's departure, Father Kennedy also returned to the priests' house at Mazowe. It did not take long for him to discover the disorder that had been caused to 'his' vinyl record collection. His face turned red; he went ballistic with consternation as he charged at all of us to give him the name of the culprit responsible for what he called the 'the murder of civilisation' in the communal lounge. We all knew who had spent most of his daytime hours in the lounge playing those records one after the other over the previous two weeks. Father

Kennedy did not quite know who Reverend Father Gregory was because they had never met; but he was familiar with the Father Superior at Campion House. Wasting no time; to vent his feelings, he picked up the landline telephone and dialled the Campion House number. The phone was promptly answered. Father Kennedy did not waste time.

Going straight to the heart of the matter, he shouted into the mouthpiece, "Hullo, is that Father Superior? Please forgive me if my voice is a bit too loud. This is Father Kennedy I'm phoning from Mazowe Novitiate to complain about one of your priests, a Father Gregory, who has just returned there following his two weeks' retreat here. I have to inform you that while I was away on retreat myself somewhere, and he was visiting us here, the man caused untold damage to the superb collection of our vinyl LP classical music records. I'm the one who takes care of these records here and I'm very disappointed with that man's care-lessness. I'm therefore phoning to offer my protestations! May I please request that before that man comes for another retreat here next time, kindly telephone to warn us so that we can hide our records!" And he replaced the receiver back on its cradle without giving the speaker at the other end a chance to say another word. But breathing out heavily once and resting his bulk on the back of the easy chair, Father Kennedy looked mighty relieved. He was satisfied he had made his point and vented his feelings sufficiently to whoever was listening at the other end of the line.

One of the purposes for which Reverend Father Mangan had been transferred from Salisbury Cathedral to Mazowe Novitiate was that, as a Jesuit Priest, he could share with two other resi-dent priests at the mission station the task of going around the surrounding large-scale farms, including as far afield as the deep end of Mashonaland Central Province, celebrating Holy Mass to non-English-speaking congregations made up largely of farm workers and Shona-speaking villagers. A challenge that Reverend Father Mangan was faced with on leaving the comforts of Salisbury (Harare) suburbia was that he could not communicate in the lo-cal language of Shona.

The truth was that celebrating Holy Mass in English to Shona or Chewa-speaking congregations was not quite the ideal thing to do if his sermons were going to have any meaningful impact. To resolve that problem for Reverend Father Mangan, I volunteered not only to go round with him when he went on those outreaches to say Holy Mass, but I also offered to translate his English sermons into the Shona language in which I was versatile. I would stand beside him in front of the congregations as he preached the word of God, and I translated portions of his English version into the local vernacular language.

Unfortunately, I was not versatile with the 'Chichewa,' dialect which was the medium of communication among most of the farm workers on large commercial farms. I was sure though that many of the congregations at stations where Reverend Father Mangan said Holy Mass around Mazowe Novitiate understood my translations in Shona. Over a period, Reverend Father Mangan noticed an improvement in the way he communicated with his congregations, so he decided to spread his wings. I recall, quite often, accompanying Reverend Father Mangan when he went on these outreaches to say Holy Mass in distant places from Mazowe Novitiate like Umvukwes (Mvurwi), Bindura and Mount Darwin. The farthest I went with Reverend Father Mangan as his Holy Mass server and translator in Mashonaland Central Province was a place called 'Marymount Mission', a remote mission outstation located several miles along gravel roads north-east of Mount Darwin. The liberation war had started across the Zambezi River from Zambia, so as Reverend Father Mangan drove his small Volkswagen around in the Zambezi Valley, we feared for our safety, fearing that we might run into skirmishes and exchange of fire between Rhodesian security forces and 'terrorists,' as Rhodesian authorities preferred to describe armed guerrilla fighters. We did not experience such exchanges, nor did we meet any of the guerrilla fighter groups; but we frequently met Rhodesian army personnel in heavily armoured vehicles patrolling along the roads in the Zambezi Valley. The moment they saw Reverend Father Mangan wearing his priest's collar, they waved us on. He even penetrated 'Protected Villages' to say Holy Mass, for example, at 'Nzvimbo Protected Village' – which I have heard is now a big growth point? Some of the outreaches would be for up to three- or four-days' absence from the Novitiate.

That meant we could not possibly do the round trips back to Mazowe Novitiate, so arrangements were made for us to spend nights and have meals at safe stations like St Albert's Mission etc. Being Black, I was surprisingly always made to feel welcome and well-accommodated at these stations, even if the religious community at such stations might be all-white, mostly all-Ger- man Priests, Brothers and Nuns. Reverend Father Mangan made sure that I ate my meals together with the religious community at every mission station where we stopped to eat our meals. In a country where the relationship between black and white com- munities was tense and volatile, my travels with Reverend Father Mangan immersed me in my first taste of true diversity. I was never treated differently because of my darker skin pigmentation.

The main summer rains in Zimbabwe start falling from about the middle or end of November, so Reverend Father Mangan sus- pended the outreaches from Mazowe Novitiate into Mashonaland Central Province until further notice. On our way back from Marymount Mission, we found the Ruya River in flood and had to wait for the water levels in the river to go down. Following a few 'Hail Marys' and feverish 'signs of the cross' by both of us, we succeeded in crossing the river. Thank God also to the German-made Volkswagen Beetle, Reverend Father Mangan was driving appeared to have been built with capabilities placed along the bottom of its chassis which seemed to enable it to 'swim' across the wild turbulence of a strong river current. Otherwise, we risked being swept off the low-level bridge whose markings were completely submerged in swirling grey waters. We hardly could hardly see these markings as we crossed the bridge.

One bright November morning in 1968 after Reverend Father Mangan had said Holy Mass which I served in the beautiful little Church at Mazowe Novitiate; he made a surprise announcement to me which caught me completely off-guard. I had passed my

Rhodesia Junior Certificate examinations the year before with impressive grades in the eight subjects I had sat for my examinations. Harare Community Secondary School was not yet ready to provide Form 3 and 4 classes.

While Reverend Father Mangan was prepared to fund the next level of my education, problems of enrolment continued to dog me, so I gave up the effort to continue wasting time looking for places in Harari Schools. With the encouragement of Reverend Father Mangan during 1968, I had begun studies privately for my General Certificate of Education 'O' Levels through the University of London and he even generously offered to pay for my bookings to sit for the examinations.

Then came the bombshell in November of that year. Arriving in his large room-cum-office after he summoned me on the intercom. Reverend Father Mangan started, "Lawrence, it is I who called you. While you travelled around Mashonaland central with me, I have been thinking hard about the next steps forward for you in the coming year. I don't think I'm wrong, but it is my considered view that you possess great potential to be a successful classroom teacher. You may not realise this, but my view was strengthened by the massive support you have given me for the past two years in carrying out my 'Sodality' work. In addition, Lawrence, you impressed me beyond measure with your fluent translations of my sermons from English language to the Shona language at the countless Holy Masses I said all over Mashonaland central.

"Since I invited you to come and stay at Mazowe Novitiate and assist me for three or four months, these two aspects have conveyed to me the belief that you have the organisational capacity and integrity that will suit you for the role of a teacher. While you accompanied me on those outreaches in Mashonaland central, I secretly consulted with my friends, Father Cockroft and Father Hancko at Musami Mission. I am therefore pleased to let you know that I have already had you enrolled for a three-year teacher training course at St Paul's Teacher Training College starting in January next year."

Reverend Father Mangan had undertaken these arrangements almost conspiratorially, without me knowing anything about them. It wasn't that I had issues with that, but I have to say that nothing had prepared me for his announcement that I would be training as a teacher. In an earlier chapter of this memoir, I referred to a conversation in which Uncle Rodrick, my father's young brother had playfully asked a group of children in which I was part of to name the jobs we wanted to do when we were grown up and finished school. Being so very young then, I had not quite formed an opinion regarding what my job prospects would be, so I told him that I wanted to become a 'headteacher'. Of course, he scaled those high hopes down and suggested that I should think of becoming a teacher first before I could rise to the lofty position of headteacher.

That conversation with my uncle was a long time ago when I was probably in year two or three of my primary school education. The entire incident had fizzled into thin air, and I never thought about the idea of becoming a teacher again. I had never discussed my professional ambitions during my trips with the reverend priest either, during my work with him in Salisbury (Harare), at Mazowe Novitiate or when I travelled with him during the outreaches in Mashonaland central. Somehow, at the back of my mind I had still entertained the hope of returning into the school system at the beginning of 1969, either as a day boarder or as a boarding school student to complete my General Certificate of Education 'O' Levels. Father had mentioned to me informally that he had chatted with the principal of St Ignatius College who had indicated there was a possibility that I would attend my Form 3 as a boarder at that school. So, I had still nursed this prospect that I would return to school in the coming year. With this sort of background and if any discussions for employment or training were to come up, teaching was nowhere near the top of my bucket list. Then came this sudden announcement: it hit me like a bolt from the blue.

Looming vertically up before me, its summit lost in what looked like low-level cloud, the entire prospect of becoming a teacher frightened me at first.

However, Reverend Father Mangan, who had made huge strides in setting this whole scheme up, went on to give me some assurance, and to inform me that while the government would pay my school fees for the three-year teacher's course, he would generously offer to pay my boarding fees at the college for the three-year duration of the course. He was offering me a sort of scholarship! "There's a huge demand for qualified teachers in the school system, Lawrence. So, I organised for you to take up training as a teacher because I felt that you have what it takes for that kind of role. Also note, I am taking full charge to ensure that you will have all the clothes and bedding you will need at the college before the new term starts in January." Concerning the plan for me to complete my General Certificate Examinations, he said, "You don't need to worry about that, Lawrence, because I have it all planned for you. I want you to be mentally ready to work doubly hard during your teacher training because I am going to have you registered with the University of London to sit for your General Certificate of Education 'O' Level exams at the end of the second year of your three-year teacher training course."

Sooner rather than later, I realised that I had to embrace the reality of my situation. As the conundrum had been cracked and the die was cast, I did not see any point in continuing to wrestle with my dilemma. I accepted Reverend Father Mangan's offer which, after all, I realised was a wonderful and God-given opportunity for me to take part in changing other people's lives. Here was somebody, a total stranger, doing everything he could to give me a boost. I pinched myself to check whether I was dreaming or not! To take you back a little, it had never really crossed my mind to take up teaching as my profession. The whole thing had caught me completely off-guard. For a long moment after Reverend Father Mangan's surprise announcement, I was speechless. I was astonished this was happening to poor me. Finding a few words to say in the end, I expressed my gratitude for his generosity and Christian charity. A few days after new year celebrations in 1969, Reverend Father Mangan drove with me on the passenger seat on his left into Salisbury city centre in his 'Volkswagen

Beetle'. Ticking off items from a list of clothing and bedding he had received from the principal at St Paul's Teachers' College, he bought everything that I needed as a proper would-be teacher trainee boarding student and not the fake 'boarder' I once had been in Standard 5 (Grade 7) when Uncle Rodrick dispatched me to 'Donga Farm Boarding School' about seven years before.

Reverend Father Mangan bought me a large black metal trunk, an item I had never ever owned before. The metal case was capacious enough to carry all the items the reverend priest had bought for me, including, among them, a black suit, that is, a well-fitting jacket and trousers, two black pairs of the correct size shoes, four pairs of stockings, underwear, four ties, two blankets, two sets of quality sheets, a pillow and pillowcases, four milky white shirts, bath towels, toothbrushes, and toothpaste and toiletries galore.

In my studies for the Rhodesia Junior Certificate examination in English, I had read a book entitled 'Up from Slavery' by Booker T Washington. In that 1901 publication, the author reflects on his struggles to eventually live his dreams of attaining a university education at Hampton Institute in Alabama, USA. In the same book, I remembered the author referring to receiving assistance from other people, who included teachers and philanthropists, to overcome the many obstacles and difficulties in his way as he struggled to obtain an education. It was as if the same thing was happening to me. If the people I have mentioned in this chapter so far, some of whom were total strangers to me, had not intervened and thus became my stepping-stones to help me utilise the potential I possessed, maybe I would not have reached the stage at which I had arrived in my quest for an education. I certainly would never have been able to start enjoying the good quality of life that I had always cherished throughout my entire childhood and adolescence. With an odd mixture of enthusiasm and excitement, 1969 had intriguingly started with a big bang and I waited to see how the invisible future ahead of me would pan out.

# Initial Teacher Training, St Paul's, Musami

We had a bright set of lecturers in the teacher training department at St Paul's Teacher Training College who possessed and displayed exceptional ability in the different specialisms they taught us. Hailing originally from Czechoslovakia (now either Czech Republic or Slovakia), Reverend Father Hancko was initially the principal of the teacher training department. We used to call him affectionately 'Czecho' to reflect his country of origin. By mid-1969, he had acquired a doctorate in education (Ed D) through private study. His new professional qualification appeared to have added more credentials to his integrity as an educationist. From then onward, students began addressing him variously as either 'Doctor' or 'Czecko'. Father Hancko lectured us in 'Principles of Education', and he was highly knowledgeable about his subject. He introduced us to the art of writing assignments that contained research-based argumentation. He was the first to warn me and my colleagues in the cohort against generalising information in our assignment presentations. Telling us that research on issues dealing with educational matters had started a long time before and was ongoing, he repeatedly asked us not to 'operate in a vacuum' and stressed that any points or suggestions we raised in written assignments had to always be backed up by verifiable evidence.

Reverend Father Barr was one of several British Jesuit priests at the mission station. He lectured us in 'Classroom Organisation.' Aged somewhere around sixty or seventy years, Father Barr's physical appearance made you want to laugh. He was of medium height, had a small physical frame and two very large ears that disproportionately protruded from both sides of his small bony and hairless head. His trademark pair of khaki trousers were almost always too big for his small frame. Two to three well fed and healthy men could easily fit into his one pair of trousers which, from the waist going downward, widened profusely as they reached his ankles. My friends and dormitory mates Charles Jambaya, Desmond Kadzura and I used to watch in wonder whenever we saw this gentleman walk from the priests' residence to our classrooms. As he hobbled along in a weird gait, his oversize trousers remained straight as a ruler, and we could not detect his legs move backwards and forwards inside the widened garment. It simply produced howls of laughter from us. His appearance aside though, Reverend Father Barr was an effective lecturer in his subject.

Next on the list of our staff was a Reverend Father Finnieston a rugged-looking old Irish gentleman who was also probably in his seventies. The hot African temperatures appear to have been unkind to this man because his white man's complexion had transformed into a lifeless brown. Reverend Father Finnieston was a heavy cigarette-smoker. The heavy, rancid smell of tobacco that hung over him as he smoked in the corridor outside the lecture room, just before his lectures started, could easily bowl you over if you stood too close talking to him. Even after he had extinguished and thrown away the cigarette stub, the odour that came off him was a heady mix of fruit and pencil shavings. He was one of our lecturers in English. All in all, Reverend Father Finnieston was a pleasant and even-tempered gentleman who could afford to crack jokes and laugh together with us throughout all his lectures. I recall him leading us on 'text analysis' during which he used Nicholas Monserrat's 1951 novel 'The Cruel Sea'. We took turns round the class to read the seven chapters in the book and followed the lives of a group of Royal Navy sailors fighting the Battle of the Atlantic during the Second World War. At the end of nearly all his lectures and as he walked out of the lecture room, he would gleefully ask us to sing with him the three-line refrain of the song 'Bon Voyage' the sailors sang:

*This is not the end of the world*
*I wish you a nice trip*
*have a nice trip*

Fifty years later since I last interacted with that man, I do not know whether he still lives. May God bless his dear soul wherever it lies as I write this account. Mr Phillip Mhundwa (long before he became Doctor Phillip Mhundwa) and a Reverend Father Mark Hackett arrived in the teacher training department either in the middle of or towards the end of 1969, if my memory serves me. Mr Mhundwa replaced Reverend Doctor Hancko who suddenly left to return to his country of birth for some reason.

Mr Mhundwa took over the teaching of 'Principles of Education'. He was also our lecturer in 'Psychology of Education' and 'Research Methods' during which, for the latter subject, he added his own input into the massive amount of work we had covered with Reverend Doctor Hancko on 'Piaget', one of the earliest researchers on child learning and development, as well as similar work done by Vygotsky, Eriksson, Dewey, Freud and others. In addition, Mr Mhundwa lectured us in English during which he displayed his expertise on the stylistics and pragmatics of language use. This was only at T3 teacher training level, so Mr Mhundwa did not go into too many details of the applied linguistics element of the subject, lest we all became confused. However, the material he presented to us was highly organised, challenging and of the highest quality ever.

To my mind, Mr Mhundwa's lectures were inspirational. They filled me with so much motivation sufficient to ignite my curiosity and to form the bedrock upon which 'applied linguistics' became the focus of my first and second university degrees, years later. Amazingly and fortuitously twelve years following completion of my teacher training, I was to bump into Mr Mhundwa at a staff development workshop in Harare. I will talk about my accidental but wholly fruitful meeting with Mr Mhundwa in greater detail in a later chapter. It is hard to believe that he ended up as my supervisor for the dissertation that I was writing for my first university degree at the University of Zimbabwe.

Reverend Father Mark Hackett had recently arrived from the UK. Following a brief stay at Prestage House to learn a bit of the local vernacular, he was posted to St Paul's Mission (Musami) to work as a missionary and as a lecturer in the teacher training department. Although he looked a lot younger, he was probably in his late thirties or early forties. He soon took charge of the teacher training department as the principal. Besides administering the department, he lectured us in English language, where he placed emphasis on syntax, i.e., how we arranged our words in sentences. While there was nothing pedantic about his demands, he was very English in that he wanted us to express ourselves in clear, simple and correctly structured English sentences. At the end of each of our written assignments, Father Hackett's comments were simple, straightforward and written with the aim to convey meaning and to motivate us. He had an open-door policy and allowed us to knock on his office door at any time he was 'in,' if we had any matters of concern to communicate to him. He welcomed suggestions – inserted into a 'Suggestions Box' beside his office door – from students in the department on ways the department could best be run to serve the needs of the students and for the department to meet its goals. Consequently, he regularly attended Students' Union meetings which we held on Saturday mornings every week, so he could adequately respond to students' queries and keep his finger on the pulse of suggestions to improve communication between his office and the students in his department.

Of the permanent lecturer staff in the teacher training department, we had a Sister Evangelista, the one and only female lecturer in our department. She lectured us in 'Art and Classroom Displays.' She shared work with Reverend Father Barr on 'Organisation in the classroom,' and she displayed expertise on the examples teachers should portray by the ways they wrote on the board. Her work on producing learning aids from 'papier mâché' comes back to me with a flash as I write these pages. Regarding Art, Sr Evangelista taught us about 'caricaturing' which in short meant making quick drawings on manilla or on the board which exaggerated people's features, for example, the appearances of their noses, ears etc., resulting in making those watching laugh. Like Reverend Father Barr and Reverend Father Finnieston I have talked about earlier, Sister Evangelista was no longer a spring chicken. She probably was in her seventies when she taught me in the department at Musami. Sadly, she was one of the six members of the religious community at St. Paul's, Musami Mission, who were killed in an incident at the mission during the liberation war in 1976, years after my cohort of teacher trainees had finished our training course and had started teaching. The news of that incident was broadcast on radio and television.

For our lessons in 'Music', Mr DA Murota – headteacher of the small St. Paul's Primary School which was located at the north-eastern edge of the mission grounds – popped in once or so every fortnight, to take us through the paces of 'Staff Notation', etc. The many insights he taught us in 'music' as a subject, including some of the little songs he introduced to my group reminded me of Mr Reginald Tsimba who taught me almost the same things in Standard 3 (year 5) nine or ten years previously. I cannot forget some of these little nursery rhyme gems Mr Murota taught us such as 'Row, row, row the boat, gently down the stream, Merrily, merrily, merrily, merrily, Life is but a dream!' He taught us several others, making his lessons such a joy to attend and to look forward to. I would meet with Mr Murota again twenty years later when he had become and was among a team of six education officers stationed at Kadoma District Office and I was education officer (staffing) at Chegutu District Office, thirty kilometres away along the Harare-to-Bulawayo Highway. Both districts were under Mashonaland West Province.

Then there was a Mr Nyazika, an elderly Teacher of the Shona Language from the secondary school department at St. Paul's. He would also pop in to lecture us in the teacher training department on 'Shona' as a subject in our curriculum, once a week or every fortnight. Curiously interesting about Mr Nyazika was that at the start of each of his lectures, he would walk into the classroom, usually late for the start of his lectures by up to ten minutes. Looking lost when he finally arrived and before he sat in the chair behind the lecturer's desk, he would look at the class in front of him and always ask, "Pane ane mubvunzo here?"

("Has anybody got any questions?"). As we would have not had any lessons with Mr Nyazika often for days on end, this way of starting his lessons caused all of us in the class to guffaw in up-roarious laughter – not quite the best of models to start lessons for student teachers, was it?

Some of our timetabled activities included 'Swimming' and 'Football' although we did not have anybody among the staff who led us in those activities. The swimming baths were in a walled enclosure north of the senior secondary school classes. It was shared by both students and religious staff.

At no time were males and females allowed to swim together. Religious staff, mostly male priests, preferred to have their dips in the pools first thing in the mornings. As those of us in the 'Male Dormitories' went for our breakfast in the dining room nearby, we usually saw Father Hackett, Father Donovan or Father McCabe walk back to the Priests' Lodge, following their swimming sessions in the baths. We went for 'swimming' as per timetable once in the middle of the week or on Saturday or Sunday afternoons. As no one was specifically charged with the teaching of swimming to those of us who were adults, the routines we followed at the swimming pool were entirely of our own making. I enjoyed prac-tising my 'freestyle', 'backstroke' and leaps into the deep end from the diving boards. As far as 'football' was concerned, again that area was left to the whims of those who were interested enough in the game to organise themselves. For years in the 1960s, there had been a St. Paul's Football Club which was in the National Premier Soccer League. Big teams in the Premier League like Dynamos, Tornadoes, CAPS United etc had been known to come out of Salisbury (Harare) – over forty miles away – to play league games at the mission in the large sports stadium behind the male students' sleeping quarters. Regrettably and now that St. Paul's Football Team had wound up and no longer existed when we started training as teachers, the huge sports stadium had slowly become derelict due to non-use and poor maintenance by mis-sion authorities. Thus, groups of students sometimes organised themselves at weekends and played totally unsupervised football games. It was in order for me to watch others playing football and not to participate in playing the game, so I did not join the teams who volunteered to play friendly games against each other in the crumpling stadium.

My friends, fellow teacher trainees and a few of the students from the secondary school department were important to me. They played a key role in the formation of my communications network during the three years I spent at St Paul's, Musami. Desmond Sidwell Kadzura was already a friend of mine from the onset of my training course as a teacher. He and I had met and become friends back in Salisbury (Harare) shortly before we set out to start training as teachers. On the same day that I arrived at St Paul's Mission, I got together with Charles Jambaya and quickly formed a close friendship with him. There was an immediate rapport between Charles Jambaya and I from the first time we met. The three of us, i.e., Desmond, Charles and myself always sat close to each other in the lecture rooms. In the dormitories, occupants of whom changed every year, we invariably slept side by side with my bed always in the middle. We remained a solid and indestructible group of friends throughout the three years of our stay at St. Paul's, Musami. Our perspectives on life, that is, our hopes and aspirations, our joys, hobbies and interests seemed to coincide, so they united us. Charles Jambaya was a cigarette-smoker while Desmond Kadzura and I were non-smokers. As I grew up in Harari (Mbare), I had never been attracted by the smoking habit although most of my agemates when I attended primary school and secondary school in Salisbury (Harare) did so secretly. Desmond and I tried to copy Charles because he looked so smart puffing away at a cigarette just before lectures started. But in less than two months of trial and error, I found smoking unappealing and despicable, so I kicked the habit for good. Even Desmond who also had be drawn into smoking stopped the practice at about the same time as I did.

Vitos Katsukunya jumps back into my mind straight away as a classmate who contributed the most in lecture room discussions across the whole range of areas in our curriculum. He was gregarious and outspoken. His general knowledge and insights on assignment topics given by our lecturers, peppered with numerous examples and practical ideas, was encyclopaedic. All lecturers liked him for that. Patrick Macheka and Desmond Kadzura did not hurry to offer responses during discussions. However, when they deemed it appropriate to speak up, they offered well-thought-out ideas and carefully measured inputs into discussions going on during lessons. Somewhere in our second year of training, I was not surprised when these two gentlemen volunteered to start a 'club' or movement they curiously dubbed 'Joint Board of Philosophers'. The formation of that club arose from topics that we discussed in Psychology of Education lectures on child learning and development and how they linked with the teachings of Greek philosophers, Socrates and Plato as well as the Swiss Psychologist, Piaget. Throwing more light on Piaget's 'cognitive conflict' when he taught us in educational psychology, Mr Mhundwa (who is probably a professor of sorts if he is still alive) would repeat:

"Language provides a means for generating a motivating kind of conflict and also a means of resolving it by engaging in thinking together with others."

Since we were all training to become teachers, Mr Mhundwa encouraged us to engage in the use of the socio-cultural approach as a basis to produce the best results on collaborative learning in our classrooms. Of course, what he did not go into too much detail about – as group work in classroom settings was still being researched upon at the time – was the nature of the interactive or discursive practices taking place between experts and peers or among peers on their own and how the nature of the practices would contribute to facilitating guided participation. The 'Joint Board of Philosophers' Club was formed just for the fun of discussing matters that were rooted in philosophy and thus test each other's cognitive reach. Membership was free and with time the club became quite large, sucking in the likes of Vitos Katsukunya, Charles Jambaya, James Sithole, Titos Bhauti and others. I never quite became a 'registered' member of this group.

But out of curiosity one day, I attended one of their club gatherings where they could spend hours exchanging viewpoints on issues of a mundane, humdrum existence! They met on Saturdays. Without laying down any rules for conducting their discussions, they simply divided into two groups. They didn't have a leader or a chairman to lead the discussions nor was there a secretary to take down notes, etc. One group was pushing the idea of having it on a Sunday while the other group argued that they should be held on a Friday, rather than a Saturday but the Friday supporters appeared extraordinarily enthusiastic to offer jumbled proposals. However, I noted that their talk was largely dominated by several appearances of cumulative talk tended to degenerate into open quarrels between participants. The participants rigidly held to their opinions. Without offering any visible signs of reasoning, they did not seem to want to obtain information from others; for example, "We were in a Psychology lecture with Mr Mhundwa yesterday, Friday, so today is a Saturday. It's a no brainer, isn't it guys?"

Participants did not try to listen to each other. Often, the group participants spoke at the same time. Patrick Macheka and Desmond Kadzura who were the more mature and reasonable among the group made useful suggestions towards solving the problem, but their justifications for proposals were not clearly articulated. By failing to build on each other's proposals in a mutually supportive and uncritical manner, this merely helped the group to construct common knowledge and understanding by accumulation. The less dominant participants in the group attempted to make suggestions, but they were rebuked; "Who told you that it was Wednesday three days ago?" "Guys, the plain truth is that it is Saturday today because it was Friday yesterday. Period!" Another of the less dominant in the group complained, "To say that on the basis of your reasoning yesterday was a Thursday doesn't make any sense to me."

The more assertive members of the group ignored the quieter speakers. The result was that they scuttled back into their burrows, frustrated at being snubbed. One day, Titus Bhauti had arrived late, meaning that he had missed out on several points of argument raised by others in earlier submissions. He became the most loquacious in that discussion group. Instead of choosing a side, he adopted an independent position in which he disputed the two groups and advanced theories by Plato and Socrates, asserting that the day the group should meet was Monday, rather than any of the alternative days suggested by his other friends in the two groups. Titus Bhauti sought to control the direction which the group activity was taking. At that stage, there were frequent cycles of short assertions and rebuttals by him when others offered proposals that conflicted with his own: "No, no, no. Both of you Vitos and Gideon are very wrong. My reading of the thinking by Socrates on the position of the moon does not support the views you expressed that Saturday was best."

Proposals during the discussion were unclear and tended not to become outcomes of supported agreement. Joint acceptance from one of the range of proposals was totally absent. *What a jumble of disorganised ideas and waste of valuable time,* I thought and convinced myself. The discussion terminated prematurely without the group reaching a mutually agreed conclusion. I was not impressed by the haphazard manner with which they conducted their discussions, so I did not see the value of joining this group despite the potential it carried in stretching my imagination and associated mental capabilities.

Elsewhere and in many of our Psychology of Education lectures at T3 teacher training level, our lecturer, then a Mr P H Mhundwa had stated that tests of truth are standards and rules that are used to judge the accuracy of statements and claims that people make. In carrying out their discussion, I noticed that although constant references were made to philosophers such as Socrates and Plato by my colleagues, The reliability of arguments or tools (facts) drawn from a haphazard understanding of such philosophies could be disputed, so understanding of a philosophy's tests of truth is fundamental. When I was reading for the Master of Education Degree (Applied Linguistics) in the UK, I came face to face with aspects of validity and reliability in quantitative studies. My mind was taken back to the years of my initial training as a teacher at St Paul's, Musami, fifty years before.

I realised that 'The Joint Board of Philosophers' was not a waste of time for the members who participated in its discussions. In their discussion to seek agreement on what the day of their meeting was, I am sure my colleagues were determining what standards distinguished truth from falsehood. Of course, what they might not have recognised at their elementary level of understanding was that not all criteria (facts) are equally valid.

In putting forward their claims, they were unfortunately trying to use a mixed bag of data based on certain philosophies. If for example I were to decide what is right and what is wrong, there is a need to ask how something stacks up against the original, the standard. Christians would claim that the reason they know that love is good, and hatred is evil is that God who created all of us is a God of love. Honesty is right and deceit is wrong because God is true. Sexual purity is moral while sleeping around is immoral because God is pure. With that understanding between right and wrong, I would be unwise to keep my money at a bank that lets robbers walk in at will and demand my money just because they think it is the right thing to do. But that is how some people think we should decide what is good and what is evil.

Please place the foregoing in juxtaposition with the fact that I participated more in the 'Students' Union' and 'Debating Club' activities when I trained as a teacher at St Pauls. The meetings of these important conduits were held after ten a.m. on alternate Saturday's fortnightly. For a period during my three years' training at St Paul's Teachers' College, I was an elected chairperson of this important body which acted as a medium through which students communicated their needs and grievances for resolution to the college authorities. With one or two others of my classmates as chairperson of the body, I also spent an extended period as an elected secretary or minute-taker of the Students' Union. The latter was a demanding responsibility because it involved plenty of writing and compiling of minutes which would be read out and analysed by large gatherings of all the students at the next general meeting.

Additionally, I was an active participant at properly organised 'Debating Club' meetings that were held on selected topics between groups of our own as teacher trainees or between selected teams from the Teacher Training Department and Secondary School Department, Forms 3 and 4 students. Behaviour changes were noted among learners resulting from new knowledge they acquired from traditions passed down to them by their seniors. We learnt a lot from a senior group of T3 teacher trainees who had started their teacher training a year earlier than those in my cohort and completed their courses in 1970. From that cohort were the likes of Peter Parirewa, Gideon Mujati, William Mutyambizi and Peter Mhlanga (?) – my memory fails me on the exact surname of the second 'Peter'. From the point of view of their sharp mindedness in open debate and how they organised their points of argument, some of these movers and shakers should have pursed studies in law rather than just teaching. I am reliably informed that Peter Parirewa ended up as a Public Relations guru, employed by a large blue-chip multinational organisation in Harare, Zimbabwe.

Peter Parirewa and Peter Mhlanga were motivational speakers' par excellence! They left a legacy of meetings during which our debating sessions were lively gatherings where opposing speakers engaged in veritable exchanges of new knowledge. Depths of genuine linguistic development in English language were reached. Serious points of disputation were proffered in debating settings that were fashioned along models followed in the Houses of Parliament and the Senate. We conducted our debates or discussions using properly constituted ground rules. The tone in these meetings was less combative and there was a clear orientation towards collaboration and intersubjectivity.

Dispositional talk continued to feature in terms of propositions arising from the nature of the topics that we debated. Indeed, we had occasions when the atmosphere was charged with tension. But that would be in an atmosphere of a free fight for all where participants felt free to give and take ideas. There were fewer outright rejections of ideas. Typical of an increase in the use of exploratory talk, participants were ready to listen, evaluate and build on each other's ideas, Although I differ with the sentiments expressed by William Mutyambizi, let me begin by endorsing some of the important points that he has raised; Participants engaged more critically and constructively with each other's ideas. An interesting feature that became apparent was that there was increased cohesion between competing groups and the emphasis was on collective responsibility with the use of 'we' and 'us' being heard constantly: For example, here is an extract: "We shall begin listening to the first five chief speakers, one at a time, from both the 'Movers' and the 'Opposers' sides. Thereafter, the debate will be opened to volunteer speakers from those of 'us' in the audience" … The emphasis on inclusion was evidenced by contributions from participants in the audience who would normally not speak up much during debates. These participants played a minor role in the proceedings which were normally dominated by a 'struggle' for dominance between Desmond Kadzura who was sharp-witted and gifted with a versatile language facility and others. Through the effective use of the English language, meanings were negotiated, resulting in a corresponding increase in intersubjectivity, a critical element in working in the zone of proximal development or the intermental development zone.

These developments not only helped the participants to scaffold each other's learning but also ensured that the quality of their learning was stabilised and did not break down. As matters were reasoned out in quieter and calmer voices, there was a significant absence of cycles of short assertions and counter-assertions. Control was a matter of constant negotiation through charm offensives which, as speakers offered contributions and those on opposing sides were persuaded, determined the subsequent direction of collective thinking. Participants made suggestions for joint consideration and challenges were justified rather than just stated, for example: "Those of you on the 'Movers' side, maybe you are right in accusing science of causing humanity more harm than good. In your conviction, may I please request you to remove all the clothes you are wearing because they are products of science!"

Reasons and explanations were made as explicit as was necessary, given the contextual foundations for the topic of the debate, which were shared by the participants to enable each one of them to make critical evaluations and reach joint conclusions; "But aren't we looking at imported products only? The best way would be to bring them by plane. It is faster. Products like nectarines and bananas may rot before they reach us. Lorries and trains are slow. Drivers may be robbed." I enjoyed the debating sessions immensely during my teacher training at St Paul's. I learnt so much about organisation, presentation of ideas and body language from the likes of Peter Parirewa, William Mutyambizi, Desmond Kadzura, Vitos Katsukunya, Susan Dandajena, James Sithole, Titus Bhauti and Charles Jambaya, to name a few. Those gifted speakers may not have been aware of it, but they helped massively to develop my ability to speak to large audiences, a skill that I would fall back upon considerably in my work years later as an education officer in Mashonaland West Region of the Zimbabwean Ministry of Education and Culture. Saturday afternoons and most of Sundays were 'free time' for all students at the mission, i.e., teacher trainees and secondary school students alike. Of course, Sunday morning would be preceded by all of us in attendance at Holy Mass in the large new church. How we used the rest of the Sundays after breakfast was left pretty much left to us. The free time on Saturday afternoons and on Sundays allowed us the choice to do a series of things including washing our clothes, ironing them, mending those clothes which needed mending or just relaxing in our dormitories talking about family matters, assignment work, etc. Quite often Charles, Desmond and I would talk quietly about personal matters like encounters with girlfriends we had had in our lives.

Some of our colleagues in the dormitory would howl with laughter as they talked about their 'conquests'; meaning the number of girls they had bedded up to then. Some of those conversations were sadly lacking in intellectual vigour. That is why Charles,

Desmond and I did not become part of them. One senior teacher trainee who lived in a dormitory next to ours, Charles Bvumbe, owned a tape recorder on which he had tape-recorded the then popular 'Soul' music tunes by Otis Redding, Percy Sledge, James Brown and Wilson Pickett. Charles Jambaya and I simply adored Wilson Pickett's husky voice as he sang and in step with the rhythm of his music, we imagined his wild dance moves on the stage. The two of us would thus often be found in the dormitory next door on Saturday or Sunday afternoons, listening to music played on Charles Bvumbe's tape recorder. He was a friendly person and he welcomed visitors by his bedside, so he did not mind us sitting by him on his bed and enjoying the privilege of listening to his choice of recorded music. Alternatively, those of my friends with girlfriends would go for what was commonly known as 'timing'. That meant that you and your girlfriend – who could be any female student from either the teacher training department or the secondary school department – would meet at an agreed open spot on the mission grounds.

At around two o'clock in the afternoon, the girls, prim and appropriately dressed to meet their male heartthrobs, usually emerged from the 'Girls Dormitories' in the south-west of the mission grounds. Then they walked daintily to the appointed meeting places either at the 'Grotto' – a holy shrine hidden under the canopy of a grove of tall evergreen trees behind the large new church, or the girls in their finest of attire walked along what we referred to as the 'Appian Way'. That was a straight but dusty road that ran east to west for a possible two kilometres. That road sharply divided the buildings where the Priests Lodge, the large church and the 'Girls' Dormitories were located and all those building structures in the north including all our lecture rooms, the 'Male Dormitories', the Kitchen and the Dining Room attached thereto. Then when the two lovers met each other, the girl usually resembling a Christmas tree, the male gentleman would take his girl out on a date by either walking with her to the nearest business centre, Musami Township which was about a mile away. After purchasing fizzy drinks or packets of sweets, the man would slowly walk his girl back to the mission. Or the date involved the two 'lovers' walking into the bushes surrounding a little kopje near the mission called 'Beta'. Between October and December, the forests of 'mizhanje' trees which grew wild in the Musami area became laden with ripe and juicy 'mazhanje' fruit. Getting lost in those forests with your girl were pleasurable adventures in which the participants seemed to enjoy indulging in their fancies.

Accounts that some of my associates gave when they returned from outings with their girlfriends did not disappoint, indicating that none of them ended their dates with their hopes diminished. On taking his girl on a ripe 'mazhanje-picking' date, the man made sure he returned with the girl into the mission grounds well before sunset. That generalised time limit was where the 'timing' element of that game applied. I have indicated somewhere in these pages that, probably by virtue of the way I was nurtured as a child and adolescent, it took a long time for my sexual maturation to wake up from its slumber. For this reason, I did not have the 'girlfriend' I had left behind in Harari (Mbare) when I started training as a teacher at St Paul's, Musami. Having not slept with anyone of the opposite sex in my life, I was practically still a virgin. In my second year of training, I suddenly emerged from my slumber, only to discover that the world was so beautiful, that there were all these beautiful two-legged creatures that God had decorated it with for those of us males to benefit from. I suddenly realised there were several of these unattached lassies in the female dormitories on the other side of the mission grounds. I was gripped with an urgency; realising that it was high time I had a girlfriend of my own. However, Reverend Father Mangan's voice spoke to me quietly although he was not with me physically, 'Tread with care, young man. Some of these girls will look amazingly beautiful on the outside but may be like rotten apples inside.'

Towards the end of my first year of teacher training, I started an intimate relationship with one girl, Gloria, who was in the same T3 teacher training class as I was. I doubted whether that was the right thing to do. I took her out on dates once or twice and discovered that although she was a beautiful girl and very pleasant to interact with, there was nothing exciting about her at all. Our relationship was doomed to fail because there was not the slightest hint of a spark in it. I did not hate Gloria by any means. Yet the truth was palpable: there was no chemistry whatsoever to draw us towards each other.

To this day, I cannot recall how our relationship ever started, resulting in her becoming my girlfriend and I, her boyfriend. She neither seemed to share my world view nor did she share my sense of humour. We were as distant from each other as the north and south poles, so I slowly drifted away from her on the pretext that I had no excuse for overstaying a potentially wilting welcome. In the end, we quietly broke up and left the matter at just being classmates. We remained friends and only spoke to each other in group discussions during lectures.

Before long, however, I connected with a very beautiful Form three girl called Mecrina. She was a member of the Ballroom Dancing Club which I administered on Sunday afternoons assisted by a Mr Uzande, a senior teacher in the secondary school English Department. Mecrina always preferred me as her dancing partner; and I preferred her. That girl was such a fantastic dancing partner. Mecrina had verve. She always brightened up a dull atmosphere just with her presence. Our conversations were packed with wit and intellectual vigour. When I told her one Sunday afternoon that I did not find her ugly at all, she laughed off my remark, but readily succumbed to my romantic advances, thus we started a romantic relationship, my first significant romantic connection so to speak, which lasted the best part of a year. Then one day, I dropped her like a hot brick. It happened like a thunderclap when I came across evidence she was 'double-crossing' me with a visiting and unmarried male Postgraduate Certificate in Education trainee-lecturer (Mr Friday) from the University of Zimbabwe who was teaching us English in the teacher training department. I never gave her a chance to explain herself and our relationship ended abruptly. I had enjoyed my two years of a relationship with Mecrina. However, there was no way I was going to put up with a deceitful, scheming and two-faced girl-friend, so I dropped her without any feelings of regret.

Before long, I fell head over heels with another very beautiful girl who went by the name Elizabeth, a Form 4 student who had been born and bred in Harari (Mbare). Being a Harari (Mbare) product myself, I felt it would be easy to strike up areas of common ground in conversations between her and me. Just her light-skinned complexion and cheerful persona were like the flick of a light switch. She literally lit me up. But the relationship did not amount to much besides exchanges of photos, dancing with her on Sunday afternoons, stolen 'good night' snogs at the end of 'Evening Studies' in the empty and dimly lit corridors of classroom blocks, holding of hands and occasionally taking her out on those silly and occasionally aimless weekend walks. However, among the girls I flirted with at St Paul's, Musami, Elizabeth stands out as one girl with whom I enjoyed the most intimate of human connections. She left St Paul's at the end of her Cambridge School Certificate Examinations in December 1970. The beautiful young woman I once truly loved fizzled into the void leaving me without someone of the opposite sex with whom I could do 'timing' once more. Having completed my second year of teacher training, I still had one more year of staying at the mission. Halfway through my final year of teacher training in 1971, I vigorously pursued another attractive Form 4 (year 11) girl, Olivia, who I plainly told I admired her beautiful and curvaceous features. Regrettably, she stiffly resisted all my advances, never mind the sheer determination with which I stalked her and repeatedly pursued that girl. In the end I had no choice but to give her up as a lost cause. Both of us parted ways amicably when we left St Paul's Mission for good at the end of 1971 with no contact addresses exchanged between us. I had completed my three-year teacher's course and she, her Cambridge School Certificate Examinations. Olivia disappeared into the void. I concluded her as a closed chapter and deleted her from my subconscious completely.

Two years after my teaching career started in Highfield, Salisbury (Harare), I happened to be walking innocently along 'First Street' in the capital city, Salisbury (Harare) one Saturday morning. The street was packed with frenzied Christmas shoppers. From the opposite side of the street, I heard a woman's voice calling my name above the noises of other shoppers by-passing each other as they hurriedly walked in opposite directions, 'Lawrence! Lawrence! Lawrence!' Stopping in my tracks, I looked round and saw a woman wearing baggy, ill-fitting clothes. I did not immediately recognise who she was. Because I had stopped walking in response to her calling, she instantly started walking across the street to come and talk to me. Almost reaching where I stood, I remembered, a-ah well, it was Olivia. She was completely transformed in appearance and had become a pale shadow of the beautiful and curvaceous girl that I had proposed love to two years previously. She was shabbily dressed and walked in a clumsy and unattractive shuffle. There was this distant, vacant look in her hollow face suggesting something had gone seriously amiss in her romantic life. The collapsed features of her whole physique suggested she might have recently suffered a still birth.

Olivia would have wanted to throw her arms around my shoulders in a gleeful greeting, but I stiffened and quickly backed off. Resulting from her flat rejection of my romantic advances at St Paul's, Musami, we had never contacted each other for exactly two years, and I had completely forgotten all about her. But Olivia, totally oblivious of other shoppers passing by, was adamant. She loudly declared her love for me on the open street that morning. Nearly grovelling on the windswept pavement, she begged me to revive my affections for her. However, remaining calm but firm, I told her politely but firmly, "Olivia, I find it hard to do what you're asking me to do. Much as I would have loved to do that when I loved you so much two years ago at St Paul's, and you rejected me, I cannot possibly do that now. I'm terribly sorry, Olivia, it is too late for me to do that now because someone else (without revealing the identity of my present wife, Margaret) has filled the vacancy that was in my heart to replace

315

you. I need hardly tell you I offered you such a golden opportunity two years ago that could have led to great things for both of us, but as you will probably remember, you spurned all my heartfelt signals of affection for you; you absolutely blew that chance. I'm really sorry, Olivia love."

She clumsily walked away from me, all her hopes to bring back to life my love for her punctured and flattened like a pancake. It's hard to believe this: a fortnight later, I was surprised to see her arrive at 'New Hope Flats' where I lived in Highfield Township, Salisbury (Harare). I did not remember giving her my physical address at our last accidental meeting in First Street, Salisbury (Harare). But here she was neither did I send her packing, nor did I find her uninvited visit welcome. Although she spent the night with me in my bedroom, I completely blanked her out. There was very little conversation, if any, between us during her visit. She was lucky I offered her the privilege of sleeping on my single bed while I opted to sleep on the floor. With careless abandon, she removed all her clothes to go to bed in the full gleam of the room light, remaining with just her knickers on and a thin see through top that barely covered her rotund breasts and her bum. I wondered whether she thought this would act as some sort of catalyst to make both of us lose our inhibitions and unleash our potent mutual secret longings. I will leave it to the reader to speculate on what would have likely happened had that scenario, akin to the biblical 'manna from heaven' been presented to an unsuspecting male prison-escapee. It was clear that Olivia had visited me with a deliberate intention to put temptation in my way. Her plan spectacularly failed to work with me as I steadfastly maintained an attitude of complete aloofness, utterly refusing to be persuaded. Her unexpected visit felt funny to me because that was the first time a semi-naked woman was going to spend a whole night with me in the same room. I had never had this experience before; it felt surreal.

At the same time, I was constantly reminded of a lovely, beautiful Highfield girl, Margaret Nyemba, who I was then going out with. She had been my girlfriend and soulmate for nearly two years. But hold your horses, reader because I provide more details about how my courtship of her panned out in Chapter 16. In sharp contrast with Olivia's forced visit and her indicating to me she was sleeping over for the night in my single bedroom, Margaret had never attempted to spend even a single night with me at the block of bachelor flats where I lived. The girl would only arrive and spend a few hours with me on most of the afternoons at weekends and then return to her parents' home before six o'clock in the evening. It was clear that Margaret's appearances to see me were not with a deliberate intention to persuade me to sleep with her. In truth, there had been an implicit understanding between Margaret and I that indulging in sex before marriage served purposes either to procreate new species or merely to satisfy our quests for the pleasures of the flesh. To avoid turning this ethical wrestling into a purely academic and confiding in each other's trust and honesty, we mutually agreed not to consummate our relationship for either purpose until a yet unknown date in future when we would legally become husband and wife. Sticking rigidly to what I believed to be the truth, I committed myself never to be tempted to engage in a physical relationship with Margaret until after she and I were married, and I had paid lobola to my future in-laws. Also, fortunate for me at that time, Margaret was spending some time off on a visit to her older sister at a small mining town called Dete near Wankie (Hwange) – approximately two hundred miles away in Matabeleland North – and would still be away for another fortnight or so. I can imagine there would have been a big row if Margaret were around town and had pitched up on that fateful Saturday afternoon and found me entertaining a woman stranger in the flat where she virtually had staked her claim. Olivia left the following morning empty-handed and more disappointed than the last time of our accidental meeting in Salisbury (Harare) city centre. That was the last time I heard of Olivia. I believe that she had assumed, with one last throw of the dice, that I could be smothered and change my mind if she appeared in person where I lived. I was sure she had gone through some trouble, but I could not help to ameliorate her situation, whatever it was.

Before I leave this section of my story, I must confess that my affections for Gloria, Mecrina and Elizabeth during my days as a teacher trainee did not assume any physical form. I supposed, from a Christian way of looking at these things, that it was the right thing to do. I steadfastly remained chaste and unblemished until I married my present wife, Margaret. In another sense though, suffice it to say that perhaps responsibility for what other men would regard as a weakness on my part must be placed on the poor diet of the restrictive upbringing in which I grew up, denied exposure to all forms of entertainment and leisure.

Thank God, though, that I fundamentally remained a 'virgin' and completely untainted by the pleasures of the flesh. Back in my adolescent days in Harari (Mbare) as well as in my young adulthood at St Paul's Teachers' College, some of my agemates had reported variously of having already had to seek medication to treat sexually transmitted diseases contracted from 'one nightstands' or carelessly sleeping around with girls. That my sexuality was still untainted often made me chuckle quietly to myself with pride.

# Chapter 15

# Some memories from Teaching Practice attachments

A strong component of my teacher training course was 'teaching practice'. In line with this expectation, it was a requirement for us to pass as part of the assessment process. The Department of African Education demanded we spend up to two months every year staying at surrounding primary schools. During that time, we were required to 'shadow' experienced teachers at work besides actually taking classes ourselves. Also, the idea was for us to become familiar with the lifestyles and habits of the people who lived in the villages and compounds in the catchment areas of the schools we would work in on completion of our training course.

In my first year, I remember being in a contingent of six male and female student teachers who were dispatched for our 'teaching practice' at schools in the Rota Villages, fifteen or so miles away, north of the teacher training college. Other small groups of our colleagues were posted to various other schools or centres scattered around the college. The most distant of these centres from the teacher training college was a place called 'Chemapango Primary School' which some people said was twenty-five miles away. That distance was probably exaggerated. The school was maybe only fifteen miles away from the mission station. I was never posted to that school for the three-year duration of my teacher training course at St Paul's. Our attachment at Rota Primary School would be for four weeks. School or College buses then were still a phenomenon of the future or a figment of one's imagination, so when it was our group's turn to be transported to our station, we were piled up in the back of a small open lorry, together with all our luggage, food provisions and any equipment we might want to use for food preparation.

The poorly maintained feeder road to the Rota reserves from St Paul's was untarred and full of corrugations, so that our first taste of rural teaching was like a baptism of fire. The fifteen-mile ride to Rota Primary School at the back of the open lorry was rough, bumpy and pretty unsettling. We, together with our equipment and luggage, were thrown about hither and thither as the lorry driver literally flew over the numerous corrugations on the surface of the uneven road to manage his driving of the vehicle. Arriving at our destination covered in layers of thick dust and grime, all of us resembled long forgotten scarecrows in fields of maize following the harvesting season; but the headteacher was expecting us and he gave us a warm welcome. The four men in my group were allocated their own living quarters in the 'Teachers' Houses' section of the school. The two women student teachers were allocated theirs too where they would be safe and secure from harassment by unmarried male members of fulltime staff or indeed total strangers from surrounding villages.

Rota Primary School was a fully-fledged rural primary school, so we drew our water from a borehole sited a little distance away at the edge of the school compound; there was no electricity, so for heating or cooking our food and lighting our rooms at night we were left to our own devices. Fortunately, we had brought with us appropriate equipment including pails with which to draw water, pots, dishes and various forms of cutlery and candles, to meet these challenges. The headteacher had allowed us to make use of dry logs of wood that were piled up on an open space beside his house. We relieved ourselves in communal toilet facilities in 'male' and 'female' outbuildings that were sited somewhere just outside the 'Teachers' Houses' compound but a distance away from our source of water. Every morning, Monday to Friday, hundreds of children arrived at the school from the local villages to attend classes, some of them in double streams, from Grade 1 (year 1 in the UK) to Grade 7 (year 6 in the UK). The term 'Standard or Sub-Standard so and so' in Rhodesia (Zimbabwe) had been overtaken by events and phased out and replaced with the new term 'Grade' when I trained as a teacher.

The efficiency and professionalism with which the headteacher administered his school reminded me of Mr Reginald Tsimba, my Standard 3 (Grade 5, year 5) teacher at Maronda Mashanu Primary School. Mr Tsimba subsequently promoted to the position of headmaster of the school despite remaining our class teacher. The headmaster at Rota School was a non-teaching headmaster by virtue of the large size of his school. He communicated well with all his staff, pupils and the parents who sent their children to the school. Apart from chairing fortnightly staff meetings with all his teachers, he spoke to the children at school assemblies that were held twice weekly. Otherwise, on every other school day after the school timetable had started, his authority was clearly visible by seeing him walk around the school premises to supervise his staff and ensure that learning was taking place in the classrooms.

At the school, there was a large headmaster's office where he hosted meetings with teachers. When education officials or individual parents visited the school for one reason or the other, he hosted them in that office. There were cupboards and shelves that contained stocks of new textbooks and exercise books in the same building. Other storage facilities contained sensitive records regarding reports pertaining to school inspections, teachers' lesson observation, enrolment figures, etc.

I was busy at one of the desks near the teacher's table, helping a little boy with his written work, when there was a loud knock, knock, knock on one of the open rear classroom windows. The loud knocking was so shattering that all the pupils stopped what they were doing and turned their heads to look in the direction where the noise had come from. I did likewise. Simultaneously, a man's hoarse voice called from somewhere outside the back of the classroom, "John! Hey John! Are you in there somewhere? What're you still doing here? School finished nearly an hour ago and you're supposed to have returned home by now!"

The pupil named John was not in my class but in the other Grade 7 class, somewhere in the block of classes opposite our own. The stranger had knocked on the window using the axe-handle which he now hung on his shoulder. When all of us, the pupils and I, looked at him askance, he was peering through the window and his eyes were sweeping across the rows of pupils sat on wooden benches. He hoped to see if he could locate where his own son, John, sat in the classroom so that he could fish him out and take him to his home. Suspicious of his next move, the group of pupils sat at the back row of the class near the window sprang to their feet and rushed forward for their safety. I quietly told the children not to panic while I walked in the opposite direction to try and talk to the man.

Reaching the middle of the classroom, the man saw me and then suddenly exclaimed, "Well, so there is someone here who keeps other people's children hidden in classrooms after school has ended?

"Hey, who are you?"

"You're going to see who I am today." …

And he began walking angrily towards the main classroom entrance door at the far end of the wall, brandishing his axe menacingly and mumbling things like a demented man. While I still kept my cool, all hell broke loose with the children. The class all stood up haphazardly, leaving their seats to pace up and down like cats on hot bricks. Exercise books, pens and rulers dropped to the floor as some of the boys began randomly jumping over desks while the girls gaped at the man with their palms unclasped behind their heads in awe.

Seeing that the man was approaching the door at the front of the classroom, groups of both boys and girls stampeded towards the only exit points available to them, the open windows in the one wall to their left. In a melee possibly never even heard of before the dawn of civilisation, screeching groups of marauding children climbed up and hurriedly squeezed through the open windows in a confused jumble. In twos or threes, they leapt to the safety of the outdoors without a care in the world whether they landed on sharp or hard objects.

It was a survival of the fittest scenario. Behind them, they left a scene of utter chaos with desks fallen over and benches upside down, their legs pointing skywards in a disorderly fashion.

Filled with air as they were airborne descending to the ground, the girls' skirts resembled parachutes of escaped jet-fighter pilots after their aircraft were blasted to smithereens in mid-air enemy attacks. On hitting the ground with nasty bumps, each one of the would be bunched-up jumpers picked themselves up and started running like the wind, shouting for help and waving their hands in the air as they sprinted across the sports field in front of the school and promptly disappeared into the woodland behind it:

"Oh, oh, oh, can anyone please come to Mr Moyo's rescue! We've a mad man with an axe! That man is bad! He has disturbed our lesson! Anyone out there, please help Mr Moyo! That man means harm to him! Over there by his class!"

Satisfied that the classroom was empty, that all the children had left the classroom and that all of them were nowhere near the man with the axe, I threw all caution to the wind and walked over to meet my nemesis who I thought would have entered the classroom during the hullabaloo of the children's hurried getaway. I was convinced if that man was a true parent of a learner at the school, he would do nothing to me. After all, he did not know who exactly I was; I was just a student teacher doing my bit to help raise pass rates for that school's Grade 7 examination results.

On reaching the door, common sense seemed to have prevailed, and the man did not dare enter the classroom uninvited. Instead, he stood a few yards away from the open door obviously waiting for me to arrive so that we could chat. Suddenly, he seemed aware of the magnitude of the commotion he had caused. Meanwhile, the loud SOS calls by my class as they fled the scene of the disturbance attracted the attention of not only the head teacher, who was resting in his home in the Teachers' Houses section of the school behind the block, following a busy day, but also that of the other Grade 7 teacher in the next block of classrooms.

Both the two gentlemen promptly responded and arrived at my classroom at the same time just when I was starting to converse with my strange visitor. Apparently, he was well-known both to the head teacher and the other teacher as one of the parents from the villages around the school. But he was one of several culprit parents who were uncooperative and always refused to attend parents' meetings when they were called.

As a result, he played no active role in development projects spearheaded by parents at the school. Although he did had a son by the name John in the other Grade 7 class, he had flatly refused to listen to his own son when he had told him of the new arrangements at school for him to attend extra lessons to help him stand a chance to pass his Grade 7 examinations at the end of the year. The head teacher invited the gentleman, the other Grade 7 teacher and I to come with him to his office. The head teacher did not beat about the bush; he was disappointed at the behaviour displayed by the parent. Although the parent apologised to me for the sudden and unceremonious break up of my lesson, the head teacher insisted that he was calling a parents' meeting at which the parent would have to offer his apologies. I still had three weeks of attachment at Rota Primary School as a student teacher. I carried on and fulfilled my commitment to participate in the 'additional Grade 7 lessons programme' at the school until my colleagues and I went back to college at the end of our attachment. That was a unique experience. I must admit that people's perceptions on various aspects of life differ. But for me, that experience was a learning curve.

Then, in the second year, I was stationed at schools in the Mabika area, approximately eight miles east of the mission station. It was another attachment that was meant to toughen us up so that we would be ready to face the challenges of teaching in the rural areas of Rhodesia (Zimbabwe). My experiences at Mabika Primary School were roughly the same as those we had had at Rota 'reserves'. The only exception was that no parent used subterfuge or deceit in their dealings with us. There was plenty to learn and we enjoyed our stay at Mabika Primary School. For the third year of my teacher training, my 'teaching practice' attachment was at another rural primary school called St Phillips in the Chikwaka Tribal Trust Lands, approximately twenty kilometres from St Paul's, Musami. I was one in a group of six student teachers who were allocated to the school where we would spend up to six weeks cooking our own meals, sleeping on the floor and were expected to cope with the hardships of working in the tough rural environments.

To soften our hardships a bit, the college provided us with food rations and a fair amount of cash which we would use to top-up on our food needs should we run short of supplies. Let me point out that when I went on the attachment at St Phillips, I had just broken up my romantic association with Mecrina following my sad discoveries that she was cheating on me with another man. I was therefore quite lonesome for most of our period of absence from mission premises for the purpose of teaching practice. Mecrina was no longer part of my life, yet I missed her so much. My group put me in charge of the small portable radio which college authorities gave to each group to provide us some entertainment and listen to the news while we were in the bush, so to speak. I seemed to be the only one in my group who had any interest whatsoever in listening to that radio, whether it be to listen to music or to tune in to stations that contained news bulletins. For that reason, all my colleagues would fall asleep at night while I continued to enjoy listening to pop music tunes that were belted one after the other by South African disc jockeys on what used to be 'Lourenco Marques Radio' (before politics took over and the station became 'Radio Maputo' when Mozambique gained its independence from Portugal in 1974). Of course, you can be sure that I played the radio at very low volume most of the time to avoid disturbing my colleagues who would be fast asleep. I would sometimes stay awake all night listening to the non-stop music. As I had severed my romantic links with Mecrina – some of the pop music tunes played by those South African DJs made me feel very lonely indeed.

My teaching practice at St. Phillip's Primary School took place from 1 June of 1971 and ended on 16 July of the same year. That was right at the onset of the short but cold Rhodesian (Zimbabwean) winter season. It was therefore indeed very cold in terms of our climate and weather patterns in Southern Africa.

Staying awake all night listening to music without wrapping up against the cold weather resulted in exposing myself to the risk of catching a cold. Those six weeks were the coldest part of our winter in Rhodesia (Zimbabwe). I contracted a very bad cold that winter while at St Phillip's in Chikwaka Tribal Trust Lands. I provide some details below about my flu infection, its results and another event relating to my encounter with a river python.

The story about the river python emanates from my inability to report for my teaching duties because I had contracted a very bad flu. Arriving at St Phillip's for our six-week teaching practice, the school only provided us with an empty teacher's house which all of us would use as storage, cooking and sleeping accommodation. As for water supplies, there was a spring well a short walking distance from the school. All we needed to do was to take turns to fetch water from the spring well using the twenty-litre pails college had supplied us with on our departure for 'teaching practice'.

In the middle of my teaching practice at St Phillips Primary School, I woke up one morning feeling terribly unwell. It was clear I had been attacked by a flu bug because I had a pounding headache; dizzy spells and was coughing badly. I sent word with one of my colleagues to the head teacher telling him I would not be able to take my class for lessons for that day and possibly the next day due to my condition of ill-health. I took some of the painkillers college authorities had issued to us, and I spent all day in bed. On day two, I felt much improved but not quite ready to resume my teaching duties. After midday, the sun came out from behind a thick blanket of clouds and it shone brightly, ushering in warmth into the atmosphere following days when we had grey skies, and it was particularly chilly. As my condition gradually improved for the better, I decided to leave the house the headteacher had given us for our use as a team during our placement. I decided to walk down to the river alone and wash my clothes. I had heard of the rocky place down at the river but none of my collegemates nor I had been to that place along the river before. I hoped that the walking to and from the river about two miles from school would, as somebody had said, refresh me and give me new strength after my ordeal with the flu. I walked slowly on the path to the river clutching my small bundle of clothes in a paper bag.

I was all by myself. I did not meet anyone as I walked to the river, approximately three kilometres from the school premises. To this day, I still do not know why it never occurred to me that I should be accompanied by somebody to the place at the river which I had only heard about but had never visited.

Arriving at the spot on the riverbank and standing on top of a rounded rock, I chose to use a bigger pool that I identified, approximately five metres below the large rock where I stood upon. I was going to have to make a diversion to reach the pool I had located by jumping from one rock to the other until I reached the place I had located down below. But hold on, before I started hopping from rock to rock to reach my destination, I suddenly did not feel safe at that place. It was eerily quiet at that spot on the river. All I could hear was water tumbling down rocks as it flowed down the river. There were bits of birdsong from one or two birds high up in large trees along the river bank whose huge branches hung low into the river. A secret voice within me whispered, "Be careful, somebody is watching you." I peered into the thick bushes up the riverbank to see if indeed somebody was hidden in there watching every one of my moves. I saw nothing. But my hair stood on end and my heart was pumping hard.

Turning round instantly and still standing on the rock I stood originally, I looked back five metres below. My attention was immediately captured by the slow movement of a massive tubular snake the size of my thigh! How frightening this was! The body of the snake had rectangular patches of grey and brown colours, the same colour as the rocks I could see all around me. The snake was obviously sunbathing beside the pool I had intended to use to wash my clothes when I suddenly arrived. I presumably had disturbed its indulgence. Being camouflaged, it had not been easy for me to see it first, hence my intense feelings of insecurity. When I finally spotted the snake, it was leaving, taking itself to a place of relative safety. I did not see its head. What I saw was may have been half of its body, about three metres long, which was slowly disappearing into a dark hole at the bottom of the large rock I stood upon. Afraid that the snake might suddenly rear its ugly head from behind the rock where I stood and have a go at me, I exploded into action. Still firmly clutching the paper bag containing my clothes and filled with a rush of adrenaline, I sprang from one rocky surface to the other. As soon as I reached the riverbank, I sprinted back to our house at the school. One of my colleagues who was more familiar with that area said the snake I had seen was a river python. That type of snakes was hardly ever seen.

Some of the few such snakes spotted in the past had been notorious for killing human beings if their hiding places were disturbed. I was lucky to have been saved by the feeling of insecurity I had experienced when I had arrived at the river earlier on. Otherwise. had I encroached too close to that snake by attempting to descend to the pool below where it quietly lay, I would have been history because the snake would have killed me by constriction and swallowed me! It was a bitter lesson for me. I vowed I would never go to that river or any other river in the area again until we returned to college two weeks later.

I successfully completed my three-year teacher training course in December 1971. Reverend Father Mangan kept his pledge to register me to sit for my General Certificate of Education 'O' Level examinations. So, by 1974, I had passed eight 'O' Level General Certificate of Education subjects including English language, studying privately through University of London. In those years among my kith and kin, obtaining a General Certificate of Education 'O' Level qualification was like earning a badge of honour. University education was largely reserved for Europeans and a small number of Africans who had been lucky enough to squeeze through what was called 'bottlenecking'. Access to those stupendous levels of academic achievement for most non-Europeans was not an easy ride. The General Certificate of Education 'O' Level qualification or simply 'Form 4', as it was then famously known among the black population, was in high demand. Due to its increasing demand by employers, it had assumed great importance in both the public and private sectors of our economy. That was so because the world was changing; yet a comparatively small number of young African men and women of the time did not possess the important academic qualification. When my General Certificate of Education 'O' Level arrived from the UK and was delivered to me, I felt like pinning them up on my forehead and running around the streets yelling to whoever cared to listen to me as I shouted, 'Look, I have my 'O' Levels! Hullo everyone. I am an 'O' Level Certificate holder!' but I lacked one important subject in my General Certificate of Education line-up of 'O' Level subject passes – mathematics, so even though I had recently got married to my young wife, Margaret, I bore down on studying for my General Certificate of Education 'O' Level mathematics, and subsequently passed that subject with a Grade 'B'. A mathematics teacher at Highfield High School took me through the paces of preparing for the General Certificate of Education 'O' Level mathematics examination twice a week after school hours. I was in an initial study group class of thirteen other adult teachers from all over Highfield primary schools. When we wrote the London University final examination ten months later, only two of my colleagues, Mr S. Maguranye, Ms Mandigora and I had clung on until we finished our studies.

The rest of my colleagues in the study group had dropped out of the study programme one after the other in despair like rodents deserting a sinking ship. They gave up trying, finding it difficult to cope with the intricacies and complexities of the subject. But my two colleagues and I proved that hard work and persistence pay by scoring colourful grade passes in the final examination because we relentlessly kept going at it despite the setbacks and frustrations we encountered along the way.

# Chapter 16

# The start of my teaching career: Then, my future wife, Margaret Florence Nyemba, gets into the mix.

Within days of completing my T3 teacher training course at St Paul's, Musami, I resolved that I wanted to start my teaching career at an urban school. Having experienced both lifestyles in rural and urban settings as a primary school pupil and recently as a teacher trainee, I was convinced that working in town schools was easier and more attractive than in the countryside. I persuaded my close friend and confidante, Charles Jambaya, to make the same preference as myself and he agreed with me. He came along with me on a visit to head office (Ambassador House) of the Ministry of Education in Salisbury (Harare) city centre. Presenting ourselves there, we proudly flashed our sparkling new T3 Teachers' Certificates as an expression of our interest in being employed in urban government primary schools.

We were warmly welcomed on our visit to head office and our enquiries for teaching vacancies were politely attended to. They had plenty of teaching vacancies in Highfield. After filling out a few employment forms, both of us were allocated teaching posts at Kudzanayi School. Two or three years later, my friend Charles Jambaya would transfer to Kuwangira School in the same neighbourhood of Highfield Township. I started teaching at Kudzanayi Government School at the beginning of the school calendar year in 1972. It was a large 'inner-city' primary school with an enrolment of around one thousand three hundred pupils and upwards of forty teachers on the staff.

Freshly qualified as a teacher, I was allocated a Grade 3A Class in streams of the same grade that went up to stream 'D'. It was fifty years ago when I started teaching the class of budding little boys and girls in that class. I still recall a few of the pupils whose education was placed in my care. Some of that first group of pupils include Pauline Jaboon, O'Day Garande, Christina Shayanowako, Perpetua Nyamayedenga, Praxidia Chimanga, Paradzayi Chinyandura, Norah Ruwizhi, (Somebody) Gwasha, (Somebody) Nleya, etc.

Christopher Hakata joined that class in Grade 4 (year 4 in the UK). That boy was one of my brightest performers. I taught that fantastic group of pupils – and others I did not mention in a class of around thirty pupils – for five solid years across all subjects in the curriculum from Grade 3 and through to their Grades 4, 5, 6 and 7. Until somebody corrects me, I am probably the only holder of the record of teachers ever employed to teach at Kudzanayi Government School in Highfield, (Salisbury) Harare, to teach one set of children continuously for five years.

Some of the pupils in the group were children of members of staff at the school. I enjoyed carrying the weighty responsibility of providing for the educational needs of these children. Seeing them literally grow up together emotionally, physically, and cognitively was satisfying to me indeed. They became part of me and whatever strengths (and weaknesses) I may have possessed as a young teacher then were indelibly stamped on these budding young learners. Indisputably, if I had had any weaknesses in my competence as a teacher, that group of pupils were permanently denied assistance to achieve and progress in their journey through primary school, which they could have accessed from other teachers with superior ability than I possessed. The head teachers at Kudzanayi School in that five-year stretch were Mr Gabi in the first two years and then Mr N Puwai in the last three years. Both insisted that I continue teaching the same class of pupils year in year out, due to popular demand from parents and other members of staff who were pleased with the work I was doing with my pupils. Mr Puwai was of the belief that from an educational perspective, whatever teaching skills I lacked were by far outweighed and subsequently cancelled-out by my teaching competitiveness which he found unmatched and admirable. Most of my 'Class of 1977' pupils produced exceptionally pleasing subject grade passes in their Grade 7 results; enabling them to proceed to be enrolled for Form 1 places in local secondary schools for January 1978.

Others were enrolled to start their secondary school education at mission boarding schools scattered in provinces outside Harare. At the end of what I considered an era of its own kind, I organised a massive party for my 'Grade 7 Class of 1977 Leavers'. I held the party in the domestic science classroom, a large classroom block attached to the back of the school. From time to time in the afternoons, the domestic science teacher kindly offered her class to both staff and pupils to be used as a function room. The head-teacher (Mr Puwai) and other teachers also attended that unique event to witness these future legends gravitate together and enjoy themselves at the end of a gruelling but successful campaign.

Five years of learning together as a group had not been an easy ride for them. My teaching style and the results thereof placed me in the top tier of what the headteacher considered the most competent and effective of his over thirty-strong members of teaching staff. Selected at the beginning of each year to teach either Grade 6 or Grade 7 classes only between 1977 and 1984, Kudzanayi achieved fame among other primary schools in Highfield as the leading school in producing the highest pass rates in Grade 7 examination results.

The only other competing schools which were slotted into second position and downwards were Mbizi School, Tsungayi School and Mhizha School. The work going on at Kudzanayi School in those years was uniquely the product of teachers who worked at the school as a team right from the lower primary classes, through middle school and up to the upper primary end of the school. Nothing beats working in teams. I was proud to contribute in the best way I could towards what would ultimately become a result of group effort. The outstanding work my colleagues and I produced in those years would not have been possible without groups of staff working in close collaboration with one another. It was all-hands on deck when I taught Grade 6 and 7 classes with the likes of Mr James Chadhliwa, (the late) Mr Hosea Mahere, (the late) Mr Joachim Chirimuuta, Mr Caleb Chagwinya and Mr

Crispin Mutiro. I derived considerable pleasure and enjoyment sharing ideas on scheming, planning and lesson delivery perspectives with these gentlemen, some of whom unfortunately have sadly passed on at the time of my writing this memoir.

Also, our luck lay in having a head teacher, (the late) Mr Nicholas Puwai, who made sure that an enabling environment always prevailed at the school, thereby allowing us the freedom to excel as teachers to achieve high levels of learning and achievement among the pupils in our care. He had an open-door policy and welcomed teachers to knock on his office door at any time, to make suggestions on how we could contribute towards making sure that the pupils entrusted to us by their parents were learning. His general staff meetings were properly organised events where teachers expressed themselves freely on matters to do with the education of the children in their charge. At the end of each of these gatherings, teachers emerged refreshed, enriched with new knowledge and skills and raring to go and apply any suggested strategies received, in their lessons.

I had been hugely fortunate to be appointed for a teaching position at an urban government primary school straight from teacher training college; but one immediate challenge I faced was that I did not have anywhere to live – a place from where I would be able to attend to my duties at school and return to in the evenings to rest. Term 1 of the school year in 1972 started before I had secured a decent place in Highfield for me to use as a base. Making it worse was that I did not have any relatives with properties in Highfield to help me get round the challenge of lack of accommodation. The Teachers' Government Flats: six of the blocks that still exist along Jabavu Drive in Highfield, largely provided temporary accommodation to unmarried male teachers. I could not immediately be accommodated in these flats because they were fully occupied. They did not have any vacancies, making it a bumpy start for someone fresh from teacher training college.

Reverend Father Mangan who was still stationed at Mazowe Novitiate, learnt of my predicament, and came to my rescue. He drove over and spoke to the Priest-in Charge at St Mary's Roman

Catholic Church, Old Highfield, asking him if I could temporarily be accommodated in a room within the priests' house while I made enquiries for a room to rent. His request was kindly accepted although, weirdly, all the bedrooms at the priests' house were fully occupied by a team of other secular priests. Fortunately for me, the metal trunk Reverend Father Mangan had bought for me before I started teacher training at Musami and the few clothes inside it was the only property I carried around with me. All I needed was a small space where I could sleep at night and have a quick shower in the morning before I rushed out to work. Travelling light as I did. I immediately moved into St Mary's Church quarters at Old Highfield, sleeping on the floor of the church's Reception Room for my convenience. I would wake up first thing in the morning and do my personal care in the priests' communal shower room. Then I would share a quick breakfast with the group of priests in their communal diner before I walked to Kudzanayi School for work, just over four kilometres away. After work, late in the afternoon, I made sure I was back at the priests' house by six thirty p.m. and shared the evening meal together with the rest of the clergy.

Lying on that carpeted floor in the Reception Room of the Priests' House at St Mary's Church one night, I convinced myself that as I was setting out into young adulthood, I had a massive responsibility on my shoulders. Splitting the load into sizeable portions, I said to myself I must continue working hard and ensure that the path Reverend Father Mangan had set me on produces tangible results. Next, I realised that I had a line-up of dependants, some real and others imagined, who would depend on me to help make their lives easier and more manageable in the same way as Reverend Father Mangan had done for me. I needed to live a hassle-free life based on my solid academic and professional achievements.

I also recognised that for me to achieve my lifelong ambitions, I did not just need someone of the opposite sex, a 'girlfriend' to hang out with; I needed a strong-willed woman for many years of my life, a woman who would stand by me, not behind me, through thick and thin, as I relentlessly pursued the achievement of my mission. I imagined that the path of my life and that of the woman of my dreams would together be a 'long and winding road', like The Beatles' Paul McCartney was singing then, but I vowed that the 'winding road' in the song must lead us to a favourable destination somewhere. I was just over twenty-one years of age and as a rule of thumb, I recognised I should be in some sort of relationship with someone of the opposite sex. However, weirdly, that was not the case. It bothered me, though, when I realised that if a lass suddenly fell in love with me and expressed the wish to marry me, where would I stay with her, without a proper roof over my head as things were, currently?

I continued staying at St Mary's Church, Old Highfield, until May of that year. Despite my accommodation discomforts in those first few months of my career as a teacher, I always kept myself smart and well-presented as a professional. I always greeted my pupils and other staff with a smile and never allowed despondent feelings to interfere with the way I presented myself. Little did I allow my pupils ever to second guess that for those five months, I was a man of no fixed abode! I truly had humble beginnings, literally starting from scratch as a newly employed young teacher. Time stretches.

A Mrs Madangure, one of the female staff in the lower primary department of the school, heard about my accommodation difficulties. Apparently, she owned a house of her own just two kilometres down the road towards Kudzanayi School from St Mary's Catholic Church. She lived in that house with two small children who were also attending school at Kudzanayi School. Mrs Madangure offered me one of her spare bedrooms in the house which I could rent at a small monthly fee. I readily accepted her offer before I even went to view the room. Viewing it days later, I discovered it had plenty of room for me to fit in a single bed and a single door wardrobe which I intended to buy later because I had not raised enough money to buy those items yet. Before I could make use those savings from my meagre earnings to afford these items of furniture, I moved into Mrs Madangure's house at the start of June 1972. I occupied my new lodgings with just my metal trunk containing the few precious possessions, mostly clothing and bedding items that Reverend Father Mangan had bought me, prior to commencing teacher training at St Paul's Teacher Training College, Musami. Indeed, for the whole of June and July of that year, I slept on the hard, cold cement floor of that rented room. Juxtapose that with my sleeping conditions at the priests' house, St Mary's Catholic Church, where I slept on the softness of carpeted floors.

My confidence at the new physical address, however, grew from knowing that I had a more decent roof over my head there and a place I could temporarily call my own. Thus, I had no choice but to grin and bear the discomfort of sleeping on the hard, cold cement floor. There were a whole host of commitments that occupied me on weekends as part of my socialisation.

My older brother Roland had by then got married. He still did not quite yet own a house of his own in Harare (Mbare) yet, so he continually changed addresses in his unending search for a place whose rent charges resonated with his smaller earnings. If I knew where he rented a room or two with his wife and children, I would take time off to visit them. If I was lucky on a visit to my older brother's place, I would also run into young brother Irrigation (Wilfred) who also would have visited my older brother and his family. When that happened, though fortuitously, we would turn the meeting of siblings into an 'ad hoc meeting'. At such 'meetings of the minds' – as we sometimes termed them – we discussed and thrashed out many family challenges, finding answers to some and leaving others for consideration when we met again next time. Irrigation (Wilfred) had just finished school and had started working in a job as a delivery salesman with a company in Salisbury (Harare) while I was training as a teacher. He was still a bachelor like me, and he lived somewhere as a 'lodger' in Glen Norah Township.

Often, within my first year of teaching, I also remembered to pay homage to my cousin/Brother Douglas Ruhukwa. He lived with his wife and children in a fashionable 'middle density' suburb called Westwood, adjacent to Kambuzuma 'high density' township. This man's close links with me and my family had endured since his brief stay with us at father's farm in Enkeldoorn (Chivhu) back in the mid-1950s. I have already given a full account of this in an earlier chapter. During school holidays while I was training as a teacher, I often stayed with him and his family at their house in Mufakose. It would be very remiss of me to forget mentioning that during my three years' training as a teacher at St. Paul's, of all my relatives in Salisbury (Harare), cousin/brother Douglas Ruhukwa, was the only one who seemed to have the wherewithal to visit me while I was in college at Musami. He would invariably arrive in his shiny yellow 'VW Beetle' from Salisbury (Harare) at least twice or thrice a year, bringing me goodies such as boxes of 'Jade' bath soap, tubes of 'Colgate' toothpaste, 'Roll-on' fragrance bottles, and so on. Sometimes he left me a bit of money, too. Cousin brother Douglas would arrive without warning, usually on Saturday afternoons. Placing me in a distinct class of the 'with it' among my colleagues, cousin brother Douglas made me feel great, secure, and sometimes even proud. The goodies he brought me provided me peace of mind and a fresh injection of confidence which went a long way towards helping me to concentrate more on my studies rather than needlessly worrying about the balances remaining in my stock of 'toiletries.' None of my friends had 'special' visitors at weekends of the likes of my cousin/brother.

My parents' marriage had broken down irretrievably years before, but they were still to be officially divorced. Then Mother who was living in separation from my father, was temporarily living with her sister, Aunt Eliver, somewhere in Salisbury (Harare), I cannot be sure where. Aunt Eliver later went on to buy a property in the Jerusalem Lines of Highfield (Harare). She moved from Harari (Mbare) Township to her new property with my mother as part of her appendages. I would go out of my way to visit my mother and her sister during which I also dealt with those welfare needs pertaining to my mother which were within my means to handle. Now that I had started working and was earning a salary, custom demanded that I play a more meaningful role in looking after both my parents; especially my mother, who had no real means of subsistence after starting to live separated from my father. Furthermore, there were quite a few 'uncles' on my mother's side of the family who lived all over the place in Salisbury (Harare).

I would take trouble to pay homage to and communicate with all these important members of my extended family. Apart from the programme of family visits that I have already thrown light on, I also occupied myself in various ways during weekends. On some Saturday afternoons, I teamed up with my friend Charles Jambaya and we went to watch football matches between such teams as 'Dynamos FC' and 'CAPS United' at either Gwanzura Stadium in Highfield or Rufaro Stadium in Harari (Mbare). I was not quite a football fan myself, so my visits to the different venues to watch soccer were few and far between. On other Saturday afternoons, if I was not reading books at the main council library in the grounds where the Salisbury Polytechnic was also sited, I would regularly be found at cinemas in Salisbury city centre, usually at 'Kine 400' or 'Park Lane Cinemas,' next to Salisbury Gardens, watching 'Spaghetti Westerns' or any fast-moving secret agent movies with my mate Charles Jambaya or indeed often on my own. Both Charles Jambaya and I had already read plenty of books by an American writer called James Hadley Chase and some 'cowboy' novels, so the actors Clint Eastwood and James Bond 007 were our favourites. We also liked watching horror movies. Among the popular ones at the time was the 1971 American vampire film entitled 'The Return of Count Yorga'. Halfway through such movies, the film would stop showing and those among the audience of a nervous disposition would politely be asked to leave the auditorium and go home as the next part of the film would be more harrowing and nerve-wracking. Having spent most of my youth in which I was fed on a diet of priestly abstinence and urged to stick to the 'strict and narrow path,' I would go straight back home after watching movies.

For lack of anything better to do on some weekends, Charles Jambaya and I were members of a ballroom dancing club at

Zimbabwe Grounds Council Hall. That recreational centre was, and still is, located directly opposite Mushandira Pamwe Hotel in Highfield. We met at that venue, also adjacent to Gwanzura Stadium across Nyandoro Road, for dancing club practice sessions with a large group of other young club members on Sunday afternoons, which was also adjacent to Gwanzura Stadium. A girl named Maria was usually my dancing partner at the ballroom dancing practice sessions. Maria had plain features which by no means drew me towards her emotionally. I personally did not find her any more beautiful than her physical endowment which drew suitors to her like ducks to water. Nevertheless, there was no romantic attachment between me and her, and yet we always preferred dancing the 'waltz', 'foxtrot'. 'quickstep', and 'tango' routines together on most of those Sunday afternoons. My preference was to dance with nobody else, but Maria seemed to compensate for or counterbalance that with the fact that I did not have a girlfriend, somebody of the opposite sex I could have claimed to be romantically connected with at the time. I suppose my not having a girlfriend seven or eight months into my fulltime work as a teacher was attributable to the irregular and disorganised accommodation circumstances that I faced at the beginning of my teaching career. That situation threw me into a kind of emotional slumber that completely switched me off 'girlfriends' between January and August 1972.

However, behold what happened on one late Sunday afternoon in August 1972. My friend Charles Jambaya and I thought we needed a breath of fresh air outside the entrance to the 'Zimbabwe Grounds' dance hall. Our decision followed a gruelling afternoon of ceaseless routine after routine of ballroom dancing. Standing by the kerb facing Mushandira Pamwe Hotel across the one tarred road (Nyandoro Road), the wide gates of Gwanzura Stadium were suddenly flung wide open. Tens of hundreds of people talking in discordant voices spilled out of Gwanzura Stadium and poured into Mangwende Drive. A football game between two rival teams in the Premier League had ended. A big knot of people walked along Mangwende Drive towards Machipisa

Shopping Centre while an even bigger group of tired-looking football revellers headed northwards towards their homes in Old Highfield. And not to be outmanoeuvred, one large group of people crossed the busy Mangwende Drive, avoiding vehicles that raced past them blaring their horns, and walked towards where Charles and I stood. A sizeable chunk of the crowd walked past us, a few laughing uproariously and others whispering to each other in hushed tones.

Then when the crowd had begun to thin out, there was a sudden spark which flashed and riveted me to the spot where I was standing. At the same time, I picked out this girl bringing up the rear two hundred yards away. In her left arm, she lightly clutched the right hand of a little boy who trotted beside her as she walked. The stranger lassie was still about fifty yards from us when, continuing to look at the girl with a fixed gaze, I said to Charles who also seemed mesmerised like me, "Charlie, do you see that girl walking towards us with a little boy running beside her? She's beautiful, isn't she? Look at the way she carries herself as she walks. That's my future wife, the mother of my children!" Charles concurred with me, "Yeah, Larry. That's a beauty of a lady. Let's see if we can get her to talk to us." Just as Charles finished his impromptu little speech, the girl reached where we stood. Her amazing beauty literally bowled me over. It held the fascination of forbidden fruit for me. In that short time, I had butterflies fluttering in my stomach wondering whether that beautiful girl would ever consider a love proposal from a poor unhandsome scumbag like me.

Mumbling to myself like a mad man, I said, "I am going to need to have my wits about me about that girl. I'll commit su-icide if I let her slip by me!" Just as she reached where Charles Jambaya and I stood and before she and the little boy she towed passed us, the little voice from somewhere inside me nudged, 'Come on you, say something!' I greeted her with some trep-idation, "Uh-um-Hullo, whi—ch, which team won and what was the score?" My heart bit fiercely. Without stopping to talk to us, she nervously responded with a sweet thin voice saying the football team 'Dynamos FC' has beaten 'Sables FC'. She did not tell us anything more.

I thought she was going to carry on walking straight ahead farther westward. But she made a sharp right turn and walked straight into the dance hall, the little fellow in tow behind her. From the corner of his eye, Charles Jambaya beckoned me to go after her. I followed her into the dance hall where she quickly located an empty seat beside Maria who was chatting to a group of other girl dancers. When I was standing just behind the girl with my heart beating wildly, she rebuffed all my attempts to speak her. She completely blanked out my request for her to let me know her name, showing no interest whatsoever in talking to me. I persisted. In exasperation, the girl stood up and walked over with the little boy in tow to the other side of the dance hall where she sat distractedly in a seat just vacated by another girl dancer who had been picked up by a male partner for a dance routine. I was going to have to be brave and act quickly because my golden girl was proving slippery. I followed her there. When I again asked politely for her name, she flatly refused to tell me, spurning my attentions completely. She stood up again and returned to sit beside Maria again. Slowly approaching the row of seats upon which the girls sat, I heard the 'stranger' girl say to Maria, "I'm ready to return home if you are, Maria. I thought we agreed I would pick you up here after the football game ended. Can we go now, please?"

Ah, so Maria should know who this stranger girl is, I thought to myself. I made a mental note of that! Bidding me farewell feverishly while the girl stood with the little boy clutched in her hand by the entrance of the dance hall, Maria, who had taken note of my interest in the 'stranger' girl, leaned over to me, whisperingx that the girl who had drawn my attention was a friend of hers They lived in the same neighbourhood in the 'M Lines' section of Old Highfield and she went by the name 'Margaret Nyemba.' I offered to walk with them from the dance hall to Old Highfield, about a mile away. During that walk I did not beat about the bush. I informed Maria that I found Margaret very attractive and that I had fallen in love with her. On being informed of my affection for her by Maria, Margaret Nyemba would not hear of it. For part of the mile-long journey I walked with the three of them, Margaret looked unsettled, if not frightened. She literally dragged the little boy trotting alongside her by the hand. Soon, she began running ahead, leaving several yards distance between me and Maria. After Margaret and the little boy had disappeared round a bend, I stopped in my tracks and told Maria I was going to have to retrace my steps. Maria promised she would see if she could talk to Margaret on my behalf. Hopefully, her attitude would have softened if she came around again on the following weekend. Margaret lived in the same area of Old Highfield as Maria.

According to my informant, Margaret adored watching football games between Premier League teams in Gwanzura Stadium every Sunday afternoon. Maria assured me that Margaret would turn up again without fail on the following Sunday. I left it at that for my first meeting with Margaret Nyemba. My second and third encounters with her were almost at the same level of difficulty as the first one. Margaret Nyemba was not a registered member of our dancing club. Yet what I found encouraging was that at the end of the soccer matches at Gwanzura Stadium, Margaret never failed to turn up at the dance hall to pick up her friend for those three consecutive weekends. In the middle of the second month of my pursuit of her, I noticed cracks in her armour. Her attitude towards me began to soften and she became more generous with her remarks. At the same time, there was a clear demonstration in her behaviour which expressed her readiness to talk to me in Maria's absence. Gradually, Margaret started not only chatting with me freely and confidently, but she also laughed together with me when I cracked jokes. That was fantastic. The chemistry between us having improved markedly, she eventually spilled the beans, confessing her deep affection for me in the same way I had executed the campaign to win her heart.

After that welcome and most pleasing development in August 1972, I embarked upon a protracted programme of dating her. I was anxious to know more about her, just as I was pretty sure she was keen to know more about who exactly I was. Instead of leaving her parents' home in the afternoons, ostensibly to attend football matches at the nearby Gwanzura Stadium, I had her enrolled as a member of the dancing club. So, she teamed up with the girl Maria who lived in the same area of Old Highfield as Margaret lived. They then went for the dancing club practice sessions together.

Before long, the dancing club venue ceased to be our meeting point. Either I secretly picked up Margaret from her parents' home and took her with me to my rented accommodation, or she regularly walked over to my place, usually on Saturday or Sunday afternoons, and we would go out to see films or had romantic meals at top restaurants in Harare city centre. I cannot remember how many times the two of us watched film shows in 'Kine 400', 'Park Lane Cinema' and ate meals at 'The Oasis Motel' or 'Jameson Hotel'. These facilities were in the heart of the 'Sunshine City' of Salisbury (Harare) and they were just a sample of the posh places an aspiring man would take his beautiful girl for entertainment. As an ordinary schoolteacher only just starting out in my career, I was not earning much money, but I was prepared to impress my gem of a girl with the best that money could buy.

Times without number, Margaret and I attended the 'Salisbury (Harare) Show' held annually at the Show Grounds. I also took Margaret with me to attend music festivals, either Rufaro Stadium or Gwanzura Stadium in Salisbury (Harare). Big 'Soul Music' names like Percy Sledge visited Rhodesia in the 1970s. Margaret and I attended one of his gigs at Rufaro Stadium in Harari (Mbare) Township. We also attended South African pop singer Richard John Smith's shows whenever he staged shows in Rhodesia (Zimbabwe). Then there were the huge live stadium performances that we attended together by visiting artists such as Paul Simon who sang 'Graceland' backed by a South African singing group called 'Black Mambazo.' The late Johnny Clegg, also from South Africa, visited Rhodesia (Zimbabwe) several times, during which he laid on an impressive display of Zulu singing and dancing on the stage. Johnny Clegg was a white South African.

At around nine o'clock in the evening one Sunday night, one of my worst fears was confirmed. Walking northwards to Old Highfield along Mangwende Drive, we had just passed the main entrance gate into Gwanzura Stadium, approximately one hundred and fifty metres from the little bridge over the stream that runs down to Mukuvisi River on the right side of the huge stadium. I had my right hand protectively wrapped around Margaret's upper part of her body to ward off seduction and to emphasise my territorial authority over her. Meanwhile, she snuggled against me in utter abandon as we quietly walked and whispered to each other soulful and poignant sweet nothings. Motor vehicle traffic along the usually busy Mangwende Drive had thinned out considerably and very few people, if any, still waked back and forth along the footpaths on both sides of the road.

We still had a few metres to go before we reached the bridge when suddenly, I suppose, either a street urchin or an adult male bag-snatcher popped up along the path in the dim street lighting ahead of us. Strategically hidden in the tall grass beside the footpath on the other side of the bridge, the fellow had presumably spotted us as we walked towards the bridge past the football stadium, and he decided to strike for a kill. I noticed he walked towards us with a lot of energy, but his hands remained stretched downward beside his body. Without suspecting him of anything malevolent, I innocently assumed him to be any one of the hundreds of harmless street prowlers one meets as one walks along urban streets by day or night. Just before he passed us on our right, he lashed out with his right hand like a bolt of lightning. Acting with extreme dexterity, he reached out with his grubby fingers and grabbed Margaret's hairpiece perched on the side of her scalp.

The robber ripped it off her in the process before he swiftly ran off with the item in his claws and disappeared into the pitch darkness of the tall grass and thick bushes growing on the un-cared-for side of Gwanzura Stadium. Both Margaret and I were caught completely unawares by the robber's technique of using shock and fear. I was tempted to dash in pursuit of the fleeing man; but I stopped short of doing so when Margaret pleaded with me to 'hold my horses'. "Don't you dare follow the man, Lawrence!" Margaret screamed at me seeing the pointlessness and the increased danger of trying to execute a citizen's arrest on my own in the dark, without police assistance. Who would have guessed what weapon the ruffian of the night might have carried on his person? He probably had a gun or a knife! Besides, there was herself to think about. I could not possibly leave her standing alone on the open street after what had happened to her.

Her safety became my priority number one, so I stayed put. What if the robber was not a lone wolf and he was working in ca-hoots with a group of others hidden in the tall grass? Fortunately for her, the stolen hairpiece had lightly been attached to normal hair with pins which quickly dropped off and fell to the ground during the scuffle, so she suffered no pain or injury whatsoever except the embarrassment of having one of her items of dress be-ing ripped off her in such an uncivilised manner. Unsuspecting as we were, the entire event left us surprised and quite shaken. We would go on to arrange for the hairpiece to be replaced soon.

Agreeing that it could have been much worse, Margaret and I congratulated each other; expressing that none of us had sus-tained any bodily injuries. Continuing with our walk, we laughed the whole event off as we neared her parents' home. After the encounter I just described, let me admit that Margaret was not only the first woman I truly fell in love with and ever dated with serious intentions of marrying. She was also the first woman or 'girlfriend' who visited me for the first time in my virtually empty rented room at Mrs Madangure's house in Highfield. Coming at the tail end of that visit, Margaret was not moved in her affec-tion for me on discovering that I still had to buy a bed to sleep on and that I had nothing else to write home about except my black metal trunk and the few clothes and bedding items it con-tained. I had feared the shameful emptiness of my living quarters might scare Margaret away, but that was just my unfounded fear. It was encouraging to discover that Margaret was not put off by my bohemian lifestyle; the fact that I was only starting out in life, and I had yet to acquire anything of meaningful substance.

My romantic association with Margaret was like a rebirth. Margaret's entry into my life marked the beginning of great things for me. Her falling in love with me put a spring in my step and I began looking at the world with a different and more favourable outlook. Our love for each other kindled my dedication to the way I carried out my duties at Kudzanayi School. I was happy with myself. There was this hefty feeling of liberation, a sense to which I felt more committed towards helping my pupils to enjoy their learning. Several of my workmates provided feedback that it was not difficult for them to notice that I was enamoured of my work. I walked with a spring in my step and all my lessons were packed with verve, energy levels and liveliness. In the co-curricular life of the school, I led in every conceivable activity possible. For example, in 1973 or 1974, my Physical Education team of thirty twelve-year-old boys represented the school at the Inter-Schools Physical Education Competitions involving the eight large primary schools in Highfield. We were pipped for first position by Mbizi School. In 1975, I took my School Junior Music Choir composed of Grade 5 and six boys and girls to inter-schools' music competitions involving the same number of schools in the area. I came out top of my category. Between 1973 and 1977. Kudzanayi School was renowned for beating all surrounding schools in athletics, football, netball and tug-of-war.

By the end of 1974, Margaret was already well-known to most of the inner circle of my close relatives including my older brother Roland, his wife Faith, my young brother Wilfred and my mother, Leah. They all took to her like ducks to water. Unknown to me, Margaret would quietly visit my brother and my mother at their homes within Highfield, during which time she spent hours chatting with them, familiarising herself with my people, so to speak, as their future daughter-in-law. In turn, Margaret introduced me to her sister siblings, (the late) Mrs Judith Mashababe and her eldest sister, Tsitsi Nyemba. In terms of our Shona custom, nor was it time yet for me to be introduced to Margaret's parents nor to visit Margaret at her parents' home. However, her sister, the late Mrs Judith Mashababe, arranged it in such a way that I

346

was invited into the Nyembas' house in Old Highfield while Mr Nyemba was at home (!) not as Margaret's boyfriend, but as the older sister's former schoolmate! The old parents never discovered the trick visit. Instead, I for the first time shared an evening meal from the same table with Margaret's father.

Mr Nyemba was a big fan of the then popular Dynamos Football Club.

On that day, his team had won a football match against its nemesis CAPS United Football Club. So, my future father-in-law was in a very cheerful mood, spending the entire meal in stops and starts as he extolled the virtues of his beloved football stars. Over forty years after we became a married couple, Margaret told me that if the football team 'Dynamos' had lost the match to the rival team on the day of my unannounced visit to her parents' home, the reception Mr Nyemba gave me might have been very different; and to avoid muddying the waters, my alleged former 'schoolmate', Margaret's older sister Judith, did not dare even give a hint of my relationship with Margaret lest my visit ended unceremoniously, with me leaving in a great hurry because someone was pursuing me with a knobkerrie!

My father-in-law sadly passed on in 1977 due to a cancerous illness. That was less than two years following my marriage to his daughter. Margaret and I discovered that my father-in-law was such a peaceful man who would not even hurt a fly!

In a development linked with my relationship with Margaret when she was a mere 'girlfriend' of mine, my father paid me a surprise visit at the flats where I lived. It was the first time he had ever done so since the start of my teaching career. Of course, I was still a bachelor then and he expressed interest in knowing which lucky girl I intended to marry. His unannounced visit was for just one day in the middle of the week, so he did not get the opportunity to meet Margaret who by then had established a fixed pattern of turning up at the flats to visit me either on a Saturday or Sunday afternoon. Instead, as we sat chatting in my room, I pulled out of my photo album a black and white photograph of Margaret and gave it to him to study, explaining to him she was the girl I intended to marry, if all went to plan. Taking after her own mother's facial features, Margaret was very light in complexion. In the image I gave my father to look at, her straight nose, thin lips and light complexion made her look like a European woman.

Turning the photo in his hands around and looking at it from different angles, he suddenly burst out asking, "Lawrence, the girl I am looking at in this picture is very beautiful. But am I right in assuming that you are having an affair with either a 'Coloured' or a European girl? If your girlfriend is truly 'white' as I fear she is, is she going to be able to work in the fields at the farm?"

I assured my father of my pride and faith in Margaret and the things she was able to do with her hands. I believed she was as good as any virtuous, responsible, and beautiful young African girl he knew; however, in order to assuage his fears about whether Margaret would be able to work on the land, I assured him that with the lifestyle changes he could see happening all around him, not all our young women were destined to work with the soil. Given the skills she had, there were several other occupations our girl children could engage in with considerable dexterity and success. Asking him politely to return the photo to me for safekeeping, to put it back in the photo album, my father utterly refused to part with it, inserting it into the large pocket of the khaki tunic he was wearing. To my chagrin, I was to learn that on his return to Enkeldoorn (Chivhu) a week later, he reportedly carried the photo with him, hidden deep in his pocket, each time he went to beer-drinking parties in the 'reserves' upon which he would produce it and show it to his drinking partners, bragging that none of their children compared with me because I was going to marry a beautiful 'Murungu', (a light-skinned woman with features resembling those of a European), a thing that had never happened in that community before!

When I was absolutely convinced that Margaret was the most suitable candidate, 'the one' to march with me into the elusive future, I offered her my hand in marriage in 1976, four years after our courtship started. By then, I had long since moved from

Mrs Madangure's house and started living at New Hope Flats, which were government-rented teachers flats in Highfield. All the customary marriage negotiations were completed with the kind assistance and involvement of my father, my older brother Roland, and a Mr D P Maunze (one of the senior teachers on the staff at Kudzanayi School) as 'intermediaries' in the delegation that I dispatched to my in-law's house. To cap it all, Reverend Father Mangan solemnised my Christian marriage to Margaret in the Roman Catholic Cathedral in Fourth Street, Salisbury (Harare). Then Margaret moved in with me without further delay. Our first child, a son named Gerald, arrived in September 1976.

By moving in with me at New Hope Flats in Highfield, Margaret had unsuspectingly walked into an engine-roo where I was quietly giving momentum to the manufacture of many hopes and aspirations for both of us. In addition to my work during business hours at Kudzanayi School, I also did plenty of reading privately to improve my professional and academic standing. I rarely slept before midnight, if ever. I considered myself a bookworm of sorts and I was in the middle of reading voraciously for my General Certificate advanced level examinations in English Literature and European History. My little room at New Hope Flats was therefore jam-packed with all manner of reading material. My bookshelf contained nearly all the major classic writers in English including Shakespeare, Dickens, Chaucer, etc. Also, I read plenty of fiction for entertainment. The genre included a wide selection of authors under 'African Writers Series', books by the American detective writer James Hadley Chase and a host of other writers. My studies for General Certificate of Education 'A' Level history involved European History (1786 to 1914) and British history for about the same period. I suppose the rich reading culture Margaret found herself surrounded with in our little flat at 'New Hope' had an influence on her of which she was unaware.

Within a short time of her moving in with me, I noticed her attention was not just focused on the upcoming baby Gerald and her responsibilities as a housewife. She immediately embarked on serious reading, too. When we married, she had not quite completed her General Certificate of Education, so she sought to deal with that unfinished business and get it out of the way. I quickly discovered that she was naturally an intelligent person who needed just a bit of support and encouragement to spruce up her academic credentials before she entered the world of work.

The first thing I discovered about her academic background during our courtship was that she had been a boarder pupil for two years at the highly reputed St Augustine's Secondary School in Manicaland. She had not quite completed her 'O' Level General Certificate of Education at that school, due to the evil of 'bottlenecking' that I already described. As she prepared to polish up her General Certificate of Education 'O' Levels, for example, in English language, I do not recall ever having to sit down to teach her aspects of language skills like 'essay writing' and so on. Instead, the wide range of written literature in her environment and my preparedness to pay for her examination registration fees did that for me, providing Margaret a strong base from which to take off into the stratosphere.

In a very short time, Margaret's General Certificate of Education 'O' Levels were done and dusted. I remember asking her at that point to think about taking up training as a schoolteacher. Although she admired my role as a teacher, she did not find my suggestion terribly exciting. While she was still turning things over in her mind about what she was going to do with her General Certificate of Education 'O' Level qualification, our second child and first daughter, Audrey Shingaidzo, arrived in April 1979. About two years before I married Margaret, I travelled to Enkeldoorn (Chivhu) on an important mission. Information had reached me to the effect that the younger of my two sisters, Winnie (Phyllis) – now happily married as Mrs Bonga – had performed exceptionally well in her Grade Seven examinations. My parents' marriage having irretrievably broken down, although they were still to be officially divorced, my mother had left home years before and was living with her people in the Nharira Tribal Trust Lands. It was a surprising to me that my sister passed her Grade 7 examinations so successfully, even with the trauma of looking after herself and preparing her own meals in what ought to have been Mother's hut. Then my father's psyche was still locked in a past in which he believed Grade 7 or Standard 6 was the cut-off point for all his girl children. After that, they should live at the farm until they got married to any of the suitors in the local community, including 'herd boys' or other lackeys with very little formal education. Strangely, he believed that educating a girl child (who would eventually get married to a stranger) was like donating riches to the in-laws' family! I strongly objected to this narrow perception and discrimination against girls.

On reaching home, I discussed the matter extensively with my father now that I was an adult and more mature as a qualified teacher. I was surprised that he was prepared to engage in a grown-up conversation with me. I pointed out to him the benefits that accrue to all the children, male and female, when they are treated equally. He was grateful that I had helped him see the light. I had succeeded in breaking down his discrimination against our sisters. The new school term at the beginning of the year was still a fortnight away, so I moved quickly and secured Phyllis Winnie a place for Form 1 through the head teacher in the secondary school department at St Paul's Mission, the Reverend Father Cockroft who I had worked so well with when I trained as a teacher. Returning to Salisbury (Harare) after my successful meeting with my father, I brought her with me. Then at the start of that new year's new school term, (I cannot remember which year it was exactly), I personally travelled on the bus with my sister to St Paul's (Musami) and handed her over to the mission authorities for the start of her secondary school education.

Before I took Winnie Phyllis to St Paul's Mission, I bought her the full kit in the way of uniforms and other clothing and bedding necessities for a young girl in boarding school. My sister successfully completed her Cambridge School Certificate Examinations (Form 4) as a boarder at St Paul's. After that, she trained as a State Registered Nurse in Harare (now Sally Mugabe General Hospital.) I was pleased that I had played a role in my sister's education, thus transforming her life. If I had not prevailed upon my father and made him change his mindset, my sister Winnie Phyllis's trajectory and progress through life might be totally different today. Worse still she might have ended up falling victim to the romantic whims of any of the horribly undereducated herd boys and labourers on Kerry's farm next door or any of the village idiots who were in plentiful supply in the adjacent African 'reserves' of Mutasa, Dzvova and Dhobha!

I stayed on at Kudzanayi School (Highfield), continuing with my teaching duties diligently besides also studying hard at home after working hours to improve my academic and professional competence. I had continued riding on the crest of a wave in Highfield as one of the achievers of good results in the Grade 7 examinations. Having been a classroom practitioner at my school since starting work as a trained teacher, I believed I had acquitted myself well enough to be favourably considered for promotion to any of the advertised deputy headship positions within the Harare metropolitan area. Between 1980 and 1984, a number of these vacancies were advertised in Regional Circulars sent to all urban government schools in Harare.

Peculiarly, my counterparts at other government schools in Highfield were being promoted to those positions while all my applications flopped. One day while I was visiting Harare city centre, I plucked up enough courage to pop into the Regional Offices to find out why all my applications for promotion had been unsuccessful for a period of five years, despite the fact that after teaching at my present station for over ten years, I had produced such an impressive record as an effective and efficient practitioner. At the reception desk, I asked to speak with the Regional Director of Education, Mr Molife, himself. He was in and I was given the green light to walk through to his office. As soon as I entered Mr Molife's huge office, he welcomed me graciously, offering me a chair to sit directly in front of him.

As an educational official, the Regional Director usually only entertained headmasters of schools at his offices in Salisbury (Harare) city centre, so being just an ordinary classroom teacher who had never before been privileged to have an audience with a person occupying such a high office, I felt rather nervous in the brief interval before

Mr Molife could attend to me. While I arranged myself on my seat, he quickly remarked that he rarely, if ever, was visited by ordinary teachers but that usually, headteachers from schools in the region put in appearances at regional office to speak with him on important matters associated with how they were running their schools.

"I wonder what it is that brings you to these offices, Mr Moyo?" he quipped questioningly, looking at me directly in the process. I responded immediately and surprisingly confidently. "I was wondering if your office could put my mind at rest, Sir. As you may be aware I am probably one of a few teachers in your region who have contributed massively towards high Grade 7 examination pass rates for quite a while now. For the past five years, I have been submitting applications for promotion to some of the advertised vacancies for deputy headmaster one in circulars issued by this office. However, for reasons that have not been communicated to me, all my applications did not achieve the desired result. I would appreciate it very much, Sir, if your office could kindly put me in the picture about where I am falling short so that I can polish up on my weaknesses." I made those remarks looking directly at the Regional Director, sitting opposite me behind his huge desk.

"Ah, Mr Moyo, it's the first time in my experience such a query is being presented to me. I agree with you, you may be justified in your effort to get to the bottom of why you have not been accorded progression as you would have wished."

He instantly reached out for the intercom on his desk to call the Records Section somewhere in the filing department of that building to bring my personal file over.

It was promptly delivered and placed on his desk by a young male clerk who looked frightened. Asking me to be patient, he perused my fat folder as I sat directly opposite him in his office. Lifting his head and adjusting his spectacles, he agreed with me that on the strength of his findings, the record held by regional office about my outstanding performance was inconsistent with the notion that I was 'not promotion material,' as had been scribbled on many of my original application forms which were in the file. He went on to pull out of the fat folder five separate older application forms I had previously submitted in response to advertised deputy headship positions.

In the 'headteacher's Recommendation' section of each of these applications was written in bold letters 'Unsuitable for promotion'. Those types of entries on these forms would have played a key role in dashing any hopes that I could ever have had to be considered for shortlisting and thereafter be invited to promotion interviews that my other colleagues had been invited to attend one after the other, leaving me in a complete lurch.

The shattering discovery had me reflecting on the extent of how unfairly I had unfairly been treated and the fact that while my contemporaries were already in positions of substantive deputy headships and earning better salaries and managing to buy houses in the more affluent and former 'Europeans Only' suburban areas of Harare, I was still just an ordinary classroom teacher and had lost out irretrievably on climbing the housing ladder. That was a serious indictment on the part of my headteacher, a Mr – He was deceased as I write this entry, but I was livid with anger against him; I felt betrayed. This was the outcome after all the hard work I had put in over the years to produce good Grade Seven results for the school.

The Regional Director's own personal view was that while I had qualified for promotion years previously, it was not in the interest of my headmaster for me to be promoted and thus leave the school. Leaning forward in his chair to speak to me with a quiet voice as if he did not want the walls around us to hear, he said, "Your headmaster may have deliberately sabotaged all your efforts for upward mobility, Mr Moyo, perhaps because he wanted to retain you on his staff for his own kudos, his own fame and popularity, rather than facilitate your movement upward. That is sad. You see, Mr Moyo, human nature is very strange. My suspicion is that whenever Grade 7 examination results were announced by head office and your school was always found to be among the top performers, it gave your headmaster considerable pride, phoning all his colleagues from his office, telling them about how well his school had beaten his rival schools in the neighbourhood. There's little I can say, but to apologise to you profusely for what might have been the reason leading to your failure to be promoted to the deputy headship positions you applied for."

I found it hard to believe that somebody would hatch such an evil scheme aimed at inhibiting; literally standing in the way of my professional growth and development. It was heart-wrenching; I felt so very disappointed with it all and about being let down by the headmaster of my school. As time went by, I resolved to exploit any opportunities that might arise for me to leave Kudzanayi School altogether; either on transfer to another local school or by securing a place at the University of Zimbabwe and pursue studies for a university degree.

While I was pondering these ideas of flight or escape, my third child with Margaret, Lorraine Vimbai, was born in September 1982. Our daughter, Lorraine, was born when we had moved to a rented three-bedroomed house in the New Canaan Section of Highfield. It was probably at the start of the following year when I accepted a request for one of my cousin/sisters, Benhilder Mudyara – a much younger daughter of Uncle Rodrick – to come and live together with my young family at a 'Jabavu Drive' address in Highfield where I rented a three-bedroomed house while she attended day school GCSE classes at Kwayedza Secondary School, three kilometres away. Benhilder was 'family'. Her father, my uncle Rodrick Mudyara, had played a big role in promoting the primary school education of his older brother's children including mine. I felt there was no problem with accepting that request given to me by her older sister Praxedes, who lived with her husband and children in faraway Chitungwiza Township. After all, Margaret and I, with our young family, had enough room to accommodate Benhilder. She lived with us for the best part of two to three years? I cannot remember exactly how long it was

In April/May 1984, the University of Zimbabwe worked in collaboration with the British Council to mount short courses in the effective teaching of English as a Second Language, with a special focus on the teaching of poetry and text analysis. The short courses were targeted at primary and secondary school teachers. Renowned for my love of development programmes associated with anything 'English', the headmaster at Kudzanayi School selected me to represent the school at one of these short courses. The understanding was that I would report back to the entire staff of forty teachers on the skills I had picked up at the short course. I had no issues about speaking before large audiences. That skill had already been sharpened in me by my ten-year teaching experience and the experience I gained in debating sessions during my teacher training years.

For the 'Staff Development Workshop', there were four co-presenters on the short course which was held over two days at Seke Teachers' College. Two of the presenters were from the British Council; specialists in English language development who appeared to have travelled to Zimbabwe, all the way from the UK. The other two –co-presenters were from the Department of English at the University of Zimbabwe. One of the co-presenters from the UZ was none other than the then Mr Phillip Mhundwa who had lectured me in English at St Paul's Teachers' College fourteen years previously! We were delighted to meet each other again after such a lapse of time; under a completely different set of circumstances.

Before the end of the three-day course and seeing how well I had acquitted myself in the group activities, Mr Mhundwa called me aside for a quiet chat. Without beating about the bush, he expressed his disquiet that I was still just a classroom teacher since he had last taught me as a student teacher at St Paul's, Musami an odd eleven or twelve years previously. I apologised to Mr Mhundwa in embarrassment that luck had not smiled on me although I had repeatedly submitted applications for promotion! Without further ado, he went on to inform me about a new Bachelor of Education Degree programme across several subjects in the secondary school curriculum that would be launched in March/April 1985.

The advertisement for applications for the degree programme would appear in the press shortly and Mr Mhund said that I should keep my eyes peeled. Already in possession of a General Certificate of Education 'A' Levels in Literature in English and History and a Grade 'B' General Certificate of Education 'O' Level Mathematics, Mr Mhundwa said I already qualified to apply for admission to pursue the 'English' component of the Bachelor of Education Degree programme. On my completing the UZ application forms, he said he would not mind if I named him as one of my referees.

# Chapter 17

# First university degree at the University of Zimbabwe and immediate transfer from my old school thereafter

Just before Christmas 1984, I received a letter from the University of Zimbabwe confirming their offer to me of a place for a three-year Bachelor of Education Degree in English and Psychology of Education. I was granted full-paid study leave for the first twelve months of my studies, which was the fulltime 'taught' component of the programme. When I married Margaret in 1976, I was in the middle of studying and completing my second General Certificate of Education 'A' Level subject, 'Literature in English.' I had done away with General Certificate of Education 'A' Level 'European History.'

The process involved juggling time between fulltime work as a teacher and attendance at evening study group classes at one of the government primary schools in Highfield Township. There were initially fifteen of us in the mixed group of male and female teachers. However, as the degree of difficulty in our studies intensified, the class enrolment gradually decreased to a much smaller number. My colleagues and I met for two-hour lessons three times a week. A Mr Roger Musewe, a fulltime teacher of 'English Language & Literature' at Highfield High School, guided us through Julius Caesar's 'Winter's Tale', and 'Julius Caesar'. We also studied as our set books for the final examination Charles Dickens's 'Hard Times', 'Bleak House' and 'Great Expectations,' along with Jane Ayre's 'Mansfield Park.' To complete that marathon, we looked at and analysed some of Geoffrey Chaucer's 'Canterbury Tales.' Up until I went to start training as a teacher, I had only specialised in learning the four rules of English language and come across bits of 'poetry' contained in English language work and in the music lessons that I taught in primary school. Having 'poetry' per se as a stand-alone subject in my General Certificate of Education 'A' Level studies opened a whole vista which exposed me to a whole body of literature, the like of which I had never known before. I agree with those who argue that poetry in any language is the purest form of human expression.

Fast forward this whole story, and the journey seems to take a lifetime, but I found myself at the University of Zimbabwe eventually, to study for a Bachelor of Education Degree in English. I was excited to have passed the General Certificate of Education 'A' Level 'Literature in English' examination when I took it; but that excitement was extinguished in the first few months of my university degree studies when I discovered to my horror that my general education had not prepared me adequately to cope with the intellectual demands of the university experience; particularly in work that involved poetry analysis. Surprisingly, I performed remarkably well in Mrs Ruth Moyana's English fiction and non-fiction novel analysis classes. I understand that she still lectures at the University of Zimbabwe and is now a professor. Thirty-three years ago, she was my lecturer. It is hardly surprising that she achieved the professorship. With her assistance and guidance, we read and analysed novels written by African writers in English, namely 'Things Fall Apart by Chinua Achebe; Dambudzo Marechera's 'House of Hunger'; Ngugi wa Thiongo's 'Devil on the Cross' and 'A Fighter for Freedom'. We also looked at Zimbabwean authors in general, but with specific attention to Charles Mungoshi's fiction novels (e.g., 'Waiting for the Rain') and Chenjerai Hove's books on 'protest poems' such as 'Up in Arms', 'Decolonising the Mind' and 'Red Hills of Home'). My Class of 1985/86 in the Faculty of Education at University of Zimbabwe will probably be the only ones on record who were lucky to have had direct interface with the famous Chinua Achebe, Ngugi wa Thiongo, Dambudzo Marechera, Charles Mungoshi and Chenjerai Hove.

The authors separately appeared in person on different dates in the Faculty of Education by invitation of course, courtesy of (Professor?) Mrs R Moyana. Her breadth of knowledge about writers from various parts of Africa was hard to beat. More than thirty years later, she had turned into an undisputed 'guru' and authority on the subject. To this day I can still visualise her sitting in front of our lecture room, doing the job that she knew best, that is, helping us to have a clear grasp of the theme(s) and plots of given novels, providing scholarly commentary or giving a balanced critique of why character so and so from novel X behaves in this way and not in another, or how that might impact positively or negatively on societal values, beliefs and practices etc. Long live Mrs Moyana. You are a star in your own right.

Working alongside Mrs R Moyana in the English component of our degree studies was Doctor Magura. He was one of the several UZ staff who had returned home to Zimbabwe from the United States of America in answer to the Prime Minister's (Robert G Mugabe, who was still constitutionally a Prime Minister and not yet assumed the title of 'President'), clarion call to patriotic, skilled and experienced Zimbabwean citizens in the diaspora to come back home and participate in the rebuilding of their country to repair the damage caused by the vagaries of colonial rule and the liberation struggle that led to independence in 1980. Doctor Magura lectured us in 'metaphysical poetry' by seventeenth century Western European authors John Donne, Andrew Marvell and others. He labelled their poetry 'poetry in abstraction'. However, in developing our understanding of metaphysical poetry, it was made clear the poets make use of metaphorical 'conceits' to explore the relationships between lovers. Such poems also place more emphasis on the spoken word rather than on the lyrical content of the poem. To successfully produce balance in one's analysis of a metaphysical poem, the onus is on the student to identify the 'conceit' first before he or she goes to unravel the overall meaning or message conveyed by the poem.

In a lecture room discussion and analysis of Andrew Marvell's 'To the Coy Mistress', one student's response was to accuse the poet of being a misogynist trying to get into his mistress's knickers by banging on about 'Time's Winged Chariot' and refusing to take no for an answer! I disagreed with the student's extreme suggestion that the poet had a natural hatred for women. Instead, I offered the view that in that poem, his rhetoric made him appear probably rather foolish – the extremities to which he goes to persuade his lover to succumb to his advances make him a figure to laugh at, thus making it a comedy of sexual frustration and romantic humiliation.

Nevertheless, in the first few months of my Bachelor of Education Degree studies, Doctor Magura returned to me my marked assignments reflecting high marks for 'construction' and low marks for 'content'. I needed plenty of practice to put my finger on the metaphorical 'conceit' of any metaphysical poems in order to analyse them appropriately. Furthermore, he was concerned that while my work showed potential, most of it clearly betrayed my lack of a strong grounding in Literature in English before I entered university, and that I should concentrate and work hard on poetry as a literary form and to try to discover my own distinctive voice. I had no choice but to fall back on my relentless determination to achieve and make progress in my studies. Fortunately for me, we had the wonderful university library that was literally groaning with the weight and breadth of human knowledge it contained. I would invariably be found reading in that building or borrowing books to read at home; or consulting with my lecturers on the best way forward and seeking advice or discussing issues on assignments with my course colleagues.

Like most of us 'students of colour' in the cohort who were having our first experience of being in a multiracial class of students, I felt somewhat nervous and doubtful about expressing my thoughts coherently, both in the spoken and writing media; but here we were. I had been afforded this grand opportunity to study these beautiful, timeless and awe-inspiring works of art, yet my responses to them were clearly inadequate, certainly nowhere any more profound than the responses of the few bright 'white' students in our midst who would stick their hands up during lectures and trot out intelligent answers and suggestions. Not only that; all of them were getting high marks in written assignments, too.

To those of us heaping all the blame on our being 'black' for our shallow responses or clearly bad performances in his lectures or written assignments, Doctor Magura was unsparing in his comments to condemn what he summarised as 'reverse racism'; our hollow excuses, whining self-pity and shoddy thinking. Often talking to us as a separate group, he did not mince his words. He went on saying – "I'm unhappy with you guys continuing to be obsessed with the past under colonial rule and the inequalities you may have suffered from it. I'm afraid you will have to get off your arses, roll up your shirt sleeves and get down to serious work to improve your lot in post-independence Zimbabwe. The few privileged 'white' students in your class may have inherited a lot from their dead ancestors, but they do not have to apologise for that." Asking a rhetorical question, he continued, "Did you want their dead ancestors to be buried in their graves, together with their riches? At the end of the day, people are people wherever they find themselves in the world; they rise and fall by their own talents and merits. I'm simply bored with people who try to pass old envy off as if it is some sort of virtue." You cannot say we were not told off!

Narrowing it down to myself, the absence of appropriate learning facilities and resources, the limitations and insecurities that were brought to bear upon my progress through the poor quality of education I had acquired prior to my starting university experience, all of these factors had not armed me sufficiently to deal with or do justice to my existence as an undergraduate student of English in the Faculty of Education. I was convinced that the two education systems operating in my country before independence in 1980 had nearly compromised me, that is, denied me opportunities to compete with my black or white counterparts on an equal basis. Meeting one of my teacher colleagues (who had never been to university for his education before) in Harare city centre one Saturday morning, he asked me, "Tell me, Lawrence, what do you spend the day doing in that place called University?"

*What a funny question*, I thought. What if I tell him we spend all day asleep in lecture halls? Anyway, the fellow had asked a question, so it was only fair I should give him a fair answer. "My friend, we spend the day doing all sorts of things: we attend lectures, work in groups discussing topics or assignments given to us by our lecturers; provide feedback to our whole class on our findings; talk; discuss; argue; conduct research in the university library; attend one-on-one tutorials with our appointed lecturers, etcetera, etcetera."

The remainder of the two years of study would be on part-time coursework, during which we attended a tight programme of weekend tutorials at the university and submitted assignments. With me back in the classroom part-time over the next two years, university time was largely devoted to attendance at weekend tutorials, writing and submitting assignments, conducting a small research project and writing up my dissertation. Year I of my degree programme was significant in that I sat examinations across the various modules of the 'taught' component which the Faculty of Education assessed as either PASS or FAIL/DISCONTINUE. I was one of the several students in my cohort who successfully passed the examinations. I had passed both examinations and assignment options, so I was given the green light to proceed to the second and third years of the study programme. In the second year, I kept up to date with the submission deadlines of written assignments as required.

Assessments in this area measured one's ability to collect data on given topics and present the data in written form that reflected scholarship. 'Waffling' or operating in a vacuum in written assignments was looked down upon and did not earn anybody any marks. Your references within and at the end of each assignment indicated that while your own ideas and suggestions were welcome, you could only express them in the context of findings by other researchers in the same areas. Before you came on the scene, other scholars who had reached more deeply into similar topics might possibly have published their findings in books, manuals or other scholarly publications.

Attendance at weekend tutorials was compulsory and it carried considerable weight too. Non-attendance for no valid reason marked you down on the total score for the segment. The third and final year of my Bachelor of Education Degree was assessed on my ability to research and present a narrative report based on a scholarly topic in the form of a document called a 'dissertation'. One of your lecturers acted as your 'supervisor'. Mr Phillip Mhundwa – who was then a lecturer in Educational Foundations Department of the Faculty of Education at the University of Zimbabwe – kindly offered to be my 'Supervisor' during the collection of data and the writing up of my dissertation. He provided me the guidance I needed on the collection of data and the organisation of that data into portions that I would include in the writing up of the final report. The mark you obtained in the 'dissertation' area depended to a large extent on the depth and relevance of your study and the extent to which your study was corroborated within and at the end of the research report. You would also earn additional marks from the quality of your presentation. Except for that grey area in 'metaphysical poetry', I did not experience any drawbacks or encumbrances with most of the segments of my first-degree studies at university. Admittedly, the three years of undergraduate study of my first degree were a hectic period for me, but I sailed through it and passed my semesters for the Bachelor of Education Degree in English and Psychology of Education at the end of 1987. I was one of thousands of graduates who, for the first and probably the only other time, were capped in receiving our degrees by the then Chancellor of the University of Zimbabwe, His Excellency, President Robert Gabriel Mugabe, in the sprawling grounds outside Sheraton Hotel, Harare.

Two other developments came in as Christmas surprise announcements for the family just before my graduation day arrived. Before our church marriage in 1980, Margaret had expressed a wish to train as a State Registered Nurse. Indeed, there was a brief period in 1974 when she travelled to and from a place in Matabeleland South, Mnene Hospital, to enquire about chances of training as a nurse there. In August 1987, our fourth and lastborn child, Valerie Hazvinei, arrived. By then we had moved from the house where Lorraine Vimbai had been born five years before to a family flat, 'Hollywood Flats', one in several blocks of teachers' government-rented flats along Jabavu Drive in Highfield. Margaret still expressed enthusiasm for a nursing career rather than training as a teacher, an option that I had once dangled before her, and she quietly turned it down. Following submission of application forms to train as a nurse when she was pregnant with our fourth child three months previously, she received a surprise letter from Parirenyatwa Group of Hospitals in October of that year confirming that her application to train as a nurse had been successful. Her three-year diploma course would commence effectively from the beginning of January 1988. We celebrated Christmas 1987 and new year 1988 festivities with mixed emotions of hilarity and anxiety.

At the start of Margaret's nurse training course, Valerie Hazvinei would only be four months old, so we hurriedly searched for a mature and responsible woman who would provide for the adequate childcare needs that our suckling infant would need during the day while her mother pursued studies for her dream career at Parirenyatwa Group of Hospitals. We found one and her name was Unita Mutingwende. Margaret and I will forever be grateful to that gentle woman for taking full charge of the baby's childcare needs while we were away from home all day, me at work in schools and she in pursuit of her nurse training. Unita Mutingwende, who was Margaret's House-help was remarkably and exceptionally caring for an ordinary baby-minder. To this day, I still have not met anybody with character traits that match hers. Taking on the care of our baby girl as if she was her own, she would carry Valerie Hazvinei behind her back when she was a mere infant and walk to local clinics/healthcare centres and back on appointed dates for post-natal vaccinations and immunisations. People with such devotion and dedication to their duties are hard to come by these days. When Margaret returned home in the evenings, Unita Mutingwende would, with our support and encouragement, leave to attend evening lessons at a local government primary school. She was studying for her GCSE 'O' Level examinations, so over and above the small wages we paid her, I volunteered to pay for her registration of the subjects she was studying with University of London. When she left our employment in 1991, she had passed most of her GCSEs. Reports we have received years after we relocated to the UK say Unita Mutingwende happily got married, passed her 'O' Level exams, and went on to train as a teacher. To be honest, I am convinced there is a God somewhere up there who has a lot of power to work wonders.

Prior to the beginning of the first school term in 1988, the Headteacher of Mukai High School, Highfield, approached me through one of the teachers at his school, asking if I wanted a job at his school as teacher of English. Word had gone round in Highfield that I had just completed a Bachelor of Education Degree in which English was my area of specialisation. He was desperate for the immediate replacement of one of his teachers who was also the head of department and had suddenly left before Christmas on securing a better-paying job in the private sector. Most, if not all, of the teachers in his English Department did not possess degrees, so I fitted his requirements perfectly. I doubted about my fitting the bill to run the English Department, but I grabbed at the opportunity to leave Kudzanayi School where I had been for twelve full years, if I took away the three years I was at university. A few days into January 1988, I rushed to inform the headteacher at Kudzanayi School of my immediate need to transfer to Mukai High School. Surprisingly, he did not object to my request, and he scrawled his signature on the relevant transfer paperwork. In retrospect, the twelve years I spent at Kudzanayi Government School were the best and most productive years of my career as a classroom practitioner.

I started duties in January 1988 at my new school as a proud holder of the Bachelor of Education Degree, teacher of English and Acting Head of the Department of English! The headteacher of that oversubscribed inner-city government secondary school was an elderly gentleman. He was among the earliest of the staff to arrive at school in the morning. Once his car was parked in a space strictly reserved for the head teacher, he promptly escaped into his office dangling a basket with his tea and possibly his dinner things in it. As soon as he entered his office, he slammed the door behind him and he would rarely be seen again for the rest of the day unless, for example, visitors from regional or head office arrived and wanted to be shown around the school. Otherwise, the man would only quietly resurface from his office at the end of his office hours, four thirty p.m. or five p.m. Then he would lock his office, get into his car and leave the school for his home.

The running of the school was left on the shoulders of the Deputy Headmaster, a Mr Mutsekwa, if my memory still serves me. He efficiently handled all the administrative functions, including addressing students and staff during school assemblies, chairing general staff meetings, dealing with pupil behaviour matters (most of the pupils being adolescents, there were always many of these) and attending to parents or visitor enquiries which were beyond the capacity of the reception office staff.

The head teacher's presence in the school was observable through Mr Mutsekwa who walked round the school structures tirelessly after lessons had started, ensuring that learning was taking place in the classrooms. As he walked round, he would frequently stop at a class and ask if everything was moving on smoothly. I was merely acting as Head of English, so he would always advise that I should not hesitate to knock on his office door if I needed his assistance. I was one of a group of departmental heads who met with him regularly to put forward suggestions on how best the school could be run effectively as a unit.

Mr Mutsekwa made you love your work. He would never pass by and speak to you because he was looking for trouble. Of course, if there was anything wrong, he would discuss it with you in a professional manner and offer suggestions to rectify the problem. His Liaison Meetings with Heads of Department and Staff General Meetings were some of the best organised learning events I was ever lucky enough to be part of. At the end of each of these gatherings, staff left satisfied, professionally enriched, and adequately informed to continue conducting their lessons to the advantage of the pupils in their charge. I recall frequently interacting with the likes of Mr Nyamunda and (the late) Mr Mushapaidze who were star performers in their departments. I was especially drawn to Mr Nyamunda (head of department geography) because he and I were of the same 'Moyo Dehwa' totem of the VaRozvi dynasty. Both Mr Nyamunda and I were quite chuffed by all the references to our belonging to the 'royalty' of the 'VaRozvi' people, sometimes even making us feel proud because of that historical reference to kings and other minions or minority tribes who were once ruled by us in those by-gone years before the Matabele Tribe and Europeans arrived to disturb our peace!

Away from the forced camaraderie of business hours at school, I would meet with some of my workmates at 'watering holes' during weekends, especially Saturday afternoons, e.g., in the open space at the back of 'Pavakwa Panaka General Dealers' Shop' or 'Mwamuka Bottle Store' at Machipisa Shopping Centre, Highfield, where we shared bottles of 'drinks' and exchanged clean jokes which made everybody howl with laughter. On some month ends when I was slightly more 'liquid', I was friends with much of the weekend floatsam and jetsam that washed up at and frequented 'Seven Miles Hotel' in the nearby suburb Waterfalls; an entertainment venue steeped in the tradition of a country hideout. '

Seven Miles Hotel' attracted both men and women revellers like moths to a flame. The hotel resident music band 'The Real Sounds of Africa' belted away tune after tune of the 'Rhumba' genre of music. None of the clientele departed to go home at the end of their shows with their enjoyment of that type of music unquenched. Otherwise, the rest of the revellers I socialised with in such glittering venues would dance, drink, carouse, gossip and entertain one another with their anecdotes. Some of the stories a certain Mr Tseriwa — who always talked about the poor people enjoying good health as they sit on the ground while the super-rich suffer poor health sitting on the balconies of their mansions — narrated sometimes gave rise to mythical events that never actually happened. One of his anecdotes went thus:

"Two rich men happened to be on a six-month hunting expedition somewhere in the remote jungles of north-eastern Democratic Republic of Congo. You need to be reminded that itt is only the rich who can afford such costly jaunts. Those familiar with the Geography of Central Africa will know that it is intensely hot all the time during daytime in the Democratic Republic of the Congo, so the best time to do your own thing is during night-time, preferably between midnight and sunrise when temperatures drop to manageable levels, thus allowing a span of oxen pulling a carriage not to become tired too quickly. At around one a.m. one very dark night, the white 'bosses' awoke their band of Congolese servants from the tents where they slept. They instructed them quickly to dismantle all the tents, pack things into the carriage and yoke in a team of oxen to the carriage so that the whole party would embark on a journey and reach their next stop of the expedition more than one hundred and fifty kilometres away before sunrise. While one group of the servants disentangled the sleeping tents, rolled them into neat bundles and loaded them together with bits and bobs of the camp's paraphernalia into the carriage, another group of servants rounded up the oxen and inspanned them onto the carriage. All these procedures were taking place in the pitch blackness of the night where nobody could see anything beyond fifty centimetres away from them. For that reason, one ox proved quite difficult to inspan, no matter how much the servants shouted and hollered for it to cooperate. Fortunately, the servants were experienced in these matters, so at last the aggressively defiant ox was yoked in side by side with another ox right at the back of a span of eight oxen. Soon after starting the journey, the 'bosses' noticed that their carriage was bobbing along at higher speed than they had ever known before. The other white man nodded in agreement, acknowledging the fact that they had been wise in starting their journey in the dark of night when temperatures were still low. As the span of oxen galloped and hopped along at great speed, the carriage they pulled literally flew over the corrugations of the gravel path the metal wheels traversed, knocking everybody and everything in the carriage hither and thither. Even the two servants on the box seats in front of the carriage could not comprehend the effortlessness of their work that night. Not a single ox from the span of eight needed urging on. They had never seen anything like this before. On reaching destination sooner rather than later and waiting a little bit until there was enough light, the mystery was unpacked. The 'ox' that had become truculent just before the party departed from the old camp was really a lion! The oxen did not innocently pull the carriage as the servants on the box seats assumed. Fear of the lion drove them mad." Nevertheless, part of the charm was Mr Tseriwa's tendency to embellish, enlarge and even create conflict in his anecdotes. By the time I returned to my home sometimes late at night following these informal gatherings, I would be very light-hearted, having disgorged the disappointments and frustrations of my hectic, energetic and rigorous routines during the week.

After the tea-break at school one morning in June 1989, the Deputy Head Teacher, Mr Mutsekwa approached me as I was stacking shelves in the Learning Resources Centre (School Library) with newly delivered library books.

He handed to me a document which he said was a 'vacancies circular' the school had received from head office. The circular contained advertised vacancies for Education Officers which were being advertised nationally. Mr Mutsekwa urged me to apply because he felt I was eligible on the strength of my teaching experience and my tertiary qualification. However, I doubted whether my pitifully small post-university experience would qualify me for the advertised 'schools inspector grade' posts. I had previously endured considerable pain on the matter of applying for advertised promotion vacancies when I was teaching in primary school years before, so I displayed a lack of enthusiasm, Still, Mr Mutsekwa insisted I should 'drop your hat into the ring,' to use his exact words. I completed the application forms supplied to me. Once I had finished completing them, I handed them back to him for processing in the head teacher's office. How they would be forwarded to head office was none of my business. I have not the foggiest whether the 'headteacher's 'Recommendation' section was completed by the headmaster or the deputy headmaster. All I was informed of later was that the forms had been processed and posted to head office.

After that, I completely forgot about the application, and engrossed myself variously with work in the English Department. You will remember that apart from administering the department, I had a teaching load of my own as well. I had several GCSE English classes that I also taught. One of my weaknesses is that I regard myself as a perfectionist. Any piece of work that I embark upon must be executed until it reaches a degree of near excellence, with me paying attention to every detail until the task is accomplished. It was my contention, mistaken as it might have been, that the department, which I had been asked to run in an acting capacity, was central to determining the chances our pupils had of passing their GCSE examinations as all their subjects, including Shona, were taught through the medium of the one and only English language.

Therefore, all the work I carried out in the English Department – whether it was observing my colleagues deliver lessons, write out lesson critiques or chairing departmental meetings, etc – was pursued with a passion and professionalism, all of which bordered on a certain type of obsession. To some of my colleagues in the department, I may have projected over-zealousness in my pursuit of certain aspects of teaching and learning. However, the message I wanted to put across at all times was that as teachers, we must always strive to portray the correct models that benefit our learners. As an English language, teacher myself, I was adamant that all lessons in English had to be correctly structured.

I insisted on English being properly taught and I offered my colleagues in the department no excuse for clumsiness or recklessness. As far as I was concerned, those were the weaknesses in our students that all of us had been hired to eradicate. Well after the start of the afternoon session on a hot afternoon in November 1989, a telephone call was received in the headmaster's office. It was about me. One of the school clerks was sent to summon me from the English Department. Staff were rarely called for an audience with the headteacher unless something was seriously wrong or there was an emergency of some sort. For one moment, I thought maybe I was in trouble. Sat quietly in that large airy room behind a huge desk, Mr Molife began speaking in a measured tone:

*"Mr Moyo, good afternoon. It's me who sent for you. I have just received a telephone call from head office. They have requested me to inform you that your application for the position of education officer (staffing) was successful. According to head office, you were to have started duty in your new role at Chegutu District Office, Mashonaland West Province, on 1 September 1989, but it is 10 November 1989 (confirms by checking the date on his wristwatch), it appears they were having difficulties in contacting you and letting you know of this development, which explains this seemingly long delay in the notice reaching you. Congratulations on your new appointment, Mr Moyo."*

I sat before the headteacher with my mouth wide open, aghast at the unexpected turn of events. I had completely forgotten about the application for promotion to an administrative post. I had submitted the application for that promotion post nearly six months previously. Head office had instructed that I leave Mukai High School immediately as my assumption of duty at Chegutu District Office was long overdue. But Mr Molife made further contacts with head office requesting for a breathing space of at least a week to allow me time to wind up my operations at Mukai High School through a properly organised handover/ take over procedure.

I also needed time to organise and re-arrange issues that related to the security of my family who I could not immediately take with me to Chegutu. I was going to live outside of Harare for the first time since I started my teaching career. Also, because my wife's nurse training at Parirenyatwa Hospital was still in progress, I had no option but to leave my family behind in Harare. But their security of tenure and convenience at the family flat were of the utmost importance to me and I made sure that those arrangements were carefully sorted before I left Harare. Margaret was only completing the second year of her three-year nurse training course. I left Mukai High School at the end of November 1989 with my head high. I had spent nearly two years at that school doing the work that I knew best as a practitioner and acting Head of the English Department.

Little did it occur to me that the experience I gained at that inner-city high school was a form of apprenticeship for the humongous responsibilities I would assume on starting work in my new role as District Education Officer at Chegutu District Office.

# Chapter 18

# Education Officer and the effect of political intrusion in my work role as an officer and civil servant

Arriving at Chegutu District Office of Mashonaland West Province at the end of 1989, my immediate challenge was to find somewhere to stay. The District Education Officer (Mr Fundira) hurriedly booked me in Chegutu Hotel where I stayed for three weeks at government expense. Then, again with the District Education Officer's assistance, arrangements were made with the Headteacher of Hartley No 1 Primary Boarding School – formerly a 'Europeans Only' school in the suburban area of the little town – to accommodate me if he had spare room for staff at the school. I was installed in a self-contained flat, but in the mornings and evenings, I shared my meals with boarder pupils. A separate space was set aside for me as a senior member of district office staff. I was well looked after at Hartley No 1 School where I stayed for the best part of six months. Both boarding and kitchen staff and all the pupils treated me respectfully throughout my stay. Preparing for Margaret and the whole family who would come over from Harare to join me in Chegutu at the beginning of 1991, I moved out of my living quarters at Hartley No 1 School and temporarily lived in a large, privately rented house in Queen Street, Chegutu, before I relocated to one of the government houses then recently built for 'civil servants' in the Zimbabwe Mining Development Corporation Area of Chegutu.

There were seven other education officials and other ancillary staff at Chegutu District Office of the Ministry of Education. The education officials included the District Education Officer who essentially was the head of the district and six District Education Officers. All the Education Officers were from the old school of former headmasters of primary schools, not just in the district itself but also from other provinces in the country. Nearly all the officers I found out that Chegutu, education officers were in their early to middle fifties. I would like to think that I was the first and the youngest education officer university degree-holder to be appointed at these offices. It is important to point out that my experienced colleague-EOs did not have university degrees. However, when the EO grade at district level was created by the ministry it should have included how the applicants had firstly distinguished themselves as school administrators in mostly rural primary schools. I had been promoted to the 'inspectorate grade' straight from the school system. That is, I did not have any experience whatsoever of running a school in the same way as my counterparts did.

So, notwithstanding considerations of my university qualification and the huge age gap difference between me and my older colleagues, I accepted that I was going to be working side by side with a diverse group of highly skilled and experienced officers. By appointing those of us with university degrees and planting us among groups of already experienced officers and former practitioner headmasters of schools, the expectation by policymakers in Head Office of the Ministry of Education in Harare was that we would add to the quality, synthesis and analysis of issues pertaining to the overall task of delivering the core objectives of the ministry. The manpower strength I found at Chegutu District Office comprised Mr Fundira (education officer and head of the district), Education Officers who included (the late) Mr Zimani, Mr Munemo, Mr Gasura, (the late) Mr Muchetwa, (the late) Mr Magandi and (the late) Mr Mwela. The late Mr Malunga was to join the staff at the district office as an acting EO two years down the line to replace Mr Magandi who had sadly passed on.

Each one of the gentlemen above oversaw a 'circuit', i.e., a designated area of the district containing a group of schools for which he was the dedicated District Education Officer. The day-to-day school supervision activities would be the remit of the District Education Officer allocated to that area. Meanwhile, Headmasters in that circuit needing direction and guidance on issues pertaining to the running of their schools would consult with their District Educational Officer. To assist us with our work at the district office was a remarkable team of other officers which included (the late) Mr Chirobo who worked with Schools Psychological Services, Mrs Mvura and (the late) Ms Ncube who were ancillary staff with the Early Childhood Education and Care section, a lady typist/receptionist (whose name I have forgotten) and two Office Orderlies, (the late) Mr Macherenje and Mr Chibaya. From the foregoing, we were an inclusive community and each one of the men and women I have mentioned above was regarded by all of us as an important cog in the wheel of Chegutu District. The 'Office Orderlies' were accorded the same respect as everybody else who was employed at the district office of the Ministry of Education.

Chegutu District was (and still is, I believe) one of five districts which made up Mashonaland West Region of the Ministry of Education and Culture. All our reports were for the consumption of and submitted to the Regional Director in Chinhoyi, the capital of the province. The district into which I was appointed was huge. It consisted of a hundred small and large primary schools and forty-seven small and large secondary schools. All these schools served within vast swathes of areas that sprawled across Mhondoro Tribal Trust Lands, Norton Urban and surrounding large-scale farms, Chegutu Urban and surrounding mines and large-scale commercial farms, Chakari Mines and surrounding commercial farms, Musengezi Purchase Area and Chevarozvi Resettlement Area. While the rest of my EO-colleagues monitored and promoted good standards of teaching and learning in circuits allocated to them within the district, I was appointed specifically as education officer (Staffing) with a diverse set of duties associated largely with the human resources component at each of the primary and secondary schools in the district. A key element of my job description was to ensure that all schools were properly staffed with the teacher numbers they needed vis-à-vis their enrolments. Emphasis was placed on providing schools with qualified teachers. In the absence of that, I was required to employ untrained teachers who held at least GCSE passes at

Grade C or better in subjects that included English language, mathematics, Science and any two others. To make my work on qualified teacher recruitment and placement in schools easier, there were two Education Officers – one primary and the other secondary who I worked in close consultation with. To avoid overstaffing in schools, heads of schools regularly provided me with their updated enrolments.

These enrolment updates resulted in continuous number-crunching with figures that caused either more requests for teachers from schools or my having to effect transfers of staff to schools where there were vacancies. It was a mammoth task calling on me to consult constantly with school heads or my seniors in regional office either by telephone or in writing. Besides just effecting teacher transfers from one school to another to avoid overstaffing, my job also dealt with all the general transfer requests from both primary and secondary school teachers.

Teachers would submit requests for transfers between schools in the district. Or they would request permission to transfer to other districts in the region or indeed to another region which we called 'inter-regional transfers.' The bulk of transfer requests I received from teachers were those that requested transfer within the same district. Teachers asked to be transferred for a cocktail of reasons: teachers at rural schools were attracted by the bright lights in towns, so they would apply to be transferred to work at schools in urban areas; they wanted to join their spouses who would be in other parts of the district; they were unhappy with the quality of teachers' accommodation offered at their schools; or they were unhappy with continuing to work at their schools due to disputes with their headmasters, fighting with other members of staff, etc. I considered each transfer request purely on its merits. If I received a bunch of similar requests, say from Mhondoro Rural and felt that I needed to establish the exact circumstances surrounding the requests, my job immediately ceased to be desk-bound. Accompanied by the Circuit EO, I would on a set date travel to the area in an all-terrain vehicle. This approach usually helped to resolve problems.

Discussions and consultations with the teachers concerned almost always reversed transfer requests. In issues to do with teachers' housing needs, I succeeded in getting the headmasters to rope in the support of the local community leadership to play their part in retaining trained teachers at their schools by improving the quality of their accommodation providing a supply of fresh water, etc. The process of effecting transfers was quite a hectic one, but I am sure I managed to stay on top of it. I authorised many of the transfer requests on humanitarian grounds, while I turned down several others if, on studying the requests more carefully, I was convinced those transfer requests had been submitted for frivolous reasons.

The District Education Officer of Chegutu often held liaison meetings with all the Education Officers in his office once every fortnight. However, depending on the urgency of the information the EO wanted to disseminate or the reports he wanted to receive from EOs, some of these meetings were 'ad hoc'. Whatever meeting it was, I was always the minute-taker at those important gatherings which afforded me opportunities to learn from piercingly intelligent contributions from the likes of Mr Gasura and Mr Munemo. Revealing their wide experiences as former headmasters of schools themselves and of working with headmasters, teachers and children in different school settings, Mr Gasura's sharp mind as an educational administrator was unmistakeable while Mr Munemo's measured and well-thought-out ideas on effective lesson deliveries confirmed that he was an intellectual giant.

The Education Officers were also a 'Promotions Committee' at district office level. Again, I was always the rapporteur at all the Promotions Committee meetings to identify suitable candidates who would fill advertised promotion posts in the district primary schools, e.g., head teacher Grade 1; headteacher Grade 2; Deputy Head Grade 1 and Deputy Head Grade 2. When final selections had been made and appropriate written recommendations had been provided by the relevant Circuit EOs, my job was to produce a detailed record of all selections made for filing and future reference and bind up the batches of completed application forms before forwarding them for finalisation by the more senior committee at regional office.

Headship promotions at secondary school level were dealt with exclusively by regional office, with district office giving them any additional information they required. I was the substantive education officer (Staffing) for Chegutu District from the beginning of 1990 until October 1992.

Then there was a sudden change in the chain of command at Chegutu District Office at the end of 1992. The substantive head of the district (Mr Fundira) had on his request transferred to Harare Region. Since I was the only one among the remaining officers who possessed a university degree, the Regional Director requested me to take up the challenge of acting temporarily in the weighty role of District Educational Officer (Chegutu). I reluctantly accepted the request made to me to act as District Education Officer presuming the appointment would be for a short period. I also agreed to the Regional Director's request, feeling that I should help as he had no alternative but to pick on me, since I was the only university educated officer available. Besides, my acceptance of the request arose out of my quest for the leadership experience that would accrue to me from such an exposure. Little did I know about the bureaucracy and slow movement of processes in the public service then. Three, nearly four years later, I was still acting in the position of District Education Officer for Chegutu!

If I may take you back a little bit, when I relocated to Chegutu on promotion towards the end of 1989, I had left my wife Margaret and family back in Harare. Then she still had to spend another full year in Harare completing her State Registered Burse training at Parirenyatwa Hospital. She was not in residence at the Nurse Trainees' Hostels at the hospital. That necessitated her having to commute daily between Highfield Township and Parirenyatwa Hospital – an approximately twenty-mile round trip – by bus or 'kombi,' unlike her first two years when I ferried her both ways in our first motor car ever, a Datsun 120Y. Now that I had gone to Chegutu, she had also lost out on the travel convenience and had to get used to travelling in less style. For the whole of 1990, both she and I moved backward and forward like a 'yo-yo'. Nearly every weekend, I travelled to Harare to be with my family. On the weekends I could not go to Harare, Margaret occasionally visited me in Chegutu, but I was a more regular visitor in Harare than she was. I remember complimenting her on her bravery and on how quickly she had adapted and had taken into her stride the inconvenience of bus and 'kombi' travel between Highfield and Parirenyatwa Hospital. In 1990, our son Gerald was in boarding school doing his Form 1 or 2. His little sister Audrey Shingaidzo was finishing primary school in Highfield Township, Harare. In 1991, I secured a place for her as a boarder to do her Grades 5 to 7 at Hartley No. 1 One Primary School, a former Group A school within the small town of Chegutu. The other little sister Lorraine Vimbai had just started primary school. Valerie Hazvinei was still a three-year-old toddler.

In the last week of August 1990, I recall spending all week in Harare at the invitation of the Zimbabwe School Examinations Council. I was in a large group of teachers – most of them secondary – who had been invited by 'ZimSec' to train as markers/examiners for the GCSE 'O' Level English language. I passed the training and started marking 'live' scripts in the November examinations of that year. That is how my association with 'ZimSec' started. I was their marker once or twice every year thereafter until June 2002 when I left Zimbabwe to relocate to the UK. When Audrey completed her primary school attendance at Hartley 1 School, I recall taking a special 'day off' to have her enrolled and start her secondary school at Queen Elizabeth Girls' High School, another former Group A school, right in the heart of Harare. Margaret successfully completed her training as a nurse at the end of 1990. She wasted no time in arranging to join me in Chegutu and was quickly absorbed at Chegutu District Hospital, thereby bringing to an abrupt end to my pretended bachelorhood.

Despite my relatively young age and inexperience, I worked very well with my team of older and seasoned Education Officers. I constantly reminded myself that I was lucky to lead a team of officers, all of whom possessed wide-ranging experiences and backgrounds of running their own schools before they were promoted to their current posts. Each of my meetings with them individually or as a group was a learning curve to me. I also realised that my short stint as acting head of department (English) at Mukai High School in Highfield three years previously had given me a foretaste of the massive responsibility I would assume later. In fulfilling our supervisory role, I led teams of Education Officers on outreaches into schools throughout the district from time to time, carrying out school inspections most of the time. On these visits, not only did we check on the effectiveness with which headmasters ran their schools, but we also used recommended checklists provided to us by the Regional Director to conduct these inspections; during which we checked literally everything that was associated with the headteachers' efficient running of their schools, including observation of lesson presentations by individual teachers at schools visited.

After each visit to a school, we immediately produced narrative reports which reflected widely on our observations of the quality of teaching, the behaviour of the children, the effectiveness of the headmaster's leadership style and how it impacted the tone and ethos of the school. At the end of each of our inspection reports, we offered recommendations wherein we highlighted suggested improvements and/or suggested teaching methodologies whereby teaching could assist in contributing towards the achievement of learning. Originals of these narrative reports would be forwarded to the Regional Director. I would also capture aspects of these team visits to schools and include them in my annual report for the district to the Regional Director at the end of each year.

Between 1992 and 1996, HIV/Aids infection was rapidly spreading among young adults in Zimbabwe. In my capacity as acting education officer (Chegutu), I held countless all day 'HIV/Aids Awareness Workshops' with both primary school and secondary school headmasters and teacher-audiences. Invited attendees would assemble at various venues. For Chegutu Urban, Musengezi Purchase Area, Chakari and surrounding large-scale farms and mines, the venues would either be Rukawo Motel or Hartley No I Primary School. I would meet attendees from the Norton Urban and surrounding commercial farm schools at Dudley Hall Primary School. For Mhondoro Rural, the venue would always be Mubaira Primary School or some other suitable venue at Mubaira growth point. The hope and expectations were that the new knowledge and awareness we provided at planned workshops would filter back into schools and subsequently into the communities where the schools were situated. At such gatherings and others like school management and teacher development conferences, I always gave the keynote address in my capacity as head of the district and the Regional Director's representative. Once every month, the Regional Director met with all the five heads of districts in person, so the five of them, with me as one of them, travelled to attend the Regional Director's meetings in Chinhoyi. The meetings also included heads of sections in the regional directorate. The main objective of such meetings was to consolidate our activities and to promote cohesion that would ultimately be echoed in the Regional Director's reports to planners and policy makers in head office (Harare). These round-trip liaison meetings in regional office in Chinhoyi, ninety kilometres away, were repeated at the end of each month.

As I did not have a government truck allocated to my district office, the District Education Officer (Kadoma) frequently dropped by to offer me lifts in the government issue truck allocated to his district office. Back in the district, I attended many Parents and Prize-Giving functions. I presided over several such functions on behalf of the Regional Director when for some reason he could not attend due to other commitments elsewhere. Attending some of these functions at schools that were far-flung from the district offices was often accompanied by all sorts of inconveniences and perils and pitfalls. An example of such is highlighted in the following account. The Regional Director had been invited as the guest of honour at one of our rural secondary schools in Mhondoro Rural, approximately one hundred and fifty kilometres away, which was holding a 'Parents and Prize-Giving

Day'. The Regional Director could not attend that function due to a previous engagement on the same day. He therefore telephoned and asked me as acting EO for the district to stand in for him. Provided with a four-wheel drive vehicle, I was on one hot day driving along a gravel road to the venue of the function, eighty kilometres away from Chegutu town. My sweet wife Margaret sat beside me in the government truck. She was going to help at the function with the giving of prizes after I had given the main speech. Suddenly, as we went up a rise along the road that was full of corrugations, the engine started coughing and spluttering. It eventually stopped running altogether. We were barely half-way on our journey to the school when the engine broke down. About forty miles from Chegutu, my wife and I were deep in the countryside where we knew nobody. I knew absolutely nothing about truck-engines, so I did not bother to open the bonnet of the vehicle to find out what the problem was. Very few vehicles from both directions, passed by.

Whenever I flagged the few passing vehicles down, the drivers seemed to ignore me. Instead, they passed us and our packed vehicle at high speed, leaving us covered in thick clouds of dust. Completely at a loss on what to do next and worried about my wife's convenience and security, let alone the possibility of missing my attendance at the school function, I said to Margaret in a tired voice, "We're lost, my dear." This was in 1995 if I am not mistaken. Mobile phones, or 'cell phones' as we in Africa were calling these hi-tec objects then, had arrived and were already widely in use. However, only a tiny minority of corporate executives in cities and towns had been given them by their bosses as company perks. I was only just a senior civil servant and not a company executive, so I did not have a mobile phone nor any other means with which to communicate my predicament to the school, district office or the Regional Director.

Margaret and I were stranded at that deserted place for almost three hours. I remembered that before our vehicle broke down, we had passed a small primary school by the roadside about seven miles along the road we had come along. Suddenly, three young men with three dogs appeared from round the bend in the road ahead of us. Arriving at the spot where we were stranded, they only carried knobkerries on their shoulders and looked tired and hungry after what seemed to have been an unsuccessful hunting expedition. They greeted me and my wife politely. After listening to my story, they said they lived in villages near the school that I talked about. The oldest of the three men said, "It's mostly downhill all the way to the school you passed on your way up here. If you don't mind, my mates and I will give your vehicle a push to the school with you and your wife sitting in it. Is that okay, guys, (talking to his colleagues), we'll disperse to our homes nearby once we have left these people and their truck at the school."

The other fellows nodded in agreement. Well, looking at my wife without uttering a word, I thought to myself, 'Here's a Daniel come to judgement!' I had certainly not expected to obtain that high quality of assistance in these deserted, dusty, and backward parts of the countryside. We were traversing another steep gradient along the road as we approached the school, and our volunteers were sweating heavily as they pushed the four-wheel drive vehicle, while my wife and I looked bemused as we sat in it. I could see more human beings as we got closer and closer to the school. But I felt embarrassed by the spectacle of people gazing at our vehicle having to be pushed with us in it. We reached the little school two hours later, covered in dust, thirsty and hungry. Before the young men dispersed to their homes in the villages, I thanked them in very few words concluding my remarks saying, "I simply do not know what we would have done without your help gentlemen."

Fortunately for me, the head teacher at the small school was within the premises. But on checking with him, I discovered that his school did not have a fixed line telephone which I could use to phone around and let people at the District Office and Regional Office know of my predicament. He said that neither he nor any of his teachers had acquired the new-fangled 'cell phones' quite yet. I had no choice but to leave the government vehicle parked in front of his house for the night. My wife and

I hitched lifts back into the town of Chegutu, some forty miles away. Vehicle Inspection Department people in nearby Kadoma picked up the vehicle on the following day and towed it to their site for repairs. I encountered many of these engine or mechanical breakdowns during my tenure as acting education officer for Chegutu District. Some of these engine breakdowns involving the government trucks we used occurred while I was in the company of my colleague District Education Officers. As a result, proposed trips to supervise schools or attend school functions in rural schools were subsequently aborted or cancelled altogether.

I never received an explanation from the section in regional office who dealt with the issuing of vehicles for use by some of us on government business. No clear explanation was given as to why most of the vehicles issued to us at Chegutu District Office were nearly always unroadworthy, and so consequently broke down. In many ways, I felt that this one issue alone impacted negatively on the smoothness with which I could have run the district more effectively and efficiently. I was not too sure about whether Kadoma District, thirty kilometres down the Harare to Bulawayo Highway from Chegutu, were as hamstrung by these transport drawbacks as we were. At least they had a two-tonne truck permanently allocated to the district office for their exclusive use while we had none.

One of the District Education Officers at Kadoma district office, a Mr Murota, seemed to be always spinning between Kadoma District Office and Regional Office, one hundred and twenty kilometres away, without any hassle. Nobody could explain to me why we at Chegutu District Office did not have a government vehicle allocated for our specific use instead of being temporarily issued with unroadworthy trucks, part of the pool of such vehicles that were kept at the regional office.

As a little boy, I was staying with my older brothers in Highfield (Salisbury then) in January/February 1963 when the political party, ZAPU split down the middle. A new rival party, ZANU, Zimbabwe African National Union, was formed; but being only about twelve years old myself then, I refused to be

dragged into the political activism prevailing then, wherein little boys even younger than me were encouraged by adults from
rival political groups to engage in a senseless orgy of throwing
home-made petrol-bombs into people's houses because of their
allegiance to rival political groupings. Resulting from that,
terrible things happened at night in Highfield (eponymously
nicknamed 'The Dark City' then) and African townships like
Harari (Mbare). Many houses were torched at night, due to
the absence of electric lighting, both in houses and in streets
throughout the whole of the African Township of Highfield.
Many homeowners and their children were victims of death,
or they sustained life-changing injuries. Being the young person I was then, my older brother Roland had firm instructions
which required me to stay indoors and never ever to become
directly involved in what was going on. I could feel the dangers
and the tensions that were all around me, even as I walked in
the streets of Highfield in broad daylight.

It was at that stage of my life that I vowed that I did not want to
be entangled in matters to do with politics. Just ten years thereafter,
I returned to Highfield as an adult, a qualified teacher and started
teaching in the same township with a clear conscience that I was a
civil servant and that dabbling in politics was, for me, completely
out of the question. My role was to contribute in the best way I
could towards the achievement of the Ministry of Education and
Culture's aims and objectives. On that score, my seventeen years
of teaching in Highfield (Salisbury) went off smoothly because
no politician interfered with my work as a teacher. Neither did
I cross paths with their work. I worked extremely well with my
superiors at school, regional office, local council and head office
in Harare. I was the Zimbabwe Teachers' Association (ZIMTA)
Branch Secretary for the Highfield/Southerton Branch from
1980 to 1984, inclusive; but my activism as a ZIMTA member
required me to merely participate in branch meetings where I
wrote minutes and reported back to the members on proceedings. Apart from advocating for, among other things, improved
conditions of service for teachers, we carefully avoided dabbling

in the highly volatile and contentious business of politics, leaving it to those who were in it as their profession.

Fast-track that to 1995 when I was acting as the Regional Director's representative for Chegutu District. I started experiencing difficulties with a senior politician and member of parliament for one of the political constituencies in Mhondoro West, one of the large rural extensions under my sphere of influence as Acting District Education Officer (Chegutu). The member of parliament for the constituency had recently been appointed Deputy Minister of Education and Culture. In terms of the protocols, I was familiar with, the most senior person I was permitted to communicate with, either by telephone or in writing, if I needed clarification or guidance on matters of ministry policy, was my Regional Director. I was given rigorous instructions never ever to communicate with, or issue statements to the media, anyone else, or any section in head office without prior permission or clearance from my immediate superior. Similarly, any directives or head office circulars were channelled down to us in district offices through the Regional Director. That was the standard practice in those years. I am writing this having resigned from the public service in Zimbabwe just over twenty years ago, so I do not know whether the system has changed. As I have said, I am writing on these pages as a former and very senior member of the public service. Curiously, the new deputy minister began phoning my office in Chegutu directly from her office in head office (Ambassador House), Harare.

In her first telephone call, one hundred kilometres away, which caught me by surprise, she introduced herself and asked me to be ready because, in about an hour or so, she was picking me up in her chauffeur-driven 4x4 government vehicle. She wanted me to accompany her to a political rally in her constituency that afternoon. I should attend the rally with her and be ready to answer questions from the audience on 'government's education policy,' which she would find hard to answer as she had just been appointed deputy minister. The whole thing was a bolt from the blue for me. Up until then, I had never attended political rallies of any party in Chegutu or in Harare where I had come from five years previously. I soon realised that the deputy minister's request was not going to be my first appearance at a political rally. I would gladly have volunteered to speak to an audience at an ordinary gathering of may be parents, without the politics involved. Apart from recognising myself as a civil servant who was non-partisan, I simply hated the raucous singing, the repeated chants of support and sloganeering that I had watched going on at such gatherings on ZBC/TV news bulletins after hours in the evenings. Speaking politely in response to her invitation, I responded thus: "Thank you very much for your invitation. I appreciate your wish for me to be present with you at your political rally in the Mhondoro area. However, I'm sorry I am unable to come with you in your vehicle without permission to do that from my Regional Director in Chinhoyi."

There was a loud click at the end of the line. She had suddenly cut me off. I quickly telephoned the Regional Director on his direct line telephone number, and I was lucky enough to find him in his office. After updating him regarding my telephone conversation with the new deputy minister, he confessed, "Nobody in head office has contacted me about what you're talking about. I need hardly remind you, Mr Moyo, that you are always answerable to me only and no one else."

Without giving further details or advice, the phone clicked, signifying that my conversation with my senior had ended. Meanwhile, the newly appointed Deputy Minister of Education and Culture would not easily be shaken off. Barely two hours after I had spoken by phone, both with her and my Regional Director, she promptly arrived at Chegutu District Office and was directed into my office, walking in unaccompanied by anybody else. I expected to see one or two other junior head office officials in her entourage. Anyway, I received her warmly in my office and expressed my appreciation for her huge personality to bless our simple offices with her appearance. When she insisted on my coming with her to Mhondoro, I stuck to my guns. She ended up saying the Regional Director was too far down the protocol ranks for her to grovel or give instructions to. Before she was finished with me, I noticed a streak of bad temper in her voice when she said:

"Uh-h Comrade, you're one of these bad eggs who do not follow the party way. From today onwards, I'm going to have you watched."

Following that event, I said to myself, *'Here's the beginning of a classic case of political interference from the big fish in the corridors of power. Tread with care, Lawrence.'* She departed to preside over her political rally in a brand-new all-terrain vehicle. As the truck was being driven off, I noticed there were two other male strangers who had remained sitting in the vehicle while I talked to my superior in the office. *Could it be that those men were the junior officials I expected to see in her company when she walked into my office, or I suspected they were her security officials.* Three months further on, the acting headmaster at one of our schools called Saruwe Primary School decided to hold a 'Parents and Prize-Giving' function at his school. He invited me as his guest of honour. Accepting his invitation, I advised him that I would also travel to the school for the occasion with my wife, Margaret, as well as the education officer of the circuit in which the school was located, (the late) Mr Magandi. Before the date of the function arrived, I dutifully informed the Regional Director of my commitment on that day, lest he phoned me to be updated on information about other administrative matters on the same day. The Regional Director thanked me for informing him about the upcoming event at Saruwe Primary School. He also expressed the hope that everything would happen as planned. Colourful and well-organised, the event was fully supported by parents, most of whom were lowly paid labourers who were employed at surrounding large-scale farms or with local 'BHP Mine' authorities. A few of the mine officials also attended the function.

None of the large-scale 'white' farmers attended the school function although I understood that invitations had been sent to them. After giving my speech – punctuated by numerous standing ovations, handclapping, and ululations from the audience –my wife, Margaret, gave out the prizes to winners of class positions. As this went on, I chatted quietly with the headteacher. Margaret was assisted to hand out the prizes by the deputy headteacher and other senior female teachers at the school. It was not my business to investigate where the school had sourced funds to purchase the many book prizes that the winners walked back home with, clutched in their hands. Nor was it my brief to query who had donated the funds which the school used to buy the refreshments that the visitors consumed after the function. All I noted was that the function was marvellously well-organised. To this day, I have no recollection of any politician or businessman being given special mention or praised during the introductions by the acting headmaster as having donated any money or helped in cash or kind with any assistance towards helping the occasion to succeed.

After partaking of the refreshments, my party bid our farewells and we hit the road to return to Chegutu, thirty kilometres away. Before the end of the following week, it was brought to my attention that by my mere attendance at Saruwe School function, I had walked into a hornet's nest.

During the week of the event, I attended at Saruwe Primary School, I also got to know that Rural District Council by-elections would be taking place soon to replace a councillor who had died. The by-elections were a political process, so campaigning by candidates of rival political parties included the area in which Saruwe Primary School was located. Whoever was the candidate for the ruling party needed the support of the member of parliament for Mhondoro West constituency. Allegations started flying around that I had turned the Saruwe Primary School function into a political rally where, it was alleged, I chanted slogans in support of an unnamed candidate for one of the opposition political parties! The books my wife had handed out as prizes to winners had allegedly been bought and donated to the school by the unnamed political rival with my blessing! The allegation went on to say that I had used the authority vested in me as Acting District Education Officer at the gathering to let the stranger address the parents and enlist their support for his

390

candidature at the forthcoming Rural District Council elections! Of course, all these allegations were complete hogwash which I responded to with a great deal of surprise. The allegations were clearly false, unfounded and a figment of the imagination concocted by someone or their proxy who had been planted in the audience at the Saruwe Primary School function.

Whoever that person was, I have yet to discover, to this day. That person had twisted the truth in line with his or her hidden agenda. The agent of destruction spewing all that nonsense obviously had instructions to ensure that I faced ultimate doom. Meanwhile, during the week following my attendance at the prize-giving event, the Regional Director telephoned me to inform me that this time around, head office (Harare) had telephoned him informing him of the same allegations. It appeared as if the Regional Director had been intimidated by someone in head office when he was contacted by telephone. I was ordered to attend an interview with him in his office at regional office, ninety kilometres away that afternoon. At the tense interview, he was sweating more heavily than me as he sat glowering at me behind his massive desk.

Reminding me as if I did not know about my role as a civil service manager, he remarked, "As a civil servant, Lawrence, I need hardly remind you, you have to be politically impartial. Yet in the allegation I have received from head office, it is said that you campaigned against the ruling party and in favour of one of the opposition parties."

I fiercely contested the allegation that I had done anything of the sort as insinuated; I had not in any way politicised my presence at Saruwe Primary School. Respectfully though, I shot back at the Regional Director, "Whoever has made those allegations should prove them, Sir."

"And that, Lawrence, will be your case for the defence if this matter were to end up in a court of law," he said. I replied, saying that if push came to shove, I was prepared to stand up in a court of law to prove my innocence. On the contrary, I suspected that the spurious allegations against me had their source in someone politically powerful in head office whose previous attempts to involve me in her political agenda had been strongly resisted by me. Reader, I must remind you that the suspected character had spectacularly failed in her attempt to drag me to her political rallies, and I refused because I knew what my role was as a civil servant.

The Regional Director, who was nearing retirement age, suddenly turned round, and said he did not want to be drawn into discussing personalities in head office as it could interfere with his retirement benefits: "Lawrence, I do not want sensitive matters like this one to burn my fingers. If for any reason I sink as an outcome of matters like this, bear in mind you also go down with me! Do I make that clear, Lawrence?"

Clearly, the honourable gentleman had been spoken to and probably intimidated by someone in the corridors of power. He informed me he had been directed by 'the powers that be', without mentioning any names in head office, to have my 'wings clipped' by removing me from the acting appointment as District Educational Officer for Chegutu District and transferring me with immediate effect from Chegutu District to Karoi District – two hundred kilometres away from Chegutu! On reporting for duty at Karoi District, I would, as a punitive measure, revert to my original role as education officer (Staffing). But the Deputy Regional Director (Secondary Schools) – a Mr Mudonhi – who was present in the meeting interjected saying that the allegations the Regional Director had received had not been proven with facts and that he believed that I had not committed the alleged offences, and thus should not be treated so harshly.

Concluding his observation, the Deputy Regional Director (Secondary) politely remarked in the following words: "I have known Mr Moyo as one of our young and hardworking officers not only in Chegutu District, but also in the region. Suffice it to say, even in the presence of some of the wildest of allegations. Therefore, I beg you, Sir, in your capacity and honour to endeavour to be seen as expressing a willingness to protect officers like him from the wilful intentions of some of our political leaders who want to involve themselves in activities that have nothing to do with translating political goals into workable plans." In response to the Deputy Regional Director's plea for my protection, my transfer to Karoi District as originally decided upon was cancelled; but in conformity with instructions or orders that had been received from 'the powers that be' in head office (Harare), the Regional Director insisted that my immediate transfer from Chegutu still stood. Instead, I should assume duty at Chinhoyi District Office as District Education Officer (Staffing) where there was a vacancy waiting to be filled; and that I should assume duty at that office first thing on the following Monday morning. My meeting with the Regional Director and the Deputy Regional Director (Secondary Schools) was scheduled for a Friday afternoon!

Without suitable accommodation immediately available in Chinhoyi, there was no way that I would travel to and start working in Chinhoyi with my family in tow. I left Margaret and my children at our rented house back in Chegutu. Meanwhile, as I had nowhere to live in Chinhoyi, fresh arrangements were quickly made by regional office for me to be temporarily accommodated in one of the self-contained bachelor flats at Chinhoyi Government Primary School, a former Group A boarding school. My new living quarters were within walking distance from Chinhoyi District Offices. I shared some of my meals with primary school pupil-boarders.

I have to say that for the period I stayed free-of-charge at the former Group A boarding school in Chinhoyi, I was well looked after by both the boarding and kitchen staff. Henceforth and for the next eight months, I commuted in my small Renault 9 car to and fro like a 'yo-yo' between Chegutu and Chinhoyi – a round trip of one hundred and eighty kilometres – to spend weekends with my wife and family. It was tough for both me and Margaret. I had no choice but to grin and bear the inconvenience while it lasted. Eight months later, while the substantive Regional Director was away on an extended vacation, one of his two Deputy Regional Directors who was then acting in the absence of the Regional Director, revisited my issue without me pestering him about it.

Convinced that the reason for my transfer from Chegutu District Office to Chinhoyi District Office lacked substance and validity, I was transferred back to Chegutu District Office where I carried on in my original post as EO (Staffing).

I was grateful to the Deputy Regional Director (Primary) concerned for his kindness in transferring me back to Chegutu where I had a family home; but since resuming work at Chegutu District Office, I no longer felt secure in my role. Even when I carried out my duties at Chinhoyi District Office, quite often, unknown individuals or groups of people with no qualifications would suddenly turn up in my office, purporting to be former liberation war fighters who some senior politician(s) somewhere (some names would be dropped) had sent to me to be considered for jobs as untrained teachers. Some of these suspicious characters approached me with money or other enticements, hoping that I would give in to the temptation of accepting bribes. I steadfastly stuck to my 'honesty is the best policy' mantra and the stand-ard practice of following laid-down employment procedures for trained and untrained teachers. I continued to feel insecure in a job where I suspected that there was a hidden hand somewhere out there waiting for me to make the first mistake before they came down on me like a hammer.

Unhappy and disillusioned by the continuing intrusions, har-assments, and interferences in my work as a dedicated manager and role-player in the public service, I voluntarily resigned from my substantive post as District Education Officer (Staffing) for Chegutu District effective from 31 December 1996. Since join-ing the public service and starting work as a classroom teacher in 1972, I had always held the view that the civil service, unlike, for example, the judiciary, was not independent of the elected government and that the political leadership and the civil ser-vice must share the same major beliefs, values and ideals despite each playing their distinctive roles. While ministers look after the politics, i.e., articulating clear strategies and selling policies to the public, the technocrats in the civil service – of whom I was one – must be permitted to use their skills uninterrupted by needless interference by politicians to design programmes of action that reflect the political context and the thinking of the political leadership. At the time I decided to resign from the public service altogether, it was my sincere hope that the Ministry of Education and Culture (then) and/or Zimbabwe in general would strive to maintain the fine balance in the relationship and functions between the political leadership and the civil service. It remained crucial to me that effective implementation of policies depended on these two areas sharing the same beliefs, values and ideals.

On ejecting myself from my role as an educational administrator, I opted to return to the job that I had a university qualification for and loved best: teaching English Language and Literature in English at secondary school level. My first six months back in the classroom were at a small rural school called Mkwasha Secondary School in Msengezi Purchase Area, about ten miles out of the town of Chegutu. I was initially placed at that school because there were no vacancies to accommodate me in Chegutu Urban secondary schools. Trailing my movements, as it were, after I resigned from my job as a senior schools' administrator at Chegutu District Office, regional office (Chinhoyi) intervened, it was directed that a suitable vacancy be 'created' for me in Chegutu Urban and that I be transferred back to town schools without further delay. I taught GCSE 'O' Level English Language and Literature at Pfupajena High School, together with the likes of Mrs Zano and Mr Cheta. I will always remember the respect that was accorded to me when I – a former education official at the local district office – arrived at Pfupajena High School to report for duty as an ordinary classroom teacher! Instead of sharing spaces with the rest of the teachers in the Staffroom, the young head teacher recommended I be accommodated in the 'annexe', a small office next to the headmaster's office which I believe would otherwise have been the deputy head teacher's office. When I arrived, the school did not have a substantive deputy head teacher, so the 'annexe' was being used by Senior Teachers Mr Chakamanga and Mrs Zano until further notice.

A little space was created and made available for my use, along-side the two senior teachers who were already using that annexe. I was comparatively more senior in age and experience than the young teachers and I tried my best to make them feel less intimidated. However, the two young teachers seemed to have quickly taken my seniority and overbearing presence in their strides. In that tiny one room world, the three of us, Mr Chakamanga, Mrs Zano and I would often be found gossiping our lives away in a sort of psychological pressure cooker! It turned out to be fun working and interacting with them professionally. During the five years I stayed on at Pfupajena Secondary School, passes in GCSE 'O' Level English Language and Literature improved significantly, thanks to some of the infusion from my experience as a Zimbabwe Schools Examinations Council (ZimSec) Marker/Moderator of the GCSE 'O' Level in English since arriving at the school. After each ZimSec 'live marking' session at the end of each year over the next five years, I would return to Pfupajena High School armed with tips and suggestions on those areas of language teaching and learning examiners on which emphasis was placed during the examination process.

I would hold staff orientation workshops in the English Department which focused on these aspects on the way teachers taught English and promoted the quality of output when it came to examination results.

A few months before the end of the year 2000, the oldest of our three daughters, Audrey Shingaidzo caught us by surprise when she suddenly relocated to the UK. Many young people then seemed to be leaving Zimbabwe to seek greener pastures in the diaspora. During the 'yellow route', those heading to the UK always hopped on their non-stop flights at Harare (now Robert Gabriel Mugabe) International Airport with London as their destination. That city somewhere overseas also had the fascination of a forbidden fruit for me. On leaving Zimbabwe, Audrey left her two-year-old daughter, Yvette Chenai, in the care of her mother. Towards the end of 2001, Audrey frequently phoned saying she missed her daughter so much. She sent her mother an air tickets and some money so that her mother and her daughter could travel to the UK and spend Christmas of that year with her. Accompanied by several members of the extended family, I saw Margaret and Yvette off to the UK aboard 'Egypt Air' at the then Harare International Airport. In a related but seemingly fortuitous development, just after Margaret and our little niece Yvette had left for the UK, I received a letter from University of Zimbabwe informing me that my application for a fulltime two-year master's degree in English had been successful and that the study programme would commence in February 2002.

Even more surprisingly, Margaret telephoned me from the UK shortly after new year in 2002. She informed me that she had found work as a nurse in the UK. To that end, she had scrapped all plans of returning to Zimbabwe soon! In the abruptness of that announcement, we did not discuss the way forward for me at that stage. That development caught me in mid-stride and for a few days I could not quite tell whether I was coming or going. Gosh, there were so many things happening simultaneously and it was proving difficult for me to stay focused. Without giving the matter further thought, I finally resolved to pursue the advanced degree studies at the University of Zimbabwe after the Ministry of Education and Culture kindly granted my application for study leave. I did not therefore quite resign from my post as a teacher then. I left my job as a teacher at Pfupajena High School in February 2002 and returned to Harare, bag and baggage, before embarking on my studies for the Master of Education Degree in English at the University of Zimbabwe, come the beginning of March 2002.

# Chapter 19

# Advanced Degree (English) briefly at the University of Zimbabwe before I relocated to the UK

The exact name of the programme of studies I started at the University of Zimbabwe in February 2002 was 'Master's Degree in Curriculum and Arts'. The advanced degree had a special focus on English and Language Education, with particular emphasis on 'Applied Linguistics.'

In the first semester that I attended fulltime (February – July 2002), lectures were taught by highly skilled lecturers some of whom I had met when I studied for my first degree in the same university. Mrs (she is now Doctor) Ruth Moyana, was one of my lecturers when I studied at the University of Zimbabwe for my first degree, the Bachelor of Education Degree, eight years previously. When she taught me in 2002, she was probably also working on her studies for the Doctor of Philosophy Degree (PhD). In my M Ed Degree studies, she taught us English and components of Language Education. The other lecturers included Mr O.P. Ndawi who was then the Chairperson of the Curriculum Department. His area of specialisation was in 'Research Methods and Statistics' (I understand he also obtained his Ph D before the end of 2002, so he is now Doctor O.P. Ndawi!); there was Doctor V Nyawaranda who taught us both English and Language Education. Also, there was a Mr D Matsvai who lectured us in Curriculum Studies and (the late) Doctor I Chikalanga who taught us English and Language Education.

By the end of my first semester in July 2002, I had written three-hour examinations and had successfully passed three courses in my area of specialisation (English and Language Education), as required. The courses were English, Language Education, Theory of Language Teaching and the Psycho-and Socio-Linguistic Aspects of Language. I had also written three-hour examinations and successfully passed two Foundation Courses in Historical and Philosophical Foundations of the Curriculum and Psychological and Sociological Foundations of the Curriculum. I also studied and was also assessed via an examination in Developments in English: Implications for the Curriculum. I was assessed in Research Methods and Statistics, but I did not perform as well as I had expected. Those six months of my M Ed Degree were extremely busy. I was adequately rewarded for my hard work by the large number of good passes I scored except in the Research Methods and Statistics component which I subsequently passed as 'Educational Enquiry' when I studied for my Master of Education (M Ed) Degree in Applied Linguistics with a different university in the UK.

A few months into 2002, I thought I was living in a dream: I had already pocketed a bachelor's degree; Margaret and I had four gorgeous children; she was full of ambition and raring to go: she had just started work as a qualified nurse in the UK and here I was, studying fulltime for my MA Degree in English at the University of Zimbabwe. I was toying with the idea of joining my wife in the UK at the end of 2003 on successfully completing my MA degree. It was going to take me two years to complete the master's degree study programme. As I had been working for many years prior to my the then current study programme, I liked the fact that I could continue working and earning while also studying. I had clearly hit a crossroads. That order of events was soon short-circuited by Margaret who brought forward my plans to join her in the UK to happen sooner rather than I anticipated. She phoned me on her mobile phone somewhere in May 2002 saying that she and our daughter, Audrey, had carried out research of their own and discovered that I could complete my master's degree studies in the UK while I also worked as a part-time secondary school teacher and earned a handsome salary at the same time. Margaret literally 'instructed' that I shelve everything I had been doing at the University of Zimbabwe so far and start arranging to relocate to the UK in earnest. If possible, she wanted me to arrive in the UK at the end of July. That would be two months later!

While I was arranging to join her in the UK, Margaret specifically asked me to bring with me her lastborn daughter, Valerie Hazvinei. The latter was then a fourteen-year-old-girl in the middle of her Form 3 (year 10) studies for the GCSE examinations the following year at Chegutu High School. That whole development came to me like a bolt of lightning. The turn of events happened completely out of the blue. I had never travelled out of Zimbabwe since birth, so I did not even have a passport. It was the same for our lastborn daughter, Valerie. I wasted no time dealing with the trauma of sorting out Valerie's and my passport. It was a bit tricky obtaining these important travel papers, but I managed to do so in record time through assistance given me by some of my communication networks at Passport Office in Chinhoyi, capital city of Mashonaland West Province. Before long, I received paperwork and flight tickets from Margaret which indicated that Valerie and I would travel through the Republic of South Africa to link up with an 'Air France' flight at Johannesburg (now Oliver Tambo) International Airport. That complicated my preparations further because I also had to obtain Republic of South Africa visas from the South African Embassy for both Valerie and I to be allowed to travel through South Africa. Furthermore, I needed to tidy up Valerie's transfer documents with Chegutu High School to enable her to be enrolled in school when we finally landed in the UK. I had done all that by the end of June 2002.

In the first week of July 2002, I had finished with our first semester attendances at lectures in the Curriculum Department. Instead, I was one of the Zimbabwe Schools Examinations Council (ZimSec) markers/examiners who were residing in students' hostels at the University of Zimbabwe and marking the 2002 June Examinations GCSE 'O' Level English language live examination scripts. Even if I was a fulltime student at the University of Zimbabwe, Zimbabwe School Examinations Council still searched for me. On finding me, they asked me to take part in what they labelled a 'national effort'. One day late at night during that first week of my 'in residence' marking of ZimSec exams at the University of Zimbabwe, my second daughter, Lorraine Vimbai, contacted me on my 'brick' mobile phone. At that time, 'Lo' – as all of us in the family used to call her affectionately – had gone more than halfway through her training as a State Registered Nurse at Gweru General Hospital. She went straight to the point in her thin, soft, persuasive voice, just like that of her mother's, "Dad, I've heard you're making frantic arrangements to leave Zimbabwe shortly and join Mum in the UK. Please know that I'm happy for you as you prepare for your departure." Without dithering, Lorraine went straight to the heart of the matter, "Dad, I've phoned to ask you please to marry me to my boyfriend, Cossam Penyayi, before you leave for the UK. I know there is very little time left within which you would have been properly informed of these arrangements. I also know you might say my uncles (your brothers here) can easily marry me to your future son-in-law after you've gone to the UK, but I'm making a personal request. Dad, I would very much appreciate if you, as my biological parent, can preside over my marriage, please Dad."

Our daughter, Lorraine, had caught me completely unawares by proposing that I mount such a major family event amid other things happening at the same time. I remained quiet for a moment thinking of how I could give her an appropriate response. I pondered over the fact that Lorraine was still a student nurse. I did not like the future she was investing in her studies for that she might lose by a silly rush into marriage. Besides, her Cossam boyfriend of hers had never been introduced to me and I had never heard of him from anyone. Overriding everything else was the fact that I only had two weekends before Valerie, and I would be departing for the UK.

At first, I told Lorraine that I would find it hard to squeeze her into my programme of arrangements. Refusing to be shaken off, she persisted with her request, audibly crying from her end of the phone connection. To avoid disappointing her and putting her off completely, I promised to return her call early on the next day after I had studied my arrangements again. Just after ending our conversation, her aunt (my sister), Winnie Phyllis, weighed in supporting her niece on the same matter when she phoned me separately that same night. I had no choice but to bend over backwards and accommodate my young daughter's request. I did not have to phone Lorraine to say all was in order, her request was granted. Her aunt (my sister) did so on my behalf. Lorraine phoned me on the following day to say she was over the moon.

On the last weekend prior to my leaving Zimbabwe, I presided over my daughter's customary marriage to the 'husband' of her dreams at Hollywood Flats in Highfield, Harare. It was a big family event, so all my brothers who lived in Harare then were present, including my older brother Roland, my young brothers Wilfred (he was the master of ceremonies) and my youngest brother (Reuben Norman), the lastborn of my siblings in the family. My son, Lorraine's brother, was also present at that occasion. My family delegation assigned Gerald the task to take notes of the goings-on as the rapporteur. From my future son-in-law's side came a large delegation of men. The large size of the delegation who were keeping an eye on my future son-in-law indicated the seriousness on the part of their relative to take my daughter's hand in marriage. Margaret's older sister, Tsitsi Elizabeth Nyemba filled in nicely as a representative of Lorraine's mother, Margaret. My sister Winnie Phyllis had travelled from Gweru for that occasion in the company of the delegation who came to marry my daughter.

I especially invited several of our uncles on our mother's side of the family to give weight to the occasion by their presence. I am sure that Uncle Noel who lived in Glen Norah was present on the night of Lorraine's marriage. Lasting well into the night, the programme of events went off like clockwork. I made it abundantly clear to my son-in-law 'elect' that he had just won the battle but not quite the war yet. Yes, he had indisputably paid 'lobola' as a token of his marriage to my daughter. I said however, that I would be greatly honoured if he and his 'wife' would consider delaying starting a family until after Lorraine had completed her training as a nurse at Gweru General Hospital. That undertaking was carried through to the letter with Lorraine and Cossam starting to live together as husband and wife almost two years after I had arrived in the UK.

In the last few days before Valerie's and my departure for the UK, there were a few loose ends which still needed to be tied up. On the penultimate night before we left to start our journey to England, I had a long chat with my son, Gerald. At the time, he was employed in some clerical job with Old Mutual, a big multinational insurance company in Harare. Although I stayed with my son at Hollywood Flats in Highfield, I must confess there were no indications that he was doing any serious reading of any sort. He seemed to spend or devote most of his spare time at some Pentecostal Church near Harare city centre praying and singing. He seemed quite fanatical about his attendance at that church. I said to him that although I did not see anything wrong with what he was doing I advised him to remember to keep his feet on the ground and faced up to the harsh realities of everyday life. Gerald had received a boarding school education for both his GCSE 'O' and 'A' Levels.

He had achieved three very good passes at advanced level which unfortunately did not qualify him for the medical degree he wanted to pursue. Gerald was still unmarried at that time, so I urged him to take advantage of the situation and utilise the small window of opportunity remaining by studying and obtaining a degree in an alternative field before some unknown girl joined him as his wife. I remember giving him fatherly advice that if he did not use the opportunity available to him profitably then, the increased responsibilities of having a wife and children would make it difficult or indeed might slow down his progress towards the achievement of his intended study objectives. I was happy to leave him not only the free and indefinite use of our four-roomed family flat, but I also gave him full charge over the collection of my rich library of books. I hoped Gerald had paid heed to my advice to 'cut hay while the sun shines.'

There were several small tasks that I could not complete as I prepared to leave Zimbabwe. The biggest omission amongst those things was my failure to squeeze into my time schedules enough time to visit and book seats on a bus that would ferry Valerie and myself at 'Roadport', a bus terminus in Harare city

centre for buses which travelled to distant destinations in different directions out of the capital city.

That bus would have reportedly transported us from Harare and
directly to Johannesburg (Oliver Tambo) International Airport.
Having failed to book a ticket on the bus early enough, the only
option we had was to use ordinary buses that travelled from Mbare
Musika through Masvingo and then reached Beit Bridge. The
suggestion was that there would be plenty of other options available to us to reach Johannesburg once we had crossed Limpopo
River and had been cleared through border posts on both sides
at Beitbridge.

The date for my youngest daughter Valerie Hazvinei and I
to start our journey to the UK arrived. It was on 29 July 2002. I
had arranged with my young brother Wilfred to pick us up in his
car from Hollywood Flats, Highfield, and transport us to Mbare
Musika Bus Terminus. He arrived first thing in the morning.
Margaret's older sister and my sister-in-law, Tsitsi Elizabeth,
had spent the night with us at the flat. She also came with us in
the car to the bus terminus. The bus we boarded had a destination notice of 'Beitbridge' on the front and above its large front
windscreen. That would be our last stop on the Zimbabwean
side of the border with South Africa. When we boarded it at just
after eight a.m. at 'Mbare Bus Terminus', my daughter, Valerie
Hazvinei, almost failed to get seating places on the bus because
it was nearly loaded to capacity with cross-border traders. Like
us, most of them had also missed the buses which travelled across
the border at Beitbridge and directly to Johannesburg thereafter. At eight fifteen a.m., both Valerie and I waved Wilfred and
my sister-in-law frantic goodbyes as the bus edged out of Mbare
Musika on the start of its five-hundred-kilometre journey to
Beitbridge. The bus made brief stops at Chivhu, Mvuma and
Masvingo. Thereafter, the only other place it stopped was Ngundu
Halt, about half the distance between Masvingo and Beitbridge.

During the brief stop for refreshments at Ngundu Halt, my
daughter and I had no choice but to force down our patched
throats lukewarm bottles of Coca-Cola which had been served

to us straight from the shelves. There was no fridge for fizzy drinks in the one and only shop at that rural bus stop. Our bus reached our destination just after four p.m. After clearance on the Zimbabwe side of the border post, it proved a bit difficult for us to get transport just to cross the Limpopo River and reach the South African side of the border. In the end, one kind lorry driver allowed us with our luggage of two heavy suitcases to climb onto the open back of his vehicle which was laden with a mixture of logs of wood and bags of coal. The lorry moved very slowly in a long queue of traffic that stretched for almost a mile to cross the Limpopo River into South Africa. It was almost five p.m. when we finally reached the opposite side of the great river. After being cleared by very polite and friendly officials manning the South African border post, I started the trauma of looking for transport that would take me and my young daughter from the South African border post to Johannesburg. On leaving the South African border post, somebody had directed us to go and wait at an open piece of ground for commuter omnibuses which travelled to Johannesburg. What surprised me was that there was not a vehicle in sight at that site. A motley collection of bystanders we found standing aimlessly at that spot hinted that there was a 'strike' involving omnibuses and that the last few omnibuses operating on the Johannesburg route had left two hours earlier!

Prior to leaving the South African immigration offices, I had announced loudly to people standing in the long queue, some of whom I suspected were motorists, that I would be grateful if any kind person could give me and my daughter a lift to Johannesburg. Besides most of my audience looking at me with blank faces as they moved slowly in the queue to have their travel documents checked and stamped, nobody had responded to my request. In the absence of omnibuses arriving to pick up passengers, I decided that there was no wisdom in continuing to wait in the open space. Meanwhile the sun was setting and before long, it would be dark. I did not have the foggiest idea where and how my daughter and I were going to spend the night. It was my first time I had been a foreigner in a country I knew absolutely nothing about. With all these fears of the unknown and the threats the impending darkness promised, my heart began beating from the sudden fear for my daughter's security in the strange surroundings. She was only about fourteen years of age, and I was concerned more about her safety than mine. About three hundred yards away, I spotted a garage and diesel station which seemed a hive of activity as mostly passenger vehicles arrived and left after having their tanks filled with fuel.

Leaving my daughter Valerie standing by the two heavy pieces of our luggage and making sure that she remained directly in my line of sight, I quickly walked to the petrol/diesel garage. I briskly made enquiries about lifts to Johannesburg from some of the car owners who sat in their vehicles while petrol/diesel station attendants filled their vehicles with fuel. Nearly all the vehicle owners were filling their tanks to full, an indication they had long journeys ahead of them. I had no luck at first. None of the drivers seemed interested in my queries. When I had almost given up hope, a car owner at another tank nearby overheard me talking to his neighbour about my desperate need for a lift to Johannesburg. My mentioning of the fact that I had a little fourteen-year-old girl with me may have strummed that man's heart strings. Besides, the sun had set, and it was gradually becoming dark. The man felt pity for me, especially when I pointed in the direction where I had left Valerie standing. He said he was travelling towards Johannesburg but that his journey would end at Pretoria, leaving us with another journey of about thirty kilometres.

Without suggesting how Valerie and I would overcome the challenge lying ahead of us on reaching Pretoria, he quietly offered to give us a lift in his car where his young wife and a baby daughter quietly sat. Introducing himself, he said he was a South African citizen, but his wife was Zimbabwean. He had just crossed the border back into South Africa from Zimbabwe where he had visited his in-laws somewhere in Masvingo Province. I exchanged greetings with his wife in our Shona language and she replied in the same language, heavily tinged with the Karanga dialect. After filling his car with petrol and having his car tyre pressures checked, the driver personally packed our two suitcases in the back of the car. Assured that my daughter and I were comfortably seated in the back-passenger seats, he started the engine of his car and we set out on the wide tarmac to Johannesburg at about six fifteen p.m. But ten kilometres from the border post, the driver exited from the Johannesburg highway into a road to the left and drove for a short distance into a small town that was clearly signposted 'Messina' (now 'Musina'). He drove to a block of buildings which had a row of modern-looking restaurants. Saying he was feeling peckish, he parked his car outside one of these restaurants. His wife and baby left the car together with him and they went into the restaurant.

Returning to the car immediately and finding me and my daughter still quietly sitting inside, the driver beckoned us to join him and his family for a meal as well. I had a bit of money in Zimbabwean Dollars on me which I was reserving for our fare to Johannesburg. By the way, that man still hadn't told me what he was going to charge me and my daughter for the lift to Johannesburg in his car. On the other hand, I certainly did not have enough money in South African Rands to buy ourselves meals at that stage of our journey. So, when the man invited us for a meal with his family, I feigned being full, although I was beginning to feel the pangs of hunger after travelling for the whole day on the rickety old bus. Besides, I was thinking of the hassle of border-crossing we had gone through earlier that evening and the near disaster which would have arisen if we had failed to find transport to Johannesburg. I was also quite sure that Valerie would have begun to feel hungry after her experiences of that journey from hell! The driver persisted with his invitation, "My friend, you're as good as my in-laws, so I'm offering you and your daughter free meals. Please come into the restaurant and have some food. You don't have to worry about paying anything. I'll take care of the cost. From what you said, you've had a long day and we still have a long way to go before we reach Johannesburg."

Valerie and I each ate a large hot beef burger, a large packet of freshly made potato chips, a portion of salads and drank fizzy drink from an icy cold 300 ml bottle of Coca-Cola. We enjoyed eating our meals, our first solid meals since breakfast in Zimbabwe that day. The burger filled me up and the fizzy drinks were cold and refreshing. After all of us were fed, the driver politely asked everyone to use the toilets available in the modern restaurant because the journey ahead of us was going to be a long one. The driver and I used the male toilets while the driver's wife (with baby in her arms) and Valerie used the female toilets on the other side. Before we boarded the car again, I thanked the driver for his generosity and kindness in buying meals for Valerie and my-self. Since we had caught that lift well after dark, I had not been able to see exactly what type of car the man was driving. But I am sure it was one of the latest Japanese passenger car sensations of that time; one of the new-fangled Toyotas or Hondas of that time, maybe. From the sound of its engine, it was still in mint condition despite having already been on the road for some time. Edging into the Johannesburg highway and starting our journey at approximately seven forty-five p.m., the driver handled the car with remarkable ease. I could feel the firm grip of the rubber tyres on the tarmac as the vehicle zoomed and lunged forward at the speed of an arrow with the engine roaring and growling proudly like a lion. On account perhaps of the quality of the car's engine, the vehicle seemed to pick up more velocity whenever it was going up a steep gradient without the driver accelerating for more fuel to reach the combustion chambers in his car engine.

After or before Pietermaritzburg (Polokwane?), the road had been built in such a way that it went through a tunnel below a range of mountains for something like four to five miles before emerging on the opposite side of the mountains. It was at about midnight when the driver stopped at a town for us to have re-freshments and for us to use the toilets. Valerie and I were still holding our own, so we stayed put in the car. With everybody back in the car, the driver hit the road again and he drove the vehicle non-stop for the next one-and-a-half hours.

When we reached Pretoria, the driver by-passed the exit point of the highway that would eventually lead him back to his home.

Instead, he offered to drive with us all the way into the brightly lit city of Johannesburg. I had never seen such beautiful glory at night. The City of Harare with which I was familiar was nowhere near half the vision that was before me as the car snaked its way into the extra-large metropolis. The 'city of gold' as it was often affectionately labelled as looked deceptively beautiful, with its galaxy of glittering street lighting against the shimmering morning darkness that blanketed the city. During our long journey, I had told the driver that that was my first time to come into the Republic of South Africa and that I knew absolutely nothing about the city of Johannesburg.

On that score, he said that if he had let us enter the city on our own at night, we would have been obvious targets of thieves, crooks and the whole array of bad humanity who infest Johannesburg's nightlife. The driver wended his way through brightly lit roads, streets and pathways that were still largely bereft of vehicular traffic, considering we were in the wee hours of the morning. He drove me and my daughter to a 'bed and breakfast' place that belonged to some trusted person he knew in the backstreets of the city. At the 'bed & breakfast,' the driver and the attendant conducted their conversation in Afrikaans. The driver arranged with the night attendant for my bedding and that of my daughter for the remaining hours of that night. They also agreed on arrangements for us to be picked up after breakfast by taxi and ferried to Johannesburg International Airport. When I offered to pay him for our travel expenses from the Messina (Musina) border, he utterly refused my offer, saying that the Zimbabwe dollar by then lost value and he would not know what to do with money that I would have given him. Feeling more pity for me for carrying around money that nobody in South Africa could accept, he paid his own money for our bedding, our breakfast and for the taxi that would take us to the airport that morning! I was flabbergasted.

I had heard of Good Samaritans before, but that man left me completely tongue-tied. I expressed my thanks in very few words. Then at three thirty a.m., knowing for certain that we were safely deposited at the bed and breakfast, the man bade me and my daughter farewell, wished us a safe journey to the UK and off he and his wife disappeared back into the remaining hours of the night to return to their home in Pretoria. After having a hot shower separately and feeling refreshed, Valerie and I ate a hearty breakfast, not in the bed and breakfast itself, but at another restaurant a street or two away. On our return to the bed and breakfast, a taxi was brought as arranged and we left the bed and breakfast at around nine a.m. to be transported to international airport. The airport is several miles out of the city centre, so it took the taxi some forty minutes to reach it. We checked in as soon as we arrived at the airport, thus getting rid of our two pieces of heavy luggage because they had been taken inside.

Our flight on Air France – a Boeing 747 Jumbo Jet – would only be departing for Paris at eight p.m. that night, so we had arrived far too early and literally had the whole day to ourselves in the massive airport lounge. Finding a spot where my daughter could sit, relax, browse through magazines and even snooze if she preferred, I went on a sight-seeing walk along the lengthy airport lounge. The Harare (Robert Gabriel Mugabe) International Airport I knew was nowhere nearer the size of that gargantuan airport my daughter and I had arrived at. More large passenger aeroplanes were parked at the airport terminal. Looking across the massive runway, other equally large aeroplanes were either landing or taking off one after the other in rapid succession. As a result of 'arrivals' pouring into the airport and thousands of others queuing up to catch flights to destinations scattered in distant parts of the world, there was a constant flow of human traffic within the airport buildings. Tens of hundreds of people filed up the flight of stairs towards the 'Departures Hall' to board their planes. At intermittent intervals, hundreds of other tired-looking and travel-worn passengers including airline staff crews in smart uniforms, spewed from the 'Arrivals Hall' on the ground floor, trundling their luggage on trolleys. Along the airport lounge was a mixture of restaurants and coffee shops, all of them strategically positioned to arrest the attention of both departing and arriving passengers.

As all this was going on, there was soft music continually filtering through speakers fitted in hidden panels of the high-ceilinged roof. The music from the speakers would regularly be interrupted by announcements about flights arriving or about to depart. With such arrangements in place, passengers waiting to catch flights and others waiting for family and friends on arriving flights were kept abreast of events. If passengers were late for their flights and departing planes were waiting for them to come aboard, their names were called out loudly through the speakers. If they had fallen asleep while sitting on the benches in the airport lounge, the announcements would wake them up and suddenly they would collect their hand luggage and dash like frightened hares up the stairs labelled 'Departures,' to catch their flights. Johannesburg's (Oliver Tambo) International Airport was a large airport. It had been designed to handle large volumes of big passenger airlines and human traffic arriving from and leaving to travel to distant destinations in faraway lands.

Before we left Harare in the morning of the day before, my sister-in-law, Tsitsi Elizabeth Nyemba, had prepared a packed lunch for Valerie and I which included cooked chicken, 'boerewors' sandwiches and potato crisps (spuds). Valerie still had remnants of that packed lunch in a paper bag. Curiously, when we had checked in earlier, she had retained the paper bag containing the packed lunch as part of her hand luggage. On 'Checking-in' Valerie reminded me that we still had unfinished food with us. I had forgotten all about it. Other commitments of greater import preoccupied my mind. She and I sat down to eat the remnants of that packed meal as our lunch for that day. I found it strange that the food was still fresh, edible and did not give off any smell of rottenness despite having been carried in a bag for close on one thousand kilometres and more than twenty-four hours later! We washed the meal down with small plastic cups of hot coffee that I bought from one of several vending machines I found along the hallway of the airport lounge. Then I enquired from the reception desk not far from where we sat whether the small change of Six Rands I had in my pocket was sufficient for me to make a quick overseas call from a nearby telephone booth to Margaret. I was assured that the sum of money I had was more than adequate. After dialling her number in the UK which I knew by heart, I waited patiently for it to go through, "Hullo, Margaret Moyo speaking. Can I help you?"

She spoke with her usual thin, soft voice. It sounded surprisingly crystal clear considering that she was over ten thousand kilometres away from South Africa. I was tempted to walk out of the telephone booth to check if she was not standing behind it. "Hi, Maggie. It's me, Lawrence," I hesitantly spoke into the mouthpiece.

"Oh my God, I'm so delighted you've telephoned because I was so worried. Where are you? I heard you left for Johannesburg by bus yesterday morning."

Beginning by telling her I was speaking to her from Johannesburg (now Oliver Tambo) International Airport, I quickly gave her an update on the sad tale of our travels up until then.

"I'm so very sorry, Lawrence, you went through all those travel inconveniences. I told Audrey here that I did not want you to take such a roundabout route to reach here. Anyway, I'm happy both of you are still okay. So, what's happening next? What time is your plane leaving for Paris?"

Then I updated her with our travel itinerary for the remaining twenty hours or thereabouts before Valerie and I reached our destination.

"I'm so happy for both you and Valerie, Lawrence. At least I'm now assured you're finding your way here," she said sweetly, "I'll be waiting for you when you arrive at Birmingham International Airport tomorrow. Safe journey, honey. See you when you get here – bye for now."

And the phone clicked. I could not believe I had just spoken to my wife. That had been the most reassuring telephone conversation I had ever had with Margaret or anybody else over the previous twenty-four hours. I felt not only refreshed after my brief telephone conversation with Margaret. I was also given hope to face the remainder of the travel challenges ahead of us with renewed conviction.

Our flight on 'Air France' was on a Boeing 747 Jumbo Jet, the first and the largest aeroplane my daughter and I had ever travelled in. Its seating capacity, almost the size of a football pitch, in the Economy Class alone, was as I was told somewhere just below five hundred passengers. Valerie had been allocated a window seat and, with me sitting beside her on her left, we had full view of the half-wingspan which stretched for one hundred and fifty metres as far as the eye could see. I wondered whether at full capacity, i.e., laden with its full cargo of both luggage and passengers, that huge metal bird of the sky would be able to take off from the runway and become airborne. After Valerie and I had been admitted and directed to our seats by polite and friendly air hostesses, we sat on the plane for almost an hour while it continued loading. Entering the plane individually or as couples or families after their travel documents had been checked, passengers rapidly filled all available seating spaces.

By eight p.m., the plane had filled up with passengers. Then the main entrance door near the pilot's cabin was closed. Almost simultaneously, the jets were started. All we heard was a muffled humming and whirring sound, which was overridden by a dominant whistling. A brisk message was relayed via a public address system within the plane. In that message, the pilot who would take control of the plane for most the journey and his co-pilot were introduced. Our journey from Johannesburg to Paris was starting, so all of us were requested to fasten our belts. Peering through the window from our side, the staircase we had used to come aboard had been detached and was being wheeled away by a small human operated vehicle. In a few moments, the huge aircraft became mobile. It slowly moved away from its parking bay and the pilot presumably steered or taxied it towards the runway, farther away from the main air terminal. It glided smoothly to the end of the runway from where the airport buildings and other parked aeroplanes were all in full view through our egg-shaped window. The huge aeroplane stopped at that end of the runway for about eight to ten minutes with its jets hissing and whistling more loudly than before it left the airport terminal.

I guessed that the pilot was awaiting instructions from airport control informing him all was clear for the jet to commence its mad race along the runway before it took off to climb into the air. The green light was presumably given and the aircraft's mad race started. Engaged into full throttle by the pilot, the humongous mountain of steel and zinc hurtled along the runway, rolling on its twenty-four rubber wheels at first. Before reaching the middle of the runway, the aeroplane had picked up so much speed that it felt as if it was going at the speed of the wind. All its jets were whistling at such a high volume that it would be ear-shattering to a listener outside. Simultaneously, the front of the plane gradually tilted upwards. As it continued its mad race at supersonic speed, it surged and swayed sideways before we realised that the entire body of the plane had left the hard tarmac on earth and was now airborne. Soon, we heard the wheels of the aircraft slot back into their compartments below the plane's carriage. Looking farther down below us through the dark night, the bright streetlights of the City of Johannesburg slowly became a carpet of patterned dots as the plane made a circle round the city below and continued to increase its altitude. Approximately ten minutes after the plane reached stratospheric height from the ground and the plane had been set on course for the journey to the northern hemisphere, we were advised to unfasten our safety belts. Meanwhile our Jumbo Jet whooshed and pierced through the darkened high heavens at the speed of light.

To repeat myself, our flight was headed for Paris International Airport in Western Europe. Once it had reached the recommended altitude for the plane of its mammoth size, the passenger jet seemed to float on air. The only sound I could hear was a compressed buzz as it glided and swished through the air. Mountains of clouds below us seemed to form an impenetrable fog. Yet the gargantuan aeroplane we were riding in zoomed and powered on over those clouds at a high speed some of us on the pane had never known before. My daughter Valerie had had a long day at Johannesburg (Oliver Tambo) International Airport. Ten hours' waiting to catch a plane following eight hours on the bus the previous day was too much for a fifteen-year-old girl, so as soon as our plane was airborne, Valerie went to sleep beside me. Not me; I stayed fully awake and kept my eyes peeled. That journey by air was my first aeroplane-ride. For that reason, I vowed I wanted to derive maximum enjoyment from it. Before we flew over the Mediterranean Sea, I had watched two 007 James Bond movies on the TV screen in front of me. I had also done justice to some of the lovely meals and drinks that were served on that flight.

Accepting my nudges once or twice to wake up during the flight, with her face laden with sleep and possibly tiredness, Valerie would wake up to eat some of the food. However, she immediately resumed sleeping thereafter. There was just one minor incident which left me shaken a bit when the plane was flying over the Sahara Desert. The whole plane shook very badly for about three minutes. The incident woke many passengers who had been asleep for most of the journey. The pilot was overheard apologising to passengers on the public address system, requesting us to stay calm as he had the plane under control. The 'aeroplane-shakes' were what he briefly described as normal phenomena that happens when aeroplanes flew over big rivers or mountains, causing what he described as 'mechanical turbulence.' He did not go into too many details about that for fear of boring passengers. We flew over the Mediterranean Sea without any hassle. After departing Johannesburg at eight fifteen p.m., our journey to Paris took us all night, without landing or stopping anywhere. The big steel bird circled over the twinkling early morning streetlights of the City of Paris twice before it finally landed and taxied to the airport terminal, as the 'prince of the sky' peeped from behind the eastern horizon at five thirty a.m.

Our stopover at Paris International Airport lasted four and a half hours. There were stricter immigration checks at that stage of our journey. Some of our fellow passengers who did not possess the correct immigration documents, for example, passports and visas, which would allow them to pass through France and enter the UK, were either detained at Paris International Airport or indeed put on the reverse trip back to Johannesburg! Valerie and I had the right immigration documentation, so we were allowed to proceed with our journey uninterrupted. We finally walked from the airport lounge to board a plane with many returning British holiday makers who had been to different parts of Europe. Our flight from Paris to Birmingham was in a much smaller British European Airways plane. It took just about two and a half hours to complete the journey. On arriving in the UK on 31 July 2002, it took Valerie and I and a few other passengers arriving from countries outside Europe, quite a bit of time to be cleared for entry into Britain. However, as in Paris, Valerie and I possessed the correct immigration credentials that allowed us unfettered entrance into the UK. My daughter and I finally emerged through 'Arrivals' at Birmingham International Airport at exactly one thirty p.m. Margaret and a family friend called 'Frank' awaited our arrival at the airport.

Frank had generously offered to carry Margaret in his car to Birmingham airport and to transport the two of us to West Bromwich – one of several towns in Birmingham – where Margaret and Audrey lived.

# Chapter 20

## Our children, our bundles of joy

My marriage to Margaret was richly blessed with four wonderful children namely Gerald, Audrey Shingaidzo, Lorraine Vimbai and Valerie Hazvinei. While they are united by a bond as our children, each of them possesses personality characteristics that are unique to them as individuals. They arrived in this world one at a time over a period of twelve years of Margaret's and my happy union as husband and wife. As I write these pages, all our children have grown up to become adults who stand on their two feet and look after themselves in a world that is fraught with a coterie of challenges. Some of our children are in distant parts of the world where, like us, they have taken over the baton in pursuit of opportunities that will improve the quality of their lives. Margaret and I credit ourselves with leaning over backwards as young parents in Zimbabwe to ensure that our three older children, that is, Gerald, Audrey Shingaidzo and Lorraine Vimbai, received the best education possible in top schools up to the higher end of secondary school before both of us emigrated to the UK. Valerie Hazvinei, our youngest and the lastborn child in our family, was a mere fourteen-year-old year 10 (Form 3) little girl when I travelled with her on my migrant journey from Zimbabwe to the UK in 2002.

Gerald is the oldest and firstborn ('Nevanji' in the Shona language) of our brood of children. He was born in September 1976, nearly five years after I started teaching. Then Margaret and I lived in a single rented room of a government-owned four-roomed flat in a block of flats named 'New Hope Flats' in Jabavu Drive, Highfield, Salisbury (Harare). We shared the use of that flat with two other male occupants, each of whom had his own room and family dependants. We used the kitchen, toilet and bathroom facilities communally. It was inconvenient living in those filthy and overcrowded conditions. Yet after Gerald was born, we continued staying at that address for another four years. Then the oldest of our three daughters, Audrey Shingaidzo, arrived in April 1979. Packed like sardines in one room with my wife, Margaret and two small children, it just would not do for us to continue living at New Hope Flats. In the other spare bedroom next door to us was a family who played their radio so loud that my family could hardly sleep at night. Literally squeezed for space with my ballooning family, a single bed, a single door wardrobe as well as a huge 'Supersonic Stereo', all of these items in one room, urgent action was needed to improve matters. A few months after Zimbabwe attained its independence from Great Britain, opportunities for many people to venture into business projects were opening up. I wasted no time. I moved my family and the few belongings we possessed to a two bedroomed house that I had found in the nearby township of 'Glen Norah'. The opening up of opportunities appeared to be the reason why my 'landlord' had left his place of abode. Things were much better there, for a change. At least Margaret and I had exclusive use of 'our' bedroom while the two children slept in the spare bedroom. Even better than that, Gerald and Audrey had some space outside the house where they could play and run around; but our feelings of happiness were short-lived. Our stay at that house was for barely eight months. For reasons associated with the failure of his business project, the owner of the house suddenly turned up and gave us short notice to move out because he wanted to move back into his property. Despite the short notice to leave the Glen Norah house, I only just managed to find one very large 'lounge' in a four-bedroomed house in the 'New Stands' section of Old Highfield, Harare, where a new home-building project by private developers was in progress. Four other people and their families also rented single rooms each at the house, while the large lounge I occupied with my family served as our bedroom, living room and kitchen all at the same time. We had to go right round to the back of the large house for laundry, toileting, and bathing purposes, where we also mixed up with a horde of other 'lodgers' occupying rooms at the house.

The whole situation was unwieldy and very inconvenient, to say the least. As you can imagine I did not find it ideal and suitable for a young wife who had two little children. Gerald was only about four or five years old then and Audrey was two to three years of age. Unfortunately, that address was too far for me to commute on foot to and from Kudzanayi School daily, where I worked as a teacher, four or five kilometres away. After making enquiries over something like ten months, I secured a detached two bed-roomed house, back in Jabavu Drive, a stone's throw away from 'New Hope Flats', Highfield, where I had originally lived as a bachelor and young married man. Again, I had no choice but to move my family to that new address which thankfully reduced my walking distance to work by half. In short, in a short space of eighteen months, I had moved house three times. When we moved over in July 1982 from the 'New Stands' in Old Highfield to occupy 'Mukotsanjera House' – because the property belonged to the owner named Mr Mukotsanjera – Margaret was seven months pregnant with our third child, Lorraine Vimbai who was born a week into September of that year. Her birth gave us plenty of joy and happiness.

Now, knowing that for the first time we had a place for our exclusive use, a house consisting of separate facilities such as a living room, a kitchen, separate bedrooms for us parents, two spare bedrooms for the children and occasional visitors; Margaret and I enjoyed peace of mind we had never known before, ever. Also, by a strange coincidence, it happened that I had managed to save a bit of money from my meagre schoolteacher's salary. To celebrate our happiness at the two events of Lorraine's birth and, at long last, our finding a little house to rent that had a boundary fence around it and a large space outside where our children could play, I bought our first second-hand family car, a Datsun 120Y Sedan. The little white car was second-hand, yes, but it was still in pristine condition, having been used with care by its original owner who I was given to understand happened to be an elderly white woman who used it on grocery shopping errands at month ends only. That car was our first prize possession which I would use to drive the family around and about in Harare for the best part of the following ten years.

I surprised Margaret and the children when they saw me enter the gate driving the little shiny milk white vehicle and parked it carefully in the driveway at the side of the house. Margaret ululated shrilly while Gerald and Audrey leapt up and down, their eyes wide open in disbelief, in their childish expression of joy. I had passed my driver's licence' after just one driving test attempt nearly a year before. Two weeks before Christmas in 1982, I rented our first 'black and white' television set from a shop in Harare city centre called 'TV Sales & Hire'. With our salaries improving bit by bit in the following year, I replaced that 'black and white' TV set with a colour set from the same suppliers. More of the colour television sets were arriving in different sizes from outside the country. I finally bought our own brand-new TV colour set which was boxed in a rectangular wooden prism. The wooden doors of that TV set could be closed and locked, and the entire prism stood on four wooden legs! On arriving back home from work in the evenings, I recall my ears being regaled with squeals and screeches of laughter and joy being the noises the children made when watching early evening TV children's programmes.

The first four months of 1983 were not altogether a happy period for us because Margaret and I nearly lost our daughter, Audrey Shingaidzo. From about her first six months after birth, Audrey persistently suffered from a form of toxic diarrhoea affecting young children called 'gastroenteritis'. Right up to her fourth birthday, repeated visits to the family physician, a doctor Mazhindu, were proving unhelpful although we continued visiting him each time Audrey's condition deteriorated.

We held a birthday party for her on 18 April 1983. Several little children of her age from houses in the neighbourhood attended that party. A beautiful and quiet fifteen or sixteen-year-old girl, Fiona Musvosvi, from next door helped with organising the children at the party for the whole afternoon. As I sat outside the house draining bottles of cheap wine, I had bought for myself, I could hear a cacophony of happy children's voices from inside the house as they ate cake and danced to vinyl record music being churned out from my huge 'Supersonic' Stereo record player that I had allowed the more grown-up Fiona Musvosvi to use for Audrey's occasion. At the end of the party, all the children went back to their parents' homes by half past six in the evening. At around eight p.m., Margaret drew my attention to Audrey who generally looked disoriented and unhappy. We both wondered whether it was because she had eaten too much cake with some of her friends at the party. While lying on her mother's lap, she began pouring out watery stool. As she did so, she writhed and wriggled sideways holding her stomach area with her palms to indicate she was in abject pain. It was late on a Saturday night and all doctors' surgeries had closed for the weekend. We were at a loss what we could do to ease Audrey out of her pain. At around eleven p.m., Audrey lay limply in her mother's arms with eyes sunken in her hollow sockets. This followed repeated episodes of passing a watery fluid. I called out her name holding her arm up, but no response came from her deathly face. Margaret did not know what to do and she expressed fear that something terrible might happen that night:

"Baba vaJerry, ndavekutya kuti mwana wangu angangofa nemanyoka ake aya. Toita sei? Ndinokumbirawo munondidaidzira Mai Musvosvi vachimbidze kuzondibatsirawo." (Margaret said to me; "I am suspicious that my daughter might die from these bouts of dysentery. What can we do? Please dash along to Mrs Musvosvi next door and ask her to come here urgently and help me with Audrey's dysentery.").

I ran like a mad man to Mrs Musvosvi's house next door to us and banged on her door and summoned her to come to our house urgently and help us out with Audrey's deathly condition. She had fallen asleep, but she woke up immediately. Noting the urgency and fear in my voice she wasted no time. As soon as she set her eyes on Audrey's face and acknowledging that it had lost colour, she quickly walked out of the house and into the small garden in front of the house. She pulled up armfuls of smelly green plants. Rushing back into the house, she grabbed Audrey's whole body as she literally lay lifeless in her mother's arms and placed her horizontally on her lap. She expertly removed whole sections of Audrey's clothing and promptly began rubbing the strongly perfumed green leaves and stems of the plants she had pulled up outside the house on Audrey's thoracic area, face, palms, thighs, the back of her thorax and finally the bottom of her feet. The atmosphere in the house was filled with the pungent but strongly scented smell of the plant leaves she had used.

Allowing her procedure to take effect, Mrs Musvosvi continued holding Audrey in her arms. Moments later she looked up and spoke to Margaret reassuringly:

"Don't be afraid, my dear. You did the right thing when you called me to help. Audrey is alright. She'll get better and will playing with her friends again tomorrow morning, okay. After all the fluid she has lost, she must be quite hungry. Can you please cook a little bit of maize meal porridge so she can eat it before I return back home?"

Mrs Musvosvi, Fiona's mother, stayed on in the house until well after one a.m. the next morning when Audrey slowly came alive again and ate a whole plateful of maize meal porridge that Margaret had cooked. Audrey slept like a log but breathing well, the rest of that night. She did not open her bowels again until mid-morning the following day. When she did so, her stool was thick as a brick. By midday the following day, Audrey could be seen playing games with her friends as if nothing had happened the night before. Her bouts of 'gastroenteritis' which had affected her from her early childhood appear to have reached their climax and ended on that fateful day of her fourth birthday. From then onwards, we experienced no further toxic dysentery challenges with her ever again.

Valerie Hazvinei was born in August 1987. At the time of her birth, we had just moved from "Mukotsanjera" house after staying in that dwelling for over five solid years. The family were then housed in a government-rented four-roomed family flat in a block of similar family flats curiously named 'Hollywood Flats' in Jabavu Drive Highfield, Harare. When Margaret fell pregnant with Valerie, we had hoped that at birth, the pregnancy would produce a boy so that our only son, Gerald, would have a little brother. However, Valerie turned up as a girl. Both Margaret and I accepted her as another of God's blessings to us, hence the name 'Hazvinei' meaning 'It does not matter' in the Shona language. There is more about Valerie Hazvinei in the paragraphs that follow later; but at the time of Valerie's birth, her other siblings were all growing up rapidly. All of them had started school at the local government school called Chengu School; leaving only Lorraine attending kindergarten at Chengu School because she was too young to walk the longer distance to Kudzanayi School. I pulled both Gerald and Audrey out of Chengu and had them attending school at Kudzanayi School where I worked as a teacher. I wanted them to be taught by teachers at Kudzanayi School whose teaching strengths I was familiar with. That gamble seems to have paid off handsomely because both Gerald's and Audrey's results at Grade Seven examinations were quite impressive, qualifying them for secondary school admission at high performing schools without any hassle.

Time passed by gradually and I was promoted to the senior administrative post of education officer. That promotion necessitated that I transfer to take up my new post in the town of Chegutu, one hundred kilometres away from Harare. I could not move house immediately to Chegutu with my family because my wife, Margaret, was in the middle of a nurse training course as a Registered General Nurse at Parirenyatwa Hospital. I had no choice but to move on my own, leaving my family in the flat that I rented in Harare while Margaret completed her nurse training. I cannot remember too well, but I think our son Gerald had started his secondary school at St Paul's High School, Musami. That Roman Catholic School in Mashonaland East Province was then a giant among some of the top schools in that province which produced outstanding GCSE 'O' Level passes. A year or so later, Margaret finished her training, found a job as a nurse at Chegutu District Hospital and promptly moved bag and baggage to join me in Chegutu. As I have said, I maintained very high expectations for all our children. Although I lived in a three-bedroomed house in Chegutu – first at an address in Queen Street and then later in the Zimbabwe Mining Development Corporation of the municipality – my daughters could attend Hartley No. 1 Primary School as day boarders if I wanted. So, I quickly organised for them to be admitted as 'boarder' pupils, a former 'Europeans Only' (Group A) School. This was in the early 1990s and teaching and learning standards were still comparatively higher at that school amid an increasing collapse of same in similar schools in the surrounding area.

I had my two older daughters enrolled for the rest of their two or three years of primary school at that school. Even if Valerie started her primary school when she joined me in Chegutu, two or three years after she arrived from Harare with her mother, we made it a point that she also attended only the best schools the little bit of money we had could buy. For Valerie Hazvinei, such schools included Sir John Kennedy Government Boarding Primary School (a former Group A school) in the Kadoma District area. Valerie had a brief stint at that school, some details of which I will provide later). Another good primary school through whom Valerie would pass through later was Hartley No. 1 Primary School. For their secondary school education, Audrey spent her first two years as a boarder pupil at Queen Elizabeth Girls' High School in central Harare. In those days, that school was included among the higher end of the best schools at which girls were recommended to obtain a balanced education.

Then for logistical and tactical reasons as well as what we saw as Audrey's need to draw from the benefits of 'mission' education – a route both her mother and I had passed through – I moved her two years down the line from Queen Elizabeth Girls High School. She joined her other siblings Gerald and Lorraine (who was starting Form 1, year 7, UK) at Sandringham High School in the Norton area. The 'logistical reason' for which I found it appropriate to move Audrey from Queen Elizabeth Girls' High

School to Sandringham High School for her Form 3 (year 10 in the UK) was so that my children would be based in one school to avoid the expense of having to drop off Audrey in Harare and then proceed to Sandringham High School to drop off Gerald and Audrey's sister, Lorraine. If I had not done that, it would have resulted in rigorous and expensive movements in circles at the beginning and the end of each term. I also transferred Audrey to Sandringham as I wanted the superior quality teaching and 'mission' ethos at Sandringham High School to boost her performance before she wrote her GCSE examinations two years down the line. It looked ideal having Gerald, Audrey and Lorraine attending boarding school at the same school. But carrying them all in one trip with their metal 'trunks' jam-packed with clothes and food provisions on a journey of approximately seventy kilometres in a small family car that I had – an old Renault 9 Sedan – frequently proved to be quite a tricky business. Imagine the rickety old banger of a car laden to capacity with its cargo trundling along the uneven tarmac, its boot bearing down heavily and the body of the car from the middle to the bonnet looking like the front of an aeroplane about to take off on the runway! That would be me on several occasions for two years going to drop off my children to school at the start of each term.

Gerald had passed 10 GCSEs with a string of '9A' grade subject passes at St. Paul's High School. There being no Lower and Upper Sixth classes at St Paul's High School, I brought him over to Sandringham High School the following year. Sandringham High had a reputation for producing high quality 'A' Level examination results and it was known that most successful 'A' Level students from that Methodist Church mission were university education material. Most of the 'A' Level products from Sandringham High School were quickly absorbed for undergraduate studies at the University of Zimbabwe. Gerald had always expressed a wish to work in the medical field as a doctor. But the lower points he attained in his Upper Sixth science subjects did not qualify him for admission in his area of first preference. However, for the past twenty years Gerald has been seized with an unrelenting determination to break the evasive conundrum that is linked with entrepreneurship and the actuarial sciences. Unfortunately for my son, the rugged political and business environment in Zimbabwe has not been of meaningful assistance to his ambitions. He possesses a plethora of business ideas. As rumour has it, business ideas and methodologies to break into business originated exclusively by my son, have occasionally been pilfered by some of his competitors. Some of these fellows have, in turn, secretly used his business plans to start their own business ventures and gone on to achieve astronomical heights of success.

I have no doubt that my son is an intelligent young man. He is loaded with a fantastic array of management skills and experience acquired in the intervening period since he completed his 'A' Levels. Provided with an equal playing field for business, there is nothing to stop Gerald from reaching for the sky. I regularly chat with him on the phone from the UK on miscellaneous family matters and on others regarding businesses. The image that he presents to me each time is one of an aspiring business executive with a burning ambition to succeed. At the time of writing these memoirs, Gerald is based in Botswana pursuing his dreams. My son got married in Zimbabwe some fourteen or fifteen years ago. He has two lovely children, Daniel 'Danny' who is completing his GCSEs as I write these pages, and gorgeous Abigail 'Abbie' who starts Form 1 (year 7, UK) in 2022.

Audrey and Lorraine went on to complete their GCSEs as 'boarders' at Sandringham High School, both passing their examinations with flying colours. Audrey finished her stay first and departed, leaving her sister Lorraine to stay on at the school for another two years. Armed with her GCSEs, Audrey was employed in the sales department of the Topics departmental stores. She then moved to the mobile phone company 'Econet' in Harare. It was sometime in 1999 when she bought me my first 'cellphone,' a big brick-size heavy object which did not fit in any shirt or trouser pocket! Other than perhaps company executives like managers, sales executives, and accountants etc. (who were given these 'things' as part of their 'perks' for the big job roles they held), very few other people, if any, owned 'cell' phones as we called them in Zimbabwe then. Audrey bought me one of these technological innovations. I was the first among a staff of six Education Officers at Chegutu District Office to walk about with the object in my hands. Arriving at the government offices one Monday morning holding the thing against my right ear and talking to Audrey in Harare, everybody left their offices and rushed over to mine where they gaped at the object. Some of them even frightened to touch it. It was a mystery to them that I could talk to somebody as far away as Harare without any wires or cables connecting us as in the case of the telephone system they were used to.

Another four or so years later, Audrey suddenly packed her bags and jumped on the bandwagon of thousands of other young Zimbabweans who were deserting their motherland in droves in search of jobs that paid them better salaries so that they could buy houses, cars and send their children to school. They were desperate for opportunities that would make it easy for them to 'bring food to the table' and generally help to improve their quality of their lives etc. etc. The vibrant economy that once held so much promise at independence in 1980 was crumbling little by little and the centre could no longer hold. The disgruntled young people were leaving with their skills and heading to various destinations in Africa or across the seas into the diaspora all over the world. Audrey's mother and I saw our eldest daughter off at the then 'Harare' International Airport and gave her tearful 'goodbyes' as both of us felt the adventure she was undertaking was like a shot into the dark. She caught a flight headed for London (Heathrow), UK on 'Kenya Airways.' That was in December 2000. By so doing, Audrey may have not realised she was acting as a catalyst. Little did she know that she was thrashing out a path along which in less than two years, her mother, her little daughter Yvette Chenai, her younger sister Valerie Hazvinei and I would use to follow suit.

Meanwhile on completing her primary school education at Hartley No. 1 Primary School and passing Grade 7 (year 7 in the

UK) examinations with exceptionally good grades in English, Mathematics and Shona, we had Valerie Hazvinei enrolled at Chegutu High School for her Form 1 (year 8 in the UK). Chegutu High School, a government-run day secondary school, still competed favourably with other top boarding schools in the district in offering a comparatively higher quality of education. Another reason we consciously enrolled Valerie at Chegutu Government High School, nearer our home rather than the schools further away as those her older sisters had attended, was so that we could keep an eye on her 'eczema', a stubborn and bothersome skin condition that had erupted on her body just when she turned six months old. Those eruptions had persisted throughout most of her childhood, resulting in our having to have dermatologists or skin disorder specialists in Harare attend to her from time to time. Recently in Grade 3 (year 5) of her primary school, we had been forced to pull her out of boarding school at 'Sir John Kennedy', a former Group A government boarding primary school in Kadoma District because her 'eczema' was getting in the way and interfering with her concentration and focus on schoolwork.

Valerie was in Form 3 (a General Certificate of Secondary Education, year 10 Class) at Chegutu High School in June 2002 when I requested her registration to be withdrawn so that she could travel with me on the journey to the UK in the following month or so. To say Valerie Hazvinei was excited at the unexpected prospect of continuing her education overseas, 'in England' is putting it in the fewest words possible. Following a tortuous two-and-a-half-day journey, a thousand kilometres by land on a bus first and then in a motorcar to Johannesburg, South Africa and on the next day by air through France, Valerie and I finally landed at London (Heathrow) in the UK on 31 July 2002. Details of that hazardous and tiresome journey can be found in a whole chapter of this book. Surprisingly, even if Valerie faced new learning arrangements altogether in multiracial classes when the new term started in September of that year, she adapted to these changes amazingly quickly, tucking all the challenges in her stride. She was enrolled and warmly received at Manor High School where she was placed in year 11 (Form 4), a class higher than the Form 3 (year 10) she was in in Zimbabwe because it was felt that on the strength of the report Chegutu High School had issued to her on her transfer, she had already finished year 10 work and that she should proceed straight into the final General Certificate of Secondary Education, year 11 class. Her new learning environment was well endowed with an assortment of resources, e.g., the use of educational technology and 'white boards', etc.

The classrooms Valerie attended at Manor High School were well-resourced with textbooks and writing materials and all her teachers were highly qualified and experienced. In the 'Information, Communication and Technology' department, each pupil had access to a desktop computer. In addition, year 11s, Lower and Upper Sixth students were each issued with personal computers in the form of laptops. They were however not allowed to take the laptops to their homes. In three short years, Valerie passed both her GCSEs and Upper Sixth Form (Form 6 or 'A' Level) examinations with very high grades in the latter which automatically qualified her for admission to Wolverhampton University, a short tram ride from West Bromwich to Wolverhampton City, to study for her first undergraduate degree, a B Sc Honours Degree in Business Management. Despite earning a 2.1 (Upper Second) score at the end of her first degree, she decided to have a go straightaway at another degree programme at Birmingham City University, a B Sc Honours Degree in Adult Nursing which she passed with another Upper Second-Class qualification. Having done justice to her quest for more knowledge, Valerie has been working in the medical field for the past six to seven years. She is happily married to a Zimbabwean man, Daniel Mpehla who is a Gas Engineer. They have two lovely children, a son Justin and a gorgeous daughter, Jessica. Ever since she flew the nest over five years ago, Valerie has never forgotten her roots, where she came from. She and her family live a few streets away in the same neighbourhood as us.

From time to time, Valerie and her family visit us. Her elder sister Audrey also lives with her family a short walk from Valerie's home and pretty much in the same neighbourhood where we live. Being the two of our children Margaret and I have virtually lived with for the past twenty years, Audrey and Valerie are not however necessarily at our beck and call. They are adults with decision-making faculties of their own and we as parents respect that. Particularly unique about Audrey and Valerie thus putting them in a class of their own is that they have always been the first to respond – and they do so promptly – when I send out 'SOS' calls for assistance like in two or three episodes in recent years when their mother, Margaret, fell seriously ill and she needed to be hospitalised. The girls also jump quicky when I call for help in those instances when we run out of cash to meet the payments of some of our bills. Occasionally, they combine efforts with Lorraine (Mrs Penyayi) in Australia when there is need for us to lay off huge costs of one sort or another.

I suspect the smoothness of our life in the UK as retired persons would be quite a rough ride without the wonderful support these 'girls' provide us. I do not know whether it is because Audrey is the oldest of our three female children. She does not want to hear that we are experiencing any form of hardship. Suffice it to say that our girls in the UK have done us proud and we are eternally grateful to them. We suspect that some parents may not have been as lucky as we have. We have welcomed them all back home whenever they report in person or call us on the phone seeking advice and assistance, either on putting the best foot forward to resolve tricky issues confronting them or to find their routes through the intriguing mazes of their lives.

On finishing her GCSEs at Sandringham High School, our daughter Lorraine Vimbai did not stay on to proceed to Lower and Upper Sixth at the same school. She spent close on ten months attending 'A' Level classes at St Francis High School in Chegutu. Just before the end of that year, she boldly announced to both me and her mother she did not want to continue with her classes at St Francis High School. Instead, she opted to take advantage of an opportunity that had arisen for her to immediately start training as an Adult Nurse at Gweru General Hospital. My own blood sister and Lorraine's aunt, Winnie Phyllis (Mrs Bonga) who was employed as a Registered General Nurse, appears to have influenced matters leading to Lorraine being enrolled for the nurse training course at Gweru General Hospital. Events moved at a fast pace. I remember taking a day off from my duties at Chegutu District Office to visit Lorraine in Gweru and assess how she was getting on as a student nurse. She seemed to be getting along fine. Her training course was still in progress in June 2002 (?) when – aware that although officially I was still a student at the University of Zimbabwe pursuing a master's degree in English – I had however quietly set a date to leave Zimbabwe at the end of July and emigrate to the UK.

Her sister, Audrey, had already been resident in the UK for eighteen months and had engineered for their mother, Margaret, to come over to the UK also. At the time Lorraine made her 'marriage' request, Margaret had been staying in the UK for six months and was already working as a nurse. She surprised me when she asked me to preside over her marriage to the love of her life, Cossam Penyayi. She caught me completely by surprise. At first, I turned her request down. With her aunt supporting her in her request, my excuses that she must complete her nurse training first and that after that, my sibling brothers I was leaving behind in Zimbabwe could always supervise at such an event were quietly overturned.

Lorraine wanted me to marry her to her future husband and nobody else.

I had no choice but to submit to her request. She was married at a family gathering, details which I have already outlined in an earlier instalment of this memoir, two weeks before I caught my flight out of Zimbabwe to the UK in July 2002. In events that followed briskly when I was already settled in the UK, my daughter completed her nurse training and with her aunt's assistance, she was immediately employed as a Registered General Nurse at the same hospital where she had received her training. In a few years following the end of Lorraine's nurse training course, we heard Cossam Penyayi, who officially was now my son-in-law, and Lorraine, were living together and had started a family. Their first child, a son named Dylan and my nephew, had been born.

Upon arriving in the UK at the end of 2000, Audrey did not let the grass grow under her feet. The environment she found herself in presented to her new challenges and routines to her, which demanded that she should respond in ways that corresponded with those demands. Following a gruelling period in her personal life, combined with many hours of fulltime study, Audrey finally emerged with advanced level qualifications which qualified her as a BSc Honours in Law & Social Policy Degree and Level 7 Credits in a Masters in Lifelong Education at the University of Wolverhampton. She opted to pursue a career in education, so she completed further studies at the same university for a fulltime Postgraduate Certificate in Education, a qualification which made it possible for her to work as a lecturer in Further Education Colleges in the UK. Audrey is employed in a senior management position at a local further education college as I write on these pages. In pursuit of achieving educational excellence and the fulfilment of her personal ambitions, Audrey has worked consistently hard over the past seven or so years. I have observed that to meet some of the onerous demands of her tasks at work, it seems that at times she tends to punish herself. She is passionate about the nature of her work, yet by all appearances, my daughter lives a very private live and hardly ever seems to have any social life at weekends whatsoever as she is invariably deeply engrossed in college work of one sort or another. I have warned her to be careful that her dedication to duty does not impact negatively on her health. She is a hardworking child and has managed to achieve a lot in life. She is strong and continues to support the family. Her firstborn child, Yvette Chenai, is following in the mother's footsteps; she is in the second year of study for a tertiary qualification too. Her second child is a son by the name Takunda. My grandson has just finished writing his GCSE examinations and is now in the sixth form. Finally, Megan is Audrey's third and the lastborn of her three children. Megan is in her early years of high school.

By around 2006, some of the key elements of Lorraine's imme-diate family, including her mother, Margaret, her sisters Audrey, Valerie and I had left Zimbabwe to go into the diaspora. Even her aunt and my sister, Mrs Winnie Phyllis Bonga, has probably also migrated to the UK. I have no proper record of the exact-ness of my sibling's movements. Yes, Lorraine then had the la-bel 'Mrs Penyayi'. That was lovely but besides her GCSEs and nurse training diploma, which seemed to be all of it there was and nothing more. Deserted, so to speak, with no nearest family member to interact with other than her husband, the economic situation in Zimbabwe was worsening every day. The value of the Zimbabwe dollar had begun to slide down rapidly. It was proving hard to buy anything with it. Prices of groceries, clothes, medical expenses etc had shot up to alarming levels. The rate at which everything was falling apart was stultifying. More and more young Zimbabweans, most of them at around Lorraine's age, were leaving the country like rats fleeing a sinking ship. Lorraine made up her mind also to escape her splendid isolation which she found increasingly hard to get accustomed to.

Using tips and suggestions from former friends and work col-leagues who had already crossed the blue oceans and settled on pastures new overseas, Lorraine sent out countless applications for nursing jobs to employers scattered across the world. Most of her applications were not answered. The few that were replied to were mere 'regrets.' There was one promising application to Ireland that raised Lorraine's hopes. But leads generated from that one exit point eventually led nowhere, crushing her hopes of ever succeeding in achieving her goal to leave Zimbabwe, as everybody else seemed to have done. All her applications to the UK returned a nil response. By the time of submitting her ap-plications to the UK, thousands of young Zimbabwean nurses and people from all over the world had arrived in that country and filled whatever few vacancies existed in the healthcare sector. The UK was, and still is, a favourite destination for immigrant job seekers from right across the globe. Job seekers flock to it like moths to a flame. Support from her sister Audrey and her mother with hints and suggestions were helpless, but she remained hopeful. When she had given up all hope, a lifeline came in the form of an invitation from an organisation from Australia for Lorraine to attend a 'bridging course' for an unspecified period after which she might be deemed 'qualified' for a job as a nurse at an unknown location in Western Australia.

One hurdle to be leapt over was that a fee of ten thousand Australian Dollars (then approximately six thousand British pounds) would be needed for her attendance to be authorised. Lorraine's mother and I pitched in there and then, as both of us were in paid employment in the UK. I remember taking plenty of trouble – and I was using an old desktop computer – to download loads of forms, complete the A4 hard copies and scan them before I sent them back to Perth in Australia by email. We sent them the money required by bank transfer directly to the persons we had been asked to communicate with by Lorraine. That was weeks before Lorraine herself left Zimbabwe alone; to travel to Australia. What I have written here is a summary of events that happened nearly eleven or twelve years ago.

Once Lorraine set foot on Australian soil to attend her 'bridging course', the sequence of events that followed became history. Before long, her husband 'Cossam' accompanied by their son, Dylan, joined Lorraine in Australia. Of course, after her 'bridging course', she fitted nicely into a new job as a qualified nurse in terms of Australian requirements. The couple have been in Australia ever since and it appears that they are very happy there. A few years ago, they were successful in buying a small piece of land, a 'stand', on which they built a great big house consisting of four very large bedrooms, a walk in wardrobe for the master bedroom, two en-suite bathrooms, an extra-large open plan lounge-cum-kitchen, study, games room for the kids, a large veranda at the back for parties and to entertain visitors and plenty of storage facilities. There is still plenty of space outside of the main house for other outbuildings if they wished to add any. In Zimbabwean terms, I would call it a 'mansion' by virtue of its massive size and the beautiful design structure. Its final touches and décor are the height of designer chic, the sort of house you would find in the airy and leafy suburbs of Mount Pleasant or Borrowdale in Harare.

At Christmas 2016, our son-in-law, Cossam and his family including his wife, Lorraine, and their two sons Dylan and Dawson visited the UK.

They spent the best part of a month visiting us here in Birmingham besides also spending some time in London with Cossam's older brother's family. It was such a joy having Lorraine reunite with the bulk of her family in the UK during that time. Then in February 2018, Lorraine's mother and I were privileged to be invited to spend the whole of that month enjoying the hospitality of the lovely family in Geraldton, Western Australia, where the couple and their children live. They invited us also so that both Margaret and I would physically be present at a grand ceremony to witness her being capped for obtaining her Bachelor of Science 'conversion' degree in Adult Nursing at the University of Western Australia in Perth, the capital city of that state.

On arriving in Australia, our flight touched down at the international airport just outside the city of Perth where Lorraine and her husband and their children waited to welcome us. We spent two full days in Perth living in a private residence. During our short stay in Perth, we were taken round on sight-seeing visits around Perth. We walked round the massive park on the outskirts of the city with well-maintained flower gardens and many trees which were full of a whole range of wildlife including birds, squirrels, insects, etc. The graduation ceremony itself was a colourful occasion which will remain imprinted on my mind for a long time to come. On day three before we set out on the journey by road to Geraldton, around three hundred and fifty kilometres away, we went on a boat-ride for the best part of three hours which took us to a historic town and seaport called Fremantle. That boat-ride was one of the most memorable experiences of our visit to Australia. Three short years after her graduation ceremony in 2018, Lorraine did not rest on her laurels. She studied hard and at the end of 2020, she successfully passed her study programme earning her a Master of Science Degree in Clinical Practice.

Although Margaret and I were unable to be in Australia to attend her graduation this time around, she and her family returned to the University of Western Australia in February 2021 once more to attend the graduation ceremony for Lorraine's new tertiary qualification. I need hardly say that Margaret and I had a wonderful time during our visit to Australia. We toured many places of interest in and around the City of Geraldton and the City of Perth. We will never forget the numerous drives with our son-in-law and his family to places like 'The Pinnacles' and the tourist town of Kalbarri, about forty miles north of Geraldton. While we were in the City of Geraldton, we became part of the Zimbabwean community who live in that city. For too many times to enumerate, we joined Lorraine and Cossam when they attended family get-togethers at the houses of other Zimbabweans.

When their numerous friends and associates literally descended at their house and the Penyayis hosted them. It was such fun and entertainment attending these grandiose banquets where camaraderie, music, food and drink co-existed in a riot and abundance that their agemates in other parts of the world may never know. There was a rapport from the first time I met Uncle or 'Sekuru' Dzoma who was a relative, family friend, confidante and very close to the Penyayis. My conversations with him whenever I was a visitor at his family home, or I was involved with him anywhere during our visit to Australia, were so vital and witty. His wit seemed to come from so much more than just his words. It would also be remiss of me not to mention Doctor Mandishona who was unfailingly sympathetic to the sensitive and insecure (typical of a medical doctor!) and his conversations which were always tinged with intellectual vigour. Then there was Mr Stima, a lively cheerful gentleman who, at their family get-togethers, had a knack for getting everyone pissed!

Memories remain fresh of Margaret and I providing Cossam and Lorraine much needed childcare support for the four weeks we stayed with them as a family in February 2018. Margaret would wake up early every weekday and ensure that the little boys Dylan and Dawson, our nephews, were tidied up and fed before I did the school-run driving a vehicle specially reserved for my use to drop off the boys at schools in the city in the mornings, four or so miles away, and pick them up again after school in the afternoon. Both Margaret and I were happy that we were being supportive and provided a much needed service to Lorraine and Cossam, thus allowing them space during our short stay with them to concentrate more on some of their employment responsibilities.

It infused in us a good feeling that we were playing a useful role as grandparents. We had a wonderful time in Australia and time moved so very quickly. We were surprised when the four weeks of our visit to that beautiful country suddenly came to an end, and we bade the Penyayis our goodbyes and caught our twenty-three-hour flight back to the UK on 'Qatar Airways.'

By any comparison imaginable, our four children are our biggest achievement as husband and wife. Margaret and I are proud at having been blessed with all of them in their particulars as individuals. We therefore did not hesitate in investing heavily in each one of them so that they would become the responsible, mature and self-supporting individuals they are today. Even in our old age as their biological parents today, we are also proud to continue giving them whatever emotional and material support and encouragement that are within our means to provide for them as they chase their dreams.

# Chapter 21

# Striking a balance between work, life and study in changed environmental challenges

I arrived in the UK when all the schools, colleges and universities were on a six-week vacation, the longest between the end of the old calendar year and the autumn term starting in the first week of September 2002. The Easter and Christmas breaks are just two weeks. Arriving therefore virtually in the middle of school holidays in the UK when all centres of learning were shut, it was pointless for me to start making enquiries about teaching vacancies or the situation in universities so I could complete my Master of Education Degree in English.

Instead, I spent most of that month of August settling down really, i.e., getting to know my way around within the satellite town of West Bromwich and the metropolitan City of Birmingham. Totally unlike in Zimbabwe, the first thing I quickly learnt soon after I set foot in the UK was that urban travel by most commuters was either by train, tram or bus. Those who owned motor cars were better off leaving their vehicles parked at home because, on the one hand finding spaces for parking your car all day was one big nightmare. On the other, parking your car all day either in West Bromwich town centre or Birmingham City Centre was very expensive for most of the wage or salary earners. I got to learn that the city of Birmingham where I lived was the second largest UK city after London, approximately one hundred and thirty miles due south along either the M6/M1 motorways or the M5/M40 motorways. Even if the City of Birmingham was smaller than the City of London, the large volumes of both human and vehicular traffic that I saw on a normal working day were far in excess of anything that I had witnessed in Harare, the capital city of Zimbabwe. All motorways were almost all the time, choc-a-bloc with haulage vehicles of all kinds, carrying assortments of cargo. On these super-highways were also trucks and passenger cars, all of them moving in opposite directions at breakneck speeds.

I want you to imagine a conveyor belt system from which hordes of commuters boarded buses at strategically positioned termini and bus-stops. Then they would be disgorged in their hundreds of thousands at designated train and tram stations. Henceforth, the loaded electric-powered vehicles moved intermittently forwards and backwards between key link points following rigidly controlled timetables. Hissing quietly along roads of steel, they picked up and finally dropped off the commuters to their intended destinations along the tram/train lines or places that were scattered ubiquitously in the concrete jungle of the city centre skyscrapers, places of work close to industrial sites and shopping centres in satellite towns. I made numerous of these observations quietly to myself and arrived at the conclusion that if the same of what I saw was being repeated every day in London, Manchester, Liverpool, Glasgow, Edinburgh, Swansea etc., that confirmed why the UK was indeed regarded as an important part of the developed world in Western Europe. I did not have a shred of doubt in my mind that the UK was a thriving, well-organised and functioning economy compared with the comatose Third World economy I had left behind in my motherland.

By the year 2000, emigration to neighbouring countries in Africa or indeed to destinations overseas had become a way of life for many young and skilled professionals as well as other ordinary Zimbabweans. They were leaving in droves to search for greener pastures for several reasons. Chief among them was the dramatic fall in the quality of their living standards caused by an economic implosion. Many wage earners had begun to see their earnings rapidly shrinking in value, rendered almost worthless by runaway inflation. This factor alone, accompanied by a shrinking employment market as an outcome of company closures and general mismanagement of the economy by the political elite, prompted people to decide on relocating elsewhere where there were jobs and more money. By choosing to emigrate, they also

hoped that their future earnings would be protected from deval-
uation caused by galloping inflation. The skills brain-drain that
characterised the first ten years of this millennium pointed to the
all too obvious loss of faith, by young and skilled Zimbabweans,
in the political class to find solutions that would stem the tide
and prevent them from escaping the looming poverty and economic hardship.

Like many other Zimbabweans who had quit the jobs they had
and emigrated to other countries in the diaspora then, Margaret
had quickly been head-hunted to fill a nursing job vacancy within
weeks of arriving in the UK. She had only visited to spend a few
weeks of the Christmas season of 2001 with our oldest daughter,
Audrey Shingaidzo, before she returned to Zimbabwe. That was
not to be. As for me, it had previously never been within my
scheme of things to emigrate from Zimbabwe to any part of the
world. When Margaret started working as a nurse in England, I
was deeply engrossed in studies as a fulltime student for an MA
degree at University of Zimbabwe. The hope I had on completing that two-year study programme was to pursue a lectureship
role in the Faculty of English at University of Zimbabwe itself
or in any one of the many universities that were sprouting all
over Zimbabwe then. It was commendable I had all these high
expectations, but what I seemed to be ignoring was that I was
also growing older before Margaret, and I earned enough money
to start climbing the property ladder. The small family homes
we lived in both in Harare and in Chegutu were rented government properties. In persuading me to accept that we stood to
make more money while I worked part-time while I also studied to complete my Master of Education Degree in the UK, she
dangled the following juicy apple as an example: the basic starting salary for a newly qualified teacher in the UK in 2002 was
eighteen thousand pounds per year. That was a far cry from the
approximately six to eight thousand pounds per year that I was
earning, thirty years since I had started teaching! That was how
I quickly made up my mind to shelve the degree for which I was
reading at the UZ. The fact that it seemed that Margaret and

Audrey had settled in and embarked upon a new lifestyle in the UK, added an aspiration value to my moving and joining them there, too. Take note however that I was in my early fifties when I made the life-changing decision to emigrate to the UK. Most of my immigrant counterparts who had gone or were escaping into the diaspora were comparatively younger than me. Most of them were in their mid-thirties or early forty-somethings.

I came face to face with racism within a few weeks of my arriving in the UK. Some of the incidents of racial abuse or slurs that I experienced were direct while others were more subtle. In those first few weeks as a newcomer before I shifted my focus onto schools and universities, I hated spending all day twiddling my fingers. To avoid that, I looked for a 'holiday' job to keep myself busy. I was offered a temporary job as a 'Driver's Mate' with a large logistics company in Oldbury, not far from West Bromwich where I lived. Their job was to collect and deliver massive amounts of packed goods, e.g., boxes full of tins of canned beans. To move large amounts of such packed products between points of collection and delivery, logistics companies in the UK – and there are hundreds of them – use what are called 'pallets', wooden structures on which the boxes or trays with products are transported on large haulage lorries or moved about by forklifts. 'Rhys Davies Logistics' was the name of the logistics company that employed me for those few weeks. Although their head office was at Oldbury in Birmingham, the lorry drivers travelled to various towns and cities in West Midlands, East Midlands and as far afield as the Yorkshire counties, nearly two hundred miles in the north and north-east of England. My job was a very simple one: sit beside the lorry driver and keep him company and chat with him so that he did not fall asleep at the wheel.

In the UK of 2002, satellite navigation had not quite become the 'in' thing, so many drivers still needed assistance to read the large road maps they travelled with to avoid getting lost. Reading the maps to assist the lorry driver was therefore one of my jobs. I did not have to lift anything when we collected or delivered the pallets. On arriving at a delivery depot, both the driver and

I simply pressed buttons on the mechanised trailers. Parts of the trailers carrying pallets full of heavy boxes or trays would either go up or go down, depending on what you wanted to do. There were mechanised forklifts which could either load the pallets onto the lorry or they could also do the unloading. It was so very simple and there was no back-breaking work to be done. The truck driver and I had spent most of the morning covering quite some distance between towns and cities in North Yorkshire. We dropped loaded pallets and picked up empty ones for re-use back at the main depot. At about twelve thirty p.m. one day, we were at a location just by the sea in the town of Whitby. Before we could proceed with our deliveries and collections to another town called Scarborough, the driver said he was hungry and suggested we leave our lorry parked while we walked to a food kiosk that we could see, a short distance away, just by the beach. Being August, the weather was warm and sunny. The Whitby seaside town we were at, close on two hundred miles away from Birmingham, was jam-packed with hundreds of seaside revellers, i.e., men, women and children, all of whom were 'white'. The lorry driver I was travelling with was a white man. Looking around, I noticed that I was probably the only dark-skinned person not only at that place but probably for miles around! That did not bother me at first. My black pride told me I did not have to be apologetic about my black complexion. However, my sudden appearance on the beach with the white driver appears to have sparked some anxiety amongst the mothers and their children three hundred yards away.

The groups of women and their children stopped messing about and stood still looking directly in the direction of the food kiosk. Some of the women stood with the palms of their hands spread across their eyebrows to prevent the sun from blurring their sight. It seemed they were checking to be sure they could see correctly and that I was a proper human being. After my white colleague driver had finished buying food for both of us, he suggested we stand around a bit while we ate the burgers, potato chips and drinks he had bought. Meanwhile our group of 'admirers' decided to suspend their merry time by the seaside and walk over to the food kiosk. They arrived where we stood. Ignoring the white man, one of the women spoke to me directly, with the group of other women and small children beside her giggling annoyingly, "Hi. Hullo, are you alright, mate?" I had food in my mouth, but I managed to respond to her greeting. "Hi, Mam. I'm very well, thank you. And you?"

The group of women looked at each other, eyebrows arched, surprised I spoke English. One of the four or five-year-old children with them suddenly huddled up to his mother and quipped, "Mummy, he can speak good English, too."

But the mother blanked him out and shot back at me, "Mate, how did you come here? We do not get visited by people like you here, ever."

My white colleague driver intervened, telling them I was with him and that they should leave me alone. They walked away looking rather embarrassed. But as they receded into the distance, the little children kept on looking back and pointing at us as their mothers literally dragged them by the hand back to the sandy beach by the sea. Just before we walked back to our parked lorry, my friend asked if I could excuse him for a bit because he wanted to use the loo. I said I did not mind.

Munching the burger and drinking from the bottle as I stood quietly for my colleague's return from the toilet, I also listened to an impenetrable dialogue between two men in their late twenties standing behind the food kiosk. Their conversation seemed to consist entirely of the 'f-word' interspersed with glottal stops and weird diphthongs which were punctuated by finger-pointing and much gesticulating towards my direction. I sensed that they were talking about me, but I remained unmoved. Then one of the two men, a stockily built man, suddenly popped up from behind the huge food kiosk. I thought he was going to buy some food from the kiosk and go away. He did not do that. Instead, he walked up to where I stood and began addressing me in very rude and uncivil terms. I did not see any sense in answering him back, but I looked at him askance as he dressed me down, so to speak. Looking satisfied he had given me my marching orders to leave the area reserved presumably for white people who lived in that rural setting, he swaggered off and disappeared into the crowds by the seaside. Telling my friend about that incident when he returned from the loo, his advice was for us to return to our lorry and avoid starting a fracas with people who suffered from racial prejudice. We hurriedly left Whitby and headed for our next job in Scarborough before we drove back to Birmingham.

With the re-opening of schools for the spring term in September of 2002, I focused my attention on finding a teaching job first before I could pursue opportunities to complete the Master of Education Degree that I had cut short mid-stream at the University of Zimbabwe two months previously.

It is a matter of policy in the UK that nobody will just enter a classroom full of pupils and start plying your trade. Apart from one being in possession of appropriate academic and teaching qualifications, you would still need to be cleared by a specially appointed body for contact with children against possible previous child abuse convictions. In those years, the body which cleared anybody for permission to work with pupils in schools was called the Criminal Records Bureau. Still carrying the same functions, the body has now been renamed DBS (Disclosure and Barring Service). If you do not obtain clearance from DBS to work with children, you may for obvious reasons be prevented entry to any of their learning spaces where there will be children.

For overseas trained teachers arriving in the UK from any part of the world, one would have to have UK Qualified Teacher Status to be employed in State or Private comprehensive schools as a fulltime teacher. Without that qualification, you might probably be allowed to work in the UK education system as an 'Agency' or 'Supply Teacher'. I started my first teaching job in the UK working as an 'agency' secondary school teacher. That job equated me to a 'temporary' teacher in Zimbabwe. Teaching agencies are employers of teachers who are registered through the Department for Education and Skills. They are found everywhere in towns and cities. Their specific role is to provide schools in their locality with their needs in respect of teaching staff.

If you are lucky while working in the school system as a 'Supply Teacher' in the UK, a school might take note of your teaching competencies. Then they might express a willingness to sponsor your training for the Qualified Teacher Status part-time bridging course through a designated local university. Time to acquire the qualified teacher's status for overseas' trained teachers with university degrees varies depends on one's commitment to achieve your objective and arrangements put in place between the university, the sponsoring school and the trainee. For some, the part-time course may take as short a time as six months, while for others, it may take longer than a year's study. That is the route I used to qualify for entry into fulltime teaching in the UK National Curriculum.

However, before that could happen, I was still forced to swallow my pride and start off as an 'Agency Teacher'. This was despite the Bachelor of Education (English) and the part-Master of Education Degree qualifications I held and the thirty years of work in education that I had acquired in Zimbabwe. I was employed by a teaching agency in that status for the best part of eight months. In the first six months they literally tossed me about, sending me to teach at different schools within the Birmingham area on a day-to-day basis. One morning, I would wake up and receive a telephone call from my agency telling me about my job for the day would be at a school in the town where I lived. That would be in order and agreeable as I probably knew where the school was. Tables would be turned on the following day when I would be posted to a school twenty miles away on the other side of Birmingham where I had never been before. I had not yet bought a vehicle, so most of the time I depended on the use of public transport for commuting between places. This entailed my often having to wake up and depart from my home at the crack of dawn to catch trams, buses and trains.

It was a hectic programme into which I ran the risk of getting lost from losing my way because I had picked the wrong train route or taken the wrong bus number! At the end of it all, I am amazed that I managed to reach my destinations albeit long after school lessons had started. In those eventualities, I had no choice but to apologise to the school authorities for arriving late for duty. There was one day when I arrived quite late at one school in North Solihull, east of Birmingham. The Executive Headteacher, a genial looking but heavily built gentleman, whom I quickly recognised as the supreme authority at the school, was standing by the reception desk in front of the school. Sweating profusely and breathing heavily after getting off the bus and trotting for a mile from the nearest bus stop, Mr – did not respond to my half-hearted greeting. Instead, he quipped deprecatingly, "You're Mr Moyo, aren't you, Sir? The sun seems to rise late where you've come from. Go on, please dash along. Your class has been waiting for you for the past twenty minutes or so."

These incidents of my lateness for work occurred all too frequently for my comfort. They were humiliating and very embarrassing, to say the least. Following a tiresome and energy-sapping two terms of my peripatetic work as a day-to-day Supply Teacher, my teaching agency improved matters somewhat by placing me in a long-term job where I stayed teaching at one school for the last term of the year. Even then, however, my day job in that school was not admirable at all as it consisted of numerous pinpricks and inconveniences to myself.

You see, I had arrived in Great Britain the year before with high hopes of achieving success as a teacher of English. Instead, I had so far only achieved the lowly and despicable status of a 'Supply Teacher'. I had only been a stand in teacher, a 'cover' teacher for fulltime teachers who would have been absent from duty at a given school on that day for a variety of reasons. For example, they were either 'off sick', or they were attending external staffing development training courses somewhere away from the school premises, et cetera. Large comprehensive secondary schools in Birmingham had staff complements of up to eighty teachers. There were therefore many such absent staff on every day at different large schools; hence the call for agency or supply teachers by schools concerned to ensure some degree of learning continuity, thus cutting down on the prevalence of behavioural issues affecting the learning of others, when their fulltime teachers were briefly absent from their posts.

Stationed in one school location for a change and thankfully not dashing about all over Birmingham metropolitan area, my job role in the school still made me feel like a person of no fixed abode as I was thrown about from pillar to post in carrying out my duties. In one lesson, I might be covering for an absent Mathematics teacher in Class M4 of Block A; in the next lesson, I could be found standing in for an absent teacher of English in Class A5 in Block C. In the next lesson when I thought I had a free slot, I might suddenly be called to rush over from the Staff Room to attend to a Music Class in Block E whose lady teacher had fallen ill and had returned home. So continued the rigmarole.

Fortunately for me, most of the absentee teachers always left prepared work on their teachers' tables for their classes to do. As it would usually be my first time to stand before such classes, prepared work, guidance notes which I quickly read through before the lesson commenced made it easier for me to establish rapport with the classes. My worst nightmare as a Supply Teacher was finding myself thrust before, say a Science Class, a history Class or some subject I had never heard of before and the absentee teachers concerned had left no work to occupy their classes. Placed in that predicament, cleverer pupils quickly noticed that I was completely at sea in the subject of their lesson on the timetable.

Such a scenario did not augur well for the maintenance of classroom discipline. To avert trouble, I would quickly get the class into their established groups. Using their textbooks for the said lesson, I would get group leaders to conduct contests within their group, during which pupils revised some of the work they had covered with their teachers. That also made it easier for me to ensure that there was wider participation in the activities by all learners in the classroom. Gaining more experience in my new role and the surprises it offered, I adopted the habit of carrying round with me in my bag readily prepared worksheets across all subjects in the curriculum. Confronted with a situation where absentee fulltime teachers had left no work for their classes, I simply pulled out from my bag of secrets those mysterious worksheets, and quickly handed them out to the class with accompanying instructions. Sooner rather than later, I had the lesson under way. Just before the lesson ended, I would get the class to swop their worksheets and pupils marked each other's answers that I provided, having quickly sourced them from somewhere. A resourceful teacher should be able to find ways or routes of escape from tight situations. That is how I think I succeeded in riding the challenges of Supply Teaching in the UK. I found out that using some of these clever little techniques assisted me in helping me to effectively circumvent having to grapple with classroom management issues that might otherwise have arisen in lesson(s) or during the rest of my duties as a Supply Teacher. As this was all completely distinct from my thirty years of fulltime work in education in Zimbabwe as both primary and secondary school teacher, as well educational administrator, I had no experience whatsoever of working as a 'temporary' teacher when I arrived in the UK.

Being 'new' in different school settings as a 'supply teacher' almost daily often overwhelmed me with a suffocating feeling of utter hopelessness. It was like I was fighting a lonely battle. On some days in the middle of my 'agency-teaching' stint, I wondered whether I had made the correct choice in leaving my country of birth to come and work as a teacher in the UK. Arriving at one school where my agency had posted me at the beginning of another week, I politely greeted the ladies at the reception desk, "Good morning, ladies. I'm Lawrence Moyo. I'm booked here for an all-day job with '-Education' (a Supply Teaching Agency), if that's in order with you."

There was no problem. My agency had done the booking and they were expecting me. Henceforth they simply handed me a batch of papers which I discovered later to be class lists of pupils who would attend lessons in the class where I was going to be based for the morning. They asked me to go to my class which in the end I discovered was hidden in an isolated and remote part of the large school. The complex was spread over an area that was close on ten to fifteen football fields in extent. None of the staff or pupils I asked for directions would volunteer to tell me exactly where my class was located.

I ended up wandering in the meandering corridors of that large complex like an atom lost upon the sea. It was probably fifteen to twenty minutes until I finally reached my destination. The class could not be sure whether their normal class teacher was turning up for their lesson that day or not. Fifteen or twenty minutes is a long time for school children – (especially when you are dealing with a low ability year 9 (or Form 3) Class) – to be without an adult supervising their behaviour. By the time I arrived in the classroom, they had turned into a noisy and disorganised rabble. As soon as I entered the classroom and stood behind the teacher's table, it didn't take them long to conclude that I was a 'Supply Teacher' replacing their teacher for the lesson. Sitting huddled in small groups as friends, many of them pretended to be unaware of my presence and continued talking in hushed tones. Speaking above their talking, I greeted the class and introduced myself in a few sentences, "Good morning, year 9. My name is Lawrence Moyo. Can I announce that your teacher, Mr – cannot take you for your lesson today. But I'm standing in his shoes, so maybe you've no reason to worry. I'm sorry for arriving late for your lesson. Let me quickly say if you can't address me as Mr Moyo, just say 'Sir', thank you. Now. Ee-r …" (There was a muffled shout of the word 'Mayo!' from among a clutch of boys sitting on the far-left corner of the classroom. Another of the boys echoed derisively, 'Mayo, Mayonnaise!'). I ignored this remembering that many of the 'white' folk I worked with mixed up my name 'Moyo' with the Irish name 'Mayo' and that generally they found it difficult to pronounce the 'o' in my name Moyo. But I also quickly made a mental note of the fact that some among the cleverer pupils in the class had recognised that just from the sound of my name, I did not belong to the small group of non-white teachers of

Caribbean origin they had on the fulltime staff. One of the boys sprang to his feet and piped out, "Are you African? Please speak to us in your language if you want to say 'Good morning, how're you'".

Frankly, I didn't think this this was the point of the lesson, so I politely told him to set aside that kind of talk for another day. Pandemonium broke out before I could get the lesson under way. From somewhere in the middle of the class, two or three boys were struggling to contain their excitement to see me arrive to take them for their Science Lesson instead of their usual teacher. "Whoo-a, Sir's not in today. Sure, we've a fun day!" one of the fellows told his friends. Meanwhile, there was a continuous rubbing of trainers' rubber soles against the shiny ceramic floors near the back wall of the classroom. Some of the students/pupils took advantage of my not knowing their names. How exasperating that was! Before I could open my mouth to call the house to order and get the lesson going, two big boys stood up simultaneously and started imitating the 'Monkey whack' with both their hands emitting clapping sounds in the armpits while they grinned foolishly, looking round to draw attention from their classmates in the process. Taking a quick look at the class timetable reception desk had given me earlier, I noted their next lesson after that one was 'Physical Education', so I shot a remark at the two boys involuntarily, "My good friends, why don't you wait to play your silly game until your next lesson which I believe is PE? Perhaps, then you can have as much fun with your antics as you want. Come on, come off it, boys!"

Some of these students could test your patience to the limit. However, if you were truly professional in these circumstances, you could not afford to lose your cool. At that sharp rebuke, the two boys promptly sat back down as if they had been pulled down by powerful magnets placed under their chair seats. Then one little girl with blonde hair sitting on the front row of chairs and desks suddenly gushed away, "Thank you, Sir. Well said. You surprised me though. I thought you could not speak English!"

Surprisingly, the lesson got under way and the class completed all the tasks assigned to them. There was this realisation and suspicion that I was operating in the deep end of a community in the grip of serious misconceptions about people of colour, especially those concerning my colleagues from Africa. I convinced myself that I would have to draw heavily upon my maturity and understanding in dealing with what obviously were issues of hidden racism in the UK. At the end of it all, I hated Supply Teaching with a strong and definitive passion. I worked in the UK as a 'supply' or 'agency' teacher for the best part of a full year, not because I was underqualified as a teacher.

Even though I had a Bachelor of Education Degree and several years of teaching and administrative experience in Zimbabwe, my qualification was regarded as 'overseas trained' and therefore did not qualify me for fulltime employment in the 'National Curriculum.' I needed to study and complete a 'bridging' course that would align my 'overseas trained' qualifications with the British teacher qualification called 'Qualified Teacher Status'. I was lucky enough to find Smith's Wood Academy (then known as Smith's Wood Sports College), a school in North Solihull who offered to employ me as a fulltime temporary teacher while I was being assessed for Qualified Teacher Status through Newman University in Birmingham. That would have been impossible if I had remained an 'agency' teacher.

However, for me to be admitted by Newman University to study for the UK Qualified Teacher Status, the Bachelor of Education Degree which I had obtained in Zimbabwe presented problems of its own. Staff in the 'Admissions Department' at that university conveyed the impression that they had never heard of a country called 'Zimbabwe.' Following frantic searching on computers, the name of the country, 'Zimbabwe', finally popped up and was confirmed to exist. However, there were doubts still whether the University of Zimbabwe that I had attended was fully accredited to issue valid university degrees! It was like I was applying to enter the gates of heaven. At the end of it all and to confirm my degree was not fake, I had to submit my degree certificate for scrutiny by the UK National Academic Recognition Information Centre. That body cracked the conundrum by confirming that:

(a) The University of Zimbabwe existed and that at its founding, way back then during (the then) Federation of Rhodesia and Nyasaland, it used to be part of the University of London!

(b) The University of Zimbabwe was an accredited university and therefore that my three-year Bachelor of Education Degree in English was valid and equivalent to any of the UK bachelor's degrees. However, 'UKNARIC' went on to recommend that for me to be eligible to teach 'English' in British secondary schools with my Zimbabwean Bachelor of Ed degree, I would have to study and pass the qualified teacher's status bridging course which would normally take a full year to complete. I was finally accepted by Newman University in Birmingham and immediately commenced my part-time studies for the all-important Qualified Teacher Status. But, oh my word, what a roundabout way to reach my destination!

My qualified teacher's status supervisor in the English Department at Smith's Wood Academy was Mr Craig Lamb. I do not know his current role and status in the school at the time of committing these thoughts to paper, but then Mr Lamb was an 'Advanced Skills Teacher' in the department. Mr Lamb, if you are still alive and lucky enough to read this account, please be reminded of the huge pride I still have in having had the opportunity to have you as my qualified teacher's status supervisor. I still possess the skills I learnt from you on the effective teaching of GCSE Shakespeare's plays 'Romeo & Juliet', 'Julius Caesar', 'Macbeth' and 'Merchant of Venice'. Once every month, an external supervisor – usually one of the senior lecturers in the Teacher Education Department at Newman University – visited the school to observe me teach one or two lessons while he wrote out a critique. I have already indicated it would take approximately a year to study and complete the qualified teacher's status course for overseas trained teachers. In my case however, it took only six months. Both Mr

Lamb and my external supervisors were agreed that I had reached the standard required to pass the course.

On attaining the qualified teacher's status qualification, the principal of the academy, Mr – requested me to stay on in the school as a qualified teacher of English in the department. As a 'Thank You' to him for facilitating my attainment of the qualified teacher's status qualification at his school, I accepted his request. I lived in West Bromwich, twenty miles one way from Smith's Wood Academy. Nearly fifteen years since I left Smith's Wood Academy in North Solihull, it still puzzles me how I managed to travel forty-mile round trips on every school day between my home and the school, mostly using public transport, for the seven years I was employed in the school. I can only say that was made possible by the sheer joy I derived from teaching in the English Department at the school. The Head of English then was a Mrs Brazier. She was hardworking and possessed fantastic leadership qualities. The wonderful staff at Smith's Wood Academy, the hardworking Assistant Headteachers and most of the more mature and well-behaved multiracial classes that I taught at that school, mostly Years 10 and 11 classes, gave me an experience that I shall treasure for the rest of my life. In around 2009, I transferred to a high school that was closer to my home in the Sandwell Education Authority where I stayed for quite a while before I began moving up and down between high schools in the Black Country.

Let me not forget to mention also that it was during my years at Smith's Wood Academy that I succeeded in squeezing in time for studies after work to complete the Master of Education Degree I had embarked upon but aborted after my six-month First Semester at the University of Zimbabwe in 2002. The 'Open University' in Milton Keynes (UK) accepted my application and the work I had covered as 'previous learning credits' in the six months I spent at University of Zimbabwe. Despite intense work commitments and an extremely demanding travel schedule between my home and place of work, I fearlessly read well into the night during semesters 'Language in a Changing World' and 'Educational Enquiry' before finally completing the advanced degree officially as Master of Education (M Ed) Degree with a specialisation in 'Applied Linguistics'.

On transferring to Sandwell Metropolitan Borough schools, I said to myself that what was important was not about what my new location would do to change my mindset, but rather about how I responded to the new challenges my move would throw in my path. The early experiences of racism I had in the town of Whitby that I described earlier in this account were like a wakeup call for me. Having just arrived in a foreign land, I prepared myself to be in the minority at various locations and to expect unavoidable derogatory attitudes based on assumptions and stereotypes deriving from perceptions about race and/or skin colour.

Once I had been living in and worked in the UK for close on ten years, I became more aware of the anti-discrimination laws operating in the country and I realised that anti-discriminatory laws were continuously being reviewed in the British parliament; but from my other subtle experiences of racism from teachers and pupils alike when I was teaching at Smith's Wood, I was alive to the fact that despite laws against racism being passed, some attitudes and habits die hard. I had also expected that there would still be large sections of the British population, both black and white, who still held perceived remnants of cultural power, due to modes of thinking, that were rooted in colonialism, that continued to give them the illusion that they had the right to think that they were superior to people of other races, based on the colour of their skin.

Notwithstanding, I have to say, despite being the only black teacher of African descent on the staff of a large English Department at Smith's Wood Academy (in the UK), the rest of my 'white' counterparts treated me with great respect. My opinions during departmental staff meetings were valued. In a large inner-city academy with an enrolment of up to one thousand three hundred students most of whom were predominantly 'white', there was a healthy mix of Afro-Caribbean and Asian students, too. From having such a diverse range of racial groups in the mix, you would expect a range of behaviours and attitudes to be imported into the school from the surrounding community. Some of these behaviours and attitudes, revealed during my lessons with students or when they were out of the classroom during breaks, amounted to expressions of racial prejudice. Students in some years 7, 8 and 9 classes frequently presented me with behaviour challenges.

As an example, with some of these classes, getting lessons started often proved difficult because the students would be busy talking to each other. At other times, the classes would allow me to promptly start lessons; but when it came to assigning group work or written tasks, naughty students, surprisingly including girls, would start the silly game of pulling out blank pages from their writing exercise books. Then they would make paper planes which they randomly tossed at each other, thereby producing so much disorder in the classroom, reminiscent of classroom scenes in Sidney Poitier's 'To Sir with Love'. I would shout so loudly, trying to tell the class to stop the nonsense until my voice sounded hoarse, but nobody would take any notice. ... But look at what happened next: attracted by the noise and shouting in my class, one of the lady 'white' teachers next door, would suddenly open my classroom door and stand there leaning against the door frame, looking at the class of pupils without uttering a word. My class would suddenly sit up quietly in their seats as if nothing untoward had been happening. This happened regularly, especially with low ability classes in years 7, 8 and 9.

In response, I would often identify the leaders of the miscreants who would then earn what were called 'behaviour levels.' That meant that at the end of the school timetable when the rest of the pupils filed out of the school to go home, the pupils who earned levels of bad behaviour would have to stay behind isolated in a room somewhere for at least an hour. On the same theme, I am reminded of a severe classroom discipline problem that I experienced with a year 9 class – a Form 3 Class in Zimbabwe – in the first week of December 2006. I was officially a teacher of English; but then having two lessons of non-contact teaching on my timetable, I was asked to cover a Music Lesson for a Ms – who was absent on sick leave. The class normally took their

Music lessons in a room called 'MU2'; but for this lesson, the venue was switched over to MA4, a mathematics classroom, on the understanding that Mr. – who normally used that classroom as his base for his mathematics lessons, was not using it during that period as he had a free lesson.

When I reported at the venue for the lesson, the students were already inside the classroom. The rule in the school was that on arriving at the beginning of a new lessons, students lined up quietly outside the classroom entrance until their teacher for the lesson allowed them to enter. On this occasion, I was unable to establish whether Mr Stephens had allowed them in before I arrived, or whether they had simply walked into the classroom on their own. Anyway, the class were sitting in disorderly groups of friends and associates. Other students milled around talking loudly completely oblivious of Mr – who was still in the room packing and re-arranging things on the teacher's table, getting ready to leave. Soon, the man quietly slipped out of the room and was gone. My initial calls to get the class to keep quiet so that I could give them some work readily prepared by their teacher fell on deaf ears. Several boys still wore their jackets despite the ruling in the school for students to remove their school blazers as soon as they entered their classes at the beginning of lessons since all the classrooms were quite warm due to the air-conditioning.

"Good morning, everyone. Please be quiet and can I have your attention. Please stand up quietly and take up seats in your normal chairs, and you boys over there (beckoning), please remove your jackets now."

Some pupils grudgingly complied, but one Lewis Jones had vowed never to be told by anyone to take off his jacket. Indeed, he kept wearing it until the end of that lesson during which time, he frequently walked in and out of the classroom at will. Not long after Mr Stephens had left, all hell broke loose. It seemed that the class had suddenly transformed into two opposing camps at war. The arrangement of furniture in MA4 was such that classes who came into that room for their mathematics lessons sat in groups. Mr Stephens kept wooden trays on top of desks, one for each group, with an assortment of equipment, for example, rulers, pencils, protractors, dividers, crayons, felt pens and so on. For that Music Lesson, compatriots picked items from the trays and began hurling them at each other across the classroom. Except for a small minority, most of the class were active participants in the disorderly conduct.

"Boys and girls, please stop this! Can I have your attention everyone! Hey, you fellow there! (I didn't know some of their names), please go back to your chairs and sit down!" Nobody cared to listen. I was blanked out completely. They carried on as if I did not exist in the classroom even if I shouted at the top of my voice. It was so exasperating. Leading their antisocial behaviours of hurling objects at each other across the classroom was a group of boys consisting of (I got to know of their identities later) Stuart Burns, Lewis Jones, Curtis Benson, Craig Peters, Joshua Miller, Mark Blunt, Jamie Coates and Damon Coleman. Girls included Jade Small, Sian Bryant, Jade Clithole (all the names mentioned in this paragraph are fake), and a few others I could not identify were also involved. Several pencils and plastic rulers were shattered in the fracas. It was as if the classroom had been hit by a tornado. My numerous calls for calm and for all the equipment – which then lay strewn on the classroom floor – to be picked up and put back into trays that had been placed on top of desks were completely ignored. With none of the students offering to volunteer, I not only personally cleared up the mess and put the items back into the trays. I also removed all those trays from the desktops, and piled on top of each other, I carried them to the relative safety of an empty spot beside the teacher's desk. As I carried the pile of trays to the front of the classroom, missiles hit me on the back of my head, producing a peal of laughter from the majority of the class. Unidentified persons released a volley of paper planes with a clear and deliberate intention to embarrass me. The class were obviously deriving some form of entertainment from that distorted sense of humour. Twenty minutes later into the fifty-minute lesson and seeing that I was not making headway with that unruly class, I called for support from senior management group. Before anyone from senior management group arrived, Mr Stephens having heard the noises coming from his mathematics classroom, rushed over to offer some help. Order was restored as soon as Mr Stephens – who was a 'white man' – entered the classroom and stood looking at the class without saying anything!

He had barely left the classroom after his brief appearance when the uproar resurfaced. Missiles which students had hidden in their pockets earlier were retrieved and those missiles began flying all over again. Some of the missiles hit me. Caught in crossfire, others whizzed past my ears to spend their force on the whiteboard behind me before they finally dropped lifeless on the floor.

For the first time in more than my then thirty-four years of teaching both in Zimbabwe and in the UK, I felt vulnerable, frightened, and very insecure in that volatile environment. I moved from the front of the classroom and stood by the class-room entrance, awaiting the arrival of senior management group support. I no longer trusted the intentions of pupils such as one of the big boys called Joshua Merchant. Soon enough, a Mr Vickers, the Deputy Principal, arrived.

He wasted no time in restoring order and making threats to send some of the badly behaved pupils' back to their homes if they continued with their antisocial behaviour. While Mr Vickers was still around, Mr Stephens also reappeared. All the pupils started on some sort of work mumbling in hushed tones as they did so. Soon after the two men had left, most of the students stopped working on the written work I had assigned to them and opted to resume the antics of low-level disruption as in the earlier part of the lesson. As a result of reports submitted to senior manage-ment group shortly before the end of the lesson, named students such as Damon Coleman, Lewis Easthope, Joshua Merchant and Jade Small were put on Level 5 for abusiveness and disrespectful conduct towards staff. It was the highest level of misconduct at the school. Their parents were contacted and requested to col-lect their children from school that same morning. The pupils were expected to spend the next two weeks at home on a partial withdrawal from school.

There were no easy answers to student behaviour trends as those revealed in my account above. But in seeking to resolve the challenge posed by the year 9 Music Class that I dealt with that morning:

- The clique of rabble-rousers in that class – some of whose names I have highlighted in the foregoing – had to be identified and destroyed before it was too late to rectify their trail of damage.
- The attitudes of almost all the students mentioned in the account towards me as a 'black' teacher needed to be corrected. In a situation where some native 'white' people in the UK practice hidden racism, it was pointed out to me by school management how difficult it was dealing with that problem.
- I insisted that I strongly suspected that there was a mistaken perception held by the said pupils that I was not a 'real' teacher; so, for that reason they could afford to mess about and do no work whenever they met me in cover lessons!
- The use of alternative classroom venues in the school in the absence of actual subject teachers also called for critical analysis.
- A change of venue – as happened in my case – inevitably influenced the behaviour of the whole class. I recommended that all pupils in the school, not just those in the year 9 class involved in my account, needed to be helped to develop a greater sense of responsibility whenever they used furniture and equipment in other classrooms as 'visitors'.

I pointed all this out to the senior management group, and they agreed with me that it was not an easy subject for adolescents to grasp. Often, these or other strategies did not seem to help improve behaviour patterns; leading me to suspect that these students' antisocial behaviours were rooted in the sole reason of my being a black teacher. Racism would rear its ugly head again every time I was on 'staff duty' to ensure students were safe from possible harm or injury during morning or lunch breaks.

At Smith Wood Academy, my chief tormentors were two-year 9 'white' boys. These two gentlemen seemed to take pleasure in standing near the dark corners at the end of long corridors between classroom blocks. Then they would start calling or swearing at me using deeply hurtful racial slurs, e.g., 'coon', 'nig-nog', 'wog', 'Go back to Africa!' etc. After noticing that their racial insults had registered on me, from one hundred yards away, they would quickly disappear round the corner where they quickly got lost in the crowds of other students patiently waiting for the bell to ring before they filed back to their classrooms. Their sudden disappearances made it difficult for me to establish who the culprits were who were responsible for these insults which were directed at me, personally. The behaviours were repeated several times, much to my chagrin. I drew the attention of the principal of the school to the situation of racial abuse which clearly had spiralled out of control. The boys in question clearly did not like the way I looked. On another day I was on 'staff duty' again. The boys swore at me sneeringly, 'black '!'. Unfortunately for them, the principal had had a word with one of the Behaviour Managers about their antisocial behaviour. When they mouthed off their foul swearing, they were unaware the Behaviour Manager had quietly crept up on them and was standing directly behind them. He caught them red-handed before they vanished into the crowd of other students.

The culprits were frogmarched to the Principal's Office who immediately withdrew them from school for two weeks and they missed all their lessons. The boys were only admitted back into class after attending a long meeting together with their parents in the Principal's Office. As for my retaliation to other less harmful expressions of racism, I simply stood there and absorbed them. Or in cases where I entered classrooms and students repeatedly but affectionately whispered to each other about me saying how my appearances matched those of the well-known black news reader 'Trevor McDonald' or started chanting 'This is the BBC! The

News at Ten!' because of my refined English accent, I would handle the alleged racism by humorously impersonating the famous BBC Afro-Caribbean news reader. The whole class would burst out laughing. Nothing beats starting your lesson on a happy note.

Working in the UK education system for fifteen years as a secondary school teacher of English, I was often forced to cope with an assortment of racist taunts thrown at me by some of my multiracial classes. It was hard, but I believe I survived and came out on top unscathed. All in all, however, I was warmly received in most of my 'high ability' multiracial classes of years 7, 8, and General Certificate of Secondary Education pupils. Apart from a minority of 'white' pupils who presented behaviour issues because they found it incomprehensible that someone from Africa could come to England and teach English Language and Literature to the English, the bulk of my General Certificate of Secondary Education students were more mature, responsive, respectful and very well behaved. My greatest asset as a teacher of English in the British school system was that my spoken register was almost 'Received Pronunciation', the standard and quality of English medium that anyone would normally hear being spoken on BBC television and radio programmes. I was readily acceptable as a teacher of English in the North Solihull area of Birmingham because cultural integration in that area was less riddled with too many linguistic varieties. Most of the households in that part of Birmingham were better educated. On the contrary, I have lived in the 'Black Country' area of the West Midlands County for over twenty years now where people in these former coal and iron-mining parts of North-west Birmingham speak approximately seventeen different local varieties of the English language! These dialects sometimes make it hard for some of them to communicate with each other well. Amidst all these dialects and fortunately for me, my clear, fluently spoken 'Received Pronunciation' type of English that you hear spoken on BBC Radio or TV, easily warmed me up to GCSE 'O' Level and 'A' Level classes who had the quest and determination to pass their language and literature examinations with good grades.

There were many desperate learners of all races who wanted talented teachers to assist them learn and pass their examinations. To such students, the colour of my skin or the country I came from was neither here nor there. Between the years 2009 and 2016 inclusive, when I worked with a teaching agency called 'Monarch Education' in Birmingham, I was frequently given day jobs to teach year 10 and 11 classes in English at 'Oldbury Academy' and at 'Wood Green Academy' in nearby Wednesbury from my home in West Bromwich. During tea or lunch breaks, and if any students saw me walk past them as they stood talking to each other in small groups, some of them would run up to me and quietly express their appreciation for the English lessons I had taught them. They would timidly confess that the lessons had been well-taught and that they had learnt much from them. I would stop to listen to what they said, thank them politely for their kind observations and then I continue walking to the next venue of my teaching timetable for the day. I shall particularly treasure my experience and joy of teaching William Shakespeare's 'Romeo & Juliet', 'Julius Caesar' and 'Macbeth' to General Certificate of Secondary Education (year 10 and 11) classes at the comprehensive secondary schools I worked at in the Black Country of the greater Birmingham area, but more so at those schools I have highlighted in this paragraph.

Whenever I get the chance go around shopping in the City of Birmingham, both black and white students I taught especially at 'Smith's Wood Academy', where I was the only black teacher of English in the large department for a while, still recognise me, more than ten years since I transferred from Solihull Borough Council schools to work in schools in Northwest Birmingham. Unsurprisingly, most of them are already grown-up men and women who have finished their university or college education and are holding down responsible jobs besides starting families of their own. These successful and happy former students of mine are not ashamed to stop me, greet me and even introduce me to their friends and family, proudly telling them that I was once their English teacher! I find some of these forms of feedback truly fulfilling. These types of positive feedback give me the genuine feeling that I played my part in changing lives and that the work I carried out as a teacher was part of the hallmark of good teaching which hopefully contributed towards the achievement of my students' educational needs.

# Chapter 22

# Reflections on 'displacement' and how it may have affected my psyche as a retired worker

I wish I were a hypothetical or fictional being from outer space possessing limitless supplies of energy, thus allowing me to continue working as hard as I believe I have done for all my adult life. Unfortunately, not being one of these hypothetical beings, the ravages of time have gradually and unwittingly caught up with me and forced me to accept that I am a mere mortal with restrictions beyond which I am powerless to compete. Following the promulgation of the Equality Act 2010 in the UK, no persons can be discriminated against at the workplace or in the employment market due to their race, disability, age, sex, sexual orientation and so on. On the strength of that piece of legislation, I could have chosen the path to continue with the rat race in the UK until I dropped down dead! While pensionable age in the UK is currently fixed at sixty-six years old (but rising steadily), fulltime employment in all sorts of jobs and trades has no age-cap.

Regarding the issue of age, as an example, the previous age-cap of sixty-five years that forced people to retire was removed. Admittedly every sixty-five-year-old who has worked in the British economy for at least ten years, during which such a person contributed to National Insurance, reaches what is called 'pensionable age'. Rather than just depend on the meagre state pension earnings, the same person can still continue working in the same job or another elsewhere if he or she feels that their general state of health, i.e., their energy levels, their stamina and levels of concentration, etc., permit him or her to continue in full-time or part-time employment. It is no longer the employer who makes the decision that you should retire. This decision-making process has been placed in the lap of the individual. However unfortunately and perhaps due to lack of awareness, some old-aged persons in the UK are known to continue working in their job roles until they drop dead! I chose not to be included in these sorts of statistics. Just after I reached pensionable age, I quietly made the decision to hang my boots because my health would no longer tolerate the levels of stress and frustration that I was experiencing in the workplace. Just to remind you, when I arrived in the UK in July 2002, I was in my early fifties but still full of energy and raring to go. The rare opportunity afforded to me at my age to start another life in a foreign land imbued me with a sense that I was on life's threshold and that, now that I was here, I should utilise this God-given opportunity to maximum advantage. As I have already given details for that in this account, it was precisely for this reason that I hit the ground running when I arrived in this country.

Years before the thought of retiring came into my mind, I juggled time ruthlessly between my work as a teacher of English in native England, my relentless quest for academic nourishment as well as my professional growth. These rigorous pursuits and the wear and tear they incurred on me would in time begin to have a toll on my overall health. Somewhere around 2015, I was diagnosed with a severely raised high blood pressure. My doctors prescribed hypertension medication which I have taken every other day for the past seven years. Contrary to my earlier belief that I was on the cusp of a new life when I arrived in the UK vis-à-vis other health challenges that I began to experience after I was diagnosed with high blood pressure, it began to dawn on me that slowly and unremittingly, I was reaching the terminus of my vibrancy as a fulltime classroom practitioner. Of course, it was clear in my mind that deciding to retire from my fulltime job did not mean I would also retire from life. I would have loved to catch the next flight available and settled back in my motherland, Zimbabwe, when I retired from fulltime teaching in 2018. I was held back from doing such a silly thing by two significant challenges that confronted me.

Firstly, having invested close on twenty years of my life in Great Britain, I recognised the plentiful supply of opportunities still available to me in the UK for growth and development in a variety of other avenues outside the field of education. On reaching retirement, the networks I had formed while I worked in the UK would certainly be helpful in getting me started in other activities or projects totally unrelated with classroom teaching, for example, I could involve myself in work associated with educational consultancy. I could engage in research and writing and/ or start out in business after a short period of entrepreneurship training, etcetera. The sky was the limit; the environment to start new ventures was rich with opportunities to exploit. What was important was to think carefully and make the correct choices of what I wanted to do. I was resolute in deciding that, after working in education mostly as a classroom teacher for over forty-five years, enough was enough of me being a teacher. I had done all the teaching anybody could do in a lifetime. I remember telling my wife Margaret, "I hate suits, a tie and collar. I've worn these forms of dress for around forty years of my working life. From now onwards, I want to be casual. I no longer want to appear before groups of children or adults for purposes of lecturing or presenting lessons. I now want to leave younger people and business executives to indulge in those forms of attire."

I daresay the economic and political landscape then prevailing in my country of birth, most of which had clearly remained unchanged since young people had begun to flee the country in their thousands at the beginning of the millennium to seek greener pastures in the diaspora, I saw no hope of enjoying the same advantages of survival that were at my disposal in the UK. Twenty years is a lifetime of change in methodologies of doing things; people and places in Zimbabwe have changed, some of them beyond recognition, since I have been away. I was convinced my ill-advised return to Zimbabwe at that moment held the potential of placing myself in the same predicament of an infant learning how to walk. Or indeed that of someone, an adult perhaps, learning to walk again following an extended period of hospitalisation due to illness. I hated the idea of being a square peg in a round hole, competing with my contemporaries who had achieved success as astute hustlers and wheeler-dealers in a comatose economy!

My next challenge related to my concerns for my darling wife, Margaret, who has not enjoyed good health for the better part of up to seven years, culminating in her having to stop working altogether. My quest to ensure all her medical needs are met has, in more ways than one, contributed to feelings that frequently ripple through me of us as being imprisoned on these islands. Margaret has worked extremely hard and stood by me against all odds since she accepted my hand in marriage more than forty years ago. We both watched all our children grow into well-rounded, mature and responsible adults. Margaret and I have travelled the world together. We have never looked back since Reverend Father Mangan solemnised our marriage at Holy Mass in the Roman Catholic Cathedral in Salisbury (Harare). Now arising from years of bruising experiences as the mother of our four children, ten years as a Registered General Nurse at hospitals in Zimbabwe before we relocated to the (UK) and fifteen years as a Registered General Nurse in the UK, Margaret suddenly fell seriously unwell. Collected from home by ambulance when I called for emergency help, she has had to be hospitalised on more than three occasions. Finally, she was diagnosed with depression, anxiety and stress. Her state of ill-health made it hard for her to return to work, so before she reached the UK retirement age in 2020, she had stopped working five years before reaching that milestone. A few years ago, her hypertension morphed into a stubborn and debilitating blood sugar. To combat her state of ill-health and really for my wife to stay alive, she had to take a cocktail of medicines every day. Fortunately, all the medications Margaret requires are freely available in several local pharmacies near our home in the UK. It is pointless contrasting the picture I have painted above with negative reports that frequently reach me from Zimbabwe regarding a collapsed healthcare system in which there are shortages of drugs in hospitals and pharmacies. Besides there are shocking reports of the astronomical costs of the few medicines that can be found in pharmacies. If I keep any plans to return to my motherland at some stage soon with my wife, I am left in doubt whether the Zimbabwean healthcare system, with the prevailing weaknesses oft reported, gives any hope for people like my wife whose lives depend on a constant supply of certain vital medications. It is precisely for this reason I have been forced to weigh my options judiciously and avoid taking the risk of dragging my wife back to Zimbabwe where she may die due to lack of the vital medicines she requires on a day-to-day basis. If staying put in the UK therefore gives us assurance and helps to keep my wife alive, I shall gladly remain stuck in this country for her sake rather than mine, until circumstances pertaining to an improved healthcare system in Zimbabwe have been received. That is why I suggested earlier that the challenge pertaining to my wife's welfare and safety has literally marooned me in the UK. I could have relocated back to my country of birth and its beautiful weather as soon as I reached pensionable age.

As I write these final chapters of my memoir, Margaret and I remain stuck in the UK because we are comparatively happier with the better quality of life at our disposal here. From my instalment in the above paragraphs, I do not have immediate plans to emigrate back to my beloved Zimbabwe. Fortunately for me at retirement, I did not have huge financial commitments, for example, a mortgage still to be paid or unpaid debts which would keep me trapped in employment until eternity. But I needed to be able to pay my bills and continue to live more comfortably with my wife, Margaret, who herself had not quite retired as such, but had not been in paid work for years due to prolonged ill-health. To repeat myself, Margaret only reached pensionable age at the end of 2020.

For the next few years before then, I supplemented my small British Pension with a curious mix of part-time teaching using agencies and work as a part-time employee at a residential care home of young and adult people with special needs in Smethwick, Birmingham. Despite having spent around forty years' work in education, I found myself unsuited for work in this area termed 'Learning Difficulties and/or Challenging Behaviour.'

In the UK National Curriculum, I had worked in 'Special Needs Departments' where pupils/students with uniquely slow learning abilities are assisted to learn by appropriately trained teachers. That is what is done in such settings before such learners can be integrated back into 'normal' classes with fast learners. Most of these pupils have what are formally labelled 'autism spectrum disorders (ASDs).' These are lifelong disabilities that affect a person's intellectual, social and communication abilities. I had studied 'educational psychology' as my second area of focus when I studied for the Bachelor of Education Degree at the University of Zimbabwe. Meeting the term 'autism' in the English school system was therefore not a completely new thing to me. I helped some of the pupils to improve their classroom performances. Others remained permanently imprisoned in the category of backward learners until they finished (or did not finish) their primary or secondary school education. When I taught that group of learners, I was perfectly aware that autistic children/ students are not 'stupid' as teachers from the old school would erroneously label them, but that that group of learners may have been born like that as ASDs are known to have a genetic base and the disorders run in families. Their slow learning abilities are not out of choice or because they are lazy.

Having learnt little or nothing while in school such pupils/ students are absorbed back into society where they become adults as unfinished products, in many ways needing plenty of assistance from others to cope with the challenges of life. On retiring from fulltime work in education, I sought to do something else that was different from teaching. Little did I suspect that I would come face to face with a group of male and female adults with 'Autism' in a residential care home setting. I was to discover that as those affected by ASDs go through their adulthood, they also develop other medical conditions including epilepsy, dementia, sleeping difficulties, learning difficulties, loss of sight, mental health issues, etc. Nearly all the residents at the care home where I was employed in the role of 'Support Worker' had a variety of other medical conditions.

Every one of those residents I cared for my desperately needed my support to get on with their lives. Some of the clients could not help themselves to the extent that our duties called upon us to do such things as bending down onto our knees to clean their flats, helping them to bathe, cook meals for them, washing and ironing their laundry, etc. The worst of these duties that I hated most was cleaning their faeces when they messed themselves or could not use their toilets properly. Due to shortfalls in their speech development in the first five years of their childhood, some of the residents had loss of language ability with which to express themselves thereby creating all sorts of communication challenges with those providing them with support. Other residents displayed very weak intellectual ability, resulting in them either trashing their flats or becoming aggressive when staff intervened to offer them assistance. 'Support Work' was the lowest grade and the most demeaning job I have ever done. Here was a university educated man sinking down to such questionable depths of humility and lowliness. I hated my job with a passion, although I conceded the need for those residents to be assisted by staff upon whom their lives depended, in the interest of duty of care and safeguarding.

At the same time, I constantly reminded myself I was not in the right space and that I would have to leave as soon as a favourable opportunity came up elsewhere. I needed to venture into something more meaningful and respectable. Surprisingly, I persisted working in this part-time job for upwards of four years, yet I did not enjoy my duties in the sector one little bit. The irony of it was that my small earnings from that job helped me pay the bills! Finding the qualifications and the wealth of experience I possessed as an educator completely at variance with the despicable, if not entirely humiliating, nature of my job description in 'Learning Difficulties', I voluntarily resigned from my part-time duties at the care home in March 2020. Then the COVID-19 pandemic and its perils arrived in the UK. This virus found me highly vulnerable as I was included in the upper age-groups that were at high risk of infection and possible death! Thank God, I decided it was the opportune moment for me to resign from my contract as a 'bank' worker and perhaps retire from work altogether. At the rate the elderly and those of my age began dying due to COVID-19 infections in the UK from about June 2020, maybe I would have been included in the statistics of those who perished! Until vaccines were discovered at the end of 2020, people were dying in the UK and all over the world in thousands every day. It was frightening. Here in the UK, the economy ground to a halt and for first two phases of the pandemic between March 2020 and May 2021, there was very little economic activity as literally everything shut down and people stayed at home to reduce the spread of infection.

Only those people who worked in essential services, for example, policemen, hospital staff, care staff, bus/train and tram drivers, ambulance drivers, firefighters, some teachers, those who worked in pharmacies, etc were the only people allowed to move around, with strict instructions to wear face-coverings and practise social distancing, among other prevention guidelines. Because I had little else to do at home really, apart from engaging in a few walks in the open air at the local Sandwell Valley Park, that was still open to the public, if it was, at that moment. Quite often, the Parks people had the whole large park shut and none of us seeking to have fresh air and some exercises were admitted. Failing to do that, my only option would be either to spend time reading books, of which I have a huge collection; being a teacher of English, or the odd daily newspaper and a bit of gardening in the small space at the back of the house. Then I made the bold decision to start writing this memoir in December 2020. Just over a year later and twenty chapters of the book later, I am nearly done with this assignment.

It is amazing how living far away from your country of birth and its support systems of home and companions has made many Zimbabwean individuals so inventive and independent. For many of my fellow Zimbabwean diaspora dwellers, the cold-blooded environment of a foreign land seems to have caused earthquakes within individuals; thereby exposing obscure abilities they had never before known they had. Tragically, some of these young men and women have found it necessary to trade off in ways that has made their lives more difficult than ameliorating to them. Pushed against the wall by circumstances beyond their control, I have known many of them choose to take up forms of employment that they could never have considered back at home. One Zimbabwean gentleman I know was a senior magistrate somewhere in Zimbabwe before he emigrated to the UK. Now, he holds down a colourful job title which goes as 'Executive Environmental Health Director.' Simply expressed back in my country, Zimbabwe, the man in the example I have provided is just a cleaner!

"My friend, this broom is very valuable to me because it pays my rent and indeed, it helps me to look after the guys back at home in Zimbabwe," he tells me proudly when we meet for a casual chat. Another acquaintance of mine, a former headmaster of a large rural primary school in Zimbabwe, is currently an 'Area Recycling Coordinator' somewhere in the Birmingham area, which occupation is known as a garbage collector, (or 'matanyera') back in Zimbabwe. Crucially, what my former primary school headmaster-colleague earns from his current work role is what brings food to the table and pays his bills. The cost of living is comparatively higher in the UK than in the Third World countries that most of us originated from. Yet the remittances our families receive back home from time to time are just the small change giving the false impression that life is easy-going in this part of the world; that on escaping poverty and economic hardship to go into the diaspora, their sons and daughters found money lying about on the ground along streets and pathways! For many of our comrades in the diaspora, especially my UK healthcare sector colleagues working in homes for the elderly or residential care homes for the mentally challenged, their work/life balances are not as straightforward as they might seem.

A great many of my country's men and women who arrived in the UK as 'economic refugees' in the period around 2000 work so hard in twelve-hour shift jobs; apart from also living very difficult lifestyles totally bereft of any semblance of social life. Working continuously in those twelve-hour shift patterns back-to-back each week, they hardly ever find time to spare for social visits to friends' and relatives' homes; to go to the theatre or to attend any of the numerous social events that occur every weekend, save for the present (at the end of 2021), due to the restrictions caused by the COVID-19 pandemic. This is the stuff from which the saying, 'It's stressful working in the UK' comes. As a result of this unhappy situation directly affecting the human psyche, many of them end up suffering from burnout, meaning being overwhelmed by stress and depression. For the thousands of unskilled migrants who joined the 'great trek' out of Zimbabwe, engaging in jobs that they would never consider doing back at home is what keeps them alive here in the UK. Employment in these inferior jobs is not the ideal life, considering that some of these people possess high level qualifications both academically and professionally.

So overwhelmed with stress are 'migrants' in the diaspora that some of them have lost faith in the whole purpose of life, leading them to become church-going fanatics. I take my hat off to the handful of young Zimbabweans who since they came to the UK took advantage of the abundant self-improvement programmes and opportunities available in colleges and universities all over the UK and trained to become doctors, nurses, lecturers/teachers, social workers or engineers of one sort or the other etc. This small band of adventurous Zimbabweans in diaspora have qualifications which enable them to be emulated because they occupy more civilised job roles.

Upon reaching retirement age and virtually stopping work, I still needed to earn money from somewhere to supplement my small state pension income. But for purposes of expediency, I did not become so desperate as to dehumanise myself by letting my pride be swallowed in the scandalous nature of some of the jobs on offer in the healthcare sector, for example. Instead, I opted to get by in 'challenging Britain' along less stressful ways where I fell back on my teaching and writing skills in the privacy and comfort of my home. The brutal reality affecting many of the Zimbabwean diaspora in the UK that I have described in this book was a direct outcome of the erosion of human capital that occurred in Zimbabwe from the year 2000. This phenomenon involved mainly young men and women from their early twenties to their late forties. Driven by a mix of variables arising from an imploding economy, they migrated to neighbouring countries, e.g., South Africa, Botswana, Zambia, Mozambique and Angola in search of better opportunities. Some of these highly skilled professionals as well as even hordes of unskilled labour became part of the progressive emigration to far-flung destinations across oceans including UK, the United States of America, Canada and/ or Australasia. The political instability and economic tailspin that followed the Land Redistribution Programme of the year 2000 in Zimbabwe did not augur well to hold back the exodus of skills and competencies young people held. Those with skills as well as other ordinary Zimbabweans opted to leave and look for greener pastures elsewhere because they had lost faith in the politicians' ability to find appropriate solutions to a tricky political challenge. That was the backdrop against which I and millions of other Zimbabweans relocated not only to Great Britain but to various other destinations across the globe.

I have said it already. You would not believe it, would you, that I plucked up enough courage in my early fifties to hop onto the bandwagon and arrived in the UK in 2002. Upon my arrival, it didn't take long for me to mix with and get acquainted with some of the Zimbabwean diaspora community who had arrived in this part of the world earlier. I discovered to my shock and indeed a sense of dismay how young most of them were. There was an age gap of upwards of twenty years plus between me and most of the Zimbabwean migrant community already living here.

Casting my eyes around the Zimbabwean diaspora within a radius of thirty miles from where I lived in Birmingham, I could barely count any baby boomers in my age group! I say so against an intense feeling that good fortune had not smiled on me earlier when the opportunity for me to move to a foreign land arose. I also realised that I was also no longer a spring chicken, having emigrated to the land of the 'Britishers' in my early fifties! That truth was made painfully clear to me against a realisation that there was still so much I needed to accomplish in the way of my studies and so on in the few remaining years of my working life. I have already written at length about the difficulties that were the stuff of my life as a teenager to obtain an education in Zimbabwe's rural areas, towns and cities. I do not know whether those experiences might have contributed to my feeling that I was a victim of 'missed' opportunities. Anyway, that was about as far as I had come. I said to myself that there was no point in wasting time wallowing in self-pity. Throwing all care to the wind due to work and study commitments lined up ahead of me – some of which I have already briefly described – time literally flitted past me with me taking no notice of it.

True, I was a qualified and experienced teacher on arriving at the port of entry into Great Britain. Teachers were in the list of shortage skills in demand. Still though, you did not just walk into the UK without meeting certain immigration requirements. To ease my task, Margaret's employment status as a qualified nurse facilitated my entry into the UK under official channels as her work permit dependent. The great majority of approximately three hundred thousand Zimbabweans in the UK today had sneaked into the country under unusual circumstances as 'six-month visa holder-visitors'. At the expiry of those 'short stay' visas, the 'visitors' could not immediately return to the unchanged conditions of hardship they had run away from. They had no choice but to submit claims to be considered to 'stay' in the UK as 'refugees' or 'asylum seekers' from the chaotic situation in Zimbabwe. I was informed that the waiting period for responses from the home office was a slow and frustrating procedure. A sizeable number of Zimbabwean 'refugee status' applicants had their applications rejected. To this day, some of these people are suffering the humiliation of being deported back to Zimbabwe until this day in December 2021.

Most of the applicants, though, had their applications for 'refugee' status granted due to the continuing political turmoil in Zimbabwe under former president, Robert Gabriel Mugabe. The thorny issue of land redistribution in Zimbabwe remained a bone of contention between the British Government led by Tony Blair and the Zimbabwean government. The never-ending wrangle between these two opposing forces took a turn for the worse when Comrade Mugabe decided to take Zimbabwe out of the British Commonwealth of Nations somewhere between the years 2003 and 2004. Margaret and I did not suffer the outcomes of the sad developments that I have just described.

Those of our friends seeking recognition as 'refugees' might have quietly benefitted from the nastiness of the situation back in Zimbabwe. Most of those who applied to be considered as 'refugees' had their requests subsequently granted and – thanks to British tolerance and understanding – many of them have long since been granted permission to stay on 'Indefinite Leave to Remain' terms.

However, several years later since many others of my country men and women arrived in the UK have for one reason or another failed to put their immigration status in order, their stay on English soil remains an elusive dream. It is not an easy task for some of my immigrant counterparts. As I am almost reaching the end of this autobiography, there is an outcry over the scores of Zimbabweans – some of whom have lived in the UK for around twenty years – being deported back to where they came from. It is not necessarily true that the deportations by the British Government are targeted at Zimbabwean nationals alone. Indeed, plane loads of deportees have been flown back to Nigeria, Jamaica and other distant lands across the globe.

Many of these deportees are men and women who failed to regularise their immigration status. It has since been discovered that many of them, instead of taking trouble to sort out their papers, diverted their attention and focused on living a life of crime, engaging in such shameful and antisocial behaviours such as child sex, rape, money laundering, raiding private citizens' bank accounts, murder, domestic abuse, substance misuse, drug-trafficking and other dastardly crimes.

In retrospect, one is forced to admit that these acts of crime for which people are being deported were not among the 'pull factors' that dictated why they left their countries of birth to come and settle in this country. What the UK Home Office has therefore decided to do is to weed out these malcontents from the streets of this country and forcibly return them to their countries of origin. In many ways, the home office is justified in taking this corrective action. They have the support of all fair-minded people. That way, they will save the British taxpayer huge amounts of money being spent in the vicious cycle of chasing after these criminals in the 'hide and seek' game between them and the criminal justice system; apart from the cost of looking after thousands of others in British prisons and immigration detention centres. It does not serve any purpose in politicising or dragging in matters of race in this issue. The truth is that no country has the capacity or limitless amounts of money to spend on social misfits who do not adhere to its laws. It is sad that after spending decades in the diaspora, some of my countrymen and women are having to leave the UK with virtually nothing of substance to their names. I have noted with pathos how some of my countrymen are arriving back home in Zimbabwe where they have no homes or anything solid to fall back on for their livelihoods.

Also, looking back at how we arrived and settled in the UK, Margaret and I entered this country as professionals and by that fact, we quickly moved through the various stages of the UK immigration system. In a short space of time, our two daughters Audrey and Valerie, then Margaret and I had acquired British Citizenship. Long before achieving these important milestones of our immigration status, I embarked on either work or study programmes as soon as I settled in the UK and did not have to fret about setting aside time to pursue regularising my immigration status. Fast forward to my initial circumstances and experiences when I arrived in the UK to a period close on twenty years later. I am pleased with the many achievements and successes I have gained. Many changes have taken place and most of the 'youngsters' I found already working or studying here on my arrival have become older and hopefully more mature. I have progressed deeper into old age myself. But I utterly refuse to be deposited on the scrap heap as an old-aged person because I firmly believe that in a full body-workout, the punches I wield can still have a devastating effect!

My wife, Margaret, has returned to Zimbabwe on brief visits on several occasions since we settled in the UK. She has done so, driven by the need primarily to attend the funerals of some of her deceased siblings and, three years ago, her own late mother. The most recent time she travelled back 'home' was in 2019 when she went over; sadly, to attend the funeral of her mother who passed on following a long period of ill-health. In my case, you might as well include me in the category of thousands of other young and aspiring Zimbabwean migrants who arrived in this country at the turn of the century and have for close on twenty years, remained stuck on these British Islands either studying or working in one job or another. I did not return to Zimbabwe because there clearly was no motivation for me to do so. Both my parents died seven years apart between 1979 and 1986, but I still have four of my male siblings and their families in Zimbabwe. I could have made a quick visit to see them if I felt it was necessary. I did not do so because I felt that flying up and down unnecessarily between the UK and Zimbabwe would just be a waste of money. Instead of spending that money on these pointless flights, I remember saying to my brothers, it would be so much better if I sent some of that money to them to soften the blows of the economic hardships they were facing. Whenever I could afford it, I remember helping my folks in Zimbabwe with money on numerous occasions when they faced cash squeezes of one sort or another.

Seriously speaking though, I eagerly awaited, and am still awaiting, the socio-economic situation and the broken politics in my country of birth - the original causes which, more than twenty years ago, led to millions of young and desperate Zimbabweans choosing to leave their country for pastures new elsewhere - to improve for the better before I could be persuaded to decide to return home. I can confidently say that if that were to happen soon as all of us anxiously anticipate, perhaps those among my younger diaspora will heed the clarion call to return to their homeland in their hundreds of thousands and participate in putting hands on deck for the upliftment of Zimbabwe and socio-economic economic wellbeing of its citizenry.

On the contrary though, sometime in July 2008, six years after I left Zimbabwe to travel to the UK, I missed my brothers and the rest of my extended family in Zimbabwe quite a lot, so I planned feverishly to make a flying visit to that part of the world from where I had originated. I had intended to travel alone for the round trip. I booked flights and obtained return tickets with Air Zimbabwe which in those years was the cheaper option and one of a few cheaper airlines that operated direct flights between London (Gatwick) and Harare. British Airways operated direct flights between London (Heathrow) and Harare, but their flight tickets were far more expensive, compared with Air Zimbabwe and a few other airlines. As a result, most Zimbabwean travellers preferred Air Zimbabwe to British Airways. If Kenyans and Ethiopians in the UK travelled back to their countries about their own countries' airlines, what would be wrong in visiting our own country aboard our own airline? Of course, there was also the obvious pride in using our own national airline. If South Africans, Kenyans, Ethiopians and Egyptians in the UK travelled back and forth between the UK and their own countries aboard their countries' national airlines, what would be wrong in us Zimbabweans in the diaspora visiting our own country aboard our own national airline also? But behold, a few days ahead of my departure date to Harare, the media was suddenly awash with the news that Air Zimbabwe was threatened with going into administration following quarrels with aviation authorities in the UK over unpaid debts of some sort. These tugs of war – which were just a tip of the iceberg pertaining to the airline's other operational difficulties – led to the subsequent winding up of its operations. Many would be travellers to Harare on Air Zimbabwe rushed to cancel their flight bookings. Some succeeded in getting their money back. I was one of those who had obtained flight tickets using private ticket agents in London.

In the end, our efforts to get refunds for the flights we had booked in advance completely failed. It was frustrating. I personally lost the princely sum to the tune of eight hundred pounds in that debacle. To this day, over twelve years later, I am still smarting from the pain of losing that handsome sum of money to the virtually deceased 'Air Zimbabwe.' At about the same time, my hopes of ever thinking of going on visits to Zimbabwe again were further dampened by persistent reports reaching those of us in the diaspora of the deteriorating socio-economic situation in Zimbabwe. The Zimbabwe dollar of that time had lost so much value, due to inflation. That was when we heard that most of the people in Zimbabwe had billion-dollar accounts in their banks! Then there was to be a general election at the end of July that year. Related to that, were the many reports of political turmoil, resulting in some supporters of rival parties being maimed or killed during the campaign period. These negative developments had the effect of throwing cold water on whatever prospects I entertained of ever returning to Zimbabwe in the foreseeable future. Awaiting a more suitable opportunity when it would be possible for me to visit my county of birth, I have succeeded in maintaining healthy lines of communication with nearly all my family back in that country. The outcomes of advancements in communication technology over the years, have enabled me to link with my brothers and other members of my wider family through WhatsApp and other social media platforms, for example, Zoom, Facebook, etc. Therefore, I speak with my people and exchange messages with them regularly. I often exchange WhatsApp messages, especially with my sibling brothers Roland Dzenga, Wilfred Mudyara and Reuben Mudyara. I have rarely been able to communicate with one of my young brothers, Gibson, (Number Two from me after Wilfred). He lives somewhere in the resettlement areas outside the town of Chivhu, so it is not easy to reach him by phone, due to the absence of wi-fi facilities in rural areas. Occasionally, I speak directly by phone with my brothers and all the others, including cousin/brother Douglas Ruhukwa and cousin/sisters Praxedes Mudyara and Jane Mudyara. On my wife's side of the family in Zimbabwe, I regularly keep in touch with Margaret's older sisters (my sister-in-law) and Ms Elizabeth Tsitsi Nyemba and cousin brother Pianos Mashababe. The latter's wife, the late Judith Mashababe, used to be our regular contact by phone until unfortunately she passed on in September 2021, due to the ravages of the 'Delta Variant' of COVID-19. We were deeply saddened to have Margaret's beloved sibling suddenly snatched away from us.

Communication between me, my wife Margaret and all the people mentioned above has been quite vibrant at times. Very recently, the whole of our families and relatives both in Zimbabwe and in the diaspora, were thrown into deep mourning following the unexpected passing on of my older brother Roland's wife, Faith, who unfortunately succumbed to COVID-19. I successfully coordinated the goings-on at her funeral/burial by remote control from the UK, using the variety of media platforms that were at my disposal. The wonders of science! It was as if I was physically present in Zimbabwe. The same occurred when Margaret also lost one of her siblings, Mrs Judith Mashababe, a beloved older sister after whom she was born. Our beloved (the late) Mrs Mashababe was also a statistic of the COVID-19 pandemic. If the brief clarification I have given in the foregoing is anything to go by, it appears as if I never left Zimbabwe at all and that for a period spanning two decades, even though I have been and continue to be located more than six thousand miles away from my country of birth.

Some of my 'white' friends here frequently ask me whether I have become so entrenched in my adoptive home that I might never think of returning to Zimbabwe. Whenever these types of questions pop up, and they often do, I usually respond to them playfully, telling the enquirers that instead of trying to work out where I belong, they should instead ask me what I am doing now by way of contributing to the greater good of society both in my adoptive country and at 'home' in Zimbabwe. On a more serious note, though, despite my having acquired British Citizenship years ago – and I am so proud of my allegiance to the Monarch and country – I still maintain a strong sense of umbilical connection for the country of my birth, my Zimbabwean identity. Nobody can ever take this important part of my identity away from me.

To remind you of my remarks at the beginning of this book, I was born and bred in my beloved Zimbabwe.

About mid-way through this book, I devote a greater portion of it by explaining how I spent the best part of thirty years of my adult life actively engaged in working and contributing to the socio-economic development of my country as a teacher and educational administrator. Against that background and try as anybody will, nobody has the power to sever the umbilical connection that exists between me and my country of birth. There is no doubt that conditions being right, I will one day return there and reunite with my folks. Concluding this memoir with the sentences contained in this paragraph, I thought I had done due diligence to its contents and compactness.

At about Christmas time in 2021 and suspecting that the balance of the book was right, I prepared to send the manuscript to the printers. But the lifting of several COVID-19 restrictions in the UK and related developments thereto led me to re-open what I assumed to be a complete manuscript and to add a few more chapters as an addendum. The next and indeed what I assume to be the final part of this book is a summary of my reflections where my wife, Margaret, and I find ourselves on an unplanned visit to Southern Africa. It was a mad idea entirely originated by me, so please Margaret must be absolved from any blame associated with some of the sad events of that visit. There was no way I could have left out the impact of that adventure, details of which I outline, for purposes of completeness and balance of this memoir, in the following three chapters.

# Chapter 23

## Surprise visit of this Native to his other 'home'

No one would have imagined that my wife, Margaret, and I would ever think of going on a journey by air halfway around the world in the first four weeks of 2022; especially not after all the family spending in anticipation of Christmas and new year festivities. A fantastic idea that playfully originated in the removal of travel restrictions to countries formerly on the UK 'Red List' all over Southern Africa was turned into reality. The plan to travel abroad picked up more momentum with the lifting of most COVID-19 restrictions by the UK government in the first few weeks of January 2022.

As for me, I wondered what it would feel like setting foot back in my country of birth for the first time in twenty years since I originally left it to relocate to the UK. Truth be told, I felt seriously homesick; I missed most of my relatives, friends, and work associates, some of whom I collected through the rumour-mill may have perished in the ravages of an economic meltdown and challenges that have forever dogged my country since we gained political independence from Great Britain in 1980. Some of the people I refer to in this group had reportedly succumbed to the COVID-19 pandemic, especially during the 'Delta' and 'Omicron' variant phases. The travel idea was still originally mine alone, but I resolved that if the trip was going to be a success, I was going to bring my wife Margaret along with me.

Bringing the subject up for discussion during one of our after-supper conversations, she initially would not want to hear of my proposal, "Lawrence, how can you suggest such a crazy idea? You must be mad making such a suggestion to travel abroad by air at this time of the year. You know very well we have no money in our coffers now because we spent all the spare cash, we had last Christmas."

Margaret insisted that the huge cost of undertaking the ten-thousand-mile round journey by air for both of us was practically beyond our means. But it was I who was gripped by this intense, passionate and fervent desire to go on the trip, so I remained adamant that some money would have to come from somewhere somehow and that we must undertake the trip without fail.

From footnotes I wrote somewhere in Chapter 22 about Margaret, she would submit to no pressure about travelling to Zimbabwe because she had already made several trips to Zimbabwe since arriving in the UK in 2001. Her most recent visit to that country was in 2019 when she travelled down to bury her mother who had passed on. Against that background, it took all my powers of persuasion to finally obtain her acquiescence.

We were also lucky to have a benevolent son-in-law in Australia who came to our rescue by offering to meet half the total cost of our air tickets to and from Zimbabwe. Agreeing that our 'safari' into Africa would be for a brief three-to-four-week period before we made the U-turn and came back to the UK, we finalised our travel itinerary. On the evening prior to the ultimate date of our departure, Margaret and I had our COVID-19 polymerase chain reaction tests done by a registered private provider. We paid sixty pounds each for that service. Our polymerase chain reaction tests results were sent to us electronically, reading 'negative'. Our preparations seemed to have no disruptions; and they were moving on like clockwork. Last minute purchases of small items of clothing and jewellery that we would carry with us as presents for some of our relatives and friends were done, draining us completely of the small cash reserves we had set aside for emergencies during our travel. We did not have much spare cash in our pockets when our eldest daughter, Audrey, drove us to Manchester Airport to catch our flight that afternoon. Then when we least expected this to happen, disaster struck at the Checking-in Desk in the 'Departures' foyer. We could not understand it: airport staff processing our 'checking-in' documents politely informed us that while our polymerase chain reaction tests results were indeed truly 'Negative', they were regrettably unacceptable because they were forty-five minutes out of date. We could therefore not be allowed to board the plane as per our flight booking!

Our booked flight was due to depart on its journey in just over two hours. If therefore we could obtain another set of 'Negative' and 'in-date' polymerase chain reaction test results within the time remaining, there was still a slim chance we could travel on board our booked Ethiopian Airlines flight. We were politely referred to an onsite COVID-19 polymerase chain reaction tests provider, somewhere on the floor below the 'Departures' foyer where we were. That provider had strategically been made available in that area of the airport presumably to deal with COVID-19 travel emergencies such as the ones confronting us. Enquiries confirmed the provider could, with luck smiling on us, take the polymerase chain reaction tests and provide the results we urgently needed in two hours or thereabouts. That service required us to pay one hundred pounds each! We did not have that kind of money, yet we were desperate to catch our booked flight. Alternatively, we risked the added cost and inconvenience of rescheduling the flight to our named destination which would only be available three days later. I threw up my arms in the air in consternation when reality, pertaining to the possibility of my long-awaited journey to Zimbabwe flopping, hit me in the face as had happened to my failed attempt to travel to Zimbabwe by Air Zimbabwe in 2008.

Amidst our worst fears that we might miss our flight, our daughter Audrey – with us every step of our struggles at the airport – suddenly fished out of her purse a debit card which she said she rarely, if ever, used to withdraw funds from. In the interest of time, she quickly paid for the processing of our new polymerase chain reaction tests which were swiftly carried out in an adjacent facility. Then followed a period of anxious waiting for the results which would be advised to us separately by email. The entire group – Margaret, Audrey, our little niece Yvette who also had come to the airport to see us off and I – sat huddled together like automatons on a fibreglass bench with our four heavily laden suitcases and hand luggage piled up on two trolleys in front of us. We resembled people running away from a war zone to seek refuge in another country. Without talking to each other, we had our eyes peeled, continuously checking our phones for any in-coming messages. For me, it was about feeling humbled by the whole vast universe of things which I absolutely had no control over. I had no choice but to wait and watch in awe for that moment because precious time was ticking by either in our favour or against us. That was the point. However, as good fortune would have it, surprise, surprise, in just over ninety minutes, both Margaret's polymerase chain reaction test results and mine were simultaneously flashed on our phones, both reading 'negative'. The first to catch a glimpse of those results was Audrey who could not believe what she saw and shouted, "Oh, my God, the results are here, Mum and Dad! I knew my prayers would be answered and He would not let me down. Can we all quickly go back upstairs, please! You've got to catch that plane!"

Exploding into action excitedly, we sprang to our feet, collected our pieces of luggage, and literally dashed back to the 'Checking-in Desk' at Ethiopian Airlines on the next floor above us. With only about twenty-five minutes to go, all our documents were checked and found in order, our heavy luggage was weighed up and pushed into the hutch somewhere behind a screen and we were hurriedly cleared to collect our boarding passes. Without further ado and clutching just our hand luggage, we gave our daughter and niece hurried 'goodbyes' and escaped inside through another entrance. Reaching the interior, we were directed through to the 'anti-terrorism' security checks section. Here, the checking process took a bit longer than anticipated. As a rule of thumb, we were required to shed most of our outer clothing and jewellery, for example jackets, shoes, belts, rings, watches, etc. Being unsure of what exactly we were required to do, I was tempted to remove my shirt and trousers until Margaret, standing nearby, cautioned me against doing such a silly thing saying, "Oi mate, keep your shirt and trousers on, man. This is not about starting swimming lessons!"

That was a withering observation by Margaret to make and I felt pulverised. Henceforth, we piled these items in trays, together with our bits of hand luggage. Those trays, laden with the rest of our paraphernalia, moved on a conveyor belt into an electronic detector that checked if any of us carried unauthorised and dangerous items like guns, explosives and so on. While this happened, we humans with our hands raised up in the air, walked through a screen or a door that had flashing lights or electronic detectors that checked if we had unauthorised objects in our pockets and/or had swallowed such dangerous items. Once cleared we collected our belongings from the conveyor belt. By then, most of our clothes and hand luggage were in an extremely horrible mess, a perfect jumble and possibly mixed up with things belonging to other passengers completely unknown to us. In the limited time at our disposal, it took us quite some effort to separate our own items from those belonging to total strangers. Remembering that time was our most precious commodity, we put our jackets, shoes, belts etc. back on at such a speed that I ended up wearing the right shoe on the left foot and vice versa! Margaret appeared to be calmer, taking things in her stride, so she seemed not prone to make the mistakes I was making. Anyway, picking up the rest of our bits and bobs and checking to see that we did not leave anything behind, we strode on ahead, with me seemingly indifferent to the mirthless glances of a cluster of immigration staff manning a set of desks lined up on the side of the route we followed to reach our aeroplane.

Margaret and I had very little time left before our flight departed, so we literally sprinted along the lengthy passenger boarding bridge that finally led up to the plane's entrance door. Meanwhile, the aeroplane's jets were no longer just idling; they were then whistling and whining as the pilots prepared the machine to taxi to the runway before taking off into the skies. I was sweating profusely, and Margaret breathed heavily from our physical exertion of running when cockpit staff admitted us as the last two passengers to board the plane on that journey from Manchester International Airport. Just as we settled in our seats and fastened our safety belts, the huge aeroplane slowly edged out of its loading bay. Its jets whistling ear-splittingly, the huge plane taxied to the runway. Before long and presumably having been given the green light by the control tower to depart, the bird of steel, as it were, hurtled along the runway at the speed of wind. Soon, the front of the plane surged upward and the whole plane became airborne, picking up more speed and gaining height on its long and tortuous journey to Africa.

We were informed on the plane's internal communications system that our flight would stopover briefly at Brussels International Airport in Belgium to refuel and to bring on board a few more passengers. I noticed that most of the men who boarded the plane at Brussels International Airport carried laptop bags and related paraphernalia. It suggested perhaps they were businesspeople returning to their various locations in Africa, following a successful weekend of successfully closing deals with their counterparts in the European Union capital city of Brussels. We had departed Manchester Airport on the evening of the day before, a Sunday. From Brussels, the plane flew all night long and arrived at Addis Ababa (Bole International) Airport just after eight a.m. Monday. The stopover at Bole International Airport was slightly longer, approximately ninety minutes, thus allowing those of us proceeding with our journey to Harare (Robert Mugabe) International Airport to orderly transfer to another aircraft of the same airline company. The aeroplane we had travelled in from Manchester International had ended its journey at Addis Ababa. I was not surprised that Ethiopian Airlines could afford the luxury of swapping their planes like shirts.

I guessed it confirmed how well-run and how professionally managed the airline company is. From my quiet observations as a stranger passenger so far, they are a large and competitive brand who have stamped their mark and carved out a niche in the airline industry on the African market. Taxiing to the airport terminal when our flight landed at Bole International Airport, those of us who had never used that carrier before spotted through the aircraft windows dozens, if not scores, of their other shiny, sleek, and impressive-looking passenger aeroplanes of various sizes and age. They were neatly parked all over the airport complex populated in the background by clean and well painted building structures. I noticed that the airport itself was a hive of activity. Several of their large long-haul passenger planes were either parked at different loading bays, allowing for passengers to come aboard. Or others, like the one we had arrived in, had just landed and hundreds of passengers were disgorging from them to go home in Addis Ababa or connect with other flights flying to different destinations. Looking farther into the distance, many other aircraft seemed to be awaiting signals from the airport control tower to start the mad race along their several runways before they became airborne on their routes to distant destinations across Africa and overseas. Being one fellow African who was in transit, I found it satisfying and amusing, taking in the variety of these details which no doubt signalled a functioning economy. I cherished the thought that the details I was subsuming could be replicated at my destination, Harare International Airport (now named Robert Gabriel Mugabe International Airport).

I have to say, in contrast with the favourable remarks I have made about one large airport on the African continent that I had had the chance pass by, the recently renamed 'Robert Gabriel Mugabe' International Airport failed to meet the high expectations I had of it as a returning resident who had been away from home for twenty years. When I left Zimbabwe in 2002, the so-called new airport complex had probably just been built or the contractors were putting finishing touches to it. Twenty years have elapsed, and I cannot remember visiting the airport to see it, seeing anybody off or welcoming relatives or visitors in that (then) new structure. As for how I left Zimbabwe to reach the UK, I travelled by road from Harare to Johannesburg. Then I connected with Air France which I caught at the then Jan Smuts (now Oliver Tambo) International Airport.

Back in the day before I ever dreamt of emigrating to the UK, the then 'Harare Airport' (I notice they have preserved the old airport building) was the place to go to. It had a special attraction for those of us with toddlers or school-going children. Some weekends were frequently reserved for outings with the family upstairs on the balcony in that old structure during which we watched mountain-like aeroplanes like 'Quantas', 'British Airways', 'Egypt Air' and several others land and take off. Both adults and children simply enjoyed the joy of viewing those large creatures parked so very close to the airport balcony where most of us preferred to sit. There was the user-friendly 'Airport Canteen' where men and women of a certain category shared countless glasses of 'the cup that cheers' while children ate meals of a distinct, posh cuisine served by white-jacketed airport staff. It was a lavish lifestyle, the beauty and fantasy of which none of our current crop of local airport visitors will ever know.

Carrying on with the main thread of my story, our Ethiopian Airlines flight touched down at Robert Gabriel Mugabe International Airport in the finest weather ever. Besides the cool breeze that blew serenely from the east, the weather itself was mildly warm-to-hot. The vast landscape in front of both the old and the new airport complexes as well as the airport runway, running in a straight line east to west like the 'Appian Way' – once considered to be the longest runway in Africa – were all bathed in a golden sea of amazingly beautiful sunshine. The vision before me was the best any first time visitor would be blessed to behold.

For twenty odd years, the UK cold, wet, windy, and highly unreliable weather patterns had been like cattle fodder to me, so the calm atmosphere and beautiful sunshine that greeted us on arrival at the airport were simply out of this world, indeed adding value to the prospect of enjoying our little adventure back in the country of our births.

Unfortunately, my excitement about the warm weather's welcome was promptly extinguished, displaced by a certain dreariness, the outright desolation that I could immediately read in my new environment. Immediately making itself palpable, the stifling emptiness and deafening silence that pervaded the front of the new airport terminal where our aircraft, the only one of its kind occupying the vast expanse of space both left and right, had stopped to allow us to disembark. Any forms of life at this airport, seemed to move imitating the body language of the living dead. Further distraction in my mind rang bells to the effect that the whole face-front of the so-called new airport complex badly needed a fresh coat of paint. I wondered if the old coat of paint was the original one at the completion of the structure that many donkey's years ago. That somebody or some airport maintenance department had slept on their job or forgotten altogether that the walls in question needed to be repainted with a brighter colour code from time to time! The dull greyish-aquamarine paint added to the desolateness of the approaches to this important port of entry to what should be a lovely country. Except for a dusty, decrepit, clearly broken down and altogether abandoned six-seater Air Zimbabwe plane that was parked approximately five hundred yards away, there were no more Air Zimbabwe aircraft or others belonging to different airlines on site as far as the eye could see. A total stranger who heard me loudly express my utter horror as we walked in the queue to leave our Ethiopian Airlines plane quipped, "My friend, in addition to that useless object you can see on the tarmac, they have just one other medium size plane which reportedly only flies to destinations in the South African Development Community region."

In hindsight, I remembered that before I relocated to the UK, twenty years previously, Air Zimbabwe operated a thriving airline business flying on routes to several destinations in Southern Africa. Yes, they not only ran a fleet of many large and medium size passenger aircraft and competed with British Airways on direct or non-stop return flights between Harare and London/ Heathrow (for British Airways) and Harare and London/Gatwick for Air Zimbabwe. With that testimony of a single broken down Air Zimbabwe aeroplane parked at the far edge of the airport terminal, it was apparent that my country's airline flagship had struggled to recover from their management and administrative issues that seem to have pestered them going back as far as 2008 or thereabouts. Also, besides COVID-19 adding to their woes, was it possible that the persistent macro-economic challenges ravaging the Zimbabwean economy have had a direct knock-on effect on the operations of the airline company? Both the bad economic situation and the COVID-19 pandemic are reported to have adversely affected air travel by members of the public who would otherwise have wanted to travel between Harare and both regional and overseas destinations like London/Gatwick, Dubai and Hong Kong. Reports say that the political class in the 'New Dispensation' are making strenuous efforts to find ways of reviving the comatose economy. But it had been the same story for the past forty-two years since we gained sovereign independence from Great Britain in 1980. When Margaret and I arrived back in the country, the air was thick with talk of by-elections to take place on 26 March 2022 to replace several members of parliament and councillors who either had died or were recalled by their party leaders for one reason or another. I learn that there is a fever concerned with by-elections that have been pencilled for 26 March 2022, so parties are holding rallies all over the country, asking people to vote for them.

Readers, please forgive me for getting carried away and digressing into a more mundane matter against the express purposes of this memoir. I am thinking aloud as I write, so let me promptly return to my more pertinent reflections on the things I saw when our flight landed at Robert Gabriel Mugabe International Airport where I suddenly reappeared for the first time as a returning resident twenty years later. Rumours I picked up while in the UK said that out of respect for UN reports pointing to the Zimbabwean economy improving in the coming year, big airline companies like the 'Emirates', 'KLM Dutch Airlines' and 'British Airways', who have on and off previously suspended their flights to Harare for lack of business, have slowly resumed their flights and increased their landing frequencies of, even. On that score, we might have to wait and see. The evidence on the ground immediately attracting my attention do not support the claims of the so-called improvements in the economy. As these thoughts and others flitted through my mind, all passengers including Margaret and I were stood up in a very long, slow-moving queue that led to the one only exit door from the plane into the jet-bridge. Our prolonged stop-start movements in that queue, squashed like sardines in a can, were taking too long for some passengers who had not used the passenger loos during the flight.

Before long, there was therefore an unmistakeable sense, standing in that queue, that somebody had lost control of their bowels. Instead of opening them in a toilet, they had done so in their pants! I want you to imagine the putrid smell of fresh human excreta which pervaded the confined atmosphere of the aeroplane. We had no choice but to clutch our noses and fan our faces with our open palms to ward off the thoroughly unpleasant smell. As it was, it would still be a while before we left the plane to breathe the fresh air of the outdoors. To distract myself from the momentary inconvenience in the queue, I peeped through one of the small windows along the length side of the aeroplane. My attention had been drawn to a lone eagle gliding up in the sky about four to five hundred yards away from our aircraft. Then flapping its wings vigorously, the bird hovered fixedly over an object on the ground, presumably a hapless rodent forty or fifty feet below, completely oblivious that a predator somewhere up in the sky was targeting it for its next lunch meal. In another split second, a much bigger and notoriously looking eagle appeared on the scene from nowhere. The smaller bird, obviously frightened by the menacing, officious attitude of the bully bird, backed off and swiftly ducked away and disappeared into the void, never to return. Its unannounced replacement, a clear case of survival of the fittest, wasted no time in resuming the hovering from the same spot, its attention determinedly fixed on subduing and winning the trophy on the ground below. Without warning, it went for the kill. The eagle suddenly flipped over and dove headlong towards whatever was on the ground at the speed of lightning. Its sharp claws were stretched out menacingly. Reaching the spot on the ground precisely where the object was located and with one fell swoop, it picked up what looked like a small but fat rabbit whose hind legs I saw kick about helplessly in inane resistance as the eagle fiercely clutched it in its talons, flying away effusively and almost uninhibitedly enthusiastic as it, at the same time, celebrated its hunting success. It gained both speed and height as it flew effortlessly towards a clump of tall eucalyptus trees, a mile or two at the far edge of the airport grounds. The significance of the event I have narrated puzzles me to this day.

Sooner rather than later, we were cleared through immigration without any hassles. Save for one officer who wanted to make a bonny exhibition of how senior he was by asking us to remove our masks so that he could match our appearances with the photos in our passports, the rest of the immigration staff served us politely. They were cheerful, welcoming, and overall, very pleasant in their demeanour. Later, pushing our two trolleys, each laden with two heavy suitcases we had collected from the 'Luggage Delivery Section', it dawned upon me that I had my feet firmly planted back in my motherland. It was hard to believe my long-awaited visit to the country I was born and bred had finally happened. Before we walked out of the 'Arrivals' exit door, I wondered who might be out there to welcome us. I remembered that a few days before we left the UK, I had politely requested my older brother to keep our visit strictly private and confidential to immediate members of the family. I said to him I would therefore appreciate it very much if there was not a crowd or a 'rally' of people waiting to welcome us at the airport. I was aware that, just as it was in the UK, COVID-19 social distancing restrictions still applied in Zimbabwe, so to all intents and purposes, we needed to follow the guidance for the safety of all and in compliance with the law. I am however quick to recall, in jest, that if my father Timothy were still alive and was among those waiting to meet us at the airport, there would be a pretty good chance he would try to beat me up for forgetting to remember to come back home after I went away to the white man's land so many years ago!

In the end, the welcoming party was a simple group consisting of my cousin Lawson, our eldest child and only son Gerald and his two children (our grandchildren) Daniel and his little sister

Abigail. Lawson and Gerald were already adults when I originally left to go to the UK. Of course, the truth is that a period of twenty years had passed by without me or them meeting each other. It was therefore truly exciting meeting them again after such a long time. More exciting than that was my meeting for the first time with my grandchildren Daniel and Abigail who were born years after I went to England, and I had never met them. Daniel, a gangling, clever-looking young adolescent of sixteen, standing almost taller than me, had just completed his General Certificate of Secondary Education while his sister, Abigail, a beautiful, quietly spoken young girl at the innocent age of thirteen, had just completed her Grade 7, scoring impressive grade passes in her examination results. On our arrival, efforts were being made to secure her a place in one of the local secondary schools so that she could start her secondary school education. Both Daniel and his sister, Abigail, appeared extremely happy to meet their grandparents, especially me who they had never met in their lives.

We had finally arrived back in our country of origin; there was no doubt about that. In my case, at the end of such a lengthy period of absence overseas, I was so delighted I pinched myself to check if I was not having one of those crazy dreams where you find yourself flying about in the sky without wings!

Ahead of us was so much work that needed to be attended to and completed; there were relatives and friends with whom we wanted to reconnect. And there was this myriad of places that were waiting for us to visit them. Our four weeks' visit was going to be so crammed with activities that we doubted whether we had enough time to fit them all in. Phew, it was going to be crazy, if not out of this world! But first things first: our board and lodging in Harare, decidedly our would be base, needed sorting out immediately. We also recognised that our visiting Zimbabwe was also akin to us coming out on holiday, so we should prepare to take it easy, relax, have some fun and, above all, enjoy ourselves.

# Chapter 24

## Oh, my Harare, what's become of your 'Sunshine City's' sheen?

Planning before we left the UK, I had consulted with my older brother, Roland Dzenga. He had given the go ahead for Margaret and me to stay with him in his house at Hillside, Harare, for the duration of our visit to Zimbabwe. However, other events beyond his control intervened before we arrived, necessitating him to make last minute changes to the agreed plan. Instead, a well-to-do cousin brother and businessman, Douglas Ruhukwa, had been approached and he kindly agreed to offer us board and lodging for the length of our stay at his massive residential property located on a plot in the Spitzkop/Snake Park area of metropolitan Harare. In the mid-1990s, long before I dreamt of relocating to the UK, I remembered visiting my cousin/brother's Spitzkop/Snake Park address several times, either on my own or with my wife Margaret, to attend a family or other function such as a wedding, a funeral maybe or some celebratory event. Then Cousin Douglas and his wife, Chipo, had just purchased the plot which had an old house on it, so they were knocking down parts of that house and putting up extensions to the main house which included two lodges and so on. It was then a comprehensive piece of work in progress.

Basing my thoughts on those memories which unfortunately had become hazy and worn out due to the vagaries of time, I still convinced myself I should not find it too difficult reaching our would-be hosts' physical address in the Spitzkop/Snake Park area of Harare. Thinking aloud, I said to myself, "From the Harare to Bulawayo Highway less than a kilometre after passing the one and only fuel station found in the area along the highway, I will turn sharp right and drive up the vlei along a gravel road for approximately two kilometres before I turned another sharp right.

Then I will follow a stretch of another half a kilometre of dirt road which will take me straight to a gated and security-checked entrance. That will lead me to our hosts' residence."

My cousin's home is located at a plot which is plus or minus twenty kilometres out of town, thus requiring anyone living there to necessarily be mobile on four wheels for purposes of maintaining business and family contacts. It was as if our eldest daughter, Audrey, had guessed her mother and I would come to live at that address. Staying in the same neighbourhood with us in Birmingham and prior to the commencement of our visit, she had quietly planned with one Zimbabwean family living in London but operating a car rental business through their relatives in Harare, that a rented vehicle would be made available to us for use during our four weeks' stay in Zimbabwe. Knowing too well of Audrey's commitment to ensuring our welfare was always secure, we were not surprised she did that. The vehicle she had hired for us, a medium size manual-driven Hyundai i35 model, was delivered to me as soon as we arrived at Hillside that afternoon.

The changes to our accommodation arrangements were only communicated to us in the middle of the afternoon after arriving at Hillside. However, we spent most of that afternoon chatting and laughing away with the family at Hillside, deliberately post-poning our departure for Spitzkop/Snake Park until well after five forty-five p.m. Had I known about the extent of changes that had taken place during my twenty-year absence, I would have been better advised to leave earlier when there was still plenty of daylight. My delaying to leave even after five p.m. was prompted by my need to allow for the huge volumes of vehicle traffic streaming up and down Chiremba Road opposite my old brother's house to die down a bit.

Somehow, I kept saying to myself 'I know the route to Spitzkop/Snake Park, so there's no need to get stressed out about the delay in starting on the journey.' Of course, I was taking too many things for granted, overlooking the fact that objects and circumstances I had known two decades previously had given way to structural changes in both form and shape. In the end, I would not only lose my way, but also find it difficult to reach my destination at Spitzkop/Snake Park that night. The rush hour traffic wheezing past us up and down Chiremba Road had slimmed down somewhat by five forty-five p.m. However, leaving the space opposite my older brother's Hillside property to ease into the traffic going towards town was proving to be a Herculean task.

Waves of traffic endlessly poured down from farther up the road, drivers never giving way and completely ignoring the furious flick of my indicator and hazard lights to show them that I also wanted to get in and join the stream of traffic going north. As every driver had their hands firmly gripping steering wheels and looking fiercely straight ahead in front of them, they looked angry and, in a hurry, to go home after work. None of them was prepared to give any consideration to the needs of other road users. Fearlessly, my older brother who was standing outside our vehicle, had to risk being run over when he suddenly squeezed himself into a small gap that had arisen in the thick flow of traffic. He temporarily, but dangerously, assumed the role of a non-uniformed traffic police officer by standing directly in front of all on-coming traffic from the north. He raised both his hands, beckoning them to stop, his voice ringing as he called, "Hear me there! Hullo-Ooo! Please stop and let my brother get into the traffic! He also wants to go on his way like yourselves. Can you, Sir, Mam, please!" The traffic moving down Chiremba Road surprisingly complied with my older brother's frantic bidding. But their response was accompanied by a cacophony of a discordant choir of car hooters and a heap of verbal abuse and road rage. All of it directed at my older brother from a band of irate drivers. Some of those drivers removed and wore back on their baseball caps in quick succession, displaying shaven and shorn heads that spasmodically shot through wound down front car windows as they shouted in gruffly voices, "Hey, you silly 'Mudhara' (old man), you're wasting our time, man! What the hell are you doing in the middle of the road? Are you tired of living your life? Get off the road!"

Some of the bad language that came from the lips of drivers was simply unprintable. All the shouting and invectives from these people was so rough, crude, and disrespectful. I could not remember witnessing such rude manners in my twenty years of driving on British roads, ever. I wondered whether the difficulties in the economy had also spiralled down to hardening peoples' attitudes. That brief scene left me with a weird taste in my mouth. Meanwhile, my own speed of accelerating to join the stream of traffic heading north was slowed down by the inoperable manual gear box of a car I was driving for the first time. I discovered that the gear box was sticking, and I could not engage the gear lever into a heavier one so that the car would start moving. My remaining stationary, struggling with the gears, meant holding up the flow of traffic going south which stretched as far as the rail crossing, five hundred yards up the road. That provoked more anger among the waiting drivers who, individually and collectively, resumed hurling insults, that time, directed at me, alleging I was a hopeless driver and asking silly and pointless questions such as, "Are you a qualified driver, mate? Where and when did you obtain your driver's licence?" including a crude mixture of belittling, sarcastic and humiliating insults.

I ignored all of them with a stiff upper lip. My gear box eased off and I engaged the car into gear. Finally, and leaving my older brother safely out of harm's way, I waved at him a hasty 'goodbye' and slowly eased into the flow of traffic. Leaving Hillside, my car was heavily laden with cargo that included my wife, me on the steering wheel, my son and his two teenage children in the back seat and two heavy suitcases in the boot of the car. My son and his two children were dropping off at some spot where my son knew best in Milton Park, four or so miles away before I would veer back, drive along Prince Edward Street towards Samora Machel Avenue.

From a point along that street, I would make a sharp right turn into what would eventually become the Harare to Bulawayo Highway further west down Samora Machel Avenue. I had last driven around and about in Harare's central business district somewhere around 1999 or 2000. Then the City Fathers, a mere twenty years into our political independence, were still taking matters more seriously and truly taking care of the city. The roads, street lighting and traffic controls in the city were always well-maintained. Streets were clearly signposted; road surface markings were attended to with professionalism; cleaning of streets using mechanised equipment was done at night and any pilfered or broken street-light fittings were swiftly replaced. Those were the good old days. I could not be sure what sin the powers that be had committed to allow things to get to this low-level of depreciation.

In the Harare 'Sunshine City' that I knew before I relocated to the UK over twenty years ago, motorists could drive around in the city in their cars at any time of day and night with careless abandon, without having to worry about the new phenomena that have become a feature of Harare, including ugly potholes, corrugations on road surfaces, absence of street-lighting, broken street-lighting poles, missing street sign posts, missing bulbs on street lights or non-working robot controls at road intersections. Just the odd four miles of my driving from Hillside to Milton Park to drop off my son and his two children were a baptism of fire for me, a complete nightmare. Navigating my way through streets into the centre of Harare in the dim light as the sun had set, I noticed its skyline had changed very little. Apart from relatively new tall buildings like Karigamombe Centre, the Reserve Bank of Zimbabwe building in Samora Machel Avenue, 'Shake Shake' building and the 'Net One' building at the corner of Rotten Row and Samora Machel Avenue, the skyline was still largely dominated by skyscrapers built during the colonial era like Livingstone House, Ambassador House and other smaller ones. It was rapidly becoming dark because the sun had set.

In the era of my driving in Harare that I referred to earlier, darkness was alien to us because as soon as the sun set, the whole of Harare was deluged in a flood of electric lighting along all roads, streets, avenues, in houses, in offices and shop spaces. The road surfaces I traversed in my baptism of fire today were intolerable and not fit for purpose. Most of those roads and streets were covered with numerous potholes, most of them so deep they made driving around and about in what should be the capital city of our nation thoroughly inhospitable. It must be incredibly expensive for ordinary residents of this city to run their cars. Mine was a rude awakening to the appalling driving conditions people in Harare and elsewhere in Zimbabwe are having to cope with in their daily grind.

Particularly heart-breaking was also discovering that most, if not all, the street lighting has disappeared in Harare. Either the haphazard load shedding or something inexplicable has necessitated the wholesale shutting down all street lighting in Harare. Or bulbs have all blown out with the passage of time and nobody has bothered to have them replaced. In many cases, the extent of neglect at road junctions included unrepaired metal traffic light poles.

Many of the poles stood neglected, several of them at acute angles of twenty or thirty-degrees from the vertical, having perhaps been struck by speeding motorists last Saturday or Sunday night. I was shocked that the residents of Harare, nearly all of whom were rate payers, may have begun accepting this situation as the new normal and therefore would not be bothered to make noise for those responsible for the upkeep and maintenance of the city to put things right. I stopped counting how many whole traffic light units were missing from those poles, with wires left dangling carelessly in the wind. Or those units which showed missing bulbs which somebody may have long forgotten to replace. After dropping off my son and his children in Milton Park, I intended to turn right into Samora Machel Avenue at the point Prince Edward Street conjoins with Rotten Row.

That road junction is a particularly busy one because it handles huge traffic flows in the four directions of the compass. Some of the traffic lights worked while others were completely dead. Those lights which supposedly worked emitted haphazard light signals resulting in confusion where all of us in the traffic flow ended up resorting to the Zimbabwean Highway Code which dictates that at road junctions where there are no traffic signals, you should always give precedence to all traffic coming from the right. It was such a chaotic situation we were lucky not to have cars all over the road junction bumping into our car. I had never been involved in such chaos in my odd forty years' driving experience. I realised that life must go on in these chaotic conditions. For that reason, my compatriots driving on these roads daily are regrettably forced to resort to the instincts of their jungle driving skills, to drive around modern Harare that unfortunately has morphed into an utterly despicable driving nightmare. I calmly eased into Samora Machel Avenue and careered on past the Bishop Gaul Avenue junction, past the Harare Show Grounds and onwards to my perceived destination at Spitzkop/Snake Park. Edging out of Harare and even before I reached the Warren Park turn off, the generally smooth road surfaces along the highway and the near absence of those ugly potholes in Harare city centre was such a welcome relief.

As I drove my car with Kambuzuma Township, Cold Comfort Farm and Tynwald suburbs on both our sides, it had become so dark I could hardly see much else besides the blurred images in my beam as well as flashes of lighting from other vehicles passing in the opposite direction. As in Harare city centre, the tall bright lights that used to burn so brightly when I drove on that road long ago at night had all been turned off. In the far distance through the pitch blackness that enveloped us, I could only see small dots of light moving slowly past us, suggesting perhaps that they were lights emitted by electric bulbs in people's houses, now spread out more heavily into the almost impenetrable wall of darkness as one peered northward. From the anxiety caused to me by the thick wall of darkness on both my left and right, my driving along the highway seemed to go on forever. After passing what I guessed to be the Warren Park 'D' turn off, we stopped at a brightly lit garage or fuel station on our right. I parked my car on the side, about thirty yards from the fuel pumps. I did not recognise that place; it appeared to have recently been built. Adjacent to it was a large chippy shop which was also brightly lit.

Margaret said she was thirsty for a drink. Although my own throat was also parched, I decided to stop at that complex ostensibly to establish from any helpful person at the station exactly where we were and how far we still had to go to reach Snake

Park/Spitzkop. The blanket of darkness and the absence of lighting on the highway had not only thrown spanners in my sense of direction but had also played havoc with my memory. The bright neon lighting at the complex – an oasis of incandescent daylight in a sea of suffocating darkness – was like a magnet. Hordes of young men in not-so-clean grey hoodies and ill-fitting slim-wear jeans appeared to have been attracted to the complex from the poorly lit neighbourhood like ducks to water. They stood about chatting in groups of five, tight as a fist, one of those impregnable defence formations that the Roman army might have used to repel the barbarians. Some of them ate the food they had bought in cheap paper wrapping from the chippy shop, turning round furtively to peer into the emptiness of the darkness behind the complex. A group of others stood in a queue that snaked into the chippy shop from outside. Two mineral drinks I bought were quickly served me and I gave one to Margaret.

Holding my drink in one hand, I left Margaret sipping hers as she sat in our parked car while I strode over to talk to the petrol/diesel attendant standing by one of the fuel pumps a few yards away. "Hullo Sir, I saw you arrive and park your car over there. If you want petrol or diesel, you will have to bring it over here by the pumps so that we can fill it."

"Oh, hullo and thank you. I was wondering if you could please help me. I am a visitor in these parts. I think I have lost my way. I am trying to reach an address in Spitzkop/Snake Park. Kindly, if you will, please tell me how I can get to Spitzkop/Snake Park for starters," I explained. He informed me my destination was still several kilometres along the Harare to Bulawayo Highway visible in front of us, with all sorts of vehicles cruising past in both directions at high speed. It should not take me anymore than fifteen minutes to reach there in the car, he concluded his remarks.

One scruffy looking stranger, a young man, who clearly had eavesdropped on my conversation with the petrol/diesel attendant, suddenly forced himself into our conversation uninvited, "I can show you where Spitzkop/Snake Park is if you allow me to come with you in your car."

I thanked the petrol/diesel attendant for the information he had volunteered. Then turning to the other fellow, I said to him politely, "Thank you for your offer, my friend. But I do not know who you are. I cannot just give a perfect stranger like you a free ride in my car, notwithstanding your good intentions. I will find my way to my destination eventually. Goodbye, sir." There was every indication the suspicious-looking fellow was one of the desperate unemployed youths milling about at the complex searching for easy pickings. Doubting his sincerity and afraid of being robbed of all our belongings or risking Margaret's and my safety, I left him gazing emptily in the darkness and re-joined my wife in the car. And back behind the wheel on the Harare to Bulawayo Highway, I drove on past the large Kuwadzana Circle. Following a downward slope and crossing a small bridge in the vlei, we drove on until we reached the Spitzkop/Snake Park area, so I suspected but I was not too sure. It had grown much darker due to the reduced traffic on the highway. I found it hard to recognise some of the features that I caught sight of in the poor light and tried to match them with the memories of that area at the back of my head. For one thing, there was no longer just one petrol/diesel garage but three of them on the left side of the highway if I counted properly. Also, the open space on the right side of the road where I previously used to make my right turn had changed beyond recognition. In its place was a housing estate showing many houses that were already occupied. There were other building structures at different stages of construction!

Driving on well out of Harare along the highway for another six or so miles later, I told Margaret, "My dearest, I think we're now well and truly lost! We'll have to stop this wild goose chase lest we find ourselves in Norton which I'm sure is not too far from here," as I peered into the darkness surrounding the shaft of light formed by my car headlights in front of us. Looking at my wristwatch, it showed the time to be nine thirty p.m. We had left Hillside in Harare just after six p.m. before I unsuspectingly got caught up in the Harare rush hour traffic glitch in extremely bad driving conditions. I stopped and parked the car on the left edge of the road. I turned off both my headlights and parking lights completely to avoid drawing the attention of possible robbers who I suspected might be hiding in the darkness of the woods on both sides of the highway. None of us knew exactly where we were along that road. We tried to use our mobile phones to contact either my older brother, or our hosts, to let them know of the fate that had befallen us. Those efforts fell flat when we got phone messages that told us we could not use our phones as both phones were not connected to either 'NetOne' or 'Econet', the local Internet Service Providers'. As we had arrived in Zimbabwe that day, we still had our British 'EE' Sim Cards in our phones which therefore we could not use in Zimbabwe. Here I was, lost in the wilderness with my wife, carrying all the luggage we had brought with us from the UK in the car boot! The feeling that for once, my wife and I were homeless when we had arrived back home was overwhelming. Looking visibly worried as she peered into the spookiness of the serene woods on both sides of our stationary vehicle, Margaret asked me, "How're we going to handle this? Where are we going to sleep tonight, Lawrence? It's kind of scary."

I calmly responded, "Margaret, you're worried about where we shall sleep tonight? My biggest worry is what are going to do now, not in the next hour or so!" We both chuckled at the comic effect of the irony in our situation while I quickly turned things over in my mind. With the prospect of darkness all the way through approximately twenty miles to Harare city centre and the bad driving conditions I had experienced on my way out of the city that evening, I ruled out any ideas to retrace my steps. Also, I concluded that even if I was somehow able to drive back and reach Harare city centre, finding my way back to my older brother's house at Hillside would be a tall order, so I ruled that out as well. But where we would spend the night remained my puzzle, all the pieces of which I needed to find and put in their rightful places before very long. "We'll sleep somewhere, but not in the car at this spot, my love," I announced. suddenly with a new-found confidence, remembering that Highfield Township – where I had spent twenty years employed as a teacher – was nearer to where we were compared to the driving challenges that I would face if I ventured to retrace my steps to Hillside, the route to which I was bound to lose in the darkness of the City of Harare! Instead, I was seized by a new conviction that if I took the correct exit at the big Kuwadzana Circle farther back, up the highway, I would rely on my sense of direction, assisted by fading memories of that route Margaret and I still held, until I reached my in-laws home in Old Highfield. I would arrive there at whatever time of the night, ask to be given room for Margaret and me to sleep until daylight on the following morning when we would resume our attempt to reach our hosts' home at the plot in Spitzkop/Snake Park. I started the car, made a quick U-turn, and commenced the journey back along the highway towards Harare. In less than ten minutes, I reached the large Kuwadzana Circle which was an important landmark. I remembered to take the second exit and continue driving along that route until it took me to Highfield Township. I had used that route quite often, so I should be able to find my way. The trouble was that many features had changed in the time since I last drove along that route. Of course, it would also depend on whether there were no other structural changes along the route which would obviously slow me down or make me lose my way again. I asked Margaret to stay awake this time and help guide me through the darkness. From the big Kuwadzana Circle, the conditions on the road towards Highfield reverted to the terrible experiences I had encountered in Harare city centre hours earlier. I had not driven along that road for twenty years, so with the changes that had occurred in the nature of the road surface, I was unfamiliar with its tortuousness. All the way up and down that road after the railway flyover, I had never been subjected to so many potholes, some of them quite deep, and corrugations that were worse than I had ever seen before. Swerving my car persistently to avoid hitting them was a test of endurance.

The stretch of road from the Glen Eagles Circle and all the way to a place that we used to call 'Southerton Garage' was surprisingly quite good. That place was still a fuel station, but its whole appearance had dramatically transformed. It was no longer brightly lit up at night as it had been. Enquiries from a lone night security guard, who sat forlornly in dimly lit fuel station grounds, led us to a single traffic light two hundred yards down the road. That robot burnt brightly, and it also seemed to be in good working condition.

The sleepy night security guard we had suddenly roused from his snoozing kindly directed us, with a squint in his right eye, to turn right at that point and carry on down the road before we came to another badly controlled road intersection where we would turn right again into Willowvale Road and carry on towards Highfield. A few hundred yards after passing what we recognised as, and still is, 'Southerton Police Station', I connected with the road that branched off Willowvale Road and led to my in-laws' home, reaching my destination in exactly forty-five minutes of the most tiresome and exacting driving experience of my life. On a happier note, the car safely delivered us to Margaret's parents' home in Highfield despite a few gear-shift challenges with our car along the way. We had continuously been reaching out in offensive darkness and in inhospitable driving conditions for well over three hours. I personally was dog-tired, and my wife was desperate for much needed rest and sleep. Finally, we were finally back in touch with the civilised world. Upon arriving at my in-laws' home in Old Highfield, I borrowed my sister-in-law's mobile phone and contacted my older brother to let him know of our predicament since we had left his home in Hillside earlier that evening. We also got to know that my cousin, whose home we were destined to go to, was searching for us high and low. My older brother updated him on our situation.

It was maybe well after eleven thirty p.m. when these gentlemen exchanged mobile phone conversations about us. Just before midnight on that day, we were preparing to go to sleep when my cousin/brother, our would be host Douglas and his wife Chipo, arrived at my in-laws' home in Old Highfield. They were driving their all-terrain 'Toyota Fortuner' vehicle. They had been waiting to welcome us at their home all day, so they were not having us sleep in Old Highfield. They had come to collect us and all our luggage and head back to Spitzkop/Snake Park with us in their car. We would leave the troublesome 'Hyundai' car for the night at Old Highfield so that a mechanic could then be sent over to sort out its gear box issues on the following morning. Being a 4X4, their 'Toyota Fortuner' literally flew over those terrifying potholes and road corrugations which had given me such grief and made my life and that of my wife, Margaret, utterly miserable earlier, driving in the smaller Hyundai iX35 vehicle. We arrived at their security-gated home shortly after twelve fifteen a.m., bringing to a happy ending our long journey from the UK filled with an assortment of experiences, albeit some of them quite harrowing.

Even in those wee hours of the night, Chipo, our host's wife, quickly organised us some hot solid food in their diner. Later, we relaxed chatting away and exchanged reminiscences as we sipped alcohol-free wine with both husband wife in the comfort of one of their vast lounges until almost two a.m. Then they walked us to our self-contained lodge, one of the reconfigurations to the main house, ensuring that none of us fell into the swimming pool that was adjacent to our sleeping quarters aptly named 'Nyathi'. For the odd four weeks of our travel adventure to Zimbabwe, my wife and I were guests in one of my rich cousin's large home in the Spitzkop/Snake Park area of Harare. That lovely location after the turn off, approximately fifteen miles from the city centre along the Harare to Bulawayo Highway, would become our operational base. Within that period and taking just a few of our clothes with us, we spent one full week in Gweru urban to pay our respects and visit the final resting place of Margaret's older sister, the late Judith Mashababe, who had passed on six months previously due to the ravages of COVID-19's 'Delta Variant'. We returned straight to Harare thereafter. Back at Spitzkop/Snake Park, we enjoyed some of the best living conditions ever. An executive and self-contained lodge was given us for our exclusive use. The family, who occasionally included their young daughter Kudzai, shared their usually three to four course English meals with us in the family diner.

Overall, we were accorded what amounted to a five-star hotel treatment which included in-house staff services. These included, workers helping in the kitchen in the preparation of our meals, our tea/coffee things being carried on trays and brought to us to partake of before breakfast to the privacy of our lodge every morning, cleaning our apartment, washing, and ironing our laundry and having our car valeted every morning before we left to go anywhere. My 'Maiguru' (Big Auntie), that is, our male host's wife, Chipo, was always at pains to ensure all our needs and comforts were met. Rushing around in doing so and always remaining unflustered and cheerful, Chipo's energy levels were inexhaustible. Her maize meal thick porridge cooked together with vegetables and peanut butter, ('sadza nemuriwo unedovi'), was her best Zimbabwean cuisine served at the table. It was my favourite meal and Chipo's tour de force. I could not lavish enough praise on her fantastic cooking. In the evenings after supper, we invariably relocated to the expansive lounge/TV room where we relaxed, chatted, and shared jokes with our hosts as we sipped sparkling alcohol-free cocktails of wine. On most times late at night, our hosts guided us through a large door that opened into a brightly lit courtyard with a swimming pool in the centre.

They finally led us into our own comfort zone for the night before they made a U-turn to their own rooms in another part of the rambling mansion. It was like we were dreaming. We were the recipients of a lavish lifestyle the likes of which exceeded anything we had known in the UK or anywhere else. Each time we came back from some of our tiresome and circular movements in the outside world during the day, their home appropriately named 'The Green Oasis', with its riot of tweets and chirps from the multiplicity of birdlife there, was simply refreshing and out of this world. It was like escaping into a luxurious holiday wonderland in the Caribbean or somewhere that was supremely unimaginable. The many delights and comforts at our disposal during what turned out to be a holiday bonanza at the 'Green Oasis' were pleasant memories that Margaret and I will treasure for the rest of our lives. From the sentiments I have expressed in the few paragraphs above, it is easy for anyone to conclude that the posh quality of life we lived at the 'Green Oasis' was accounted for by the fact my cousin and his wife are a rich couple. Margaret and I were having it good in a world that was ironically set apart from the grinding poverty in nearby and overcrowded high density areas that included Mufakose, Dzivaresekwa, Kuwadzana, Kambuzuma, Rugare, Highfield, Mbare and Mabvuku, farther away east of the capital city. Yet I do not regard my cousin and his wife to be as extravagantly rich as the small clique of men and women politicians in Zimbabwe today.

Where in Zimbabwe today a small group of these people in the political class have turned into USA Dollar millionaires, owning so much money they do not have the slightest idea what to do with all the money they have acquired, those same ex-combatants were extremely poor at independence from Great Britain in 1980, and did not even own a penny in their bank accounts, if they had any. Side by side with the clique of those in the political class is another smaller group of honest and successful businesspeople who have slowly built up their wealth by dint of their determination and hard work. This group includes retired people, some of them retired, who were once executive employees and managing directors of big business corporations in one-time thriving Zimbabwe. Others are former chief executive officers or managers who gave up being employees and chose the path of starting their own manufacturing businesses, thus fulfilling their own entrepreneurship zeal. My cousin and his wife belong in the latter group. But even in that sense, my cousin does not own millions of United States dollars. However, while I am confident in asserting that he and his wife are not extravagantly rich, there is no doubt he can justifiably afford to enjoy the comfort and high quality of life that he and his wife have sought to enjoy.

Their home, appropriately named 'Green Oasis' in the Spitzkop/ Snake Park area, far out at the western edge of metropolitan City of Harare, just off the busy Harare to Bulawayo Highway, was our neck of the woods and strategically positioned for the entire period of our stay in wonderful Zimbabwe. Fortunately, we had a vehicle at our disposal with which to visit people and places around Harare and beyond. Margaret and I together could drive out of our comfort zone at our hosts' residence every day to re-connect with surviving relatives, friends and work associates that I, in particular, had left behind twenty years previously.

# Chapter 25

# Light still shines at the end of the tunnel
# for the millions of the disadvantaged in Zimbabwe

Visiting Highfield Township during daylight as my first port of call two days following my arrival back in Zimbabwe, I was sad to learn that several of my former workmates at Kudzanayi Government School and Mukai Government High School had passed on due to natural causes of illness and the ravages of old age. The concrete blocks of old 'teachers' flats' along Jabavu Drive, where I once lived both as a bachelor and married man still looked unchanged in appearance. To this day, they remain solid and upright structures with some tenants having been given permission by Harare City Council to put up Durawall's around their dwellings in a quest for them to enjoy a degree of security and privacy of their own. The blocks still bear the same colour of paint of dirty pink/grey on their exteriors that I left them wearing those many years ago when I left to go to the UK. Now parts of that coat of paint have slowly started peeling off or is so horribly faded from the effects of the elements. A few of my surviving friends and workmates of roughly the same age as myself, and still live in these old flats, look pale shadows of their former selves. In nearly all cases, former workmates have all re-tired from their jobs as either teachers or school administrators. A colleague of mine who long retired as a Grade 1 primary school headmaster in one of the large inner-city government schools in Highfield, unable to get onto the property ladder due to poor salaries paid to civil servants over the years, still lives with his wife and several grown up children in the four-roomed coun-cil-owned teachers' flats.

Despite over thirty years of living in these old, decrepit struc-tures, my colleague simply could not save enough money from his pittance of earnings to buy a decent home of his own when he was still of working age. I was reminded I might have been trapped in the same cycle of despair had I not boldly made the decision to jump onto the bandwagon and flee overseas in 2002. I was in my very early fifties when I fled poverty to seek greener pastures in the diaspora. The faint-hearted at the age I decided to take the plunge do not rush into making such catastrophic decisions. In like manner as my relatives and former comrade-in-arms I was re-united with when I visited Highfield twice or three times more, my colleague council-flat tenant in the four-roomed council-owned flat was excited beyond belief to see me, but he looked miserable and by far the worse for wear. "The situation here has moved from bad to worse, Mr Moyo. We are finding it increasingly hard to make ends meet. I personally have no idea where we are going. That's why you find me stuck in these abominable living conditions. I can't go anywhere," he calmly observes. He makes that sorrowful observation, reminding me that during my visit to Zimbabwe, teachers and nurses are on one of their numerous 'industrial actions' seeking better salaries from their employer, the public service. Nothing has changed. It is like crying for the moon to come down to mother earth! The latter have continued paying a deaf ear to their employees' pleas, started during my days as a teacher in Highfield back in the day, more than fifty years ago, never mind how many times teachers have complained they are finding it difficult to cope with the ever-rising cost of living. Many of those who teach in urban areas, as well as even those who teach in rural schools, are finding it increasingly difficult to travel to their workstations because they have repeatedly said they are 'incapacitated'. They simply cannot make ends meet. The Ministry of Finance and Economic Development have been known to say the fiscus cannot afford to respond to civil servants' requests for their salaries to be increased. As I drove around Highfield Township, the township I lived in for twenty years as a teacher, formerly with clean streets and roadways, was now littered with heaps of uncollected rubbish on both street sides. From those heaps, putrid smell and swarms of buzzing green flies spewed out. The whole picture was simply nauseating.

The roads along those streets and between houses, once neatly tarred and resurfaced from time to time when I used to work and live there, were now configurations of old patches of tarred road, in a mixed grill with a litany of potholes which made it so inconvenient, difficult and tricky to venture driving along such irregular surfaces. Machipisa Shopping Centre has long lost its former glory. Everybody seems to be engaged in selling something somewhere in such a disorganised fashion, resulting in dirt and grime spreading everywhere. If the picture I was looking at was so shoddy here, then the situation must be terribly unimaginable at the nearby, but smaller, Gazaland and 'The Stones' Shopping Centres. What happened to the municipal police who used to enforce control of these practices? The Makomvas and the Mwayeras who used to dominate lucrative grocery and general dealer businesses at this big shopping centre appear to have closed shop, giving way to budget grocers like OK Super Market and TM Super Market. Whatever it is, something is horribly wrong somewhere. The whole shopping complex, and its shoddy, unkempt shop fronts and heavily potholed road surfaces past the upright but albeit solid-looking Mushandira Pamwe Hotel and the seemingly crumbling Gwanzura Stadium along the route to the city, looks generally run down and a victim of a hidden corrosive force. My visits to other parts of Harare and Gweru, in the Midlands, replicated the same downward trend. We are supposed to be growing and becoming economically stronger and not regressing. That regrettably is the sad situation in my country of birth now.

It is like a baptism of fire; I am disappointed and particularly so in the absence of anyone who will explain to me why our wheels towards civilisations appear to have all come off. I remembered that since the economy of our country started going downhill more than twenty years ago, it has not been an easy ride for the powers that be to bring it back on even keel. Admitted, I had not visited Zimbabwe as an investigative journalist. Yet, the snippets of a storyline that I collected from people I quietly conversed with as a concerned citizen of this country confirmed one thing:

the economic meltdown in Zimbabwe, starting way back in the 1980s and continuing unresolved for more than forty years now, has reduced our people into corpses in the graveyard of their own country. Galloping inflation in the early 2000s, and more recently between 2018 and 2019, the local currency took a hit against the United States Dollar. Those deadly and unfortunate consequences have wiped out the value of people's pensions, insurance policies or any hard-earned savings they had kept in their bank accounts. As I continue with my visits around and about, I collect shocking information that some of my friends and workmates who had died in recent years may have allegedly succumbed, not to the ravages of COVID-19, but suspected stress-related illnesses. I felt saddened learning about this. I remembered that although I was in my early fifties in 2002, I plucked up enough courage to join millions of mostly young and skilled Zimbabweans who fled their country in search of opportunities for employment and a better quality of life in countries all over the world. Those millions of economic refugees remain stuck in diaspora to this day because there is no attraction for them to return to Zimbabwe. Our economic stagnation remains unchanged. The outlook is quite bad. So, for the past forty-two years, the thorny issue in Zimbabwe is the poor management of the economy and the extent of how that has impacted on the people's quality of life. Surrounding this issue is a tricky political matrix that is inextricably linked with it. The irony of it is that Zimbabwe, like any other country, is a publicly owned entity. So, it belongs to the people who make up the entire population of roughly fourteen or fifteen million people. In sharp contrast to that discourse, it seems there is one small group of Zimbabweans who mistakenly think the country belongs to them alone, that they hold the title deeds of the country, because they fought in the 1970s liberation struggle. One day in the not-too-distant future, which misplaced belief will have to be debunked by the citizens themselves.

As a direct outcome of that misguided thinking, some members of one political party – the same organisation who have, allegedly by hook or crook, held the reins of power in Zimbabwe for forty-two years – are publicly known to have held cabinet positions in a whole line-up of government terms for the period stated. They are the same people who, in their shamelessness, have the temerity to step up the plate on podiums and still churn out wild promises to hapless audiences, telling them they will do one thing or the other to fix the economy. It is probably unfair to heap all the blame for our people's plight on the sitting president who has only been in power for nearly five years now. I understand the eighty-year-old man is the sole candidate of his own political outfit running for the esteemed position of president in the forthcoming general elections in 2023. Yet apart from bits of road rehabilitation programmes and clinching of a few mining deals with Chinese investors, the same fellow has been part and parcel of the same cabal, the leadership who have spectacularly failed to right the many wrongs in our broken economy and to improve the lives of the people over the past four decades, effectively letting the economy deteriorate to its current shambolic charade on their watch. One is forced to conjecture or ask what other untried ideas these people have in their bag of tricks to fix the economy. Truth be said, the Zimbabwean economy died during the Robert Mugabe era. It is no use pretending that miracles will happen in the so-called 'New Dispensation' because the same old guys who were in the late Robert Mugabe governments are the ones still calling the tune.

They are running around like a headless chicken searching for solutions in a haystack to resurrect an economy that flipped over and went moribund years ago. Do they not resemble a mad man chasing a rainbow or trying to catch the wind? There is absolutely no point unnamed people playing the blame game or seeking refuge in tired and useless excuses like 'targeted sanctions'. These economic sanctions were imposed by the international community on the political leadership led by the late President Robert Gabriel Mugabe, accused largely for tinkering with the constitution to keep themselves in power forever and for their numerous human rights abuses. The 'Gukurahundi Massacre' of around twenty thousand innocent Zimbabweans in parts of the Matabeleland and the Midlands Provinces could have taken the late President Robert Mugabe to the International Court of Justice at the 'Haig.' He was lucky to go a free man, without having to answer for the horrors of his rule. One central argument put forward by their critics is that if these people were thinking 'without the box', and not 'inside the box', consequently doing the right things before, the so-called punitive sanctions would not have been imposed on them in the first place.

Notwithstanding wild and unverified claims by sources in the United Nations that the Zimbabwean economy had grown, the facts on the ground are that the key sectors of that economy, namely, Health, Education, Agriculture, public service, Social Services, Transport, Security, etc., are in an extremely bad shape now than they have ever been for not only the comfort and survival of the population, but indeed also for the political future of those leaders in the so-called 'Second Republic' who to date, four years in power, have offered nothing new to resolve our situation. If anything, the sitting president appears to be surrounded by more crooks and con men who masquerade as his cabinet ministers compared with his predecessor.

Given four years in the seat of power after the late Robert Mugabe was overthrown in a 'bloodless coup' in 2017, the sitting president appears to have failed to fulfil the promises he made on assuming power to turn things around and make life better for everybody in the country. During my brief visit to Zimbabwe, I heard many people saying their quality of life was better during the late President Mugabe's rule than it is now. The older members of the population were even saying they were happier during Ian Smith's colonial rule than what began happening when we obtained independence from Great Britain in 1980. Driving around the former 'Heavy Industrial Sites' and 'Light Industrial Sites' in Harare, many factory buildings which used to employ hundreds of thousands of people stand idle as empty shells. Those empty shells were the drivers of the large-scale business activities that were once the order of any weekday in Zimbabwe and gave our country the proud title of 'the breadbasket of Central Africa'. The big business corporations shut down their businesses due to the numerous and intractable issues with the economy. The huge machinery housed in those buildings were manned by people so that products could be produced and sold locally and in overseas markets thus bringing in the much-needed foreign currency into the country. The few former big employers of labour in Harare, Bulawayo, Gweru, Mutare, Masvingo and Kwekwe – who have reportedly attempted to resuscitate their former business operations – are only reluctantly doing so with skeleton staff and poorly equipped machinery because some of their operations need government funding which is unavailable. At all the town centres I visited during normal working hours – Machipisa, Glen View, Chitungwiza ('Huruyadzo'), Mufakose, Dzivaresekwa, Norton (Katanga), Avondale Town Centre, Gweru central business district, Senga in Gweru, Kwekwe, Mabelreign, Waterfalls, Harare Community Centre, Borrowdale, etc – whole crowds of restless and unemployed youths stood about on spaces outside shops or at 'kombi' pick up or drop off points, completely at a loss what to do with themselves.

The youths had nothing better to occupy them because the industries which used to absorb them when they finished school have all shut down. Groups of them prowled around listlessly; others sold airtime or pretended to engage in tyre-puncture mending, vehicle engine repair or panel-beating jobs for which they had neither adequate and appropriate equipment nor the requisite skills to carry out those tasks. It was a genuine case of survival of the fittest. One corner shop owner selling drinks and packets of cigarettes I spoke with commented, pointing at one triangular faced youth and his two friends disappearing behind one unoccupied tumbling down shack, "Look at those three young fellows. They'll soon emerge from behind there unable to walk straight after taking swigs of these illegal substances, 'marijuana' among them. I don't know what these youngsters get from feeling high after smoking the stuff." Expressing my own private opinion, I am convinced that there are people somewhere who must share the larger portion of the blame for failing to provide for the needs of young people in their planning.

After forty-two years of ceaseless waiting for government to provide leadership in producing good policies aimed at promoting and occupying youths meaningfully, their habits of resorting to antisocial behaviours like drug-taking and other crimes would be the best that you can get. As it was, the scene before us involving those youths was a summary of all their hopes for a future of success, happiness and achievement that were dead in the water. Some of the airtime businessmen I saw were reported to be university degree holders who due to the scarcity of job opportunities forced them to take up low-grade and utterly humiliating forms of day jobs. I will say here government is sitting on a ticking time-bomb. A whole generation of young people in their forties have never been employed. Thousands of them, if not millions, have never done a day's job in their lives.

Shockingly and in another short twenty or so years from now, this group of people will wake up as pensioners and discover they have no pensions, insurances or savings to fall back on! It is hard to imagine how our government who have buried their heads in the sand on matters about youth empowerment, among a litany of failures, will cope with such a horrific situation. I heard talk of young people being encouraged to become involved in development 'projects' like, for example, in mining, construction and agriculture. However, complaints from stakeholders are that these issues like youth empowerment, the need to provide for those in need, etc, only begin to be talked about in earnest at political rallies during election campaigns.

Thereafter, and especially when the ruling party has 'won' the elections, the same matters surprisingly are put to bed or simply forgotten about until the next round of electioneering when they are resurrected as new ideas. This has been the same uniform pattern for the past forty-two years. Were these young aspiring farmers, businesspeople, artisanal miners, etc backed up by not just sincere and properly organised government funding, but also appropriate training rendered so that they can be assured of success in their ventures, indeed none of the youth unemployment figures that are bandied about in the media would see the light of day. Most of the promises have never been followed up and in our volatile situation, no properly constituted commercial banks will give loans to aspiring 'businesspeople' who cannot provide means with which to pay back their loans.

The way I see it is that that tortured existential thing of dangling before the people 'Mickey Mouse' and myopic development programmes and slogans like 'Vision 2020' – which came and went fruitlessly – and now the so-called 'Vision 2030' by those in the corridors of power, may be fine to a point for their survival after electioneering. Nobody should waste their time formulating such meaningless policies if our youths, who are such a critically important resource for the future of the country, are neglected and subsequently consigned to the rubbish heap. That will not do and playing silly games with our youth has got to be halted as a matter of urgency. On the contrary, a quick drive through the leafy, high-end low-density suburbs of Borrowdale Brooke, New Pomona, Mount Pleasant Heights, Hogerty Hill and Glen Lorne, among others, reveals a whole landscape of extravagantly large houses, many of them double or triple storey mansions, each sitting on land large enough for an airport. Most of these houses are nearly completed and armies of tradespeople are working on other properties in the same neighbourhoods that have reached different stages of construction. Somebody quietly whispers in my ear, "In case you didn't know, mate, most of those properties are being built for the top brass in government at the taxpayer's expense." Of course, you can be sure I was not only just disconcerted, but I also felt a strong sense of distributive injustice, especially when I suspected that these myopic attitudes by the mandarins in government to public spending have gone on unnoticed by ordinary members of the public for tens of years. Instead of purchasing those expensive cars for cabinet ministers and spending millions of USA Dollars on building white elephants or other needlessly expensive ventures, some of these funds could have wisely been used to buy medicines and equipment for our hospitals or pay our civil servants in the public service decent wages.

The examples of things gone horribly wrong in my country that I cited in my illustrations are but a mere tip of the iceberg. Driving through the centre of Harare for the first time in twenty years on day one of my arriving back in Zimbabwe, the bad driving conditions I endured were one of my worst nightmares and, for me, sufficient testimony of an economy that had long since gone downhill. The rot cannot be entirely blamed on the operations of urban or rural authorities. I had assumed that local government authorities countrywide, who are largely run by councillors voted in by opposition party supporters, would have put in a better show of providing quality service to the people. However due to the conflict in the power politics matrix between leaders in central and local government, suspicion is rife that the former may deliberately be sabotaging the efforts of the junior partner who subsequently fails to carry out their political and administrative mandate. Half the time, the cities of Harare, Bulawayo and Gweru have had their duly elected mayors suspended from office on spurious grounds by the more powerful local government minister who sits in cabinet. These actions have left the said cities without their mayors for extended periods. In addition, central government has allowed several councillors countrywide to be recalled due to intra-party fissures discreetly encouraged by surrogates of disorder, leaving councils – be they urban or rural – without people's chosen representatives to advance the wishes of the people who voted for them. The most recent by-elections in Zimbabwe were held to fill vacancies created by these numerous recalls of members of parliament and councillors nearly two years after the unnecessary recalls were allowed to happen. I did not get the chance to visit a typical rural area due to time constraints and the reports I received stated that most gravel roads out there were so rugged and in disrepair I would have needed to wear a crash helmet while driving an all-terrain vehicle, which fortunately I did not have!

But on the strength of some of the observations I make in this chapter, those reflections could be relied upon and replicated anywhere both in the urban and rural areas of Zimbabwe.

In hindsight, I have just remembered that probably only one single traffic light worked in the whole of Gweru city centre for the entire week I stayed in that 'City of Progress'. I must admit though that in Harare and Gweru central business districts, low-density and high density areas, both wherein I spent time walking or driving around, I witnessed amazing things happening in the building industry, especially the building of residential housing or projects like shopping malls by ordinary individuals or people in partnerships. The bulk of the local population may be struggling with their lives in difficult circumstances. Against all odds, some of the citizens in the diaspora are investing back in their motherland. Hence the mystery of so many new houses and building projects that seem to have sprouted in most of the urban settings in Zimbabwe. It is all very simple. There is so much that patriotic Zimbabweans can do to develop their country if the overall environment were more enabling. I cannot exactly remember who said, 'Give us the tools and we will finish the job'. Against the general rot and unhappiness, I have spotlighted, here is a clarion call from an ordinary educationist, writer and citizen who loves his country like everyone else.

As the 2023 harmonised parliamentary and local government elections in Zimbabwe loom, it is my hope that our leaders in the ruling elite are sincere and honest with themselves as they approach the end of their last five-year mandate in the service of the people. Zimbabwe is blessed with enough resources for all of us to enjoy. Yet the general population continues to live in abject poverty and deprivation. I need hardly mention that people are tired of waiting. Forty-two years of empty promises by politicians is enough. Both the great majority of our people at home and in communities scattered across the whole world still cherish the quest to enjoy the true fruits of acquiring our sovereign independence in 1980.

I am sure that most of those in government are perfectly in the loop regarding the true values of the reasons why people took up arms against colonial rule. If so, the time has come for those in positions of authority in the 'Second Republic' to set aside personal interests and display genuine and unquestionable political will towards bringing closure to Zimbabwe's long-drawn argument. The sitting president does not need to have 'sanctions' imposed on Zimbabwe by the EU, the UK and the USA lifted to begin changing the lives of ordinary Zimbabweans.

Neither does the sitting president need to 'dialogue' with opposition parties on what rumour says is the possibility of setting up a 'Government of National Unity' for people to begin enjoying improved lifestyles in Zimbabwe. That will be a pointless waste of a scarce resource: time. Instead, there is a small window of opportunity left for him and his party to do a big introspection in the interest of the people that he always says he 'listens' to. He has, by far and wide, enough executive authority to start doing the right things. By 'doing the right things' I refer to the need for the ruling elite to deal squarely and honestly with the reasons why the country was ever placed on 'sanctions' by Western countries. Once all the political reforms have been implemented and aligned with the people's constitution of 2013, then we shall truly be on our way towards free, fair and credible elections in 2023 that will not stand a chance of being contested because those elections will have been held on an even playing field.

It is unfortunate that instead of implementing the necessary reforms, the sitting government appears to have already begun amending the constitution to buttress their entrenched positions. Yet truth be told, the immediate outcome of doing the right things by the current crop of the ruling elite will culminate in turning things around in the economy and people enjoying improved living standards. The missing piece to complete the big picture is 'political will' which those in government must provide without further delay. Those in the ruling elite and their advisers will need to be dissuaded against the misguided thinking that their party will remain in government forever. Most of them have amassed considerable wealth in terms of land, real estate, hefty bank balances and opportunities in business for themselves and their families over the years.

As the bureaucracy primarily consists of people who may not be alive in another thirty years from now, it is in their interest to safeguard the gains they have accumulated for the benefit of their children long after they have departed. If they continue to keep the levers of state power to themselves, thus going against democratic principles, by refusing to eliminate the imbalances in our socio-economic set up, the only option left for the masses will be a people's revolution which might include violence and even death. These are chilling possibilities and nobody in his or her right mind advocates for such an end. In that unfortunate event, the current crop of rulers may lose all the wealth they have acquired when the people take back everything, they will perceive was stolen from them, leaving their offspring walking away empty-handed, without any legacy whatsoever.

So, assuming that I was availed the chance to appeal to the instincts of those at the helm of government in Zimbabwe at the time of writing this book, I would not beat about the bush but say it straight to their faces as follows: Comrades, considering that your entrenched ideas on 'entitlement' have evolved and existed over so many years, it is not going to be easy for you to respond to the pleas of a humble, little-known wannabe ordinary citizen like me. Yet facing the courage of your convictions might even mean having to swallow your pride and choosing the route of being shunned by your colleagues for preferring the path of peacefully giving way to the unstoppable 'tsunami' of disgruntled voters, including millions of unemployed but registered young voters who, if given a chance, would no doubt vote you out of government if truly democratic elections were held in 2023. That 'tsunami' is slowly, but surely, gathering momentum and taking Zimbabwe by storm. It is still within your grasp to create conditions in Zimbabwe where people should freely choose their leaders. At nearly seventy-four years of age as I express these sentiments, it would be folly for anyone to pin the label 'young man' on me. I am perfectly in the picture of what I am talking about, having lived in both 'Rhodesia' and 'Zimbabwe.' I am not a politician by any means. I have never wished to be one and have no political ambitions of my own.

I am neither a political activist nor a card-carrying member of any political party in Zimbabwe. Yet I strongly believe it is long overdue for an appropriate response to be accorded to clarion calls to the effect that the future of Zimbabwe needs henceforth to be left in the hands of our young people who have fresh ideas that must be put to the test for the sake of posterity. I may have amply demonstrated in these pages how it has been a pain living in Zimbabwe for most Zimbabweans. Ordinary people have suffered long enough. By changing the aims and objectives of the liberation struggle to suit your own selfish ambitions when the few of you still alive went into government, the people of Zimbabwe have been let down big time. We cannot, therefore, carry on forever with a tiny fraction of politicians of a certain DNA to continue enjoying the fat of the land alone while most of the people wallow in downright poverty. One of the right things you must do and the last act of statesmanship you must display is to create an enabling environment in which the citizens must be allowed to enjoy the free will to choose or elect leaders of their choice across the party divide.

In finishing off writing the third of the last three chapters of this memoir, specifically designed to reflect on my journey to Zimbabwe, the first and the only one I ever made in twenty years of my stay in the UK, I thought it was fitting to make my concluding comments tying them up with the central theme of this book's title, "Pursuit of the Elusive Dream." Amidst the increasing levels of poverty and deprivation that I witnessed during the one and only visit to my motherland, I felt it was amazing the extent to which hope among the suffering masses in Zimbabwe surprisingly still thrives. That hope is the last sole survivor in a bruising struggle revealing the robustness and resilience with which the human spirit utterly refuses to be smothered out of existence. There is a never dying hope among the people that one day the sun will come out and everyone will smile again. Like the indomitable courage shown by farmers during extended seasons of drought, the long-suffering people of Zimbabwe keep on looking wistfully at the distant horizon, hoping that one day, the rains will arrive, thus enabling them to carry on with their normal lives again without having to struggle so much just to put food on the table and ensure that their families were provided with most of their basis needs in life.

I feel that it was wonderful having decided to embark on that trip. I enjoyed it and there was so much to learn despite the high levels of deterioration I saw. I would describe that journey as a spiritual quest for me to find the best in myself, to quietly assess the situation on the ground in my country on my own with the knowledge that the rest of my people in Zimbabwe are on the same path of relentlessly pursuing the elusive dream to live better lives. For me, the result or reward of that Zimbabwe travel adventure was a feeling of being together with my people in their never-ending struggles for economic emancipation. Like all men and women of goodwill, I cherish the hope that one day, their aspirations and struggles for a better quality of life in post- independent Zimbabwe will be richly rewarded.

Elsewhere, I also recognise that the basic motif of my relocation to the UK back in 2002, leaving my country of birth behind, and finding the source of life to bring myself forth in a richer or more mature other world, has given meaning to my everyday existence, putting my individual struggles in a noble context. I have lived and worked in this beautiful country (UK) for twenty years now, enjoying core British values of respect and tolerance, individual liberty, equality of treatment, democracy and a quality of life that is second to none. I recognise the numerous benefits and privileges that have accrued to me by the choice I made to relocate to this part of the world. To be warmly welcomed here when I arrived in the UK back in the day and to feel comfortable in two different worlds as a British–Zimbabwean is a rare inheritance indeed. I have no intention to belabour this point: I feel that I should neither exclusively be Zimbabwean nor exclusively be British by identity. Indeed, I can absolutely be both, linked or tied together in a migrant's adventures. I have neither shame nor apology whatsoever in making the confession that for two decades now, I have defined myself in terms of the challenges and realities that have confronted me rather than by my past.

We are now having to learn to live with COVID-19 in the UK. The COVID-19 virus, stubborn and mutant as it has proven, is seemingly determined to continue with its trail of needless carnage for a long time to come. As I wind up writing this memoir, Margaret and I have already received not only our two-jab vaccinations but also our booster jabs against COVID-19. While nearly all COVID-19 safety restrictions have been scrapped in the UK, the 'Omicron Variant' is still on the rampage but seemingly being contained by the NHS and all public health agencies in the country. I love my country of birth, Zimbabwe, as much as my adoptive country, the UK. In making that admission from deep down in my heart, I may have also hinted that depending on how the socio-economic environment in Zimbabwe unfolds and becomes more stable and welcoming, I cherish an undying wish one day to return forever and reintegrate among my folks in Zimbabwe. My return, and that of my other comrades-in-arms scattered all over the world, will hopefully guarantee that once we are settled back there, our past will reclaim its rightful share in our recalibrated identities. I rest my case.

# Acknowledgements

In the same way journalists would stick their necks out to collect information, I believe those who write memoirs or autobiographies are as good as their sources of data and those who offer them assistance. In writing this book, I have singularly been lucky myself in having many people who helped me subsequently emerge with this finished product.

First, there is my darling wife, Margaret. I could not possibly write this memoir without her love, patience, and encouragement. Despite my often-loud calls for her to turn down the volume on her mobile phone or the television set in the living room downstairs so that I could concentrate, she surprisingly was always there as my cheerleader whenever I felt frustrated and tended to slacken in my efforts to continue writing this memoir. For most of the last eighteen months, I was stuck on the computer in the privacy of the 'box room' of the house where we live in Birmingham (UK) instead of being in company with her and enjoying quality time together. Then, assisted by our eldest daughter Audrey, Margaret submitted herself to the painstaking reading and editing of both the early and final drafts of this book, kindly suggesting changes to its overall presentation.

Margaret my dearest, I need hardly remind you that, apart from providing the impetus for why I go on relentlessly since you put the gold on my finger more than forty odd years ago, I am hugely proud of you. Above everything else, you remain my one and only anchor, friend and soulmate.

Next, I want to single out for special tribute my older brother and sibling, Roland Kufakunesu Kaston Dzenga. In the earlier chapters of this book when I was tracing our family's ancestral background, he was always available each time I contacted him either directly by mobile phone or through WhatsApp messaging to verify the veracity of details I held. Elsewhere, Roland was my pillar of strength as my custodian, starting from my frustrating experiences in the first two months of 1963 when I could not be enrolled for Standard 5 (year 7) at government primary schools in Highfield Township, Salisbury (Harare) so I could continue with and/or complete my primary school education. Then at the end of the same year, he plucked me from the jaws of near educational extinction and depths of despair when, for eight solid months, I had been marooned at the so-called 'Donga Farm Boarding School' at Selukwe (Shurugwi). He valiantly brought me back to Salisbury (Harare). Without him, there would have been no 'Salisbury' (Harare) or 'civilisation' for me to write about. Living with my brother Roland as a teenager, I completed part of my secondary education and used Salisbury (Harare) as my base, my launching pad to fly a rocket into the unknown in my pursuit of elusive opportunities to live the good life. Older brother Roland, who was mostly a bachelor during his custodianship of yours truly, was kind enough to take care of me for nearly six years until he got married towards the end of 1967. My brother Roland, only heaven knows the huge sacrifices you made with your pitifully small earnings to keep us going. Words fail me to express how deeply I am indebted to you.

It would be remiss of me to omit mentioning other people who played significant roles, large and small, in providing the building blocks that eventuated in developments that they, in themselves, led to my being able to compile and produce this memoir. There were many such kind, honest, benevolent, highly influential, and philanthropic people. I can only manage to name a few. In no order of importance, I want, to start with, to thank posthumously and from the bottom of my heart the following three respectable and wonderful people:

1) My Uncle and father's young brother, (the late) Rodrick Tinarwo Mudyara. Without that honourable gentleman, almost everything I talk about in relation to my progress through

life would be a pipe dream. Uncle Rodrick or 'Mudhara D' as we would affectionately refer to him, was the bedrock of civilisation in my father's family. My father had numerous male children for whom it was completely beyond his financial means to send to school. I was therefore lucky enough to be one of the few 'boys' Uncle Rodrick benevolently offered to see through attending upper primary school while staying with him in Gwelo (Gweru) where he was employed as a Meteorological Assistant. His sterling efforts in breaking down barriers and literally transporting 'civilisation' and off-loading it in the utterly deprived and splendid isolation of the decrepit environment where my childhood was nurtured is etched in the records of my family history until eternity. Thank you ever so much 'Moyondizvo'. May your Dear Soul Rest in Eternal Peace.

2) My mother's young sister, (the late) Mrs Eliver Mbidzeni Ruhukwa (nee Muguto). Like Uncle Rodrick above, Aunt Eliver stamped her very big influence on the hearts of all of us who were the children of her older sister, my mother, through her numerous visits, and sometimes unannounced appearances at the farm homestead of my childhood at Maronda Mashanu, Enkeldoorn (Chivhu). As I grew up at the farm, her many arrivals, laden with all sorts of 'goodies' for her older sister and her children, thrilled us all to bits. For the duration of her short visits – and how time moved with so much speed when she was visiting – we enjoyed the comfort and convenience that she ushered into my mother's hut. Aunt Eliver offered so much solace to her older sister. Her visits lifted our spirits. We were happy. I am truly grateful to the positive contribution Aunt Eliver made to my upbringing and that of my other siblings. A fitting description of how she did this is contained in the main body of this book. May my 'Little Mum' (Mainini)'s Soul Rest in Peace.

3) (The late) Reverend Father Mangan was one of several English Jesuit priests working in Salisbury (Harare) Archdiocese of the Roman Catholic Church when my acquaintanceship with

him commenced in 1966. Were it not for that God-fearing reverend gentleman, I would not have been able to complete my secondary school education in Salisbury (Harare), gone on from there to adopt and become familiarised with civilised and sophisticated lifestyles, nor would I have carried on training as a teacher at St. Paul's Teachers' College, Musami. Through his benevolent assistance, I regard myself as one of the few direct recipients of Christian charity. Reverend Father Mangan went out of his way to take full charge of all my welfare needs for the best part of six years, including the period after I completed my teacher training. Five years into my work as a trained teacher, Reverend Father Mangan personally led Holy Mass to celebrate my marriage to (the then) Margaret Florence Nyemba who remains my wife to this day, over forty years later. Words fail me to express how deeply grateful I am to (the late) Reverend Father Denis Mangan may his Dear Soul Rest in Eternal Peace and the love of our Lord Jesus Christ.

One or two other kind people below who may have not realised the full impact of their contributions to help me move on with my life are hopefully still alive and well. Doctor Phillip Mhundwa was a lecturer and intellectual at the University of Zimbabwe in the sequence of events that I narrate in this memoir. If Doctor Mhundwa – who perchance may by now possibly be a professor in an institution of higher learning somewhere in this world! – is still alive and 'opportuned' to read these pages, he is probably unaware that from my fortuitous meeting with him at Seke Teachers' College in April/May 1984 where he was one of the presenters at a teacher development workshop on the subject of English, he unknowingly triggered processes which eventually made it possible for me to attend the University of Zimbabwe resulting in the attainment of my first tertiary qualification in December 1987. Doctor (or Professor?) Mhundwa, Sir, kindly accept my deepest appreciation for your kind intervention and changing the direction in which events pertaining to developments in my life followed. Thank you very much Professor or Doctor Mhundwa. I have provided more information on how this happened in the main body of this book.

In the UK, I had the rare luck of meeting Mr Craig Lamb. He was an 'Advanced Skills Teacher' – a Senior Teacher Grade of English in the UK, with similar status to that of a Deputy Head of department – at Smith's Wood Sports College (later changed to Smith's Wood Academy). I was an employee on the school staff as 'teacher of English & General Subjects' between 2002 and 2008, for the first twelve months of that period as an 'agency or overseas trained teacher,' who was regarded as a temporary teacher in the English school system because I did not possess UK 'Qualified Teacher Status'. In his capacity as my appointed 'Supervisor' in the English Department during my studies for 'Qualified Teacher Status', Mr Lamb provided me with invaluable support and specialist guidance that enabled me to pass the bridging course thereby qualifying me to earn 'Qualified Teacher Status' through Newman University, Birmingham, UK.

Mr Lamb's English Language and Literature teaching style helped me to fine-tune a broad variety of pedagogic approaches which assisted me to tailor my delivery techniques to the various abilities and personalities of the students in my care. On completion of that bridging course, the Executive Headteacher and Principal, a Mr Rob Hawkins, had me promptly employed at the school as a teacher of English and member of the fulltime qualified staff at his large inner-city secondary school. Without the qualified teachers' status and only holding my Zimbabwean Bachelor of Education Degree in English, I would have been unable to continue teaching in the National Curriculum, that is, the UK system of education. I have no quibble in recording it here for the sake of posterity that I began earning serious money as a qualified teacher working in the UK because of Mr Lamb's sterling and selfless efforts. I am truly and sincerely indebted to you, Mr Craig Lamb.

Last but by no means least, this book is a true story of my life, immersed at first in the ten years of my childhood at Farm No.

7, Maronda Mashanu African Purchase Area, Chikomba District in Mashonaland East Province, Zimbabwe. I am therefore truly indebted to the reference book 'Maronda Mashanu: The History of a Community' by Murray Steele. Whether the author of this reference book is alive and aware of it or not, the title of his publication 'Maronda Mashanu' appears on most pages of the first few chapters of this memoir. I grew up as a child to become the man I am today, having started making sense of the world around me against the backdrop of Maronda Mashanu or the 'Five Wounds' community that was essentially brought into existence by the pioneering endeavours of an Anglican Church missionary, Father Arthur Shearly Cripps. A simple shrine just across the Chiputya River (or River Jordan as Father Cripps would have preferred to call it) formerly a big river with fast flowing water but now a dry riverbed due to outcomes of climate change over the years, that holy place lies barely two miles from the farm homestead where I spent my childhood. The shrine marks the grave where the renowned British clergyman's remains repose after completing his missionary work in shaping the lowly sphere where the Almighty had wanted him to work and to walk.

May I also say, it is the nature of this book that certain smart remarks and observations may have probably been pilfered from friends, professional acquaintances and, indeed, other written texts over the period covered by my memoir. I need hardly mention that I live in a world where there are millions of other human beings. If any are noted in the body of this narrative, my collective thanks go to all of them – or an apology – will suffice.

MIN HERZ FÜR AUTOREN A HEART FOR AUTHORS À L'ÉCOUTE DES AUTEURS MIA ΚΑΡΔΙΑ ΓΙΑ ΣΥΓΓΡ
HJÄRTA FÖR FÖRFATTARE UN CORAZÓN POR LOS AUTORES YAZARLARIMIZA GÖNÜL VERELIM SZÍ
CUORE PER AUTORI ET HJERTE FOR FORFATTERE EEN HART VOOR SCHRIJVERS TEMOS OS AUTC
HERZÖINKÉRT SERCE DLA AUTORÓW EIN HERZ FÜR AUTOREN A HEART FOR AUTHORS À L'ÉCOU
RACÃO BCEЙ ДУШОЙ К АВТОРАМ ETT HJÄRTA FÖR FÖRFATTARE Á LA ESCUCHA DE LOS AUTOI
AUTEURS MIA ΚΑΡΔΙΑ ΓΙΑ ΣΥΓΓΡΑΦΕΙΣ UN CUORE PER AUTORI ET HJERTE FOR FORFATTERE EEN I
YAZARLARIMIZA GÖNÜL VERELIM          ÖINKÉRT SERCE DLA AUTORÓW EIN HERZ FÜI
VOOR SCHRIJVER TEMO    S A        O BCEЙ ДУШОЙ К АВТОРАМ ETT HJÄRTA FÖI

# The author

Lawrence D. Moyo was born at Dzenga Kraal, a rural village in Zimbabwe. He qualified as a High School Teacher, specialising in English. He has a QTS (UK), a B. Ed Degree (English) obtained from the University of Zimbabwe and a M. Ed Degree (Applied Linguistics) obtained from The Open University (UK). He has forty-five years' experience in education, both as a classroom practitioner and as an educational administrator in Zimbabwe and Teacher of English in the UK. He is currently retired and spends most of his time engaged in reading books and conducting research. He lives in Birmingham, UK. His favourite activities include reading, writing, listening to instrumental jazz, watching football, walking and attending gym sessions. His special skills include public speaking and writing. This memoir is his first venture in publishing. He is married with four adult children: a son Gerald and three daughters, Audrey, Lorraine and Valerie.